In Peril on the Sea

THE ROYAL CANADIAN NAVY AND THE BATTLE OF THE ATLANTIC

(Overleaf)

"HMCS *Sackville* pursuing a surfaced U-boat."

In the afternoon of 3 August 1942, while serving as part of Escort Group C-3 protecting Convoy ON 115, the corvette *Sackville*, under the command of Lieutenant Alan Easton, RCNR, obtained an ASDIC contact. Changing course to investigate, she sighted *U-552* running on the surface and immediately increased speed to ram as shown in this painting by John Alford. The U-boat commander, *Kapitänleutnant* Erich Topp, managed to avoid the attempt and crashdived but not before *Sackville* put a 4-inch round into his conning tower that so badly damaged Topp's boat that he had to break off his patrol. In a period of 14 hours, *Sackville* engaged three U-boats, and these actions brought her captain, Lieutenant Alan Easton, RCNR, the award of the Distinguished Service Cross with other medals and awards going to members of her crew. (Courtesy of John Alford)

In Peril on the Sea

THE ROYAL CANADIAN NAVY AND THE BATTLE OF THE ATLANTIC

DONALD E. GRAVES

With drawings by

Latham B. Jenson

and maps and diagrams by

Christopher Johnson

Published for

THE CANADIAN NAVAL MEMORIAL TRUST

by

ROBIN BRASS STUDIO

Toronto

Published and distributed for
Canadian Naval Memorial Trust
HMCS *Sackville,* P.O. Box 99000 Station Forces
Halifax, NS B3K 5X5
www.hmcssackville-cnmt.ns.ca
by
Robin Brass Studio Inc.
10 Blantyre Avenue, Toronto, Ontario M1N 2R4, Canada
Fax: 416-698-2120 / www.rbstudiobooks.com

Printed and bound in Canada by Friesens, Altona, Manitoba

National Library of Canada Cataloguing in Publication

Graves, Donald E. (Donald Edward), 1949-
    In peril on the sea : the Royal Canadian Navy and the Battle of the Atlantic / Donald E. Graves ; with drawings by Latham B. Jenson ; and maps and diagrams by Christopher Johnson.

Includes bibliographical references and index.
ISBN 1-896941-35-4 (bound). – ISBN 1-896941-32-X (pbk.)

    1. Canada. Royal Canadian Navy – History – World War, 1939-1945. 2. World War, 1939-1945 – Campaigns – Atlantic Ocean. 3. World War, 1939-1945 – Naval operations, Canadian. I. Jenson, L. B., 1921-   II. Johnson, Christopher III. Canadian Naval Memorial Trust. IV. Title.

D779.C2G73 2003   940.54'5971   C2003-901609-9

Excerpts from several copyright works appear in *In Peril on the Sea* and must not be reproduced without the permission of the following copyright holders or executors: Atlantic Chief and Petty Officers Association, *Fading Memories: Canadian Sailors and the Battle of the Atlantic* (Halifax, 1993, © ACPOA); Frank Curry, *The War at Sea: A Canadian Seaman on the North Atlantic* (Lugus, Toronto, 1990, © Frank Curry); Susan Easton, executor of Alan Easton, for *50 North: Canada's Atlantic Battleground* (Ryerson, Toronto, 1966, © Alan Easton); Rosamond Greer, *The Girls of the King's Navy* (Sono Nis Press, Victoria, © Rosamond Greer); Lieutenant Commander Anthony Griffin, RCN (Retd.) for "A Naval Officer's War, Episode 7," *Starshell*, Autumn 2002; Werner Hirschmann, photographs and excerpts from his memoirs; Latham B. Jenson, *Tin Hats, Oilskins & Seaboots* (Robin Brass Studio, Toronto, 2000, © L.B. Jenson); Mac Johnston, *Corvettes Canada: Convoy Veterans Tell Their True Stories* (McGraw-Hill Ryerson, Toronto, 1994, © Mac Johnston); James B. Lamb, *The Corvette Navy* (Macmillan, Toronto, 1977, © James B. Lamb); Mr. Raymond Layard, executor of Commander A.F.C. Layard, RN, for permission to quote from that officer's diary in the Royal Naval Museum, Portsmouth, UK; Naval Officers Association of Canada, Ottawa Branch, for *Salty Dips*, vols 1 to 3 (© NOAC Ottawa, 1981-1984); Major (Retd.) Terence Manuel for permission to quote copyright material from the "HMCS *Esquimalt*" website; Edward O'Connor, *The Corvette Years: The Lower Deck Story* (Cordillera Publishing, Vancouver, 1995, © Edward O'Connor); Mike Parker, *Running the Gauntlet: An Oral History of Canadian Merchant Seamen in World War II* (Nimbus, Halifax, 1994, © Mike Parker); Gregory W. Pritchard for *Memories of Basic Training and Other Dips* (Lunenburg, 2000, © South Shore Naval Association); Mr. Ronald W. Richards, executor of S.T. Richards, for *Operation Sick Bay* (Cantaur Publishing, West Vancouver, 1994, © S.T. Richards); Mr. Richard W. Stevens, executor of Allan W. Stevens for *Glory of Youth* (1995, © Allen W. Stevens); and the University of British Columbia Press, *The RCN in Retrospect, 1910-1968* (UBC Press, Vancouver, 1982, © UBC Press).

TO

ALL CANADIANS WHO SERVED

IN PERIL ON THE SEA

DURING THE SECOND WORLD WAR

AND TO

THOSE WHO STRIVE

TO PRESERVE THEIR MEMORY

AND TO

THOSE WHO HAVE SERVED

CANADA SO WELL SINCE 1910

IN OUR NATION'S MARITIME FORCES

AND MERCHANT MARINE

LEST WE FORGET

CONTENTS

FOREWORD

by Rear Admiral D.W. Piers (Retd.)

I am very pleased to contribute a brief foreword to *In Peril on the Sea*, the Canadian Naval Memorial Trust's commemoration project to mark the 60th Anniversary of the high point of the Battle of the Atlantic in 1943. It is a time that should be commemorated because, in the space of three months from March until June 1943, the Allied navies went from near defeat to the beginnings of clear victory in the Battle of the Alantic, a battle that simply had to be won, or the Second World War could have been lost.

Having been born in 1913, three years after Canada finally established its own navy, my generation of naval officers witnessed the difficult years of the Great Depression and faced the problem of maintaining even the most modest professional naval capability in Canada between the wars. Fortunately for this nation, and the great contribution it was called upon to make during the ensuing war, the Royal Canadian Navy possessed a very small but highly dedicated and professional core of Officers, Chief and Petty Officers and Men, who within months of September 1939, began to literally create a new navy. In addition to manning and fighting the six destroyers in the 1939 fleet, this meant providing the leadership, plans and training facilities required to expand a service of about 3,500 all ranks to 100,000 in the space of five years. It also meant building, equipping and commissioning more than four hundred warships and was, by any meas-

urement, an incredible achievement that was only brought about by the efforts of the professionals of the Royal Canadian Navy and Royal Canadian Naval Reserve who were able to provide the crucial leadership for more than 90,000 men and women who joined the Royal Canadian Naval Reserve and the Women's Royal Canadian Naval Service. Such a vast and rapid expansion caused genuine problems but we all worked under the imperative that there was a war that had to be won.

This imperative meant that young officers such as myself assumed immense responsibility at an age and level of experience that was unheard of in peacetime. I was the Executive Officer of the destroyer HMCS *Restigouche* when the Battle of the Atlantic began in 1939 and, two years later at the age of 28, I became her Commanding Officer and served in that capacity until 1943. It is fair to say that those two years were perhaps the worst in the war's longest battle. After acting as the Senior Officer of the Escort Force for seven convoys in which we escaped unscathed without the loss of a single merchant ship, my ship joined C-4 Escort Group in September 1942. We did so to replace HMCS *Ottawa*, which was sunk just a few hours after the burial service on her quarterdeck described in the opening paragraphs of this book. I was the Senior Officer of C-4 Group during the battle for SC 107 in November 1942 which Donald E. Graves, the author of *In Peril on the Sea*, calls "the convoy from hell." It certainly seemed so to me at the time as, during the night of 1 November 1942 alone, we lost eight merchant ships to a concentrated submarine attack and, during a battle that lasted five days, sixteen of forty-two ships in SC 107 were sunk despite the desperate and unrelenting efforts of my group to defend them.

Postwar records have revealed that Admiral Dönitz, the head of the German submarine force, had concentrated two U-boat Wolf Packs to make a determined attack on this particular convoy. Despite the heavy losses of SC 107, this battle helped point out some of the problems created by the rapid expansion of the RCN. These problems resulted from rushing ships into service with minimum training and with obsolescent equipment; the frequent manning instability of personnel in our ships; and the often unavoidable shifting of vessels in and out of the escort groups, which hindered the development of their fighting cohesion. All these concerns needed serious and immediate attention.

Our efforts to defend the convoys were also hampered by the backward technological state of our vessels – my destroyer was the only escort in C-4 Group to have a HF/DF or High Frequency Direction Finding set, a vitally important piece of equipment – and *Restigouche* only had it because I had illegally scrounged a set while she was in refit. For much of the war, Canadian warships in the North Atlantic lagged far behind their American and British counterparts in terms of technology and the RCN was too often asked to do a great deal with very little. In June 1943 I pointed out some of our problems in my "Commanding Officer's Report of Proceedings," a monthly memorandum to my immediate superiors, including Rear Admiral Leonard Murray, which was passed on with his approval to Naval Service Headquarters in Ottawa. It still took nearly a year, however, before Canadian warships were on an equal footing with those of their Allies.

These facts are now well known as in the last two decades many historians have written on the wartime problems of the RCN and the author has ably summarized their findings in the main text of *In Peril on the Sea*. I am glad, however, that he has also included so many personal accounts from Canadian sailors who fought in the North Atlantic as their stories of bad weather, worse food, U-boats, seasickness, cold, ice, survivors, gales, exhaustion, terror – and more bad weather – convey with vivid immediacy

just what we experienced during that long and cruel battle. I am also pleased that *In Peril on the Sea* contains many well-chosen and interesting illustrations that depict our life at sea in the wartime escort fleet.

For nearly half a century Canada has been at peace and two generations have not had to face the trials of war. Throughout these peaceful decades, however, the Canadian navy has continued to serve this nation in the North Atlantic and other waters because, whether we care to acknowledge it or not, the threat of war is still with us. In fact, as I write these words, at the request of our allies, HMC Ships *Montreal* and *Winnipeg* are presently stationed in the Persian Gulf and HMC Ships *Iroquois* and *Regina* are en route to that troubled area. It is my fervent hope that young Canadians never have to experience what my generation faced during the 1940s but I would like them to know about and to remember what was perhaps their nation's greatest wartime achievement – the RCN's role in the Battle of the Atlantic. It is my belief that, with the publication of *In Peril on the Sea*, the Canadian Naval Memorial Trust will admirably accomplish that purpose.

The Trust is also responsible for what is perhaps the best monument to Canada's part in the Battle of the Atlantic and that is HMCS *Sackville*, the corvette that served in C-2 Group in 1942-1943 when my *Restigouche* was in C-4 Group. Under the care of the Trust, *Sackville*, Canada's official Naval memorial, is in good hands and will be preserved at Halifax for the indefinite future. This little warship is a living record of an important event in our history and I recommend that the readers of this book and all young Canadians make the effort to see *Sackville* at her summer berth in Halifax. I am frequently aboard myself and each visit inspires reflection on the magnificent response of thousands of Canadian sailors, most in their teens or early twenties, to the great challenge of their generation. It also invokes memories of other times, grey seas and absent friends.

Rear Admiral Desmond W. Piers, DSC, CM, CD, RCN (Retd.)
"The Quarterdeck"
Chester, Nova Scotia
February 2003

INTRODUCTION

by Vice Admiral Hugh MacNeil (Retd.)

The Canadian Naval Memorial Trust (CNMT) has two principal objectives: to restore, preserve and maintain HMCS *Sackville* in her 1944 configuration as a Second World War corvette; and to operate this last survivor of the 269 corvettes built, as a Naval Museum for the benefit of all Canadians. This rather small and somewhat battered little ship is the sole remaining example of the 121 Flower Class corvettes built in Canada, as part of this nation's extraordinary war production program. Corvettes were designed and intended as a stop-gap measure to be used as coastal escorts until larger and more powerful ships could be built, but the pace of the Battle of the Atlantic, particularly in the critical period of 1941-1943, required that Canadian corvettes, largely manned by Reserve and Volunteer Reserve personnel, were thrust into the mid-Atlantic as soon as they were completed. By default, corvettes became the mainstay of the Canadian escort fleet and, in the great ocean battles, fought their way into naval immortality.

Sackville herself had a distinguished career. She is a veteran of many convoy battles in that generally inhospitable stretch of ocean between Newfoundland, the Denmark Strait, Iceland and the Western Approaches to the British Isles. She blew one U-boat out of the water with depth charges and, somewhat incredibly, badly damaged another with her First World War vintage 4-inch gun. In September 1943, this rust-streaked little warship was an early target of the German acoustic homing torpedo – one of these deadly weapons exploded in her wake and another beneath her hull, fatally damaging *Sackville*'s No. 1 boiler. *Sackville,* however, was lucky as in this same action three of her sister escorts, a destroyer, a frigate and a corvette, were sunk in close proximity with only one man from each ship being saved. A fragment of metal from the frigate HMS *Itchen,* which exploded on being hit in this action, landed on *Sackville* and is today preserved as a treasured artifact.

Sackville is a symbol of Canada's war effort. In 1939 Canada had a very small population and our national industry, concentrated in a few pockets across the country, was not capable of constructing warships that required technical and industrial sophistication. The six destroyers of the peacetime Canadian navy had all been built in Britain, as were the four large Tribal destroyers (of which HMCS *Haida* is the last and most famous survivor) commissioned later in the war. The critical need for convoy escorts led to the decision to build corvettes, simple and rudimentary warships, in large numbers. Although the Royal Canadian Navy, which grew to a strength of more than four hundred warships by 1945, had many larger and more powerful fighting units, the humble corvette, in the form of HMCS *Sackville,* is the quintessential example of Canada's naval effort during the Second World War and represents the type of vessel in which most young

Canadian sailors served. In many respects she can be viewed as a microcosm of Canada's capabilities in that period.

Sackville is also representative of what could be termed the critical role that Canada played in the Battle of the Atlantic – a role too often overlooked. The postwar Canadian navy was shaped in large measure by the experiences of the thousands of young Canadians, from all walks of life, who served aboard corvettes in the Battle of the Atlantic. For many, this was the formative period of their lives and has become the defining moment for the Canadian Navy. For all these reasons, HMCS *Sackville* was designated as the official Canadian Naval Memorial by the Canadian government in 1985 and she is to Canada what HMS *Victory* is to the United Kingdom and the USS *Constitution* is to the United States. On behalf of their nations, *Victory* and *Constitution* are held in trust, maintained, crewed and interpreted by the navies of the United Kingdom and the United States. The major difference is that Sackville is owned by the CNMT and, with some assistance from the navy, is largely maintained by the volunteers of the Canadian Naval Memorial Trust. How long such a situation can be sustained is moot.

The reasons for preserving this rather humble but important icon, HMCS *Sackville*, for present and future generations of Canadians, has nothing whatsoever to do with the glorification of war. It has everything to do with the state of Canada in 1939, its general unpreparedness for an unwanted conflict, the tools it could provide to its own sailors, and the conditions under which they served. *Sackville* is dedicated to helping Canadians understand how a previous generation of young men and women responded to a worldwide crisis that threatened our security and way of life. Lest the reader think this is an exaggeration, it is worth remembering that many Canadian ships and sailors were lost by U-boat attacks in local Canadian waters such as the Gulf of the St. Lawrence because the Battle of the Atlantic was the only campaign of the Second World War that intruded into Canadian territorial waters.

In Peril on the Sea stems from the goal of the Canadian Naval Memorial Trust to develop a dynamic, resource-rich, educational web site, for use by high school history teachers and students. The Trust has received much wise advice and strong encouragement for this project from the Nova Scotia Department of Education, from teachers, and from Veterans Canada. In the past decade, it has become increasingly clear to many in Canada that the intelligent study of this nation's history and development is not a luxury but an essential ingredient for Canadians both old and new, to understand who we are, how our nation has evolved, the values we hold dear – and the reason why. Teachers need examples, documents, primary and secondary sources, records, true stories, and facts to incite their students' interest in the study of major concerns which dominated the past but remain pertinent for Canadians today, in areas such as globalization, development and sovereignty. The Canadian navy is part of the fabric of this nation. Its history, struggles and successes are, in many ways, a reflection of Canada's interests, priorities, decisions, resources and abilities over much of the past century, and provide a wealth of material relevant to the study of Canadian history.

Such material will eventually be available on the Trust's educational resource web site but *In Peril on the Sea* will provide an excellent introduction and first class companion for teachers, students and Canadians in general, to the educational web site during its development. A specific example that teachers could use when studying the emergence of Canadian sovereignty is the whole story surrounding the appointment in 1943 of Rear Admiral Leonard W. Murray as the Commander-in-Chief, Canadian Northwest Atlantic, thus becoming Canada's sole theatre commander in the Second World War. This large area of responsibility was later reflected in the postwar NATO command structure but it did not happen without a struggle. It was gained through the grudging recognition by Britain and the United States of Canada's contribution to the war, and her growing international status. Who can forget the headlines in the world's press, "British and Americans land in Normandy," when one fifth of the assault troops who landed on D-Day were Canadian.

The Canadian Naval Memorial Trust is fortunate to have been able to commission the well-known Canadian historian Donald E. Graves to write this book. Donald Graves not only has many highly-acclaimed books to his credit, he is also a former member of the team which researched the forthcoming offical history of the RCN in the Second World War. *In Peril on the Sea: The Royal Canadian Navy and the Battle of the Atlantic* is intended for a general, not a specialized, audience. The author's text contains a brief overview of the RCN's beginnings for the important reason that one cannot fully understand the Canadian role and contribution to the longest and perhaps most cruel operation of the Second World War without understanding the early struggles to establish and maintain a Canadian Navy and that navy's status on the eve of war in 1939. The book contains approximately 65 personal accounts of the experiences of men and women, sailors and merchant seamen and their poignant, first-hand human stories amplify each chapter. In addition there are nearly 200 photographs, paintings, drawings and maps which illustrate both the history of the Canadian Navy and the war at sea in the Atlantic.

This book is largely about the navy and its involvement in the Battle of the Atlantic but it is also worth noting some additional points. The ultimate victory in that crucial battle was only made possible by the exertion of the thousands of men and women on the home front in Canada who provided the tools of war which were virtually non-existent in 1939. The decisive factor in ultimately defeating the U-boat offensive (despite the odds against which the Germans fought, many historians consider the U-boat service the only arm of the German forces that had the potential to win the war) was the crucial role played by the maritime air forces, which closed the mid-Atlantic air gap, and who made life so miserable for the U-boats transiting from their vulnerable bases. There is also the courage and determination of the Merchant Marine. At the end of the war, Rear Admiral Murray stated what many knew – and which should never be forgotten – that the true heroes of the Battle of the Atlantic were the thousands of Canadian and Allied merchant seamen who, despite their vulnerability and the terrors they were subject to, returned again and again to the convoy routes of the North Atlantic. The U-boat arm and the Merchant Marine suffered the highest attrition rate of all the forces of all nations involved in the Second World War. Finally, although *In Peril on the Sea* discusses many of the major Canadian Atlantic convoy battles which resulted in the loss of many merchant ships, it is worth remembering that the primary task of the Allied navies was to ensure the safe and timely arrival of shipping. Between 1939 and 1945, nearly 1,500 convoys crossed the North Atlantic and 98 per cent reached their destination unscathed.

In connection with the subject of this book, I would like to add a personal note. As a seven-year-old boy, I was taken to sea for 24 hours with my older brother in the corvette HMCS *Sorel*. She was based at Pictou, Nova Scotia, for the summer of 1943 where my Dad, her captain, was the senior training officer for the working up (WUPS) of new escorts joining, or those returning after repair or refit, to the Atlantic battle. The memories of the next day are still vivid. Even now, I can feel the weight of my tin hat, anti-flash gear, life vest, and how the seemingly huge naval binoculars slung around my neck bounced against my knees (I couldn't see much through them then and found many years later, that "pusser" or issue binoculars did not seem to improve). My ears stuffed with cotton wool, I peered over the open bridge during the night as *Sorel* fired depth charges, and then star shell from the 4-inch gun, and "snow flake" illuminants from launchers on the wings of her bridge, as she attempted to light up and locate a "tame" British training submarine on the surface in the dark. U-boats preferred to attack at night on the surface and from inside the convoy screen. Fascinated, I watched as other ships in the training group fired their guns, came close alongside, transferred instructions and received the occasional "drop of detail" over the radio. That was not all. A sailor, one of the cooks, took me fishing; we fired Sten submachineguns and a .45 calibre pistol, (which forever after made me very wary of them); and one of the 20mm Oerlikon anti-aircraft guns. The yeoman sent my brother and me messages by semaphore, which we had more or less learned as a cub and scout. I slept for a while in a hammock, drank many cups of cocoa, was stuffed with sandwiches, and finally remember waking up late the next afternoon, with the sun streaming through the open scuttle above someone's bunk in which a very excited but very tired little boy had finally been wedged.

It was a memorable experience for me but a safe and protected one. Now there remains only one corvette left in the world. These staunch little ships, good sea boats that they were, were not built to naval standards and would often sink within minutes of being torpedoed. Their boiler rooms, for example, were essentially coffer dams, where the stokers stood on steel plates a foot or so above the ship's bottom, and often wondered whether the crashing explosions that reverbrated around their compartment were enemy torpedoes or their own depth charges seeking a U-boat. For these men there was only one way of escape and that was up a 30-foot, greasy vertical ladder. But thousands of young Canadians spent the war in these little ships which, in the words of the British Admiralty, allowed the Atlantic convoy system to work. All Canadians, present and future, owe a huge debt of gratitude to those who fought the Battle of the Atlantic. They should also be grateful to those who had the foresight and determination, and who have given so generously of their time, skills and resources, to save and preserve Canada's Naval Memorial, HMCS *Sackville*.

Vice Admiral H.M.D. MacNeil, CMM, CD (Retd.)
Chair, The Canadian Naval Memorial Trust
Wallace Point, Belmont, Nova Scotia
February 2003

ACKNOWLEDGEMENTS

First and foremost, the Canadian Naval Memorial Trust and the author would like to thank Commander Latham ("Yogi") Jenson, RCN (Retd.) for permission to use his wonderful illustrations of ships and seamen from his memoir, *Tin Hats, Oilskins & Seaboots. A Naval Journey, 1938-1945.*

Second, we must acknowledge that this book was made possible in part by a generous grant from the Freedom Forum, whose aims are "Free Press, Free Speech, Free Spirit."

Third, we would like to gratefully acknowledge the assistance given to us in the preparation of *In Peril on the Sea* – including permission to reproduce previously unpublished drawings by L.B. Jenson – by the staff of the Directorate of History and Heritage, Department of National Defence, Ottawa, particularly Lieutenant Colonel D.S.C. Mackay, OMM, CD, Major Paul Lansey, CD, and Mr. Michael Whitby, Senior Naval Historian.

Fourth, the Naval Memorial Trust and the author wish to thank the following individuals or organizations who graciously gave permission to quote from copyright material: The Atlantic Chiefs and Petty Officers Association for their book *Fading Memories. Canadian Sailors and the Battle of the Atlantic*; Frank Curry for his memoir, *The War at Sea*; Susan Easton for her father, Alan Easton, author of *50 North*; Rosamond Greer for her memoir *The Girls of the King's Navy*; Lieutenant Commander A. Griffin, RCN (Retd.) for an excerpt from his wartime memoirs published in *Starshell*; Werner Hirschmann for the use of his unpublished memoirs; Commander Latham B. Jenson, RCN, (Retd.) for his book, *Tin Hats, Oilskins & Seaboots*; Mac Johnston for *Corvettes Canada*; Raymond Layard and Royal Naval Museum, Portsmouth for the wartime diary of Commander A.F.C. Layard, RN; Edward O'Connor for his book *The Corvette Years*; Major Terence Manuel for material from the "HMCS Esquimalt Website;" Michael Parker for his book *Running the Gauntlet*; Gregory W. Pritchard for his book *Memories of Basic Training and Other Dips*; Ronald R. Richards for S.T. Richards, his father, author of *Operation Sick Bay*; The Salty Dips Committee, Ottawa Branch, Naval Officers Association of Canada, for *Salty Dips*, vols 1 to 3; Richard R. Stevens for his father, Allan W. Stevens, for his book *Glory of Youth*; University of British Columbia Press for *The RCN in Retrospect, 1910-1968*.

The author is particularly grateful to Lieutenant Commanders Douglas McLean, CD, and Mark Tunnicliffe, CD, serving officers of Maritime Command, Lieutenant Commander Douglas Thomas, CD, RCN (Retd.), and *Oberleutnant (Ingenieur)* (Retd.) Werner Hirschmann for reading and criticizing early drafts of this book. Responsibility for ignoring their helpful advice is that of the author and his alone.

For assistance in tracking down various naval persons or their families, the author would like express his thanks to George Brown, editor of *Starshell*, Patrick Byrne of Vancouver, Dr. Shawn Cafferky of Victoria and Commander M. Cameron, RCN, (Retd.), of Ottawa.

As usual, the author must again register his gratitude to Robin Brass for his design skills, Christopher Johnson for his map and graphic work and Dianne Graves, his patient wife, for her excellent assistance in proofreading the manuscript at its various stages.

A NOTE TO THE READER

In the last two decades or so it has become fashionable in certain literary circles to no longer refer to ships in the feminine, despite long tradition in the English language. By a conscious decision of the Canadian Naval Memorial Trust and the author, all vessels in this book, with the exception of submarines, are referred to in feminine terms.

By definition, the North Atlantic is that part of the ocean which lies above the equator but, as is used in this book, the term also includes adjacent British waters (the English Channel, Irish Sea and North Sea) and North American waters (the Gulf of St. Lawrence).

German naval ranks are used in the text and the reader may wish to know the period Canadian equivalents. These are: *Funkerobergefreiter* (leading seaman, telegraphist); *Leutnant zur See* (junior sub lieutenant); *Leutnant (Ingenieur)* (junior sub lieutenant, engineering branch); *Oberleutnant zur See* (senior sub lieutenant); *Oberleutnant (Ingenieur)* (senior sub lieutenant, engineering branch); *Kapitänleutnant* (lieutenant); *Korvettenkapitän* (lieutenant commander); *Fregattenkapitän* (commander); *Kapitän zur See* (captain); *Kommodore* (commodore); *Konteradmiral* (rear admiral); and *Grossadmiral* (Admiral of the Fleet)

CHAPTER 1

CANADA AND THE SEA: 1600-1918

At sea, Sunday, 13 September 1942

The burial service took place on the quarterdeck just before sunset. The sky was overcast with a definite threat of rain but only a moderate sea was running and the wind force was just 3 or about 10 miles per hour. All members of the crew of the destroyer HMCS *Ottawa* not on watch were in attendance in pusser rig, their best dress, although the commanding officer, Lieutenant Commander Clark Rutherford, RCN, remained on the bridge. The convoy he was escorting, ON 127 out of Lough Foyle in Ireland bound for Halifax, had lost seven merchantmen in the last three days, and though the arrival of air cover from Newfoundland that morning was cause for optimism, the danger was far from over.

The body, sewn up in a hammock, had been carried on a plank by the chief bosun's mate's party to the quarterdeck and placed on the railing, where it now rested, covered by the White Ensign. The man to be buried

(Facing page) **Flagship of the Fleet: The Old "Nobbler."**
An armoured cruiser, HMCS *Niobe* was commissioned in the RN in 1898 and transferred to the infant Canadian Naval Service in 1910. She displaced 11,000 tons, carried a crew of 677 and was armed with sixteen 6-inch guns, twelve 12-pdr. guns, five 3-pdr. quick-firing guns and two 18-inch torpedo tubes. Despite the British custom of naming ships after distinguished admirals or figures from classical mythology, sailors had their own, much less glamorous nicknames for their vessels and *Niobe* was always "Nobbler" to her crew. *Niobe* served until 1920 when she was sold for scrap. (National Archives of Canada, PA 177136)

was a young gunner of the Royal Artillery Marine Regiment from the tanker *Empire Oil*, torpedoed the previous Friday evening. He had been badly wounded by fragments from the blast but his comrades had managed to get him into the lifeboat from which they were picked up by *Ottawa* a few hours later. When he was lifted on board, Surgeon Lieutenant George Hendry, the destroyer's medical officer, examined him and, discovering that he had suffered 13 wounds, including serious abdominal injuries, ordered him taken immediately to an emergency operating theatre set up in the wardroom. There, assisted by Lieutenant Thomas Pullen, *Ottawa*'s executive officer, and Sick Berth Attendant Alexander MacMillan, Hendry had laboured nearly four hours to save the boy's life. The gunner survived the surgery and there was hope that he would pull through but unfortunately peritonitis set in and the lad had died that Sunday morning.

Lieutenant Pullen conducted the service using the *Divine Service Book for the Armed Forces*. As the assembly stood respectfully at attention with caps off, the executive officer read the prayers attendant on such ceremonies, including the request for preservation "from the dangers of the sea, and the violence of the enemy." Pullen concluded by intoning the committal, beginning with the words "Man that is born of woman hath but a short time to live" and ending with "We do now commit his body to the deep."

On command, the bosun's party gently tipped up the inboard end of the plank and the body in its hammock shroud slid into the grey Atlantic, while at the same time those gathered on the quarterdeck sang William Whiting's magnificent hymn:

> *Eternal Father, strong to save*
> *Whose arm hath bound the restless wave,*
> *Who biddest the mighty ocean deep*
> *Its own appointed limits keep;*
> *Oh, hear us when we cry to Thee,*
> *For those in peril on the sea!*

They could not know it but many of those singing that evening on the destroyer's quarterdeck were in greater danger than they realized because a few hours later their vessel would be sunk with great loss of life.[1]

The story of how HMCS *Ottawa* and those who sailed in her came to be in peril on the sea that Sunday in September 1942 is actually the story of the Royal Canadian Navy and it begins nearly three centuries before, in the early days of Canada's recorded history.

Introduction: Canada and the sea to 1867

Although Canada has coasts on both the Atlantic and Pacific oceans, Canadians – the greater part of whom dwell in the interior of the continent – have never been comfortable with their maritime heritage, particularly their naval heritage. This is unfortunate because navies have played an important role in Canadian history. It was naval power that permitted European nations such as Britain and France to wage a series of conflicts in the 17th and 18th centuries for control of the northern part of the American continent. European armies could not campaign overseas without the support of their navies, and in this respect the British navy usually proved superior to its opponents. It was the Royal Navy's command of the sea and its ability to conduct amphibious operations – to project force from sea onto land – that gained success for Britain in its struggle against France for Canada.

As an example of just what "command of the sea" means, consider the siege of Quebec in 1759. This operation involved three separate squadrons with 49 warships (about a quarter of the British fleet), crewed by 14,500 sailors, escorting 134 merchant vessels carrying 11,000 soldiers and marines from ports on both sides of the Atlantic 600 miles up an uncharted river to their objective.[2] The size of this operation is best gauged by the fact that the total population of the French colonies in North America at that time was about 63,000 souls.

In the century that followed, the Royal Navy continued to protect the infant colonies of British North America, particularly against their aggressive neighbour to the south. In the American Revolutionary War of 1775-1783, the RN supported British forces fighting the insurgent colonists and built and manned warships on the Great Lakes. A similar phenomenon occurred during the War of 1812-1814 when Britain not only instituted a blockade of America's Atlantic coast that nearly brought economic ruin to the republic but constructed and manned warships on the inland lakes and rivers, including a ship of the line on Lake Ontario larger than Nelson's famous *Victory*. The many memorials to British and Canadian victories of the conflict scattered today across Ontario and Quebec bear no mention that these successes were only possible because the Royal Navy controlled the sea lanes.

Although the threat of invasion from the United States decreased as the 19th century wore on, Britain continued to maintain a naval presence in North America. The squadron on the lakes acted as a marine police force to prevent American adventurers who supported the ill-fated rebellions in Upper and Lower Canada (modern Ontario and Quebec) in 1837-1838 from raiding across the border. During the 19th century, shipbuilding and maritime trade boomed in the Atlantic colonies, impelled by the rich fishing grounds nearby and by the triangle trade between the Maritimes, Britain and the West Indies. The RN maintained a station at Halifax, blessed with one of the largest and most sheltered harbours in the world and, as settlement spread across the continent, established a second base at Esquimalt on the Pacific coast.

By 1867, when the separate colonies of British North America began to confederate into the modern Dominion of Canada, the new nation pos-

Jack Tar ashore.
The crew of a British warship on a route march near Esquimalt, B.C., between 1900 and 1905. Throughout the British Empire, the RN served as an emergency police force and British warships were often required to send armed parties ashore to quell local disturbances. For this reason, it was necessary that sailors received basic military instruction, including marching and small-arms training. (National Archives of Canada, PA-115388)

followed a continental as opposed to a maritime policy – in effect, Canada turned its back on the sea. Ottawa instituted high tariffs to protect industries in central Canada against American competition, and the Atlantic merchant marine gradually withered away, although fishing remained a strong enterprise. As a result the maritime provinces entered an economic decline from which they have never fully recovered.

Birth pangs of the Canadian navy: 1867-1914

Periodically, during Canada's first four decades, the question of a naval service was raised, usually in connection with the fisheries as this industry was a major source of employment. There was always concern about American intrusion and in 1870 the government created a Marine Police with six armed schooners to regulate American fishing vessels but it was disbanded the following year after the British-American Treaty of Washington resolved long-standing disputes over fishing grounds. In 1881, for reasons that are still somewhat obscure, Britain presented the Canadian government with a small and obsolescent steam/sail warship, HMS *Charybdis*, in the hope that it would serve as a training vessel for recruits to the RN and the nucleus of a Canadian navy. On her arrival in Saint John, however, *Charybdis* was found to be so unserviceable that she

sessed a sizeable merchant fleet and a maritime tradition, both commercial and fishing, on its Atlantic coast. It might therefore be expected that the establishment of a naval force would be one of the first acts of the Canadian government but, unfortunately, this was not the case. The greater part of the population of the Dominion lived in the interior and Canadian politicians, catering to voters rather than looking to the future,

was quietly returned to Britain in 1882. Disputes with the United States over the fishing provisions of the Treaty of Washington led to the creation of what might be called a proto-naval force – the Fishery Protection Service – in 1886 and this organization grew until by 1906 it had 30 vessels in commission. But the federal government disliked spending a dollar more on defence than absolutely necessary (while at the same time basking in the protection provided by the British fleet) and resolutely resisted all calls for the establishment of a permanent Canadian navy.

In the first decade of the 20th century, the comfortable assumptions on which this policy was based disappeared when Britain made a major change in its defence strategy. Germany had begun to construct a large and modern battle fleet, and faced with this challenge, Britain started to concentrate her warships in home waters. Since the RN also guaranteed the safety of the empire, British politicians encouraged the self-governing Dominions of Australia, Canada and New Zealand to strengthen their own naval forces or to make financial contributions toward the construction of British warships, and as part of this shift in policy, the RN dockyards at Halifax and Esquimalt were turned over to Canada and the last British garrisons departed in 1905. At a series of colonial conferences held between 1887 and 1907, however, Canadian politicians rebuffed British requests for Canada to increase its defence spending or to make contributions to imperial defence.

The climate of opinion began to change in 1908 following the passage of legislation in Germany to create a battle fleet to match the Royal Navy's home fleet. The response throughout the empire verged on panic – even the Canadian government, which had always disliked paying for its own defence, was forced by public opinion in English Canada to change course and seriously contemplate the creation of a navy. French Canada, always concerned about entanglement in imperial military adventures, opposed such a service but Prime Minister Wilfrid Laurier was skilful enough to get unanimous approval in the House of

Admiral Sir Charles Kingsmill (1855-1935).
A Canadian, Kingsmill joined the RN in 1869 and rose to the rank of rear admiral before retiring in 1908 to direct the Canadian Maritime Service and, later, the Canadian Naval Service. He commanded the RCN during the First World War and retired in 1921 with the rank of admiral. (Author's collection)

Commons for the expenditure necessary to establish a Canadian navy "with the view that the naval supremacy of Britain is essential to the security of commerce, the safety of the empire and the peace of the world."[3]

On 10 May 1910 an act was passed in the House of Commons creating the Canadian Naval Service. This new entity was placed under the direction of Rear Admiral Charles Kingsmill, a Canadian-born officer who had retired from the RN two years earlier to serve as the Director of the Marine Service, which supervised the hydrographic, navigation and fishery protection functions of the government. The act stated that Canada might acquire 11 warships, five cruisers and six destroyers, which, if possible, would be built in the country. It also provided for the establishment of a naval college to train officers, but until it was ready, Britain promised to provide two old cruisers to serve as training vessels and to loan officers and ratings (enlisted sailors) to act as instructors.

There was much excitement when these two warships, *Niobe* and *Rainbow*, arrived in Canada in the autumn of 1910, crewed by 600 officers and sailors. The newly-christened His Majesty's Canadian Ship *Niobe* displaced 11,000 tons and was armed with sixteen 6-inch guns while the smaller HMCS *Rainbow* displaced 3,600 tons and mounted two 6-inch guns and six 4.7-inch guns. *Niobe* went to Halifax and *Rainbow* to Esquimalt. At the same time, the Royal Naval College of Canada opened in Halifax to educate officer cadets and the first recruiting posters, advertising "Great Attractions" in the Canadian Naval Service for "Strong, healthy, well educated men and boys" of "Good Character," were posted across Canada.[4]

The "West Coast Fleet:" HMCS *Rainbow*, November 1910.
A protected cruiser, *Rainbow* was commissioned in the RN in 1893 and transferred to the Canadian Naval Service in 1910. This photograph shows her entering the naval base at Esquimalt, B.C., on 7 November 1910 and passing by HMS *Shearwater* in the foreground, which has "dressed overall" for the occasion by displaying flags from stem to stern. *Rainbow* displaced 3,600 tons, carried a complement of 273 and was armed with two 6-inch guns, six 4-inch guns, eight 6-pdr. guns and four 14-inch torpedo tubes. *Rainbow* served in the RCN until 1920 when she was sold for scrap. (National Archives of Canada, PA 115365)

The future looked good but, unfortunately, this promising start was soon blighted. *Niobe*, the flagship of Canada's infant fleet, ran aground off Cape Sable in July 1911 and was so badly damaged that she had to spend sixteen months in dock. Still worse was the defeat of Laurier's Liberals in the election of September 1911 because Robert Borden's incoming Conservatives placed the Naval Service in "suspended animation" while it worked out its own defence policies. Laurier's ambitious ship acquisition programme was cut in favour of providing funds to Britain to construct three battleships, but this bill failed to pass the Liberal-dominated senate (despite "closure" being used for the first time in the history of Canadian politics) and Borden was stymied. Morale plummeted in the new service (in 1912-1913, the figures for desertion surpassed those for recruiting) although, somewhat ironically, at about the same time it was given permission to assume the title of "Royal Canadian Navy." Naval matters in Canada were at a standstill.

The First World War

They remained so until June 1914 when the assassination of the heir to the Austro-Hungarian throne set in motion a chain of events that ultimately led to a British declaration of war against Germany on 4 August. At that time, when Britain went to war, so did her empire, and Canada thus became involved in a European struggle that broadened into a global conflict. The country's major contribution was an overseas military contingent, the Canadian Expeditionary Force, which in four years of bloody fighting on the western front acquired a reputation as one of the most professional combat formations on the Allied side.

Unfortunately the Royal Canadian Navy's wartime record was considerably less resplendent. On the day that Britain declared war, the Canadian government placed *Niobe* and *Rainbow* "at the disposal of His Majesty for general service in the Royal Navy."[5] In the early days of the conflict, there was concern about the threat of German surface raiders and the two old cruisers engaged in coastal patrols although neither would have lasted long in combat with modern warships. To bolster naval defences on the west coast, the British Columbia government purchased two submarines built at Seattle and these were later commissioned into the RCN as *CC-1* and *CC-2*. While Canadians supplied the greater part of the crews for all four warships, most of the officers and specialists on board remained British. Both the RCN and its auxiliary component, the Royal Navy Canadian Volunteer Reserve, were active in recruiting for the British navy – some 1,700 Canadians joined the Overseas Division of the RNCVR and another 1,118 specialists, mainly pilots and medical officers, were obtained in Canada for the RN. Ironically, the first Canadians to die in combat during the war were four young RCN midshipmen who were lost when the British cruiser HMS *Good Hope* was sunk in action on 1 November 1914.

In addition to coastal patrols by its cruisers and submarines, the RCN also assisted the British Naval Control Service, which supervised merchant shipping in time of war, and participated in the defence of Esquimalt and Halifax. This latter port was a major terminus for merchant ships sailing for Britain – and they soon sailed into dangerous waters. In 1914, German surface raiders had been viewed as the greatest menace but as the war progressed, it became apparent that the submarine was a more serious opponent. The RN had built up its prewar battle fleet in expectation of fighting a major high seas action against its German counterpart and British naval planners had largely discounted submarines because their underwater speed was too slow to catch a warship. Nor were submarines regarded as that dangerous to merchant ships since, under the international laws of maritime war, a submarine had to surface and warn its target of an impending attack. This gave the threatened crew time not only to abandon their ship but also to send a radio message with their location – and, of course, that of the submarine.

It was all rather gentlemanly but things changed in 1915 when Germany declared the waters around the British Isles a "war zone" in which German U-boat* or submarine commanders would follow a "sink on sight" policy and attack targets without warning while submerged. At this time Germany possessed a small submarine force (29 boats, of which only 6 or 7 were operational at any one time) but it was deployed most effectively in the North Sea and English Channel. In May 1915, however, the torpedoing of the Cunard liner *Lusitania*, with the loss of many American lives, outraged the United States and caused German submarine operations in British waters to be abandoned in favour of the Mediterranean. The U-boats returned in February 1916 under complicated rules of engagement that forbade them to attack passenger liners and unarmed merchant ships outside the "war zone," but the mistaken torpedoing of a small liner again caused them to be withdrawn in April 1916, although they were back in operation late in that year. By early 1917, with the war going against her, a desperate Germany decided to resort to unrestricted submarine warfare to knock Britain out of the war before, inevitably, the United States entered on the Allied side. On 1 February 1917 the German submarine force, which by this time had grown to 120 boats, was ordered to attack without warning.

This decision nearly won the war for Germany. Between February and

---

* Throughout this book, the wartime term "U-boat," an anglicization of the German *U-boot* or *Unterseeboot,* will be used to designate German submarines.

April 1917, U-boats sank around 1,000 merchant ships displacing nearly two million gross tons in British waters – nearly a quarter of the shipping sailing from British ports. In the month of April alone, 881,000 tons of merchant shipping were lost and Britain was threatened with starvation. Despite these horrific statistics, the Royal Navy steadfastly refused to implement the convoy system, the most effective countermeasure against commerce raiders. The use of convoys would have deprived the U-boats of the independent ship targets that constituted most of their victories. In addition, convoys could be routed around dangerous areas and, if located by U-boats, the Germans would first have to deal with the naval escort.

In the end, it took the insistence of the British cabinet to force the Admiralty (the traditional term for the headquarters of the Royal Navy) to institute the convoy system in August 1917. The results were immediate – by October the rate of sinking of ships in convoy was 1 in 150, a rate of losses that could easily be overcome by new construction. Moreover, since the Royal Navy had broken the German naval cyphers, they were able to listen to their opponent's radio traffic, learn where U-boats were to be deployed and steer convoys clear of them. Other measures were also taken. Increasing numbers of aircraft, the natural enemy of the submarine, were brought into service to fly patrols in British coastal waters. Scientists devised the hydrophone, a passive sonar* device, which could, under optimum conditions, detect the presence of a submarine, although it could not accurately locate it. If a submerged submarine was detected, naval escorts attempted to destroy it using another innovation – depth charges, containers filled with explosives dropped by a warship and set to explode at a pre-arranged depth. Since U-boats had to approach the convoys to find their prey, their chances of being sighted were correspondingly greater, and while Allied shipping losses declined in late 1917, U-boat losses increased. The German naval command began to look for less dangerous and more profitable areas in which to operate and the entry of the United States into the war drew their attention to the western side of the Atlantic.

---

* Sonar, underwater detection equipment, is divided into two types. "Passive" sonar is a listening device while "active" sonar sends a sound pulse that, if it strikes an underwater object, returns an echo.

U-boats In Canadian waters

The first indication that German submarines might operate in North American waters had actually occurred in November 1916 when *U-53* claimed five unescorted merchant ships off Nantucket. In the following summer, in response to a request from the Admiralty, the RCN created a local escort force to protect convoys assembling for passage to Britain and to guard coastal traffic. It was commanded by Captain Walter Hose, RCN, a former British officer who had transferred to Canadian service in 1911 and possessed considerable experience with small vessels. Hose proved to be an energetic and competent officer but he faced almost insurmountable problems building up an effective anti-submarine escort force. Its nucleus was 15 hastily-armed civilian vessels that had been carrying out coastal patrols in the Gulf of St. Lawrence and off Halifax since the beginning of war, and Hose made plans for Canada to man 36, later revised to 112, small escort vessels. A shortage of suitable craft and weapons, however, meant that the force was only completed with the loan of vessels from the British and American navies (some actually having been built in Canada), the hasty conversion of more civilian craft, and a massive programme of new construction. Personnel shortages were just as bad. Canadians serving in the Overseas Division of the RNCVR had to be called back to Canada to man Hose's force, and British and Newfoundland personnel procured on loan. Matters were not helped by the attitude of the Admiralty, which foisted incompetent British officers on both Hose and his superior in Ottawa, Admiral Charles Kingsmill, and held discussions with the United States Navy about operations in Canadian waters without bothering to inform the RCN. It was fortunate for Hose and his sailors that the expected German submarine offensive did not materialize in 1917 because, at the end of that year, they had to deal with a worse catastrophe.

On the morning of 6 December 1917, the Norwegian steamer *Imo* collided with the French steamer *Mont Blanc* as the two ships were trying pass each other in the narrows that separate Bedford Basin from Halifax harbour proper. The result was one of the greatest disasters in Canadian history. The French vessel, which was carrying a deadly cargo of 2,300 tons of volatile picric acid, 200 tons of unstable TNT, 35 tons of highly inflammable benzine and – just for good measure – 10 tons of highly explosive gun cotton, caught fire. A boat's crew from HMCS *Niobe* boarded the *Mont Blanc* and was attempting to put out the fires when its lethal cargo detonated and the resulting blast, the largest man-made explosion before the atomic bomb, vaporized the *Niobe* party, flattened much of the city of Halifax, killed 2,500 people, injured some 9,000 and left 6,000 homeless in the depths of a Canadian winter. Naval personnel from American, British and Canadian warships in the harbour were prominent in the rescue activities, which lasted for weeks, but many Haligonians blamed the disaster on the RCN, which was responsible for the control of traffic in the harbour, and it was certainly not the new service's best moment.

By the spring of 1918, Hose had managed to cobble together a force of 47 escort vessels, of which only a half dozen were capable of extended operations in all weathers, manned by 1,518 officers and men, many of them raw recruits. The only positive feature was the stationing of six United States Navy sub-chasers, fast modern craft, at Halifax and the promise of American assistance to create a Royal Canadian Naval Air Service to operate air patrols on the Atlantic coast.

The "Hun Sea Wolf:" The cruise of U-156

The long expected U-boat offensive finally materialized in May 1918 when *U-151* sank 22 unescorted ships by gunfire off Maryland. Another submarine, *U-156*, laid mines off Massachusetts that sank the American cruiser USS *San Diego* before brazenly destroying several merchant ships by gunfire off Cape Cod in broad daylight and in plain view of idling vacationers. *U-156* then sailed north to Nova Scotian waters and her first Canadian victim, the lumber schooner *Dornfontein*, in the Bay of Fundy on 2 August. Moving east, the raider sank seven fishing schooners off the southern tip of Nova Scotia after permitting their crews to take to their boats. These successes were capped by the torpedoing of the 5,000-ton tanker *Luz Blanca* just 35 miles from the mouth of Halifax harbour. When the crew of the tanker rowed ashore, their arrival created a sensation as newspapers outdid each other with headlines that proclaimed the peril of the "Hun Sea Wolf." Many Canadians, both military and civilian, falsely believed that

U-156 was being guided by German agents on land and this, in turn, incited a witch-hunt for spies.

The newspapers criticized the RCN for not preventing these depredations. In fact most of Hose's sailors were doing exactly what they were supposed to be doing – providing local escort for a large troop convoy carrying 12,500 American and Canadian soldiers that had departed Halifax bound for Britain. Of the 40 seaworthy escort craft in Hose's command when the *Luz Blanca* went down, one-third were unavailable because of mechanical problems or routine maintenance, and the remainder were involved in escort duties. The tanker's sinking, however, had immediate repercussions – the terminus for trans-Atlantic convoys was switched from Halifax to Quebec City and the convoy system was imposed on Canadian coastal traffic, but these steps forced Hose to spread his already small force even thinner. More importantly, the USN rushed surface units to Canadian waters and sent flying boats to Halifax.

In the meantime, *U-156*, the source of all this commotion, had moved back into American waters where it sank two more victims, both unescorted merchantmen. Having caused trouble enough, *U-156* then headed for home but, unfortunately for the RCN, it chose to exit through Canadian waters. During a six-day period, 20-25 August 1918, it not only sank several fishing schooners off Cape Breton Island but also put a prize crew aboard the Canadian steam trawler *Triumph*, armed the vessel with weapons from the submarine, and used this miniature privateer to sink six other fishing craft. When the *Triumph*'s coal was exhausted, the prize crew scuttled her and re-boarded *U-156*.

The RCN finally caught up with the piratical *U-156* off the northeastern tip of Nova Scotia in the early afternoon of 25 August 1918 when a patrol from Hose's escort force consisting of the converted yachts *Cartier* and *Hochelaga* and trawlers *22* and *32* were steaming abreast about four miles apart in a patrol line. The senior officer was Lieutenant McGuirk of *Cartier* and the easternmost vessel, *Hochelaga*, armed with two 12-pdr. (3-inch) guns, was under the command of Lieutenant Robert Legate, RNCVR, a two-year veteran of the east coast patrols. Legate's crew saw two fishing schooners and turned toward them, intending to warn their cap-

Not a proud ship: HMCS *Hochelaga* in 1918.
A former American yacht, *Hochelaga* was purchased by the RCN in 1914 to serve as a patrol vessel. Displacing 628 tons and armed with a single 12-pdr. gun, in August 1918 *Hochelaga* was the first Canadian warship to encounter a U-boat but the occasion was not a memorable one as her captain swiftly withdrew, an act that cost him his commission. *Hochelaga* served until 1920 and was then sold to private interests, only to reappear in the Mediterranean in 1948 when she was seized by the RN while engaged in transporting illegal immigrants to Palestine. (Directorate of History and Heritage, DND, CN 3400)

tains of the presence of a German submarine, but almost immediately one of the schooners seemed to disappear, and only then did Legate spot *U-156* surfaced near the remaining vessel. For the first time in the history of naval warfare a Canadian warship was in contact with a U-boat.

Unfortunately, instead of carrying out the tactical instructions that had been issued for such an occasion – that he should try to engage the submarine and inflict damage – Legate chose to steer in the opposite direction. As the *U-156* was armed with two 150mm (5.9-inch) deck guns which would have made short work of *Hochelaga*, this may have been wise but Legate compounded his sins when, after turning toward *Cartier* and signalling "enemy in sight" by flag (he had no radio), he refused to obey when McGuirk ordered his command to steer toward the *U-156*.[6] Instead, Leg-

ate held back and cautioned his senior officer by megaphone not to engage until reinforcements arrived. The enemy had submerged by the time this conversation took place and the action, for all intents and purposes, had ended because, although some of McGuirk's vessels were equipped with hydrophones, nobody had been trained to use them. *U-156* got clean away and sank another fishing schooner the next day while Legate went before a court martial which dismissed him from the service because he did not, "on sight of the enemy which it was his duty to engage, use his utmost exertion to bring his ship into action."[7] It was not an auspicious beginning for the Canadian navy's involvement in anti-submarine warfare.

After creating havoc, *U-156* headed for Germany, only to be sunk by a mine in British waters with the loss of all hands. Its cruise was followed by those of *U-117* and *U-157* in September 1918 but these two boats did not enjoy the same success. Stymied by the strength of the naval escort accompanying the trans-Atlantic convoys, they managed to torpedo only two ocean-going merchantmen and several fishing vessels. An attempt by *U-157* to lay mines off the mouth of Halifax harbour was defeated by the constant presence of Allied naval units and no ships were lost as a result. Although the Canadian public and newspapers complained loudly that the RCN appeared to be incapable of safeguarding the nation's coastline, what most observers overlooked was the fact that, during the period the three German submarines were in Canadian waters, more than 500 merchantmen left Halifax bound for the United Kingdom under escort and the U-boats were only attacking fishing craft and small vessels proceeding independently because better targets were lacking.

The scare, however, had been enough to move the government to action as it was expected that, despite recent victories on the Western Front, the war would continue into the following year. The Royal Canadian Naval Air Service was formed in September 1918, but when the Royal Naval Air Service refused to release experienced Canadian personnel, the new organization had to train flight personnel from scratch and this delayed it reaching operational status. By this time Hose commanded 120 small escort vessels (including the two submarines *CC-1* and *CC-2*, which had been brought from the west coast) for convoy and patrol work, as well as 50 auxiliary vessels for harbour defence and minor duties. Always a realist, Hose reported that his crews were "untrained, not only in the technical knowledge required to handle the weapons and offensive appliances on board the ships, but also in service discipline, being drafted to ships as hardly more than raw recruits."[8] He wanted the RCN to acquire destroyers, fast and relatively well-armed warships, which he saw as the most effective vessels for ASW (anti-submarine warfare), and the commander of the RCN, Admiral Kingsmill, advised the government to construct six destroyers in Canada as there was little hope of obtaining these useful ships from either Britain or the United States. The government did nothing.

The RCN's record in the First World War

When the First World War ended in November 1918, the Canadian navy consisted of 5,500 officers and sailors in its three divisions: the regular RCN, the Royal Navy Canadian Volunteer Reserve and the Royal Canadian Naval Air Service. The seagoing organizations manned 170 small vessels but its largest purpose-built warships were the aged *Rainbow* (*Niobe* had been permanently secured alongside in 1916) and the submarines *CC-1* and *CC-2*. The remainder were a motley collection of converted civilian vessels and hastily-constructed small craft. Another 4,000 Canadians had served with the RN during the war, where they had established an enviable record, particularly in the Royal Naval Air Service. Yet, the RCN's greatest contribution to the Allied naval effort had been Hose's ragged little armada. Although its single action against the enemy (*Hochelaga* versus *U-156* on 25 August 1918) was not very noteworthy, it had rendered essential service by protecting Canada's east coast ports and covering the first stages of the trans-Atlantic convoys to Britain. The point should be made that no merchant ship escorted by the RCN was lost to a U-boat during the First World War.

Unfortunately, Canadians and their politicians neither knew much, nor really cared much, about their tiny navy. In their eyes, the nation's major contribution to Allied victory had been its army – more than 600,000 Canadian men, about one in three of military age, had joined it – and throughout the war Canada's attention had been firmly fixed on the activi-

Rag tag fleet – HMCS *Grilse*, 1918.
During the First World War, Canada's naval force was largely assembled from hastily-converted civilian vessels and purpose-built small naval craft. One of the more powerful ASW vessels in this rag-tag fleet was HMCS *Grilse*, a former American yacht. Displacing 287 tons, manned by a crew of 56 and armed with two 12-pdr. guns and one 14-inch torpedo tube, *Grilse* was capable of 30 knots, making her useful for patrol duties. Sold to a member of the Guggenheim family and reconverted to a yacht, she foundered off Long Island in a storm in 1938. (National Archives of Canada, PA-133293)

ties of its fighting units on the Western Front. Canadians were proud of their soldiers' victories, sorrowful at the cost (232,494 dead and wounded) and determined that this sacrifice, which guaranteed the nation a separate signature on the Versailles Peace Treaty of 1919, would never be forgotten. Balanced against this achievement, the wartime efforts of Canada's infant navy were regarded as useful but insignificant.

What Canadians and their leaders were overlooking were three crucial lessons of the naval war of 1914-1918. First, submarines were the only German forces to significantly threaten Allied control of the sea lanes – the best estimate is that a total of 351 U-boats sank 5,000 warships and merchant vessels displacing about 12 million tons during the First World War. Second, it had required a tremendous effort to defeat the German submarine force – the convoy was the most effective defence but approximately 3,300 warships and nearly 600 aircraft had been deployed in anti-submarine operations. Third, and perhaps most important, the U-boats had been the only German naval units to attack shipping in Canadian waters. Two decades later these three lessons would have to be learned again – at an awful cost.

THE EARLY DAYS TO 1918

"Some more non-paying guests:" Joining the Service in 1915

A.H. Wickens of Vancouver was serving on a CPR steamship at Esquimalt in 1915 when many of her crew decided to join the Royal Navy Canadian Volunteer Reserve. He recalls his first hours in service:

We were conducted upstairs to the slop room which was situated at the end of the gymnasium and class rooms. Said the M[aster at] A[rms] to the bloke in charge: "Here you are, Bill, some more non-paying guests." Said Bill, "Don't worry, Master, they'll pay for it," and we surely did as time rolled by.

We were issued with the following:

1 Canvas kit bag
1 hammock
2 hammock covers
1 blanket (white)
1 round tin hat box
1 wooden ditty box
1 length of rope for lashing hammock
3 caps, round, 1 of which had a linen or canvas top
2 cap covers, linen
1 straw hat with carrying bag for tropical use (which became a damn nuisance in transportation
2 suits, underclothes
2 flannel shirts
2 blue work shirts
3 collars,

1 cholera belt
3 duck suits
2 duck suits with collars attached and blue cuffs for tropical use
3 blue serge suits (one to be kept for special occasions and Sundays)
1 boiler suit (combination overalls)
1 dozen clothes straps (short laces used to tie your washing to the forestay)
1 overcoat
1 sou'wester
1 oilskin
1 pair rubber sea boots
1 heavy woollen sweater, turtle neck, blue
1 blue woollen scarf
1 winter hat with ear protection
1 silk scarf or handkerchief, black
2 lanyards (big enough to use as tow ropes)
1 tooth brush
1 tin pink tooth powder (which we thought was pulverized holy stones dyed pink which took the enamel off our teeth)
1 razor (make a good bush knife)
1 jack knife with marlin spike attached
2 pairs of black boots
1 housewife [sewing kit]
1 hair brush
2 shoe brushes
2 stencils (1 for marking dark clothes and the other for marking light clothes)
1 white pad & 1 black pad for marking [clothing]
1 pair of gaiters
2 pair woollen socks

Now down to the armourer's stores. We were issued with:

1 .303 Lee Enfield rifle of Boer War vintage
1 bandolier
1 belt with bayonet with scabbard attached
1 water bottle
1 haversack

all numbered with the same number on the rifle racks in the drill shed.

All that we needed was a pack horse to complete the deal.[1]

"We were all dog-tired:" Cadet life at the Royal Navy College of Canada, 1917

Patrick Brock joined the RCN as a cadet in 1917 and, in later years, remembered his time at the naval college in Halifax:

We began each day at 0615 and "cleaned" into flannels for boatwork or gym after a cup of cocoa. At the conclusion of our exercise period we washed, and shaved if necessary, and plunged into a cold bath. I remember the cadet captain standing over us to ensure that we immersed ourselves completely. Breakfast was followed by "defaulters" at 0840 and divisions at 0900, at which time we were inspected by the commander. Studies, interrupted by a break for a glass of milk, commenced shortly after the inspection and continued until 1300. ……

Work resumed after lunch from 1400 to 1600, when we had milk and biscuits, before taking exercise, usually in boats or on the football field. The order was reversed in winter so that we might exercise in daylight. Supper came at 1900 and was followed at 2000 by an hour of study known as "prep" in Study 8. We were then given five minutes to undress and two minutes to say our prayers while kneeling before the seachests at the foot of our cots. Then we turned in by order of the cadet captain. We were all dog-tired, and there was little risk at this stage of Satan finding mischief for idle hands.

Work stopped at 1300 on Wednesdays and Saturdays but there was always organized sport. On Saturdays we were allowed to "go ashore," as we religiously called it, with seventy-five cents pocket money (from our parents' pockets, issued to us in a ceremony known rather wryly as "payment") until 2100. We had leave from 1300 on Sundays, and fortunately, most of us found friends who "showed willing" to give us tea or supper.[2]

"Dogs of war:" A Canadian midshipman in the Royal Navy, 1916-1917

In early 1913, 15-year-old Frank Houghton from Victoria joined the RCN as an officer cadet. Following graduation from the Royal Naval College of Canada, he was sent to serve as a midshipman in a British battleship and quickly discovered that, as far as the life of a "snotty" or midshipman went, things had not changed much in the Royal Navy since Nelson's time. After he retired with the rank of rear admiral, Frank Houghton remembered his days in the gunroom, as the midshipmen's quarters were known, in 1916-1917:

The hierarchy of the Gunroom was of long-standing tradition. The senior sub-lieutenant, if there was more than one, was known as the "Sub of the Mess," and he was all-powerful. ...... the Sub is monarch of all he surveys, and woe betide any young snottie who occupies his favourite chair, or talks at breakfast or plays the mess gramophone when the Sub wants peace and quiet. To assist him in maintaining this type of discipline, the Sub would usually appoint some or all of the senior snotties as "Dogs of War." If the Sub became annoyed at some wretched junior, all he had to say was "Dogs of War out Houghton!" or whoever it happened to be. One was then quickly thrown out of the Mess – literally – with a minimum of ceremony. Of course one was allowed to fight back, though I can recollect no case in which the victim won the battle. .....

Then there are Gunroom traditions that go

"Are we downhearted – No !!!"
Sailors from HMCS *Niobe* pose for a picture after "coaling" ship. When coal was used as fuel, every member of a ship's crew not absolutely required for other duties participated in the laborious and filthy task of refuelling. (National Archives of Canada, PA 190758)

Future admirals, every one.
Junior officers and midshipmen of HMCS *Niobe* pose for a group portrait. The seven sub lieutenants can be distinguished from the six "snotties" or midshipmen as they carry swords and wear double-breasted jackets while the midshipmen carry dirks and have single-breasted jackets with white patches on the collars. The sub lieutenants are also seated on chairs while the snotties, a considerably lower species, squat on the deck. After a certain period, an aspiring (more likely "perspiring") midshipman might secure promotion to sub lieutenant, allowing him to wear officer's uniform, carry a sword and, based on his considerable experience, lord it over all snotties. It was a very old, very traditional and very successful system of junior officer training. (National Archives of Canada, PA 126721)

back well before the days of Nelson. One of these is "Breadcrumbs." If the Sub and senior snotties happen to be discussing some matter which is not considered fit for the ears of juniors, the Sub gives the order "Breadcrumbs!" Whereupon all warts – as they are usually known – hurriedly jam their fingers in their ears. Sometimes the Sub will address some unsuspecting wart in his normal voice, and if the chap so much as twitches, indicating that he had unstopped an ear, he was for it.

Sometimes the Sub reaches a point where he feels he is thoroughly sick of the sight of all warts, in which case he picks up a fork and lays it on a beam or ledge above his head – in the days of wooden ships it would have been jabbed into a beam. This is "Fork in the Beam." Immediately all juniors make a concerted dash for the door – nor do they stand on the order of their going. There is inevitably a mass of struggling bodies endeavouring to get through the door and the last one out received the professionally aimed assistance of a senior's boot. ……

I can assure you that it was taken in good part. After all, when a new lot joined, the juniors became seniors and it was then their turn. Rough and tough at times, perhaps, but excellent training.[3]

Houghton also learned that naval discipline was swift but just after he made a witty remark when his captain appeared one morning in civilian dress, complete with a pair of plus fours with a pattern so loud that he "looked remarkably like a walking checkerboard." Unfortunately, the captain overheard Houghton and the young Canadian was ordered to the platform on top of the mast

and there I stayed – and stayed. Fortunately, it was summer, and for once the weather [at Scapa Flow]

The Halifax Explosion, 1917.
Damage to the naval dockyard caused by the Halifax explosion in December 1917, the largest man-made explosion prior to the advent of nuclear weapons. More than 2,000 people lost their lives and large parts of the city were destroyed. (Author's collection)

was remarkably fine and warm. But as the sun sunk behind the low, dark hills of Hoy, I began to feel the pangs of hunger. It was then that some of my sympathetic shipmates came to the rescue. As soon as darkness had completely enveloped the ship – of course there were no lights showing anywhere – I heard the faint protesting squeak of a signal-halyard, the block for which was attached to the Maintop. I leaned over to see what was going on, when lo and behold a package appeared being slowly hoisted to my solitary platform. With trembling hands I released it from the signal halyard and, on opening it found, to my unspeakable joy, a curious but extremely acceptable mess of sandwiches and biscuits and a medicine bottle full

of gin and bitters. Life once more became bearable. I was finally released from my perch at ten pm, only to be told that I was damn lucky not to be left there all night.

"We watched her burning, spellbound:" The Halifax Explosion, 1917

Cadet Patrick Brock was at the naval college and remembers the great disaster:

It was Thursday morning 6 December 1917. Our term-end examinations were due to start, and after breakfast most of us were in Study 8 doing some last-minute cramming. At about quarter to nine one of the cadets noticed a ship on fire in the harbour and we left our books to look.

It was the French freighter SS *Mont Blanc*. ...... Unhappily she was carrying a deckload of inflammable benzine above her cargo of TNT and picric acid. When this caught fire it provided the detonator for disaster.

We watched her burning, spellbound. Then the warning gong sounded for us to square ourselves off for divisions, and we "new kids" retired to our gunroom on the landward side of the college. Three minutes later the *Mont Blanc* blew up.

The explosion was the greatest man-made explosion on earth to that date. Many supposed that there had, in fact, been two explosions, because the first effect was felt through the earth rather than the air. People at a distance ran to their windows only to be caught up in a blizzard of flying glass. The outside walls of the college stood up, but the partition walls were badly damaged. One cadet was driven through the gunroom window while the rest of us staggered through a shower of plaster and rubble to the green outside. We cowered there with rivets and pieces of iron plate falling all around us. Later we saw that a large piece of boiler plate had come through the roof of Study 8, where we would have otherwise been. A gigantic cloud of smoke, visible for miles, rose over the harbour. Buildings were devastated for fifteen hundred yards around the explosion and there were many fires.

Although we juniors escaped for the most part with minor cuts, the senior terms and the officers who were on the harbour side of the college received many serious injuries. Commander Nixon and several others were badly cut, while two cadets each lost the sight of one eye. Chief Petty Officer King was taken to a mortuary, where he remained for two days before he could demon-

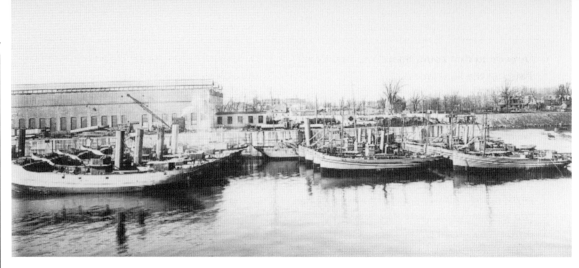

Canada's anti-submarine defence force, 1918.
Constructed in Canada, these wooden-hulled "drifters" were used as escort and patrol vessels during the First World War. Displacing only 99 tons and armed with a single 6-pdr. gun, they were no match for the large German U-boats that began to operate in the western Atlantic in 1918. (Directorate of History and Heritage, CN 3201)

strate that he was still alive. When the injured had received what treatment was available, the rest of us began to recover our gear. However, at this stage we were warned that a magazine just north of us might explode and that we should evacuate the area. Many of us fetched up on Citadel Hill, a vantage point from which we could survey the scene below. Most of the ships and craft in the harbour seemed to be under way, while visibility northward was obscured by smoke and flame.[4]

Leading Seaman Wickens was on HMCS Niobe *in Halifax harbour that fateful day:*

I was lucky enough to escape with cuts and bruises [but] almost lost my eyes. The *Niobe* was badly damaged and was almost tore away from her moorings. ...... There were quite a number of ratings aboard the *Niobe* when the blow came, many of these had families ashore. They were about to make a break for it when some officer heavy on tradition, yelled through a megaphone for "All Hands to stand fast. Keep cool and everything will be all right. There's no immediate danger. Remember the *Birkenhead!*"* So someone yells back at him "To hell with you and the *Birkenhead*, we got wives and kids ashore!" There was a general stampede for the gangplank which was somewhat out of kilter.

It was a good thing those ratings took the law into their own hands, they did a lot of good saving lives and putting out fires, after which they were commended for their bravery and in helping the civic authorities who at the time did not know that they broke ship and had a charge of mass mutiny hanging over their heads but said charge was dropped.[5]

---

* A reference to the loss of the British troopship *Birkenhead* in 1853. In a remarkable display of discipline and self-sacrifice, the officers and men of the 74th Highlanders stood in ranks on the deck while their wives and children were put in the lifeboats. There were not enough boats and most of the soldiers perished.

"Any thing that could float:" The East Coast Patrol in the First World War

Matters of discipline were more casual in "Harry Tate's Navy," as its personnel called Commander Walter Hose's East Coast Patrol after the popular music hall entertainer of the time.

Leading Seaman Wickens remembered that

anything that could float or turn a wheel had a gun mounted on it. There were the flat bottom drifters CDs* destined for overseas service, some which reached England and some which reached Davey Jones. Now there raised an incident in 1918. There were a shortage of Captains so some fishing captains were recruited up and down the coast, old shell backs I assure you, the outcome was, when they saw what they had to skipper, they immediately handed in their resignations & departed for their various homes, saying "they would sooner take chances in their bald headed schooners than those floatin' coffins." ……

Lieutenant W. McLaurin, RNCVR, recalled that Captain Pascoe, the Royal Navy officer in charge of ship repair at Halifax was "a gruff old fellow" but also had a "humane side in his make up:"

Captain Pascoe, R.N. made his headquarters and residence aboard HMCS *Hochelaga*. For us this meant having every button [buttoned] on duty with no deviation from rules contained in the so-called Naval Bible, *King's Rules and Regulations*. During this period prohibition was in force in Halifax and deliveries of evil spirits came via the underground route, the beer in bottles from the

---

* Small wooden fishing vessels converted to auxiliary warships.

Dartmouth Brewery being packed in barrels stencilled on the outside SUGAR.

One of those barrels was waiting until Captain Pascoe went ashore before being unpacked. The following morning [there] was a sigh of relief when Captain Pascoe walked down the gangway. Immediately Lieut. T. Dutton and the Chief Steward went into action. Apparently the old man [forgot] something and backtracked and caught them red handed. In a loud voice he said: "What is this?" Tommy Dutton was equal to the occasion and answered "Sugar, sir." Then the old man whispered, "Don't forget to send some sugar to my cabin."

Some time later he said to Lieut. Dutton: "Don't you think it is time to get some more sugar."[6]

"For Heaven's sake can nothing be done:" U-boats off Nova Scotia, 1918

In August 1918, the German submarine U-156 *sank a number of fishing vessels off the coast of Nova Scotia, inciting a near-panic ashore. The U-boat captured and employed a fishing trawler, the* Triumph, *as a privateer and she sank a number of unsuspecting victims, including the schooner* Francis J. O'Hara, *as her captain relates:*

The Beam Trawler approached us under full steam. I could see that it was the Trawler *Triumph* of Halifax as we had fished alongside of him on our last trip and I knew the captain of her quite well. I did not distrust anything … until they got within 150 yards of us when they stopped their vessel and the captain, through a megaphone ordered us to heave our vessel to. I thought the captain was joking with us … and the first thing we knew, four shots were fired across our bow from

rifles. [The *Triumph*] came up alongside of us and I then saw that she was manned by a German crew and had a German flag at her masthead. The captain ordered me to come aboard of his vessel with our papers [and he gave] me quite a calling down for not stopping my vessel sooner, and said that if we expected him to do the right thing, we would have to do the right thing by him. He then ordered three of his men to come in the dory with me and they brought a bomb along. The bomb was a small round thing and they had it in a bag and hung it under the stern with a line … After touching off the fuse, [they] returned to the Beam Trawler. The bomb exploded shortly after … and the vessel went down stern first.[7]

The success of U-156 *caused a panic among civilians, who were convinced that the enemy was being guided by German sympathizers on shore. One angry Nova Scotia woman complained to the authorities:*

The Men of Lunenburg are in Khaki, the dough-heads and pro-Germans are left … So it is up to the women and children to be on the look out … For Heaven's sake can nothing be done; are these devils to be allowed to carry on this work in aid of Germany and enjoy some protection and liberty as loyal British subjects? I tell you, men, if you don't take notice, we sisters, mothers, etc., who have given all will do something to those traitors, in that case I suppose the "Law" would protect the Hun and traitor, and hang its own countrymen. Send a man who is not afraid and don't herald it about as was done a few weeks ago when a detective was sent here and the traitors given every chance to keep "Mum."[8]

CHAPTER 2

LONG, SLOW YEARS: THE ROYAL CANADIAN NAVY

BETWEEN THE WARS, 1919-1939

Bright future, sad destiny, 1918-1921

In the immediate postwar period, the Canadian navy's future appeared bright although at first there were the inevitable reductions in strength. Personnel numbers were cut, the air service was disbanded and most of the hastily-commissioned patrol vessels were sold off or scrapped, leaving only the rusted-out *Niobe* and *Rainbow* and the two, by now obsolescent, submarines *CC-1* and *CC-2* on strength. In January 1919, however, the visit of Admiral Jellicoe, the former First Sea Lord, or senior officer of the Royal Navy, to Canada on a mission to co-ordinate imperial naval defence, gave hope that the RCN might soon acquire large modern warships. At the request of the Canadian government, Jellicoe drafted four "off the shelf" plans for a navy ranging from one costing £1 million that called for a coast defence force consisting of 8 submarines, 4 destroyers, 8 sub-chasers and 4 minesweepers up to a grandiose plan with a price tag of £5 million that proposed the creation of a fleet of 2 battle cruisers, 7 light cruisers, 13 destroyers, 16 submarines, 4 aircraft carriers and many smaller vessels.

Jellicoe stressed that most of these ships could be obtained cheaply from the Royal Navy, which was cutting back its wartime fleet, but Prime Minister Robert Borden's government balked at the price tag. One historian has called Jellicoe "a used warship salesman" but he was at least instrumental in arranging for the RN to sell Canada a light cruiser, *Aurora*, two destroyers, *Patrician* and *Patriot*, and two submarines, *CH-14* and *CH-15*, at bargain basement prices.[1] These vessels arrived in 1919-1920 and *Niobe*, *Rainbow* and the two wartime submarines went to the scrapyard. With five modern warships and a number of smaller vessels in commission, 1,000 officers and sailors on strength, and the Royal Navy College of Canada re-established at Esquimalt to train future leaders, the RCN appeared to be, at long last, on a firm footing.

As usual, however, just when things were looking good for the Canadian navy, disaster struck. In 1921, the Liberal government of Mackenzie King came to power and, responding to the prevalent distaste for war and the military – and the attendant expenditures for defence – began a rigorous programme of cost cutting that came close to scuttling the RCN. The navy's already small budget was slashed 40 per cent, the *Aurora* and the two

(Facing page) **New arrivals – HMC Ships *Aurora*, *Patrician* and *Patriot*, 1921.** Acquired from Britain in 1920, these three warships had seen service during the First World War. *Aurora*, an Arethusa Class light cruiser displacing 3,512 tons and carrying a complement of 318, was armed with two 6-inch guns, six 4-inch guns, two 3-inch guns and eight 21-inch torpedo tubes. *Patrician* and *Patriot* each displaced about 1,000 tons, were manned by a complement of 82 and armed with three 4-inch guns, one 2-pdr. gun and two 11-inch torpedo tubes. Financial cutbacks caused *Aurora* to be decommissioned in 1922 and sold for scrap in 1927 but the two destroyers served until 1929. (National Archives of Canada, PA 115369)

HMC Submarine *CH 14*.
For a brief period in 1920 there were almost as many submarines (four) in the RCN as there were surface vessels. *CH 14* and *CH 15* were British H-Class boats taken over by Canada in 1919 but postwar cutbacks caused them to be sold for scrap. Displacing 363 tons, *CH 14* was manned by 22 officers and men and armed with four 18-inch torpedo tubes. (Author's collection)

submarines were decommissioned, the Royal Naval College of Canada was closed, personnel strength was cut by half, and the navy reduced to the two destroyers, *Patrician* and *Patriot*, two trawlers and a very rudimentary dockyard organization on each coast. It might have been worse – at one point in December 1920, the Minister of the Naval Service, C.C. Ballantyne, became so disgusted with his cabinet colleagues' reluctance to spend money on the RCN that he issued instructions that more or less shut it down, embarrassing them into providing enough funds to keep it alive, but just barely. Money was so tight in the early 1920s that the captains of the two destroyers were ordered not to operate their generators when in port, forcing their crews to use stinking oil lamps to light the interior of their ships.

A training organization, 1922-1934

One positive event in this general tale of woe was the appointment in 1921 of Commodore Walter Hose as Director (or senior officer) of the Naval Service to replace Kingsmill. Hose was a good choice as he understood the political and financial realities that affected naval matters in Canada – the government was tightfisted and its attention was firmly fixed on central Canada, which had the largest number of voters. Hose also knew that the Canadian government, disdainful of the military and interested in industrial policies aimed at central, not maritime Canada, would never support, either financially or in any other way, even the most basic naval force, which he estimated as being six destroyers on each coast. To guarantee the survival of the navy, Hose therefore transformed it into a reserve-based organization because he realized that, although the government regarded the RCN with indifference, there was actually considerable enthusiasm in Canada for a naval service. The problem was how to mobilize this enthusiasm and raise the navy's profile among Canadians living far from the sea – in short, how "to bring the Navy to their doors, into the lives of families and friends."[2]

Hose's solution was to transform the Canadian navy into a training organization. The small regular component, the RCN itself, which consisted of only 400 officers and men, would serve as the instruction cadre for the Royal Canadian Naval Reserve, drawn from those who made their living in the merchant marine or fishing fleets, and the Royal Canadian Naval Volunteer Reserve, a force of about 1,000 officers and men, organized in companies of 100 and half-companies of 50 in most major cities. The creation of the RCNVR was an inspired move as it established a small but visible naval presence across Canada, while all three components of the Canadian navy constituted a foundation that could be expanded in time of war.

Throughout the 1920s the RCN kept the two obsolescent destroyers, *Patrician* and *Patriot*, in commission, along with four trawlers, and each summer Reserve and Volunteer Reserve personnel would participate in training cruises that maintained and polished their skills. Since the naval college had been closed, officer cadets for the RCN were trained by the Royal Navy, spending part of their time in classes and part at sea, and Britain also provided advanced instruction for enlisted personnel in the technical trades. Members of the permanent force could expect to spend part of their time with the Royal Navy, part on board Canadian warships, and the rest instructing the two reserve forces.

The RCNVR proved to be a popular institution and most companies soon had waiting lists for new entrants. These companies, later renamed "divisions," held 30 evening drills a year at their headquarters and participated in two weeks of training each summer at either Halifax or Esquimalt. Ratings were paid 25 cents per drill and received the full pay of their equivalent RCN rank during their two-week training period. Reserve officers did not receive pay for the drills but did get it for summer training, although most donated it back to their respective divisions. At a time when Canada's connection to Britain was much closer than it is today and the Royal Navy's reputation was at its peak, the local RCNVR division was sure to be part of any civic function and some divisions raised bands which further enhanced their popularity. The Volunteer Reserve also functioned as a social club, particularly during the depression when funds were limited and entertainment at a premium. The end result was exactly what Hose had hoped for – the navy had a presence across Canada.

Walter Hose (1875-1965).
Shown here as a commander in 1914, Walter Hose served in the RN for 21 years before transferring to the Canadian service in 1912 as captain of the light cruiser HMCS *Rainbow*. During the First World War, he commanded the east coast escort fleet and in 1921 he became the director of the naval service. Hose preserved the Canadian navy in the face of cost-cutting politicians during the interwar period and his decision to create the RCNVR was an inspired move that would pay dividends in the war. (National Archives of Canada, PA 141880)

By the late 1920s, *Patrician* and *Patriot* were worn out and it is an indication of Hose's skill in dealing with politicians and bureaucrats that he actually convinced the government to pay for the construction in British shipyards of two modern replacement vessels. Ordered in 1929, HMC Ships *Saguenay* and *Skeena* were built according to Canadian specifications and incorporated so many innovations – reinforced hulls for operations in ice fields, improved heating for cold weather, improved ventilation for hot weather, and larger bridges – that British dockyard workers christened them the "Rolls-Royce destroyers."[3] Until they were ready, the RN helped out by loaning two veteran destroyers, commissioned as HMC Ships *Champlain* and *Vancouver*. When *Saguenay* and *Skeena* arrived in Canada in the early summer of 1931, it was a proud moment for the RCN.

But neither Hose nor the navy could afford to relax. The worldwide depression, which began in 1929 and deepened in the 1930s, led to severe cuts in even the tiny Canadian defence budget. In 1933, the Chief of the General Staff, Major General A.G.L. McNaughton (the senior military officer in the country), faced with a government demand for a massive reduction in expenditure, proposed scrapping the RCN and instead using aircraft to provide coastal protection. Again, it is proof of Hose's good standing with the politicians that this proposal went nowhere and the Canadian navy weathered yet another storm. When Hose retired as Director of the Naval Service in 1934, he could take satisfaction that the tiny RCN, which now possessed eight vessels and about 2,000 officers and men in all three of its components, had survived Canadian politicians and bureaucrats who steadfastly ignored their nation's most basic defence needs. This was fortunate because, in both Asia and Europe, war clouds were gathering on the horizon.

The road to war: 1931-1938

In 1931 a militant Japan invaded Manchuria and set off the first of a series of international crises that would ultimately lead to the Second World War. By 1937, Japan's aggression in Asia had broadened into outright war with China, while in Europe Mussolini's Fascist Italy was on the march and had attacked the east African nation of Ethiopia. The League of Nations, the international body created in 1919 to prevent such aggression, proved powerless as none of the major democratic powers, weary from the First World War and suffering severe economic depressions, were willing to take up arms to assist the victim nations. Even worse, the United States, the most powerful democracy, had refused to join the League but had pursued an isolationist policy since 1919, hoping to keep out of foreign entanglements and wars.

The most dangerous enemy, however, was neither Japan nor Italy; it was Germany. Although that nation had been disarmed in 1919, the coming of Adolf Hitler's Nazi party to power in early 1933 signalled a programme of re-armament that included the creation of a substantial naval force. Throughout the 1930s, crisis followed international crisis as these three nations, who would later enter into a formal alliance known as the Axis, continued a policy of territorial expansion. The western powers, led by Britain and France, reluctant to use force, instead followed a disastrous policy of appeasement that only encouraged further aggression.

The gathering storm in Europe did not go unmarked in Canada. Hose's replacement as Chief of the Naval Staff (CNS) was a Canadian, Commodore Percy Nelles. Nelles had first gone to sea as a cadet in a Fishery Protection Service vessel before the First World War and had briefly commanded a British light cruiser in the 1920s. His strength lay in administration and throughout most of his career he proved very adept at manoeuvring through Ottawa's shark-infested corridors of power. Nelles was an admirer of the Royal Navy and all things British, not surprising given his background, and his overwhelming ambition was to build up the strength of the RCN's surface fleet so that it could function as an effective sub-unit of the British fleet.

Although far from the crisis centres in Africa, Asia and Europe, the Canadian government reluctantly initiated a modest programme of rearmament in the late 1930s. The RCN's budget doubled between 1936 and 1937 and by 1939 it was 360 per cent greater than it had been in 1935. Most of the additional funds went toward the acquisition of new ships. The Royal Navy, encouraged by the Canadian government's tardy interest in naval affairs, made available at a fraction of their cost, four destroyers similar to *Saguenay* and *Skeena*. They were commissioned in 1937 and 1938 as HMC Ships *Fraser*, *Ottawa*, *Restigouche* and *St. Laurent* and the obsolescent *Champlain* and *Vancouver* were paid off. These six vessels were augmented by the building of four minesweepers in Canada. For the first time, the RCN possessed a force of modern warships, although only half the basic number naval staff estimated were needed to defend both coasts.

Plans and preparations for a new war

As the new destroyers entered service, they were assigned to either Halifax or Esquimalt. Although the Canadian government emphasized the RCN's independence from the Royal Navy, it actually functioned as an integral part of that service's America and West Indies squadron and the high point of its annual training cycle was the holding of joint exercises with the RN, usually in the Caribbean. The emphasis in these exercises was on surface ship action as, despite its experience in the First World War, the Admiralty regarded surface raiders, not submarines, as the primary danger in a future conflict. Of particular concern were the German "pocket battleships," miniature battleships armed with heavy guns that could evade almost any warship powerful enough to sink them and sink almost any warship fast

German heavy cruiser *Prinz Eugen*.
At the beginning of the Second World War, the English-speaking navies considered the threat from submarines to be far less than that posed by German surface ships such as the heavy cruiser *Prinz Eugen*, with its main armament of eight 8-inch guns. The RCN's six destroyers were trained in high-speed torpedo attacks against such opponents, but in the end it was the U-boat that posed the most dangerous peril. (Courtesy, Werner Hirschmann)

fast and armed with torpedoes, were
 this threat, and in their training the
peed torpedo attacks on large surface

osed to anti-submarine warfare, was
 y and its Dominion counterparts in
 ombination of the convoy system,
 and international conventions on
 the submarine as a threat in any
 the Admiralty planned to imme-
 out the British Commonwealth
 rvised merchant shipping sail-
 marines, surface ships would
 mmeasurably improved since
1918 charges. More importantly,
in the oduction of the active sonar
devic er mounted in a dome attached -frequency sound impulse
(a "ping object within its range, an
echo (" IC operator could obtain
the loca his ship and, with this
informat bmarine and destroy it
using dep ASDIC was 80 per cent
effective at terested in ASW – and
there were almost infallible.
Finally, matic means to limit
both naval c d been a number of
international erations. The most
important of t signed by Britain,
France, Italy, J Germany and the

* ASDIC supposedly tion Committee" of
the First World War, a ow better known by
the American term "so he RCN during the
Second World War.

Soviet Union, which stipulated that submarines must conform to international maritime law. In particular, they were not to

> sink or render incapable of navigation a merchant vessel without hav-
> ing first placed passengers, crew and ship's papers in a place of safety.
> For this purpose the ship's boats are not regarded as a place of safety
> unless the safety of the passengers and crew is assured, in the existing
> sea and weather conditions, by proximity of land or another vessel
> which is in a position to take them on board.[4]

The Royal Navy and its Dominion equivalents were confident that
these measures had effectively neutralized the submarine and there would
be no repetition of the losses of the First World War. As Commodore
Nelles put it in 1937:

> If international law is complied with, submarine attack should not
> prove serious. If unrestricted warfare is again resorted to, the means of
> combatting submarines are considered so advanced that by employing
> a system of convoy and utilizing Air Forces, losses of submarines
> would be very heavy and might compel the enemy to give up this form
> of attack.[5]

The *U-Boot-Waffe*

In Germany their future opponent, Commodore Karl Dönitz, was just as
certain he knew how to offset these advantages. A submarine officer in the
First World War, Dönitz had been appointed (rather unwillingly) in 1935
to command the newly-created *U-Boot-Waffe* or U-boat arm of the German navy. Although Germany had been forbidden to possess submarines
under the terms of the 1919 Versailles Treaty, it had continued the development of this type of warship by constructing examples in shipyards in
Finland, Holland, Spain and Turkey owned by German concerns. When
Hitler instituted a programme of re-armament, the *Kriegsmarine*, or German navy, laid the keel of the first German-built submarine, *U-1*, and it
was commissioned the same year that Dönitz took up his appointment.

In September 1939 the *U-Boot-Waffe,* or submarine service of the German navy, possessed 57 submarines, and during the war that followed, the *Kriegsmarine* commissioned 1,113 more craft, making a total of 1,170 submarines, of which 863 reached operational status. German submarine casualties were catastrophic – 753 U-boats were lost from all causes between 1939 and 1945.

The Type VII: Mainstay of the *U-Boot-Waffe*

The major U-boat and the submarine most often encountered by the RCN was the Type VII in its various forms. The Type VII was based on a First World War submarine, the UB III class, modified by experience gained during the interwar period when Germany clandestinely built submarines in foreign shipyards owned by German firms. The first Type VII boat was commissioned in the *Kriegsmarine* in June 1936 and in all some 704 boats of this class were built in five variants:

Type VII	10 boats built, 1935-1936
Type VIIB	24 boats built, 1936-1940
Type VIIC and C/41	660 boats built, 1938-1944
Type VIID	6 boats built, 1940-1942
Type VIIF	4 boats built, 1941-1943

The major variants were the VIIC and C/41. The drawing opposite illustrates *U-91,* a Type VIIC boat as it might have appeared in September 1942 when, under the command of *Oberleutnant zur See* Heinz Walkerling, it sank HMCS *Ottawa.* Note the low silhouette which made the Type VII difficult to spot. In late 1942 and early 1943, the main deck gun was removed from most U-boats and their anti-aircraft armament increased to as many as eight 20mm guns.

The Type VII was a submersible warship rather than a true submarine. Until the advent of the snorkel in 1944, it could only run underwater on its electric motors for short periods before having to surface to recharge the batteries on which they depended for their power. Its powerful diesels gave it a fairly fast surface speed of 17 knots, but as the war progressed, Allied aircraft and escorts rarely let it take advantage of this asset. By late 1943 the Type VII was obsolescent and the last of the class was produced in 1944 although use of the snorkel prolonged its service life until the end of the war.

The Type IX

The Type IX was the other main ocean-going submarine of the *U-Boot-Waffe.* Larger than the Type VII, it was primarily used for independent missions. Between 1937 and 1945, 193 boats of this class were commissioned and the main variants were:

Type IX	8 boats built, 1936-1939
Type IXB	14 boats built, 1937-1940
Type IXC	54 boats built, 1939-1942
Type IXC/40	87 boats built, 1940-1944
Type IXD	30 boats built, 1940-1944

The Type IX did operate in the North Atlantic although its larger size meant it had a slower diving time, which put it at a disadvantage. Type IX boats were effective, however, in long-range patrols to distant waters, including Canadian waters. The technical information for the Type IXC/40, the most numerous variant, was as follows: *Displacement*: 1,120 tons on the surface, 1,232 tons submerged; *Length*: 249 feet; *Beam*: 23 feet; *Speed*: 19 knots on surface, 7.3 knots submerged; *Maximum range*: 13,850 miles on surface at 10 knots; *Torpedoes*: 22; *Armament*: 1 x 105mm main gun, 4 x 20mm AA, 1 x 37mm AA; *Crew*: 48-56 men; *Maximum depth*: 755 feet.

The new generation – Type XXI and Type XXIII U-boats

In 1943 the decision was made to replace the Types VII and IX with a new generation of "electro boats" (so called because they used a larger number of batteries) that represented a technological leap ahead of their predecessors. The ocean-going model was the Type XXI which had much greater submerged speed, range and armament, and a deeper diving depth than the older types, while the coastal class was the Type XXIII. Construction of these new boats commenced in late 1943 and 118 Type XXI and 61 Type XXIII submarines were in commission by May 1945 but very few reached operational status before the end of the war.

Technical information for the Type XXI was as follows: *Displacement*: 1,621 tons surface, 1,819 tons submerged; *Length*: 249 feet; *Beam*: 26 feet; *Speed*: 17.2 knots submerged, 15.6 knots surface; *Range*: 15,500 miles at 10 knots on surface; *Torpedoes*: 23; *Crew*: 56-60 men; *Maximum depth*: c. 900 feet.

Technical information for the Type XXIII was as follows: *Displacement*: 234 tons surface, 258 tons submerged; *Length*: 112 feet; *Beam*: 10 feet; *Speed*: 9.7 knots surface, 12.5 knots submerged; *Range*: 2600 miles at 8 knots on the surface; *Torpedoes*: 2; *Crew:* 14-18; *Maximum depth*: 591 feet. ■

(Left) **Late war threat – Type XXI U-boat.**
In 1943 the decision was made to replace the U-boat arm's aging fleet of Type VII and Type IX boats with more modern craft, including the Type XXI shown here. With twice the speed, both on the surface and submerged, twice the torpedo armament and twice the range of its predecessors, the Type XXI would have posed a major threat to Allied sea power but its entry into service was delayed. (United States National Archives, NA 80 G70 5562)

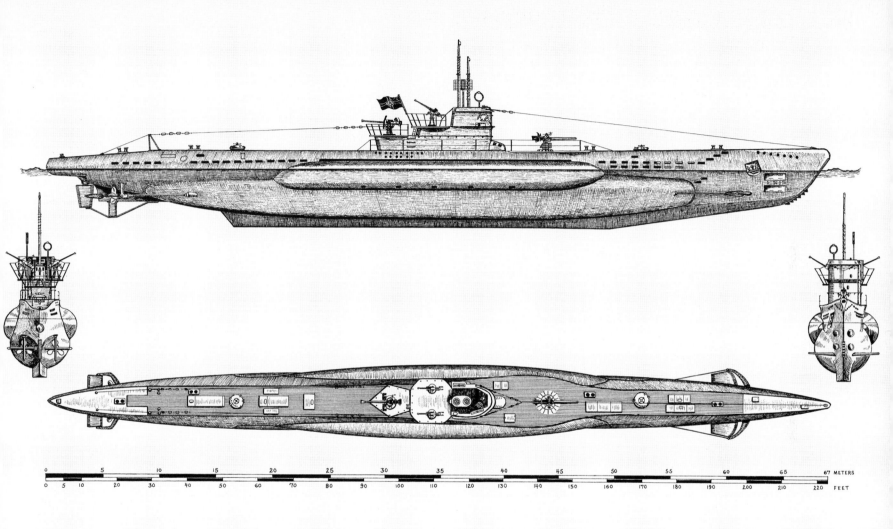

Type VII C U-boat, 1942, and the G5 "GNAT" acoustical torpedo.
The Type VIIC was the workhorse of the wartime U-boat fleet,
although as the war progressed it became increasingly obsolescent. *U-91* is depicted here as she might have appeared in 1942.
The drawing to the right shows the G5 acoustical torpedo, introduced in 1943, which homed in on the propeller noise of a target
ship. (Drawings by L.B. Jenson, courtesy of the artist)

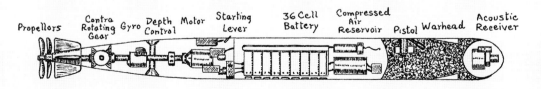

Propellors — Contra Rotating Gear — Gyro — Depth Control — Motor — Starting Lever — 36 Cell Battery — Compressed Air Reservoir — Pistol — Warhead — Acoustic Receiver

U-1 was soon followed by 14 similar craft, and although these were small 250-ton coastal boats, nicknamed "Ducks" or "Canoes" by their crews, they permitted Dönitz to begin training the *U-Boot-Waffe*.

On the basis of his study of submarine operations in 1914-1918, Dönitz believed that the most effective use of submarines was an attack in numbers against a single convoy. Confident that the new boats entering service in the 1930s were superior to their First War predecessors in speed (both above and below surface), acceleration, ability to crash dive and survivability from attack, he devised new tactics for them. His favoured method was a night surface attack. In the dark, a U-boat was difficult to spot; it could use the advantage of its superior surface speed to manoeuvre into the best firing position while at the same time having little to fear from ASDIC, which was ineffective against surface objects. Dönitz was not unduly concerned about aircraft as he believed that a submarine running on the surface in daytime would not be surprised from the sky if its commander maintained a stringent lookout that would sight approaching aircraft in time for the boat to crash dive.

From 1935 to 1939, Dönitz carried out a series of exercises that developed group attacks against simulated convoys. It became clear that the massing of U-boats against a single convoy required central command and good communications, and in a future war Dönitz planned to exercise tight control over his submarine captains by means of radio communications between his headquarters on land and U-boats at sea. Although he was aware that British codebreakers had broken German naval cyphers during the First World War, he was not concerned about a repetition of this feat because he believed that Germany possessed the most sophisticated coding device in the world – the Enigma machine. Adopted by all three German services, the Enigma machine, which resembled a typewriter, used highly sophisticated electronic circuits to convert a message into a complex code that could only be deciphered by a trained operator using another Enigma machine (see pages 166-167). Each machine possessed a number of variable settings which produced an almost limitless variety of cyphers and, as these settings were changed on a daily basis, German signals experts were confident that messages coded and transmitted by Enigma were unbreakable by any known method of deciphering.

Dönitz was convinced that Britain was Germany's most likely future opponent and therefore devoted much time to analyzing the strengths and weaknesses of that maritime power. He concluded that, with 300 ocean-going U-boats of his favoured Type VII under central command, he could bring Britain to its knees in less than two years. However, his plans for the expansion of the *U-Boot-Waffe* were frustrated by Hitler, who for much of the 1930s restricted German naval construction, particularly submarine construction, as he wished to remain on good terms with Britain. Another stumbling block was that some senior German naval officers, just as convinced as their British counterparts that the submarine was no longer a credible threat, favoured building surface warships. Still worse, from Dönitz's point of view, not only did the German navy build fewer U-boats than he requested, but it built the wrong types and not the ocean-going Type VII he felt would be the most effective vessel against Britain.

Thus when war broke out in September 1939, far from possessing the 300 ocean-going submarines he regarded as necessary for victory, Dönitz commanded 57 U-boats. Of these, only 22 were ocean-going craft suitable for service in the Atlantic, and only 20 were ready for operations.

Last days of peace, 1938-1939

The possibility of war, which had gradually increased throughout the 1930s, became imminent in 1938 when Hitler demanded that Czechoslovakia relinquish the Sudetenland, the portion of that small nation populated by German-speaking citizens. The Czechs were prepared to fight but Britain and France gave Hitler the Sudetenland in return for an empty promise that it represented his last territorial demand in Europe. In the spring of 1939, while the western democracies stood by and did nothing, Hitler overran the remainder of Czechoslovakia and, more ominously, began to make noises about reclaiming former German territory in Poland. By now, British and French leaders were reluctantly convinced war was inevitable and concluded treaties with Poland to come to her aid, should Germany invade. Hitler, disbelieving their resolve, continued to make demands and in the summer of 1939 another international crisis was being measured in the black ink of newspaper headlines.

At the Admiralty, active planning and preparation for war had, by the summer of 1939, been under way for more than a year. For Britain as an island nation, the Royal Navy represented the first and most vital line of defence, and in the event of war it had to be ready to dominate the waters around the British Isles. The Admiralty had accurate information about the size and composition of the German submarine fleet, which, given its weak strength, they did not regard as a serious threat. On the outbreak of hostilities, the RN planned to impose the convoy system throughout the British Commonwealth and to monitor German naval movements at an Operational Intelligence Centre in its London headquarters which tracked German surface and submarine units.

Although it largely discounted the submarine threat, the RN did recognize the necessity of having numbers of specialized anti-submarine warships. In the late 1930s, the standard British ASW vessel was the sloop, a miniature destroyer equipped with ASDIC, guns and depth charges. Sloops were very effective but their construction was almost as costly and as lengthy as that of a destroyer and the Admiralty believed that in the event of war there would be a tremendous demand for coastal escorts as there had been during the First World War. They therefore looked for a simpler and less costly alternative to the sloop and found it in a design by William Reed, a marine architect in a British shipyard that specialized in constructing whaling vessels. Whalers had to be seaworthy and highly manoeuvrable (qualities also needed by submarine chasers) but, being civilian vessels, also had to be cheap to construct and simple to maintain. In 1938, the Royal Navy asked Reed to design a whaling-type coastal escort and the result was the corvette.

The corvette was small (about 200 feet in length and 33 feet in beam, with about 1,000 tons displacement), but it was highly manoeuvrable and very seaworthy. Reed's design called for the use of simple piston-drive steam engines in preference to the steam turbine engines used in most warships and it was this feature that made the corvette practicable for construction in shipyards unskilled in naval construction and suitable for operation by relatively inexperienced personnel. The penalty for simplicity, however, was slow speed – about 16 knots and that only for short periods – which was insufficient to overtake either of the two major U-boat types, the Type VII and Type IX, on the surface. As the corvette was not intended to engage enemy surface ships, its gun armament was minimal – a 4-inch main gun, an anti-aircraft gun and a couple of machine guns – and its main weapons were its depth charges. The utility of such a sturdy but simple little warship was obvious and plans were made to construct corvettes for the RN in the event of war.

In Canada Commodore Nelles and his staff at Naval Service Headquarters (NSHQ) in Ottawa also discounted submarines – their minds were fixed firmly on the danger of surface raiders. Destroyers, with their high speed and gun and torpedo armament, were regarded as the best defence against fast, powerful German surface ships and this was reflected in the Canadian government's plan for the expansion of the RCN announced in May 1939. It called for the acquisition of 18 destroyers, 16 minesweepers and 8 motor torpedo boats but only 8 ASW vessels – type unspecified. The Liberal government, however, did not allocate the funds to carry out this plan and in any case it was overtaken by events.

It was standard practice for the Admiralty to station a British officer at NSHQ to improve liaison with the RN, and in the summer of 1939 the officer in that post was Commander Eric Brand, RN. He proved not only helpful in his liaison duties and the naval control of shipping but also useful in August 1939 when the time came for the NSHQ staff to draft war plans. On the 21st of that month, planning moved from the theoretical to the actual when the British government warned Ottawa that it was mobilizing because German troop movements toward Poland indicated war was imminent.

The RCN goes to war

In response, the government authorized the heads of the three Canadian armed services to mobilize in conjunction with Britain despite previous public statements that, unlike 1914, Canada would not necessarily go to war if Britain went to war. The next day, when Britain instituted naval control of merchant shipping, Ottawa followed suit and on 1 September, when word came that German troops had invaded Poland, NSHQ placed the Canadian navy on active service by sending a signal to all captains to "Ship warheads and be in all respects ready for action. Do not start an engagement until ordered ... but be prepared to defend yourselves in case of attack."[6] On the morning of that day, as one RCN officer remembered, HMC Ships *Fraser* and *St. Laurent*, then at Vancouver, received orders to sail immediately for Halifax. He recalled that "a scene of considerable activity" ensued as smoke "poured from the funnels, awnings were furled, boats hoisted and booms and gangways were secured for sea."[7] Less than three hours after receiving their orders, both destroyers were steaming out of Vancouver bound for the Panama Canal and ultimately Halifax. At noon, the two vessels received a signal from NSHQ to "prepare for war" and at 1715 hours they received a second signal informing them that the RCN had been placed "on active service" and the RCNR and RCNVR were "being called up as necessary."[8]

Two days later, on 3 September 1939, after Hitler failed to respond to British and French demands to withdraw his troops from Poland, those nations declared war on Germany. Canada's declaration came a week later on 10 September, following an emergency debate in the House of Commons, but during that week the RCN was fully mobilized.

It was a tiny service consisting of just 415 officers and 2,476 sailors in its three components – the RCN, RCNR and RCNVR – but it was as well prepared as it could be, given the fact that it had suffered from government indifference and inadequate funding throughout most of its short history. Its striking edge was the six modern destroyers (His Majesty's Canadian Ships *Fraser, Ottawa, Restigouche, Saguenay, Skeena* and *St. Laurent*), which were backed up by four modern minesweepers (HMC Ships *Comox, Fundy, Gaspé* and *Nootka*), and three small auxiliary vessels (HMC Ships

Ready for captain's rounds.
The seaman's messdeck of a prewar RCN destroyer as it would have been at its best – ready for the captain's rounds or inspection. When not on duty, sailors slept, ate and rested in this crowded space, where there was a place for everything and everything was in its place. Hammocks have been lashed and stowed and placed in the storage area in the corner and the mess deck is as spotless as the men can make it. Eating utensils are either stowed on the shelf unit by the forward bulkhead or neatly arranged on the mess table. The scuttles are open for ventilation, and beneath them are the men's hat boxes, their small wooden "ditty" boxes and their freshly shined boots. Their duffel bags are stored beneath the locker benches along the bulkhead and accessed by the hatches on the seats. (Drawing by L.B. Jenson, courtesy of the artist)

Skidegate, Gate Vessel No. 1 and *Venture*). At the outbreak of the Second World War, the Royal Canadian Navy could be characterized as a small but professional service. That professionalism would be sorely needed in the coming years as it experienced unprecedented expansion in times of almost continuous trial.

THE INTERWAR PERIOD

"I've seen a Navy die, boys:" The 1920s and 1930s

Having served for nearly seven years on board British warships, during which time he cruised around the world, Frank Houghton came back to the RCN as first lieutenant of HMCS Patriot. *It was not an auspicious time as Liberal government defence cuts had just reduced the service to a shell:*

I was returning to the RCN at a time when it was at its lowest ebb. I shall always remember the farewell party given to my predecessor, Lieutenant Cuthbert Robert Holland Taylor, which lasted into the early hours, at which time he was carried off the ship on a mattress, partly as a mark of respect to a popular officer and partly for other reasons. It had been a good party indeed, but I can still hear in my mind the last words he managed to articulate before he quietly and appropriately passed out: "I've seen a Navy die, boys; I've seen a Navy die!"

But by the grace of God it was not quite dead.[1]

But there were also good times during the long peacetime years. One such was the joint exercise held in the West Indies by the RCN's four destroyers with units of the British Home Fleet in 1934. By now, Houghton was commanding HMCS Vancouver.

I shall not easily forget one pitch-dark moonless night in heavy seas, out in the wide Atlantic east of Barbados when the Canadian flotilla was or-

dered to carry out a dummy torpedo attack on the "enemy" fleet led by the Commander-in-Chief himself. It was to be under full wartime conditions – no navigation lights and strict wireless [radio] silence.

From a position well ahead of the Fleet our four destroyers crashed through the waves at thirty knots, ships pitching madly, mast-high spray flying over their bridge. It was impossible to see more than a few yards ahead of us. *Vancouver* was last ship in line, but we were disposed quarterly to port .. so that the other three Canadians were somewhere off my starboard bow and of course completely invisible. ......

King George VI presents Colours to the RCN, 1939.
Between the wars, the Canadian navy was basically a training organization with a small regular component which instructed the reserve components. Reserve divisions were set up in most large Canadian cities, creating a naval presence across the country. In this photograph, dated 30 May 1939, King George VI presents colours to the RCN, which are received by Lieutenant J.H. Stubbs. (National Archives of Canada, PA 148552)

Suddenly a searchlight was switched on dead ahead of *Vancouver*, the sharply-defined, bluish beam aimed directly at our bridge. Luckily for us, the flagship, leading the "enemy" line, had spotted us; we were obviously much nearer our target than we had calculated. In fact, *Vancouver* was actually on a collision course with the huge battleship.

"Hard-a-starboard! Stand by to fire torpedoes!" As we swung round, we "fired" four fish, indicating the moment of firing by shooting off a Green Verey light. Whether or not, in the circumstances, our torpedoes would have struck home must forever remain a matter of conjecture. I can only remember feeling at the time that I had had quite enough excitement for one night.

"As cold as charity in October:" Enlisted men's life in the interwar period

Arthur Hewitt and William Mansfield, who joined the RCN as boy seamen at Esquimalt in 1928, recall their first days in service:

You know there were no such things as comforts in those days. We lived in *Naden* [shore station at Esquimalt] in great barren barrack-rooms with hammock-bars. They were just great bare rooms, and the Officer of the Watch came around with the Petty Officer of the Watch, and the usual routine. The PO of the Watch always carried a lantern, leading the parade and they had to open all the bloody windows in the place. It was as cold as charity in October or whatever, and so as soon as they'd gone, of course you'd close all the windows. But there was no heat in there anyway. It really was a very uncomfortable business. We sit back and laugh about it now, but in those days we

thought it was really pretty doggone grim. We didn't have any place to sit. The only place you could go and really have any comfort was down in the canteen. ......

I got 50 cents a day and they used to keep back ten dollars a month, say, enough money to go on leave. And the other five dollars your Divisional Chief took, and he doled it out if you wanted to go down town. You were only allowed two afternoons a week. Your leave started at one on Saturday afternoon and finished at a quarter to nine. ...... And you had to be in your hammock by nine o'clock. The old Duty PO would come round and check.[2]

"You weren't paid too well:" Life in the Volunteer Reserve

R. Houliston enlisted in the RCNVR in Toronto as a boy seaman in 1926 and remembered that,

when you joined the reserves in those days, you weren't paid too well. We drilled every Wednesday night and got twenty-five cents a night for the drill, plus two [street] car tickets, one to go and one to come. We put in a lot of extra time because we also had the field-gun crew. The field-gun crew used to travel pretty well all over the prov-

DEPARTMENT OF NATIONAL DEFENCE
NAVAL SERVICE

MEN WANTED

FOR THE

ROYAL CANADIAN NAVAL VOLUNTEER RESERVE

Volunteers are required for enrolment as seamen, signalmen, telegraphists, buglers, engineers, electricians, ordnance artificers, motor mechanics, accountants and cooks in the Royal Canadian Naval Volunteer Reserve.

PERIOD OF ENROLMENT—Three years.

QUALIFICATIONS—Candidates must be British subjects over 18 years of age resident in Canada, of good character, physically fit and willing to serve at sea or wherever required in time of emergency, or when undergoing annual training. Candidates must not belong to any other Reserve Force.

NAVAL TRAINING—From two to three weeks' Naval training in H.M.C. Ships or Establishments at Halifax or Esquimalt each year. In addition to annual training, at least 30 drills each year, at Company Headquarters near their homes, will be required of Reservists.

PAY AND ALLOWANCES—Canadian Naval rates of pay will be paid to men of the Reserve Force whilst undergoing annual training at the Naval bases. A bounty to cover expenses of men attending drills at Company Headquarters will be paid at the rate of 25c. per drill up to a maximum of 30 drills a year. An extra $5.00 will be paid each year to Reservists on completing 40 or more drills during the year.

WHERE TO APPLY—For further information application should be made as follows:—
Residents of Halifax, The Senior Naval Officer, R.C.N. Barracks, Halifax, N.S. or the Officer Commanding the Halifax Half Company, R.C.N.V.R.

Residents of Vancouver, The Senior Naval Officer, R.C.N. Barracks, Esquimalt, B.C., or the Officer Commanding the Vancouver Half Company, R.C.N.V.R. Bowman Building, 837 Hastings St. East.

Residents of any other town of Canada, The Naval Secretary, Department of National Defence, Ottawa.

FOR MORE DETAILED INFORMATION APPLICATION SHOULD BE MADE TO:

"MEN WANTED" – interwar recruiting poster for the RCNVR.
The decision to create the RCNVR in 1923 was an inspired one on the part of Commodore Walter Hose, the Director of the Naval Service, as it established a cadre for wartime expansion. This recruiting poster for the RCNVR contains the unwarranted optimism and misinformation usually found in such advertisements. (Author's collection)

ince and down to Montreal. We took part in the old Coliseum in Ottawa and had quite a time. ......

If there was a gun-crew drill or anything like that, that was done in our own time. If you went to the gun drill, you got an extra two car tickets and there was the possibility that you might get an extra drill thrown in with it, but you didn't get an extra twenty-five cents. ….. nearly every thing that we did as far as drills and that sort of thing were concerned, we did it on our own – although when we got our pay every quarter we used to squander it, going to a dance or something like that.

During the summer-time we had the opportunity of going to Halifax, to do training. You were supposed to do two weeks' training. At that time, if there was a ship in you'd go aboard ship or you'd go to the schools, according to your rating. Most of the trips were done in the old *Festubert* or *Ypres*. In the early thirties, because I wasn't working at the particular time, I was given the opportunity of going south on a cruise. I picked the *Saguenay*. That's the time [1934] we manoeuvred with the Home Fleet.

The turnover in the reserves at that time was very small, due to the fact that we were a very close-knit organization.[3]

Frederick Sherwood, who joined the RCNVR Division in Ottawa as an officer cadet in 1932, had similar experiences:

In those days in Ottawa, most young men joined something, the Militia or the Naval Reserve. It was one of those things you did. Nobody had any money and this was a way to get a holiday. It was certainly very popular and all the units would have dances from time to time and invite people from other units. The Militia was very strong then, there was no pay for them, but the sailors

got 25 cents a night and they turned that over to the unit fund. They would have a plain-clothes dance once a week just with a gramophone and that sort of thing. 1932 was deep in the depression; it was pretty tough going but everybody had a lot of fun and enjoyed it tremendously. ……

A lot of the chaps were pretty well trained, and they had a nice thing in the RCNVR in those days. If you could get the time off, there were two destroyers on the West Coast, two destroyers on the East Coast, and they used to go south for about four months each year. If you were lucky and you could get time off from your job – if you were lucky enough to have a job – you could do four months at sea on one of these cruises, which I was fortunate enough to do in early 1936. …… I got a Watchkeeping Certificate in that time and that stood me in good stead later. Then I had used up all my holidays, so I didn't get any the next year.[4]

Piped on board – Rear Admiral Percy W. Nelles (1892-1951).
Seen here coming on board the destroyer HMCS *Restigouche* (known unofficially as "Rusty Guts"), Rear Admiral Percy Nelles served as the chief of the naval staff, or commander of the RCN, from 1934 to 1944. He was a conscientious and hard-working man but his admiration of the Royal Navy and his inability to assimilate rapidly-evolving technology caused him to be less effective than he should have been. Nelles was manoeuvred out of his position after it became clear in 1943 that Canadian ASW escorts were poorly equipped in comparison to their British counterparts. (Directorate of History and Heritage, DHH 0-1785)

"Here, who's going to take this?"
Naval Service Headquarters, 1939

During the interwar period, the headquarters of the RCN was a modest establishment in Ottawa. Sub-Lieutenant Herbert Little, RCNVR, who joined NSHQ as an intelligence officer in 1939, remembers that it

was located on the third and fourth floors of the red brick Robinson Building, on the south side of Queen Street, between Elgin and Metcalfe. Whether by design or not, there was ample camouflage in the form of a delicatessen on the ground floor, a Department of Agriculture section specializing in swine on the second and the Department of Transport Radio-License section on top.

The principal naval room faced Queen Street. It was small and unbelievably crowded. In the west corner was the desk of Rear-Admiral P.W. Nelles, Chief of Naval Staff, where I can picture him sitting with his back to the window surveying his unlikely ship's company. To his right was a ponderous safe which only his secretary, Miss Hetty Evans, appeared capable of opening. What grand secrets it contained, I never found out, but I do know she kept the Admiral's tea caddy and biscuits there, secure from all predators. In the east corner was the desk of Commander F.L. Houghton, Staff Officer Plans. When he looked up he would see a plain wooden table at which half a dozen people could sit and write or read. There was often a scramble for a place and more than once I simply sat on the floor in the corridor with my books.

Just inside the doorway was a wicket from the next room where Lieutenant Commander Barry German and Chief Yeoman Wiseman were in charge of signals. I can still see the basic distribution system; an arm would appear through the wicket with a message form and a voice would call out, "Here, who's going to take this?"[5]

The newly-promoted Commander Frank Houghton, RCN, joined NSHQ in July 1939, as active preparations were being made for war. He recalls one of his innovations:

One of my "inventions" was a method of gaining and retaining some sort of order in the hundreds of signals sent and received every day. I obtained a 4 x 8 plywood panel and drove nails through it from the back, upon which we impaled the signal forms according to subject. This simple if not exactly ingenious solution was successful as far as it went; but owing to the restricted space in which we worked the sharp nails were an ever-present menace, and indeed my esteemed colleague, Commander Eric Brand, RN, … managed to tear a large rip in his best trousers just as the Admiral arrived to see how we were faring.[6]

Houghton's victim, Eric Brand, remembered the activities at NSHQ in the weeks immediately before war broke out:

In May 1939 my appointment on loan to the Royal Canadian Navy at Ottawa was announced. …… On 5 June 1939 I proceeded for three weeks of wandering round the Admiralty, to find out as much as I could which might be of interest to me in Canada. I bought a small black notebook at Woolworths in which to jot down the information. My little black notebook was to prove valuable!

…… after seeing my predecessor off on a hot July morning, I returned to my office … and found Frankie Houghton sitting at his desk, alongside mine. So far I had found no vestige of any "Plans" and neither had my Staff Officer. I said we had better get busy and make some because, in my view, time was short. To which he replied, "The Navy has little money for such things." I retorted: "You make paper in Canada, don't you? So let's have some of that, at least." ……

So, in those early day of August, we pushed along with the plans. …… Having pencilled the plans for the defended ports I took them to "Cuth" Taylor, the Director of Personnel, to show him what people they would require. He looked them over and grunted, "And where the hell do you think I am going to get all this lot?" I said, "I have doubled as many duties as I possibly can, but I have a hunch that, if a war starts, a lot of damn good Canadians will want to join the Navy." To which he replied, "Well, I hope you're bloody well right." I was! ……

On the 23rd [of August 1939], Admiral Nelles arrived back in the office, and I finally met him. I found him a wonderful officer to work under; he never fussed about details. If he agreed with one's proposals, he would wave his handkerchief and say, "That sounds sane to me, chappie. Go to it!" ……

By that evening, the CNS [Nelles] had been informed of the situation and the way things appeared to be going. He immediately called a meeting of the whole Naval Staff – in my big office – to try to frame some emergency estimates for greatly increasing the size of the Canadian Navy. It was agreed that we should be prepared to build fifty "whale catchers" – corvettes – and twenty minesweepers of a type known as "Bangors," which the RN were building. Since nobody had the slightest idea of the cost of these ships and their equipment, some basic price I had jotted down at the Admiralty in my little black Woolworth notebook came in very handy.[7]

"Four hours notice for steam:" Preparing for war, August 1939

Commander Wallace B. Creery, RCN, captain of HMCS Fraser, *recalled how war came to the Pacific Division:*

Towards the end of August 1939 four destroyers, *Ottawa, Restigouche, Fraser* and *St. Laurent,* under Captain G.C. Jones as Captain (D) in Ottawa, went to Vancouver for the opening of the Pacific National Exhibition. Because the situation was critical, with every indication that war was imminent, we were kept at four hours notice for steam and shore leave was curtailed.

At 1300 on 31 August, Captain (D) sent for the COs of *Fraser,* myself … and *St Laurent,* Lieutenant Commander A.M. "Boomer" Hope, and showed us a secret signal from Naval Service Headquarters, instructing *Fraser* and *St Laurent* to proceed to Halifax at high speed, calling only at San Pedro, Balboa and Kingston, Jamaica for fuel. The trip between San Pedro and Balboa was to be done at the best speed possible, having regard to fuel and endurance, and the rest of the trip at 25 knots.

Although the ships were at four hours notice, we left harbour within two hours after receipt of the signal. *Fraser* arrived in Halifax 14 days and 34 minutes later. *St Laurent* took some eight hours longer, as I had routed her through a different channel between the West Indies Islands. We did the three thousand miles between San Pedro and Balboa at an average speed of eighteen knots, a notable achievement for that class of ship. The whole voyage established a record and it is greatly to the credit of the ships' engineers that they arrived in Halifax, refuelled and were immediately available for service.[8]

"The telephone rang, and a voice from Ottawa said:" The RCNVR goes to war

Jack Anderson, a native of Toronto, was a member of the RCNVR Supplementary Reserve, which provided preliminary training for young men who might wish to obtain officers' commission in time of war. He recalls how war came to his Reserve Division:

Starting in July, 1939, the supplementary reserve officers in the Toronto Division were required to stand duty officer at night, usually being the only one there to answer the telephone or anything that might turn up. I happened to be the Duty Officer the night of the 26th of August, 1939. The telephone rang, and a voice from Ottawa said, "Commander Taylor, Director of Naval Reserves speaking; I'd like to speak to your Captain." I said, "Sir, he's over at the Exhibition Grounds, at the

Little ships – the minesweeper HMCS *Comox*.
The RCN was very much a "small ship" navy and some vessels were smaller than others. Although the escorts that fought the Battle of the Atlantic have attracted most of the attention, there were many other utilitarian little vessels that played an essential but often overlooked role. Among them were the four Fundy Class minesweepers (*Comox, Fundy, Gaspé* and *Nootka*) built in Canada in the late 1930s – the largest naval vessels constructed in the country up to that time. Based on the British Basset Class, these vessels displaced 460 tons, had a top speed of 12 knots, were manned by a crew of 38 and armed with one 12-pdr. gun. They spent much of the war serving in the Halifax Local Defence Force – unglamorous but essential service. (National Archives of Canada, PA 105183)

Tattoo. The Divisions are putting on the usual twelve-pounder gun drill over the jumps." He said, "Get hold of him, and have him call me."

We had no car, and we were about a mile or two from the grandstand, but I managed to phone over to the Exhibition Grounds and found somebody who went and informed Lieutenant Commander Shedden that he was wanted. So he came back about ten o'clock and called Ottawa, and said, "Yes, sir; yes, sir," and then hung up the receiver, turned around and said, "Well, that's it. We're mobilized. We're all on active service."[9]

Early days, September 1940.

HMC Ships *Assiniboine* and *Saguenay* (astern) escort Convoy HX 77 out from Halifax on 28 September 1940. These are still early days, the ships are in spotless condition and the sailors in proper uniform – five years of service on the North Atlantic would take its toll on the appearance of ships and sailors. The weapon is a 2-pdr. (40mm) Vickers, an oversized machine gun, with a cyclic rate of 200 rounds per minute and a maximum range of 7,830 yards. (Photograph by Glen Frankfurter, National Archives of Canada, PA 104390)

CHAPTER 3

OPENING ROUNDS: THE ROYAL CANADIAN NAVY AT WAR,
SEPTEMBER 1939–MAY 1941

Immediately following the Canadian declaration of war, the Admiralty requested that the RCN be placed under its operational control in North American waters. This followed the precedent set in the First World War but things had changed since 1914 and it was not acceptable to Prime Mackenzie King, who had a deep distrust of British entanglements. The government therefore instructed NSHQ that, although the RCN might cooperate with the RN, it was not to come under formal Admiralty control.

The Canadian government, however, was agreeable to British control of merchant shipping. On 26 August, when the Admiralty sent out the code word "Funnel" from London, the RN assumed regulation of all merchant shipping departing from or sailing to ports within the empire. Fast merchant vessels were allowed to proceed independently but slower craft were restricted to convoys that only sailed under naval escort. As part of this measure, the RCN exerted its authority over merchant shipping in Canadian ports, using the Naval Control Service, an organization that had remained in existence in shadow form throughout the interwar period. Commander Eric Brand, the RN officer posted to NSHQ in Ottawa, supervised it and appointed Canadian Naval Officers-in-Charge at major Canadian ports to oversee this vital function.

On 16 September 1939, six days after Canada's declaration of war, the first trans-Atlantic convoy, HX-1, departed from Halifax bound for Brit-ain under the escort of HMC Ships *St. Laurent* and *Skeena* although *St. Laurent* had only arrived at Halifax the previous day, after a record journey from Vancouver. The two Canadian destroyers escorted HX-1 for 350 miles eastward into the Atlantic before turning it over to two RN cruisers, which took it into British waters, where it picked up a local escort. HX-1 set the pattern for Atlantic convoys in the first months of the war.

The concern at this time was not U-boats but German surface raiders, hence the deployment of cruisers, heavy warships, to escort HX-1. At the outbreak of war the *Kriegsmarine* possessed 2 modern battlecruisers, 2 old pre-1914 battleships used as training vessels, 3 "pocket" battleships, 8 cruisers, 22 destroyers and 20 torpedo boats (small destroyers), and there were also plans to convert 26 fast merchant vessels into armed raiders. The *U-Boot-Waffe*, as has been noted, possessed just 57 submarines and of these only 20 could operate in the Atlantic, and to reach it they first had to traverse the narrow waters of the English Channel or the North Sea which were patrolled by the RN. This was a far cry from the 300 ocean-going submarines that Dönitz estimated as necessary to sever Britain's waterborne lifeline and it was his opinion that in 1939 the best his submarine crews could do was "subject the enemy to a few odd pin-pricks," which would not be enough to "force a great empire and one of the foremost maritime powers in the world to sue for peace."[1]

The situation was made more difficult for Dönitz by Hitler, who, remembering the outrage over unrestricted submarine warfare that had brought the United States into the First World War, ordered German submarine commanders to obey international maritime agreements. Unfortunately for Hitler, just a few hours after hostilities broke out, *Kapitänleutnant* Fritz Lemp, commanding officer of *U-30*, torpedoed and sank the Cunard liner *Athenia* northwest of Ireland causing the death of 118 of her 1,000 passengers, including 22 Americans. Lemp claimed that he thought the vessel was an armed merchant cruiser, which would have been a legitimate target, but few believed him. The damage was done, and although Hitler continued to restrict targets, these limitations were gradually lifted until by August 1940 the U-boats were carrying out unrestricted submarine warfare in all but American waters.

There were no U-boats in the western Atlantic in 1939, however, and the six Canadian destroyers which performed escort tasks from Halifax throughout the first autumn and winter of the war saw no action. In October they were augmented by the arrival of a sister ship purchased from Britain, which was commissioned into the RCN as HMCS *Assiniboine*. To assist the RCN, the Admiralty stationed its 3rd Battle Squadron at Halifax to add weight to the convoy escorts against possible Germans surface raiders. These fears seemed justified in December when the pocket battleship *Graf Spee* made a very successful voyage in the South Atlantic and Indian Oceans

Grossadmiral Karl Dönitz (1891-1980).
Karl Dönitz joined the Imperial German navy in 1910 and served in submarines during the First World War. In 1935, he was given the task of creating and building the *U-Boot-Waffe,* or German submarine service, and worked tirelessly to train personnel and develop tactics. Throughout the war Dönitz proved to be a clever, untiring and implacable opponent for the Allied navies. (Author's collection)

before her captain scuttled his damaged ship after an inconclusive engagement with three British cruisers off the coast of Uruguay. When *Graf Spee*'s sister ship *Lützow* carried out a similar raid into the North Atlantic late in the year, however, it intensified concern that German surface units might appear off the coast of Canada.

The RCN's plans for wartime expansion, 1939-1940

In September 1939, NSHQ initiated a regulated increase in the size of the Canadian navy for what was viewed as a limited war in Europe. The RCN had entered the war with a total strength of just under 3,000 officers and sailors and its first expansion plan, implemented in the early weeks of the war, called for a moderate rise in strength to 5,472 all ranks by March 1940, and 7,000 by March 1941. The inception of the 1939/1940 warship construction plan, however, caused the latter figure to be revised upwards to 15,000 all ranks. The problem was not finding men – the RCNVR Divisions, which functioned as recruiting centres across Canada, turned away many volunteers during the first eight months of the war – it was finding qualified instructors to train them. Fortunately, the Admiralty gave permission for retired British naval personnel living in Canada to join the Canadian service rather than return to the RN and this provided a small pool of about 40 badly-needed key officers. Another major problem was a shortage of accommodation – by April 1940, fewer than half of the 1,394 naval personnel at Halifax could be housed in government buildings and the navy was forced to take over structures at the Nova Scotia Exhibition Grounds to accommodate its sailors in what were little more than cattle barns.

Procuring warships proved more difficult. Over the winter of 1939-1940, the Canadian navy assembled a heterogeneous collection of some 60 auxiliary craft for port and local escort tasks. Many were acquired from the Royal Canadian Mounted Police or government departments such as Transport and Fisheries, and this was convenient as their crews often came with them, simply switching uniforms. Others were civilian yachts, trawlers and whaling craft converted to carry out the myriad tasks that are the small change of naval operations: coastal and harbour patrols; minesweeping; boom defence; and the examination of merchant ships. To counter surface raiders, the navy took over three modern 6,000-ton liners from Canadian National Steamships – *Prince David*, *Prince Robert* and *Prince Henry* – and armed them with 6-inch guns to act as auxiliary cruisers.

NSHQ rightly regarded these vessels as temporary expedients that would later be replaced by proper warships. In its first shipbuilding programme, submitted to the government eight days after the declaration of war, naval staff emphasized that the RCN faced two major tasks – coastal patrol and escort work; and defence against surface raiders – and asked for ships that could accomplish both tasks. Against surface raiders, NSHQ wanted fast and heavily-armed fleet destroyers that could take on major German surface units with some chance of success and it particularly favoured ships of the Tribal Class, the largest and most heavily-armed British destroyer type. For coastal escort and patrol work NSHQ, after some cogitation, settled on the Flower Class corvette and Bangor Class minesweeper, which would be joined by small motor launches, or patrol boats, for inshore work.

These plans found a positive response, as now that Canada was at war the Liberal government viewed the navy's need for new warships more favourably. For political reasons, Prime Minister Mackenzie King wished to avoid the heavy casualty lists of 1914-1918 and hoped to engage in hostilities with the minimum of human loss and the greatest financial profit. The government was therefore keen to reap economic benefits from the war and the RCN's construction programme, which would both stimulate the Canadian shipbuilding industry and create employment, appeared to fit the bill very well. The figures for new construction were thus constantly revised upwards until by August 1940 the government had placed orders for the construction of 64 Flower Class corvettes and 28 Bangors, all to be completed by the end of 1941.* It was planned that ten of the corvettes built in Canada were to go to the RN, which in turn undertook to construct four Tribal Class destroyers for the RCN in British yards as the building of such "state of the art" vessels was beyond Canadian capacity in

---

* In contrast to the RN, which gave its corvettes flower names, NSHQ named the RCN corvettes after small Canadian towns. This was an inspired decision as many communities maintained close relations with their namesake ships, providing comforts for the crews.

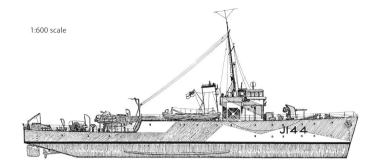

1:600 scale

HMCS *Georgian*, Bangor Class minesweeper.
Fifty-six Bangor Class minesweepers served in the RCN as coastal and local escorts, although 16 vessels reverted to their original function for the Normandy landing. Bangor minesweepers displaced 672 tons, were 180 feet in length, had a top speed of 16 knots, carried a complement of 83 and were armed with either a 4-inch, 3-inch or 12-pdr. main gun, and two 20mm AA guns, as well as depth charges. The antenna on the foremast is for the Canadian SW2C radar. (Drawing by L.B. Jenson, courtesy, Directorate of History and Heritage, DND)

A corvette is launched, 1941.
In 1940 Canada initiated a massive programme of warship construction which included many corvettes. The small size and simple design of these vessels made them suitable for construction at shipyards that lacked the facilities or experience to build larger, more sophisticated warships. Here, HMCS *Moose Jaw* is launched sideways at the Collingwood Shipyards in Collingwood, Ontario, on 10 April 1941. (National Archives of Canada, PA 037449)

1940. Determined, however, to gain some industrial advantage from the war, the government did eventually contract for four Tribal Class destroyers to be built at Halifax, but, such were the delays entailed in mastering the necessary technology, none were commissioned until 1945. Worse still, their construction occupied valuable facilities and acted as a drain on Canada's ability to build and maintain its escort fleet.

From the outset, the 1939/1940 construction programme encountered problems. Although the corvettes and minesweepers were simple to build in terms of marine engineering, the construction of such a great number was still a mighty undertaking for the small national shipbuilding industry, which was also under pressure to construct merchant vessels. Corvette and Bangor keels were laid at 15 shipyards across Canada, many on the Great Lakes, but delays in receiving plans from Britain and shortages of materials, skilled workers, armament and equipment, hampered their completion. Only 14 corvettes were ready by the end of 1940, including the 10 destined for British service, and the last vessel ordered under this program was not completed until well into 1942. Nonetheless, despite some growing pains, the RCN's expansion plans were well under way by the spring of 1940 when they were derailed by events in Europe.

The fall of France, May-June, 1940

During the first eight months of the war, while the RCN carried out escort duties in Canadian coastal waters and NSHQ planned a moderate expansion in ships and men, the war in Europe seemed distant. Poland succumbed after a valiant struggle at the end of September 1939, but thereafter the war on land

The North Atlantic, 1939-1945

KEY

⚓ Indicates Naval Headquarters

Ⓐ Area of West Ocean Meeting Point

Ⓑ Area of Mid-Ocean Meeting Point

Ⓒ Area of East Ocean Meeting Point

NOTE: The ocean meeting points varied at different times during the war. Points shown here were used during January to June 1943.

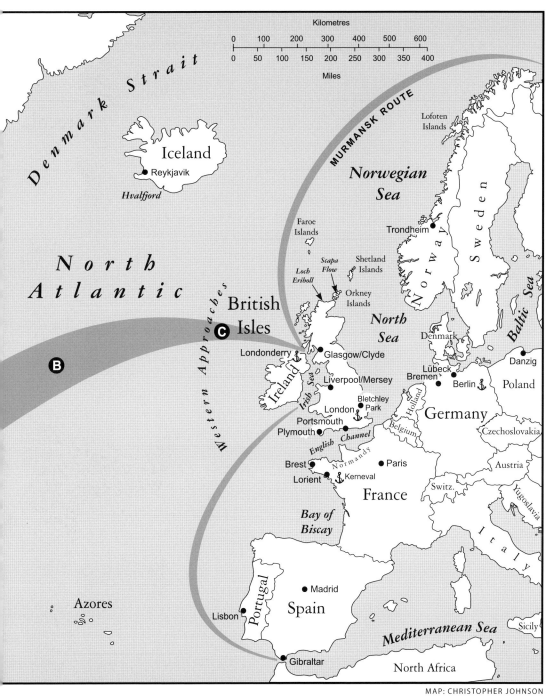

MAP: CHRISTOPHER JOHNSON

appeared to have reached stalemate. Britain and France, anticipating a rerun of the First World War, mustered their armies on the eastern borders of France to forestall a possible German invasion, but when it did not come, they settled into winter quarters. The lack of action led journalists to dub this period the "Phoney War" and there was hope that Hitler, being satisfied with his Polish conquest, might begin negotiations for peace. In April 1940, the tempo of the war changed radically when Germany occupied Denmark and Norway in a lightning campaign. In early May, German armies, using new methods of mobile warfare and overwhelming air support, launched a devastating blow against western Europe, overrunning Holland and Belgium and gradually forcing the British and French armies back to the Channel coast. Hitler's success prompted his Italian fellow dictator, Mussolini, to join the war on Germany's side at about the same time as a despairing France began to seek peace terms.

On 23 May 1940, the urgency of the crisis was underscored by Vincent Massey, the Canadian High Commissioner to Britain, who, in passing along an Admiralty request for Canadian warships to serve in British waters, noted the possibility "in the near future of [a] sea-borne invasion of the United Kingdom."[2] The Canadian government approved the British request and 24 hours later HMC Ships *Restigouche*, *Skeena* and *St. Laurent* sailed for Britain, to be followed later by the RCN's remaining four destroyers (HMC Ships *Assiniboine*, *Fraser*,* *Ottawa* and *Saguenay*). Canada's response to Britain's need was gener-

---

* Shortly after the outbreak of war, the RCN acquired a seventh modern destroyer from Britain which it commissioned as HMCS *Fraser*.

ous – she sent every modern warship in her navy to European waters, leaving, as Prime Minister Mackenzie King noted, her own coasts bare. But King had no doubts about this decision as it was his belief that Canadians owed Britain "such freedom as we have" and it was only right that Canada should strike with Britain "the last blow for the preservation of freedom."[3]

The three destroyers arrived at Plymouth a week later and were immediately armed with an additional 3-inch anti-aircraft gun which was needed as the German *Luftwaffe* was a dangerous threat. They were too late to participate in the evacuation of more than 350,000 British and allied soldiers from the beaches of Dunkirk, an operation that cost the Royal Navy 32 destroyers sunk or damaged (one seventh of its total number of this type of useful warship). Over the next three weeks, however, the Canadian ships participated in a series of hair-raising missions evacuating military and diplomatic personnel from small French Atlantic ports. On 24 June, the day after France surrendered to Germany, disaster struck when *Fraser*, manoeuvring at night in close proximity to the British cruiser *Calcutta*, was cut in half when the two vessels collided. The bridge of the Canadian vessel ended up on *Calcutta*'s forecastle and Commander W.L Creery, RCN, *Fraser*'s captain, and his bridge personnel were able to step down to safety but 47 Canadian and 19 British sailors died in this tragic incident.

The U-boats begin to threaten: July–December 1940

The fall of France irrevocably changed the nature of the war at sea. At one stroke, Britain lost the assistance of the French fleet while the entry of Italy into the war doubled the naval power arrayed against her. Britain was now threatened with invasion, and even if this did not come, German and Italian naval forces and aircraft, operating from bases just across the Channel, would be in a position to cut her seaborne lifeline. The worst menace, although it was not fully appreciated at the time, was not air or surface units but Dönitz's submarines, as they could now operate from ports on the Atlantic coast, extending their operational range 600 to 1,000 miles west and also their time on patrol. Up to this point, owing to their small numbers, the effect of the U-boats had been more psychological than actual. Between 3 September 1939 and 1 March 1940,

when they were temporarily withdrawn from anti-commerce operations to support the German invasion of Norway, Dönitz's U-boats sank 277 merchant ships with a total displacement of 974,000 tons for the loss of 17 submarines. Britain was able to compensate for the merchant tonnage by the construction, capture or charter of new vessels, but Dönitz could not replace his losses as fast, since the German wartime construction programme had only just got underway. By the end of March 1940 his operational strength was 23 boats, only marginally higher than it had been at the outbreak of war.

The collapse of France, however, tilted the scales in his favour. On 23 June, the same day that France surrendered, Dönitz made his first inspection of French Atlantic ports for possible use as submarine bases – two weeks later, *U-30* became the first boat to operate from Lorient and it was shortly followed by others. The result was that shipping losses increased steadily throughout the summer of 1940 and for the first time began to outstrip the rate of new construction.

The westward movement of the German submarine fleet and the presence of German air power over the Channel rendered ports in southern Britain unsafe and trans-Atlantic convoys began to sail instead from the northwestern ports on the estuaries of the Clyde and Mersey. The situation, however, quickly began to deteriorate. By late August 1940, Dönitz had enough boats in service to mount group attacks and he spread his submarines individually across the most heavily-travelled convoy routes. When one boat sighted a convoy, it informed his headquarters at Kerneval near Lorient by radio and Dönitz then guided others toward the target. The German submarines attacked in numbers to overwhelm the escorts, on the surface to take advantage of their greater speed, and at night when they were very difficult to see. Their tactic was to close to point blank torpedo range at the fastest possible speed, fire at as many ships as possible, and then escape before the startled escorts were able to react.

These methods brought immediate results – from July to September 1940, the U-boats sank 350 vessels, and in October alone 63 ships, totalling 350,000 tons, were lost. Some convoys were nearly destroyed. On the night of 18-19 October, six U-boats attacked Convoy SC 7, escorted by only a single British sloop, and sank 20 merchant ships totalling 79,646 tons. The slaughter of SC 7 was epitomized in the report of *Kapitänleutnant* Otto Kretschmer of *U-99*, who sank six vessels that night:

> Fire a bow torpedo at a large freighter of some 6,000 tons, at a range of 750 meters. Hit abreast foremast. Immediately after torpedo explosion, there is another explosion with a high column of flame from the bow to the bridge. The smoke rises some 200 meters. Bow apparently shattered. Ship continues to burn with green flame.[4]

On the following night, five U-boats savaged Convoy HX 79, sinking 12 of 24 merchantmen although there was a strong naval escort. It is small wonder that the German submariners termed this period their "Happy Time."

The convoys also faced other hazards. The *Luftwaffe* began to operate long-range Condor bombers from French airfields and they proved nearly as dangerous as the U-boats, sinking 15 ships in August 1940. German surface raiders, either warships or fast armed merchant ships, continued to break out into the Atlantic, forcing, at the least, the widespread deployment of the RN's strength.

These troubles occurred at a time when the Royal Navy, having suffered recent heavy losses, had only 74 operational destroyers – far too few to escort the vital Atlantic convoys, operate with the main fleets, and prevent a possible German seaborne invasion of England. In desperation, Prime Minister Winston Churchill appealed to President Franklin D. Roosevelt

"Four-stackers" – American Lend-Lease destroyers, 1940.
More than 50 First World War American destroyers are crammed into the Philadelphia Naval Yard in this remarkable photograph taken in September 1940. In return for bases in the Western Hemisphere, the USN turned over these aging veterans to the RN and, at British insistence, the RCN reluctantly manned six. (USN Navy Photograph, author's collection)

HMCS *Laurier* – one of the smaller warships in a "small ship" navy.
Constructed in 1936 for the Royal Canadian Mounted Police, *Laurier* was one of the Canadian government vessels taken over by the RCN at the outbreak of war. This was convenient as the crews of these vessels often came with them, simply switching uniforms. *Laurier* served throughout the war as a local coastal escort between Halifax and Sydney, Nova Scotia. Displacing 201 tons, she was 113 feet long, had a top speed of 10 knots, a complement of 29 and was armed with a single 12-pdr. gun and one .303 machine gun. *Laurier* returned to police service in 1946.

(Below) Wearing gun shirts and tin hats, the gun crew of *Laurier* practise their drill in 1940. Originally designed in the late 1890s, the 12-pdr. (3-inch) gun was extensively used during the First World War as the main armament on Canada's extemporized anti-submarine escort force and was brought back into service in the Second World War as the main armament of smaller warships and auxiliary vessels. It was not a particularly effective weapon although it had a good range – 5,000 yards. (Both, Canadian Naval Memorial Trust)

of the United States for old American destroyers to serve until the RN's wartime building programme provided new vessels, and in September a deal was struck which saw the United States turn over 50 "mothballed" and obsolescent destroyers in return for long-term leases on eight British bases in the Caribbean and Newfoundland. Included in this agreement, at American insistence, was a clause requiring Churchill to make a public declaration that the RN would not be scuttled or surrendered if Germany carried out a successful invasion of the British Isles. A month later, the first of these veterans arrived at Halifax to be taken over by a British crew.

The seven Canadian destroyers (*Fraser* had been replaced by a similar vessel, *Margaree*) were involved in the rising tempo of the naval war in the second half of 1940. They served as local escorts in the RN's Western Approaches command, taking outward-bound convoys from the Clyde and Mersey to a point northwest of Ireland and then picking up inward-bound convoys. On 2 July, *St. Laurent* made a dramatic 84-mile dash to rescue 826 survivors from the liner *Arandora Star* after it was torpedoed north of Ireland – ironically, the 1,299 passengers on board were largely German prisoners of war and German and Italian civilians on their way to internment in Canada. On 5 August, almost 22 years since a Canadian warship had last been in action against a German submarine (and that was the ignominious brush between the *Hochelaga* and *U-156*), Lieutenant Commander Herbert Rayner, RCN, commanding *St. Laurent*, attacked *U-52*, a Type VII boat under *Kapitänleutnant* Otto Salmann about 300 miles north of Ireland and so badly damaged it that Salmann had to limp back to his base. Three months later, on 6 November, HMCS *Ottawa*, under Commander E.R. Mainguy, RCN, and a British warship attacked and sank the Italian submarine *Faá di Bruno* after a hunt that lasted 24 hours. This was the RCN's first submarine kill although this success was not confirmed until long after the war.

These were the triumphs but there were tragedies as well. In late October, the newly-commissioned HMCS *Margaree* sank after colliding with the merchant ship it was escorting, causing the loss of 140 Canadian sailors – tragically, many of them survivors from *Fraser*. In early December, the Italian navy exacted revenge for the *Faá di Bruno* when the submarine *Argo* torpedoed *Saguenay*, blowing her bow off and killing 21 men,

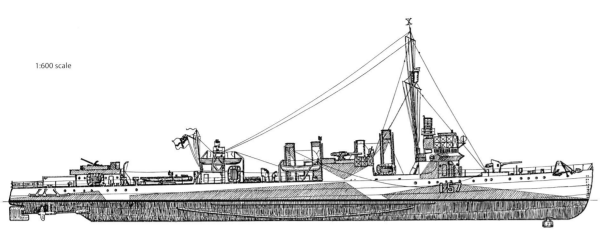

1:600 scale

HMCS *Niagara*, Town Class destroyer, 1941.
In 1940 the RCN took over six First World War American destroyers and later acquired two more. These vessels generally displaced between 1,000 and 1,200 tons, were 314 feet in length and carried a complement of 153 officers and men. Originally armed with four 4-inch guns and twelve 21-inch torpedo tubes, their armament was reduced to one 4-inch gun, one 12-pdr. gun, three 21-inch torpedo tubes, four 20mm AA guns, depth charges and, later, Hedgehog. *Niagara* is illustrated here with Type 271 Radar. (Drawing by L. B. Jenson, courtesy of the Directorate of History and Heritage, DND)

although prompt and effective action by the crew saved the destroyer and she was towed into harbour to spend six months under repair. There were now only five operational Canadian destroyers left but they soon received an unexpected reinforcement.

Problems for the RCN

At the urging of the Admiralty, which was already starting to feel personnel shortages, NSHQ reluctantly agreed to take over some of the old American destroyers. There was no great enthusiasm for these obsolescent warships, which, with their narrow hulls and high superstructures, tended to be unstable in rough seas, traits not offset by their better qualities – high speed and relatively heavy armament. It was a time, however, when any warship was better than none and the RCN commissioned six of the veteran warriors (HMC Ships *Annapolis, Columbia, Niagara, St. Clair, St. Croix* and *St. Francis*). Two proved so defective that they were only good for limited service but the remaining four, as crews were found for them, were dispatched in late 1940 and early 1941 to join the five modern destroyers in British waters.*

---

* Of the six ex-USN destroyers acquired by the RCN, only *Columbia, Niagara, St. Croix* and *St. Francis* served for extended periods in the mid-Atlantic. The other two spent most of their careers doing coastal escort work. Later in the war, at the request of Britain, Canada took over two more four-stackers, HMC Ships *Buxton* and *Hamilton*, but these ships were used primarily as training vessels.

The RCN would have much preferred using the manpower sent to these ships to man the new vessels beginning to enter service in late 1940. The first Canadian-built corvette to commission was HMS *Windflower* on 26 October, one of the ten vessels constructed for the RN, and she was soon joined by the other nine, all of which received, as was the RN custom, flower names. Under an arrangement made with the Admiralty, the RCN provided skeleton crews to deliver them to Britain and the plan was that these temporary crews, once replaced by British sailors, would then form a manning pool for the Canadian destroyers on the eastern side of the Atlantic. Unfortunately, the British replacement personnel never appeared and, given the general shortage of warships, the ten "orphan" corvettes were soon escorting convoys despite the fact that their crews were largely untrained. It was a difficult situation that persisted until April 1941 when NSHQ reluctantly complied with a request from the Admiralty that the ten vessels be retained as Canadian warships.

These developments had serious consequences. The unforeseen commitment to man 16 warships in late 1940 took much of the RCN's available manpower and totally disrupted its plans to recruit and train personnel for its wartime construction programme. The manpower required for these vessels, some 1,700 officers and sailors, may have seemed small to the Admiralty but it was nearly the exact strength of the permanent RCN in September 1939. As the newly-promoted Rear Admiral Nelles explained to his British

Convoys – the sailing of one or more merchant ships under the protection of a naval escort – have a long history that dates back to Roman times. Originally intended as a protection against pirates, by the time of the Napoleonic Wars convoys were so commonplace that Britain passed laws forbidding any merchant vessel to sail other than in convoy.

In the First World War the Royal Navy's reluctance to introduce the convoy system as a protection against submarines nearly reduced Britain to starvation, and as a result there was no hesitation to implement it during the Second World War, particularly on the North Atlantic. The first Atlantic convoy sailed from Britain four days after that nation declared war on 3 September 1939 and the last sailed in the middle of May 1945.

Although convoy organization changed several times during the war, generally only those vessels that could make more than 15 knots, which was almost as fast as a U-boat could travel on the surface, were allowed to proceed independently. All other vessels were required to sail in convoys, which were classed as fast or slow depending on their speed. Slow convoys included ships that could only make less that 9 knots while fast convoys included vessels that could steam between 9 and 14.8 knots.

The slow convoys were the most vulnerable as they were often composed of older ships, prone to making smoke and breaking down, and their lower speed meant that a U-boat could keep pace on the surface and manoeuvre into the best firing positions. It also took them longer to transit the "air gap," meaning that there was a greater chance that they would encounter the enemy.

Convoy designations and routes

Each convoy had a specific designation according to its origin and destination. In the North Atlantic, Canadian warships escorted the following types of convoys:

Designation	Route	Comment
HX	Halifax to UK, later New York to Halifax to UK	Fast convoy
HXS	New York to Halifax to UK	Slow convoy
OA	Thames via English Channel	Ceased Oct 40
OB	Liverpool outward	Ceased Jul 41
ON	UK to Halifax, later to New York	Fast convoy
ONS	UK to Halifax, later to New York,	Slow convoy
SC	Sydney to UK, later Halifax to UK	Slow convoy

Between 1939 and 1945, 1,468 convoys crossed the North Atlantic. The largest was HXS 300, with 167 merchant ships carrying 1,019,829 tons of cargo, which originated in New York on 17 July 1944 and arrived at its destination without loss, escorted only by a single RCN frigate and six corvettes.

Canadian warships were also involved in escorting the following types of convoys in North American or other waters:

Designation	Route
AH/HA	Tanker, Aruba to Halifax/Halifax to Aruba
BHX	Bermuda to Halifax
BW/WB	St. John's, Nfld, to Sydney/Sydney to St. John's, Nfld
BX/XB	Boston to Halifax/Halifax to Boston
CU/UC	Tanker, Curacao to UK/UK to Curacao
FH/HF	Saint John, NB, to Halifax/Halifax to Saint John, NB
GAT/TAG	Guantanamo to Aruba to Trinidad/Trinidad to Aruba to Guantanamo
GN/NG	Guantanamo to New York/New York to Guantanamo
GZ/ZG	Guantanamo to Panama/Panama to Guantanamo
HK/KH	Galveston to Key West/Key West to Galveston
HT/TH	Tanker, Halifax to Trinidad/Trinidad to Halifax
JH/HJ	St. John's, Nfld, to Halifax/Halifax to St. John's, Nfld
JW/WJ	UK to Murmansk/Murmansk to UK
KMF/MKF	UK to Gibraltar/Gibraltar to UK, fast convoy
KMS/MKS	UK to Gibraltar/Gibraltar to UK, slow convoy
LN/NL	Labrador to Quebec City/Quebec City to Labrador
NK/KN	New York to Key West/Key West to New York
QS/SQ	Quebec City to Sydney/Sydney to Quebec City
WHX	St. John's, Nfld, to West Ocean Meeting Point, fast
WSC	St. John's, Nfld, to West Ocean Meeting Point, slow

Convoy organization

The illustration opposite, based on Convoy ON 127 of September 1942, shows the organization of a typical convoy. The escorts – two destroyers and four corvettes – are stationed around the convoy, which consists of 32 merchantmen. The Senior Officer's ship, HMCS *St. Croix*, steams about 5,000 yards ahead of the convoy; the four corvettes are positioned on either side; and the second destroyer, HMCS *Ottawa*, is stationed about a thousand yards astern. Ideally, the escorts were positioned so that their radar, ASDIC and visual ranges overlapped but this was not always possible.

The merchantmen are steaming in six columns with three tankers, the most important and vulnerable ships, placed in the centre of the convoy for additional protection. The flagship of the convoy commodore, the naval officer who has authority over the masters of the merchant vessels, is in the leading vessel in one of the columns, the most convenient station. In large convoys, there might be one or more vice-commodores who would assist the commodore to keep the sometimes very independent merchant masters in their proper station. One or more ships in each column was usually designated a rescue ship, which would attempt to pick up survivors and for this reason usually sailed in the rear of its column. By 1942, many of the merchantmen were armed, either with AA or larger guns manned by detachments of naval or military gunners.

Despite all the precautions, Convoy ON 127 was attacked by a U-boat wolfpack on 9 September 1942, commencing a running battle with no less than 13 U-boats that lasted

Typical Convoy – ON127, September 1942
(Not to scale.)

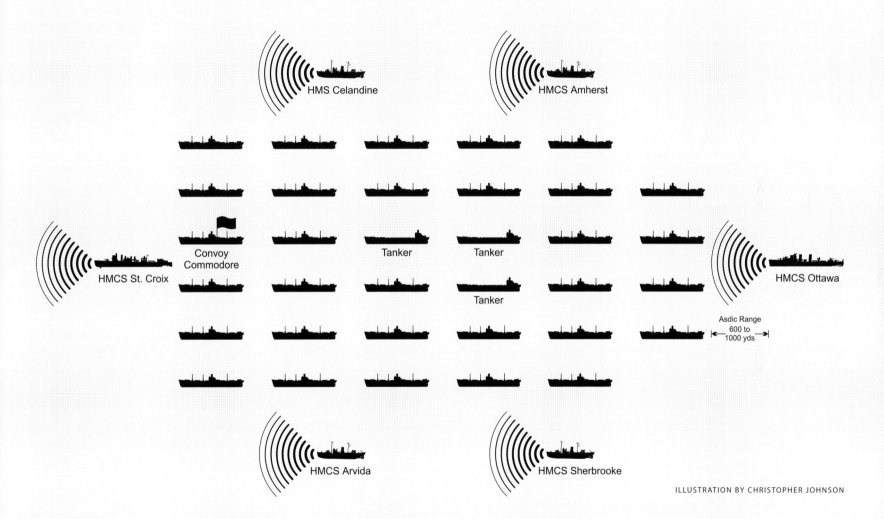

HMS Celandine

HMCS Amherst

HMCS St. Croix

Convoy Commodore

Tanker

Tanker

Tanker

HMCS Ottawa

Asdic Range
600 to
1000 yds

HMCS Arvida

HMCS Sherbrooke

ILLUSTRATION BY CHRISTOPHER JOHNSON

almost four days until air cover from Newfoundland arrived. The six escorts struggled to protect their charges but German attacks, both surface and submerged, resulted in the loss of seven merchantmen, with four more damaged. On the night of 13 September, U-91 torpedoed the destroyer HMCS *Ottawa* as she was investigating ASDIC contacts ahead of the convoy and the vessel sank with heavy loss of life.

The bottom line

Between 1940 and 1945, 7,357 merchant ships carrying 41,480,161 tons of cargo left Canadian ports in the St. Lawrence and the Atlantic coast bound for overseas destinations. Almost all sailed in convoys. Despite the heavy losses suffered by some convoys, most of these ships reached their destinations. ■

opposite number, Admiral Sir Dudley Pound, the RCN's manpower problems were such that it was trying to make "bricks without straw."[5]

In fact, in late 1940 the Canadian navy faced an almost insurmountable problem. To meet commitments for new construction, it had to train 7,000 officers and men before the spring of 1941 – including 300 officers of the executive branch, not one of which had yet been entered into the service. Even worse, the training establishments needed for this manpower had not yet been built and even if they had been, there were almost no instructional staff to man them. To add to the problem, the RCN's best warships were serving in British waters and were not available to provide at least some operational experience for what was rapidly becoming a navy of raw recruits. Sixteen months after the beginning of the war, the RCN was on a disastrous course toward a crisis that was not of its own making but one it could not avoid.

"We may fall by the way:" The background of the Battle of the Atlantic

The RCN's problems were unknown to the Admiralty, which at the end of 1940 faced its own difficulties. U-boat sinkings had tailed off in November and December as ferocious winter weather hampered operations, but the statistics compiled for the year made grim reading. During the preceding 12 months, the British Commonwealth's total shipping loss had been 3,991,641 tons. Submarines had accounted for 200 ships displacing 2,186,158 tons, and just over 90 per cent of these sinkings had occurred in the Atlantic or in waters adjacent to the British Isles – a sombre portent for the future – and, even worse, only one third of the more than 5 million tons of merchant shipping lost since the beginning of the war had been replaced. The scales were tipping against Britain and Winston Churchill had good reason to advise President Roosevelt that in the year to come the decision would lie upon the sea. It was the British prime minister's belief that, unless Britain

can establish our ability to feed this Island, to import the munitions of all kinds which we need, unless we can move our armies to the various theatres ... and maintain them there, and do all this with the assurance of being able to carry it on till the spirit of the Continental Dictators is broken, we may fall by the way.[6]

The man most responsible for this grim prediction was the recently-promoted Admiral Karl Dönitz. Dönitz had worked out his group attack tactics before the war but it was not until the second half of 1940 that he

Convoy conference.
Prior to sailing, the convoy commodore (standing on the left) held a meeting with the merchant captains who would be under his command to give them their sailing instructions and any last-minute information. There is no date for this photograph, which was probably taken in Halifax, but the relative informality of the occasion would indicate that it probably took place early in the war as later conferences were highly organized affairs including large maps and the attendance of many naval and air force officers. (National Archives of Canada, PA 180530)

had enough operational boats at sea to put them into effect. Dönitz's command method depended on radio communication between submarines on operations and his headquarters at Kerneval, and although Dönitz and his staff knew this traffic might become a source of intelligence for their enemy, they were confident that the cyphers provided by the Enigma machine could not be cracked. Fortunately for the Allied cause, this faith proved to be misplaced.

The workhorse of the German submarine fleet was the Type VIIC U-boat (see pages 38-39). Displacing 769 tons on the surface and 871 tons submerged, capable of 17.2 knots on the surface using its diesels and, for short period, up to 7.6 knots submerged using electric motors, the Type VIIC was a proven and rugged weapons platform. Its main weapon was its five torpedo tubes (four in the bow and one in the stern), for which it carried 14 torpedoes, but it was also armed with an 88mm deck gun and a varying number of small-calibre AA guns. At its most economical surface speed, the Type VIIC had a range of nearly 10,000 miles, which could be extended by refuelling and re-arming at sea from surface supply ships or Type XIV submarine "milk cows." The other major submarine type was the Type IX, which displaced 1,120 tons on the surface and 1,232 tons submerged and had a top speed of 18.2 knots on the surface and 7.3 knots submerged. Because their larger displacement meant slower diving times, these big brothers to the Type VII boats were at a disadvantage in the North Atlantic, where a delay of seconds could mean disaster, and they were primarily used for long-range independent patrols.

Defence of shipping – the priority objective

The preservation of Britain's lifeline – what Churchill dubbed "the battle of the Atlantic" in March 1941 – now became the Royal Navy's overriding concern. Fortunately, although the RN had believed before the war that the submarine was a manageable threat, it had still taken important steps to create an effective foundation for anti-submarine warfare.

First and foremost was the convoy (see pages 58-59) organized by the Naval Control of Shipping organization established at every major port in the British Commonwealth. The NCS mustered all merchant vessels –

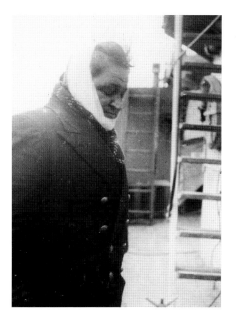

Not a happy man.
The wounded captain of a sunken Norwegian merchantman walks the deck of HMCS *Dauphin* in 1941 after that ship rescued his crew. The blast of the torpedo blew him off his bridge into the Alantic and he sustained a gash to his chin which was sewn up by Chief Petty Officer McGillivray, *Dauphin*'s cox'n. Understandably, he is not happy about the situation. (Canadian Naval Memorial Trust)

except those which could travel at speeds greater than 15 knots and thus outrun U-boats travelling on the surface – into convoys that sailed under the command of a commodore, usually a retired senior naval officer. The commodore was responsible for seeing that the merchantmen got to sea on time, formed up properly and were disciplined on passage. His was an important but thankless job as he had to deal with an assemblage of merchant masters who were very independent in their outlook. The commodore usually sailed on a large merchant vessel, well equipped with radio communications both with the shore and the accompanying naval escort. Convoys were classified according to the speeds of their constituent ships. Fast convoys generally included vessels that could steam between 9 and 15 knots; slow convoys consisted of those that could travel between 7.5 and 9 knots. The fast convoys were of more modern vessels; the slow convoys all too often consisted of older vessels, susceptible to making smoke, straggling and breakdowns.

The second important step was the establishment of a Submarine Tracking Room in the Operational Intelligence Centre (OIC) in the Admiralty headquarters in London. All information concerning the movement and operations of enemy submarines was channelled to the OIC, evaluated, and then sent to naval operational commands, escort vessels, and convoy commodores. The most important source of intelligence came from German radio traffic as Dönitz's method of command was to provide an important weapon to be used against him.

The location of U-boats at sea could sometimes be roughly ascertained by High Frequency Direction Finding (commonly called "Huff Duff"). The RN and RCN established a network of listening stations in eastern Canada and the British Isles that, if conditions were right, might intercept German radio signals and then, through cross bearings or "triangulation," establish an approximate position for the source of the transmission. These locations were fed to the OIC, which would warn convoy escorts of the number and position of enemy submarines in their area. Once it was ascertained that the DF system worked, it was a short step to mounting HF/DF apparatus on convoy escorts. Under good conditions, this equipment could provide a bearing for an intercepted radio signal and an approximation of its distance. Two or more HF/DF-equipped ships could exchange bearing information and obtain a cross-fix that would reveal the enemy's location. Beginning in late 1941 the RN made attempts to equip at least one warship in each escort group with HF/DF and the logical next step was to attempt to read German radio traffic, to comprehend enemy intentions and movements before they took place.

Seamen's mess, HMCS _Battleford_.
Accommodation in corvettes was very cramped as this photograph of the seamen's mess in HMCS _Battleford_ illustrates. This is almost certainly a "posed" shot taken in port as the sailors are uniformly dressed and the mess is suspiciously neat. It would have been quite different at sea. Note the small suitcases on the bulkhead and the round metal containers piled with the steel helmets above – the suitcases contained a sailor's personal effects and the container was used to store his dress cap. (National Archives of Canada, PA 184186)

This required cracking the Enigma machine, the German coding apparatus. It was fortunate for the Allied cause that the Polish intelligence service had started this monumental task in the mid-1930s and was actually successful in reading much of German Enigma traffic by 1939. When Poland fell, its codebreakers fled to the west and a decoding organization was created at Bletchley Park in Britain which, with the assistance of the Poles and much hard work, was soon able to read Luftwaffe and some German army traffic coded by Enigma. The _Kriegsmarine_, however, was a much more difficult proposition. The German navy used a different type of Enigma machine, called _Schlüssel M_, generated much less radio traffic and

was very security conscious. A fortunate series of captures of German auxiliary vessels and a U-boat in 1940-1941, however, provided Bletchley Park with naval Enigma machines, codebooks and cypher pads which rendered enough information to begin unravelling _Kriegsmarine_ Enigma cyphers in the early spring of 1941, using primitive computers dubbed "bombes."* By June, it was able to read German naval radio messages transmitted by

---

* One of the most important captures was that of the Type VII boat _U-570_ in August 1941. _U-570_ was the first German submarine to be taken intact during the war, and the Canadian destroyer HMCS _Niagara_, under the command of Lieutenant Commander T.P. Ryan, RCN, played a prominent role in this event, which has since been portrayed by Hollywood in the unintentionally hilarious film "U-571."

Enigma almost simultaneously, and in effect it could listen to Dönitz as he directed his submarines at sea, and then route convoys away from the U-boats. The intelligence product of Bletchley Park's work, dubbed "Ultra," was a war-winning asset and was such a closely guarded secret that its existence was not completely revealed until 1978.

Dönitz, a competent officer, soon became suspicious when, no matter how he deployed his boats, they found themselves searching empty horizons. He was certain that "coincidence alone it cannot be" but such was his faith in the Enigma machine that he refused to believe that his radio communications, the heart of his command system, were being read by his opponents.[7] He suspected spies at first but later came to believe that HF/DF was the cause of his problems, and it was fortunate for the Allied cause that he never accepted that the Enigma machine was seriously compromised, even though, in his postwar memoirs (published in 1959 before the existence of Ultra was known), he wondered whether his "enemy had some means of locating U-boat dispositions and of routing his shipping clear of them?"[8] *

In 1941, however, the advantages accorded to the British and Canadian ASW vessels by HF/DF and signal intelligence were offset by the inefficiency of their equipment and armament. The type of ASDIC on British and Canadian warships at this time required a highly-trained and experienced operator to work effectively, was often inaccurate and was almost useless in rough weather, at high speed or against a surfaced submarine.

Even if the escort got a reliable contact and depth-charged it, contact was often lost during the attack and all too often never regained. Since the U-boats' preferred tactic was to attack on the surface at night, many of the advantages of ASDIC were lost.

What was needed was a means of locating a surfaced submarine in all conditions of weather and light, and the answer, of course, was radar (see pages 112-113). At the outbreak of the war, the RN possessed a primitive radar set, the Type 286, but it was not that useful for ASW work as its range was only about one nautical mile and its antenna was fixed, meaning that it could not sweep 360 degrees but only about 60 degrees off each quarter. It was a rare occurrence for an operator using Type 286 radar to get a contact on a U-boat with only its conning tower above the surface. An improved radar, Type 271, which used a shorter centimetric wavelength that provided a more accurate return and that could locate the conning tower of a submarine, was introduced in late 1940 and the RN planned to install it on all its escort vessels used for mid-Atlantic work.

The major challenge faced by the British and Canadian navies in 1941, however, was not deficient equipment but a shortage of escorts. The RN needed its large destroyers for its main battle fleets in home waters and the Mediterranean, and it was forced to use older First World War destroyers, fleshed out by American vessels of similar vintage, in the Atlantic. Neces-

---

* To give Dönitz credit, on three occasions during the war (autumn 1941, spring 1943 and autumn 1943) he requested *Konteradmiral* Erhard Maertens, the chief of the *Kriegsmarine* signals service, to investigate whether the Allies were reading his messages coded by Enigma. Maertens did so and duly reported that the possibility of messages sent in cipher created by Enigma machines being broken by the Allies was "out of the question."

sity meant that the Flower Class corvette, designed as a coastal escort, was pressed into service in the mid-ocean and, when the shortcomings of the class became apparent, the Admiralty began to carry out modifications and to design improved ASW vessels. For the time being, however, the shortage of ships meant that Atlantic convoys in 1941 were escorted by small numbers of corvettes and aged destroyers. In the RCN, the situation was made worse by the fact that, from the outset, the Canadian navy lagged behind its British counterpart in new equipment and modification of existing vessels, factors which combined to affect its performance at sea.

The other British service concerned with the struggle against the U-boats was the Royal Air Force. In April 1941 the Admiralty assumed operational control of the RAF's Coastal Command, which consisted of a varying collection of aircraft with limited range and inadequate armament. Coastal Command suffered from a lack of suitable aircraft, particularly a long-range patrol aircraft, and even if its aircrews did spot a surfaced submarine by eyesight (the proverbial Mark I eyeball), they lacked an effective bomb or depth charge that could sink it. The aircraft, however, was the submarine's worst enemy and so effective in the "scarecrow" role were Coastal Command aircraft patrolling around the British Isles in the first half of 1941 that Dönitz was forced to shift his submarines west into the Atlantic.

The situation gets worse: January–May 1941

In the first three months of 1941, the statistics of the war at sea continued to be grim. Total losses from submarines during this period came to 833,000 tons while the Luftwaffe's long-range bombers were responsible for another 167,000 tons. The worst month was March, when the U-boats sank half a million tons of merchant shipping, losses not entirely replaced by new construction. Another disturbing trend was that Dönitz continually moved west in an attempt to avoid the range of aircraft based in Northern Ireland and Iceland (occupied by Britain in May 1940). Closer to

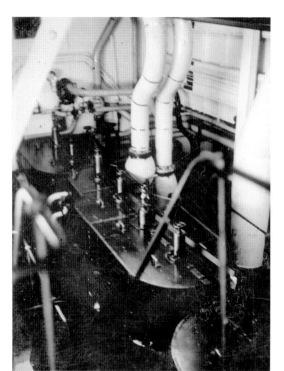

(Left) **Power plant – the main engine of a corvette.**
The triple-expansion engines installed in the Flower Class corvettes were dated in design but were robust and easy to operate – important considerations for a navy that expected to man these vessels with inexperienced crews. These engines generated 2,750 horsepower, enough to move a 950-ton corvette at a top speed of 16 knots – for short periods. (Canadian Naval Memorial Trust)

(Below) **The "Fiddley Deck."**
Stokers from HMCS *Sorel* relax aft of the corvette's funnel on a rare fine day. This sheltered area was a favourite place for off-duty crew members to congregate and, not surprisingly, catch up on their sleep. Engine rooms were noisy and hot so a chance to get some fresh air and a little sunshine was always appreciated. (Canadian Naval Memorial Trust)

Canada, the RCAF instituted aerial patrols from Newfoundland and by April 1941 only the mid-Atlantic remained without air cover.

At this time, many of the Atlantic convoys sailed either unescorted or lightly escorted in the middle reaches of the ocean and it was into this area that the German submarines moved in the spring of 1941. In response, the Admiralty created a separate naval command, Commander-in-Chief Western Approaches, with headquarters at Liverpool to co-ordinate operations in the Atlantic and also undertook to provide escorts for the trans-Atlantic convoys throughout the entire duration of their passage. To this end, they asked NSHQ whether the RCN would be willing to assist by providing mid-Atlantic escorts to be based in St. John's, Newfoundland. Ottawa's response was positive and on 20 May 1941 the Newfoundland Escort Force was created under the command of Commodore Leonard. W. Murray, RCN.

The Royal Canadian Navy was about to step onto centre stage in the Battle of the Atlantic.

Depth charge launch, HMCS *Pictou,* March 1942.
Until the advent of "ahead throwing" weapons, the standard ASW weapon was the depth charge, either dropped from the attacking ship's stern rails or, as shown here, launched by throwers. The major problem with this type of attack was that the attacking ship had to be as close to the target as possible, usually passing over it, before it dropped the charges and the resulting explosions interfered with ASDIC, often causing loss of contact with the target. (National Archives of Canada, PA 116838)

THE FIRST MONTHS OF WAR, 1939-1940

"Top hats being trampled:" The Volunteer Reserve mobilizes, 1939

The RCNVR mobilized well before Canada declared war on 10 September 1939 and most trained personnel were immediately sent to Halifax or Esquimalt. As recruiting began for wartime service, there were shortages of everything except men. Sub Lieutenant Jack Anderson, RCNVR, recalls the first months of the war at HMCS York, *the RCNVR Division in Toronto:*

We had absolutely nothing, we started completely from scratch. We had no uniforms in stores, or any sort of equipment whatsoever, except for a few old Lee-Enfield rifles and the twelve-pounder gun. ......

We asked about uniforms for the men and Ottawa said, "There won't be any available until the spring of 1940." I knew the contracts had been let to Tip Top Tailors in Toronto. So I went down and saw the general manager, whom I had known previously when I was at Eaton's, and he made a special effort and said that when these 100 men were assembled in Toronto, send them down and he would personally kit them up with jumpers and trousers. I got a hundred pair of new black boots from Eaton's. I got a hundred caps from Muir Cap Company, who also had received a contract to produce sailors' caps. ......

We found ourselves at the Division, completely trapped without any transportation. So, in discussion with the Captain and some of the other officers, we decided to hold a naval ball to raise funds. Tickets were sold at, I think, $10 or $15 per couple, for a formal ball to be held on the Drill Deck. This was in October '39, around Trafalgar Day. The only unfortunate thing, they sold about 1800 tickets, and the Drill Hall would only accommodate about 600 at the utmost. ......

The evening in question arrived. And cars, large cars, started to arrived, people in tail coats, opera hats, women in mink and sable coats. I don't know where they all came from, and it got to the state where there were hundreds outside who could not get in. ......

There were mink stoles and top hats being trampled on the floor. It ended up in complete disorder. However they seemed to enjoy themselves, and we cleared about $1800 from that dance, with which we bought a second-hand panel truck, painted it navy blue with "Toronto Division, RCNVR" on the side of it. We appointed a driver and we were in business as far as transportation was concerned.[1]

Lieutenant Frederick Sherwood, RCNVR, who commanded HMCS Carleton, *the reserve division in Ottawa, comments on the early days:*

We had some very good Petty Officers and I am a firm believer that it's the men in them and not the ships that make the difference. We had a twelve-pounder on a mounting in the gun battery and we had a twelve-pounder that we could put on wheels. That was our field gun. We had some rifles which we could do rifle-drill with, we had all kinds of equipment for knots and splices, and we improvised quite a lot of things ourselves in signals. I found an old Chief Yeoman of Signals from the Royal Navy, named Pink, who was so stiff he couldn't turn at all, but he could go in a straight line, and if he wanted to turn he'd turn like a robot. But he took on the recruits and he started teaching them signals and morse and flags and things like that. ......

All sorts of people came out of the woodwork to help. It really was a marvellous effort. ......

All that winter we were getting ready for a war which hadn't officially started yet. It wasn't until the Norwegian campaign in April [1940] that they began to realize that there was a war. Then there was Dunkirk and it was at this time that suddenly all the plugs were pulled and they said, "Come on now, we're going to have a war!" Up until then they were trying politically to put on a show of "Yes we're going to do everything we can boys, but let's not do any more than we have to."[2]

"There was no option, so we did without:" Halifax in the early days of the war

Most RCNR and RCNVR personnel mobilized at the outbreak of the war ended up on the Atlantic coast where they manned the small ships of the local patrols. Lieutenant Owen Robertson, RCNR, took over command of HMCS Fundy, *one of the prewar minesweepers, and remembers the problems he encountered with his first seagoing command:*

At first, in *Fundy*, we had three duffel coats – one that was my personal property and two that belonged to the Navy. You took 'em off and the next guy put 'em on. If it hadn't been for the IODE [Imperial Order of Daughters of the Empire] and the people like that, we would have frozen to death. They knitted us scarves and socks – the Navy didn't have any. No oilskins. We couldn't get sea boots for the men at sea. The naval stores had seaboots that were falling apart; they'd been there for fifty years – had arrived long before the Royal Navy handed over the Dockyard to the brand new RCN. But they were still "on charge" and so there was no authority to replace them. There was no option, so we did without. ……[3]

Leading Seaman R. Houliston, RCNVR, was assigned to HMCS French, an auxiliary patrol vessel, and remembers what happened when a green officer joined the vessel:

One of new arrivals was a middie at first, and then picked up his first stripe. He was detailed off as the Gunnery Officer. I remember when we were taking off from Halifax harbour on a patrol, he closed the crew up to the main armament, which was a six-pounder gun; I don't know what we'd do with it if we had come up with anything. He gave the order to train the gun to starboard, and told the lad in charge of the gun, "Load with HE [High Explosive]," which was done. The Gunnery Officer turned to the Captain and said, "Permission to fire?" And the Captain said, "Yes." The Gunnery Officer gave the order to fire and nothing happened. So he repeated the order and nothing happened. The third time he asked the Captain of the gun, "What's the problem?" The reply: "Sir, on the bearing we're trained on, Camperdown Lighthouse will be gone if we let this thing go!"[4]

Petty Officer R.M. Smith, who began his naval career as a rating in the RCNVR in September 1939, recalls the early days of the war at HMCS Stadacona, the shore station at Halifax when he was the duty bugler:

Every morning I played "Wakey-Wakey" – which I blew over the mike at the Quarter Deck, then [went] to every block and blew it again. Every time I did it in the old [barrack] block down by the dock where all the "retreads" and "ex-merchant" ratings were, I had to run through [and] between the lockers playing the bugle – and the boots, etc., were flying around my head complete with loud comments of what I could do with my bugle!

When I arrived at the block where I had been with my buddies, they were hollering as well …

couldn't I play anything besides "Wakey-Wakey?" so I chose to blow the first notes of the "Tiger Rag."[5]

How to be a plumber in one easy lesson: The navy expands

Lieutenant Owen Robertson, RCNR, was transferred to Ottawa in early 1940 to assist recruiting for the wartime navy. He remembers it being a hectic time:

In Ottawa we had nice easy working hours – seven days a week from eight until you were finished, generally about seven o'clock at night. If you were going to be later than that, you went home or went somewhere to eat and then came back and finished off. Four nights a week we went down to the basement in the RCNVR Headquarters and

Basic training – variations on a common theme.
Before going to sea, recruits in both the Canadian and German navies had to undergo military training. On the left, sailors at HMCS *Cornwallis*, near Digby, Nova Scotia, prepare to repel boarders using First World War rifles that would not have had much effect on a U-boat. Meanwhile, across the Atlantic, officer cadets at the German naval academy at Flensburg learn how to crawl through the mud although this skill would have had only limited application in the North Atlantic. On the other hand, such is life in the service. (RCN photograph G.A. Milne, National Archives of Canada, PA 128091; German photograph courtesy, Werner Hirschmann)

taught for a couple of hours. Saturday was a good day – we tried to knock off work at six or seven o'clock at night. We worked on Sunday mornings – Sunday afternoons we had off. ……

In recruiting seamen, it wasn't so difficult, because we knew how long it would take before you could ship them off to sea as seaman gunners or whatever. But the technical trades! To turn out an artificer or an artisan took six to nine months before they were fit to send to sea and manage a propulsion plant. ……

Very quickly, I had to learn what skills were required for the various trades so that I could talk glibly about them. Every night I'd go to sleep with a manual on my chest: *How to Be a Plumber in One Easy Lesson*, or something like that. ……

We'd go on these recruiting trips for a week, sometimes up to three weeks. As we stepped off the train, guys would be waiting at the station to join up. When we were leaving on the train, there would sometimes be about ten guys still with us. ……[6]

"Have sighted German, swimming strongly:" The early days at sea

For the first nine months, the war at sea was relatively uneventful for the Canadian navy. Sub-Lieutenant Ralph Hennessy, RCN, of HMCS Assiniboine *recalled that one highlight came in early 1940 when that destroyer was serving in the West Indies.*

Down in the Caribbean we did manage to intercept one German [merchant] ship. The British cruiser *Dunedin* and ourselves picked up the *Hannover*, which subsequently was converted by the Royal Navy to an auxiliary aircraft carrier. She was a brand new ship – a lovely one – but her crew tried to scuttle her. They set her on fire but made a mess of the scuttling. So *Dunedin* and ourselves went alongside her. …… For the trip from there into Kingston [Jamaica], we had *Dunedin* on one side of her and ourselves on the other with fire hoses going and eventually we put out the fires they'd set. ……

We made sure the German crew stayed on board. *Hannover*'s decks were quite hot to stand on as a result of the heat from the fires, and the German crew tried to come on board both our ships. But we said, "No effing fear – you just stay right where you are, friends." They were all into fire fighting, once they knew she wasn't going to sink. ……

At quite an early stage, one of the "better" Nazis on board, refusing to be dishonoured by being taken prisoner, dove over the side and headed for the Fatherland by rhumb line, under his own power. After things began to come under control *Dunedin* sent us to recover him. *Assiniboine* sent back a series of messages:

"Have sighted German, swimming strongly."

"German in boat. Has requested Cox'n to shoot him."

"Cox'n regrets he has no gun."[7]

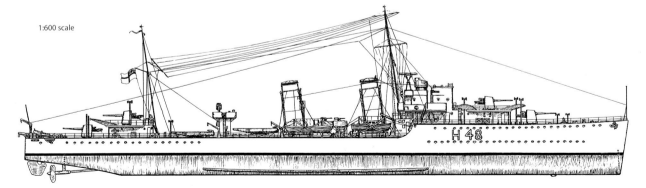

1:600 scale

HMCS *Fraser*, River Class destroyer, 1937.
In 1939 the RCN possessed six destroyers of standard British design. These vessels displaced 1,375 tons, were 329 feet long, had a top speed of 31 knots, carried a complement of 181 and were armed with four 4.7 inch guns, eight 21-inch torpedo tubes and two 2-pdr. (40mm) anti-aircraft guns, as well as depth charges. HMCS *Fraser*, the former HMS *Crescent*, entered Canadian service in 1937, participated in the early war convoys but was sunk in a collision on 25 June 1940. (Drawing by L.B. Jenson, courtesy Directorate of History and Heritage, DND)

"G-G-Good G-G-God, there's a gun!"
The fall of France, 1940

In the spring of 1940 the tempo of the war changed when Germany conquered the Low Countries and France in the space of six weeks. Canada sent all its destroyers to serve in British waters and one of the first tasks they carried out in June 1940 was the evacuation of civilians, diplomats and allied troops from small ports in the west of France before the seemingly invincible German army arrived. Commander W.B. Creery, RCN, captain of HMCS Fraser, *recalls the evacuation of the St. Jean de Luz in the Bay of Biscay in late June 1940:*

Sub-Lieutenant Landymore was sent by motor boat to try to persuade the skippers of some Belgian trawlers anchored in a distant part of the harbour to sail north to England instead of south to neutral Spain.

The evacuation party [Landymore] was obliged to leave the shore before 1300 and, therefore, be re-embarked while there were still a few boatloads of evacuees waiting passage to the merchant ships. I decided to remain until all evacuees had been embarked.

So there we were: our time was up, the Germans were known to be approaching, the evacuation was not completed and Landymore and our motor boat had not returned. We spent a miserable forenoon. At noon, boatloads were still arriving from shore and the decks of the little tramps were swarming with people who would have to live there for a week with little or no protection from the elements and a few facilities. Suddenly the Officer of the Watch, who had a slight stammer, exclaimed, "G-G-Good G-G-God, there's a *gun*!"

Sure enough, over the brow of a nearby hill a small force with a field gun and a tank had appeared. We couldn't make out their nationality but, to guns on land, ships in harbour are sitting ducks and there was only one thing to do. I sounded "Action Stations," ordered the merchant ships to sea and prepared to follow them. We watched sadly as several boatloads of evacuees turned back to shore.

Our motor boat returned and had difficulty hooking on the hoisting falls because we were light in the water and rolling badly in the confused swell. Landymore sent the boat's crew swarming up the falls and inboard as soon as the boat was hooked on, but remained in the boat himself. I was anxious to go to action stations and weigh anchor but we had no power hoists and it took all hands to hoist the boat. However, we had a try at doing all three things at the same time and, although the boat smashed badly against the ship's side as we hoisted it, all was going reasonably well until a steadying line parted, the boat canted sharply outward and Landymore was catapulted into the sea.

As if this were not enough, the Focsle Officer reported that the anchor had apparently fouled a cable on the bottom of the harbour and could not be weighed. Then the Officer of the Watch reported that there were now several guns on the nearby ridge, all of which appeared to be trained on us! Obviously we could delay no longer, so we fished Landymore out of the water, slipped our cable and departed in haste if not dignity. ......

Because of this sudden move, we had to leave one final boatload of refugees but, in all, 16,000 Polish soldiers and thousands of refugees were successfully evacuated.[8]

Canadian warships were not directly involved in the rescue of the British army from the beaches of Dunkirk but some RCN personnel did participate as individuals. One was Sub-Lieutenant Robert Timbrell, RCN, who was at the RN gunnery school at Whale Island at Portsmouth one morning in June 1940 when he and his classmates were hurriedly ordered to take command of an armada of small craft gathered for the rescue attempt. Timbrell was sent to Llanthany, *a millionaire's spanking-new diesel yacht, and later recalled that, when he first mustered his complement,*

The crew was mixed – there were a Petty Officer and four RN seamen, six Newfoundland navy ratings and two 50-year-old engineers in civvies. I found out that the civvies had come from the London Transport bus depot. I thought the Newfoundlanders were my saviours – until I found that they had put on their uniforms a month before, having been lumberjacks in Newfoundland and had never been to sea. ...... *Llanthany*'s main armament consisted of my .45 revolver, holstered in a marvellous leather belt, stamped "1914." ......

We sailed [from Ramsgate] and did the "usual" day trips to Dunkirk. ...... The RAF were over the Dunkirk beach, doing a marvellous job, but the odd German got through. The beach was also being shelled. The town was in flames.

I had two boats on davits and I sent the Petty Officer in with them to embark troops to our anchorage north of the jetty – the jetty was reserved for destroyers and cross-Channel ferries. *Llanthany* carried about 100 or 120 Allied soldiers with their rifles on each trip, and we returned the instant we were loaded. Every conceivable yacht and pleasure craft was occupied in the rescue. ......

On our third or fourth trip we got knocked about a bit near Dunkirk end – I don't know whether it was a bomb or shell – but I lost half the crew, my anchors and the fuel supply line to the engines. We ended up on the beach. We carried out some repairs -- the hull was OK – and were ready for the tide to come up and spring us loose. I kept looking at my first command, high and dry there on the beach, with the water seeming to be a mile away. ......

Mussolini's revenge, December 1940.
After HMCS *Ottawa* sank the Italian submarine *Faá di Bruno* in October 1940, the Italian navy exacted its revenge by torpedoing the destroyer *Saguenay* in December of that year. *Saguenay* was saved by good damage control and was able to reach port where she is seen in the photograph. *Saguenay* returned to sea in May 1941 as part of the Newfoundland Escort Force but a collision with a merchantman late in 1942 led to her being relegated to service as a training vessel. (National Archives of Canada, PA 114155)

A sergeant came down with about six or eight men; they turned out to be the remains of a battalion of Guards. The sergeant said they would like to get back to England – a statement we agreed on. He asked how he could help. I asked him to go off and find a tank and he found a bren-gun carrier and drove it out into the ocean until it stopped. We put a line around it and winched the yacht off.

After we got the yacht off the beach and loaded with troops, we went back to Ramsgate and were met by the [RN co-ordinating] Captain, who was still meeting every ship. I reported that I had lost half the crew and asked, "Could you make arrangements for replacements?" The Guards sergeant, there and then, said, "Sir, we would like to stay with you, if we're permitted, and go back and get our mates!" The Captain could have got replacements for my sailors but he asked the sergeant, "Are you sure you want to go back?" The sergeant said that they would stay – and they stayed the whole time, for all the rest of the runs.

Up until then, the only gun on the yacht was my .45 revolver. The soldiers were able to get machine guns and some anti-tank guns which fired something like a one-inch shell. The guns proved useful later when E-boats came down on the last two nights.

After we did the last trip back to Ramsgate, we went on to Portsmouth. ...... Then, with the sergeant and the troops and the remains of my original crew – including my two civilian engineers – we marched to the lower gate at Portsmouth Dockyard. We were asked one question, "Are you back from Dunkirk?" I replied, "Yes," and the Dockyard sentry said, "Pass."[9]

Rescuing survivors

On 2 July 1940, the liner Arandora Star *carrying nearly 1300 passengers was torpedoed and sank west of Ireland. HMCS* St Laurent, *under Lieutenant Commander Harry De Wolf, RCN, picked up many of the survivors and, as Lieutenant Ralph Welland remembers, they were in a terrible condition:*

They had been in the water about 8 hours and by the time we got back to Greenock … at full speed, 32 knots, 62 of them had died. I remember the number. De Wolf had told me … "You, Welland, take two strong sailors, and you're in charge of Category 2 people." I said, "Category 2, sir?" He said, "Yes, dead."

The ship was a shambles. Within an hour of picking those people up, not one lavatory in the ship worked. The whole thing was covered by oil. People had been throwing up. ...... There were 50 people in the wardroom, all lying down in rows, like a slave ship, and all in pretty poor shape, and dying all the time.

I and my two sailors went around and collected the people who were dead and stacked them up on the Y gun deck. That's a lot of dead people. ……

We did the best we could. Everybody gave all their clothing, all their blankets, all the canvas sheets, hammock covers, to wrap these people in to keep them warm, because most of them were on the upper deck. There wasn't room for that number of people down below, so they were wrapped up in the upper deck with the ship doing 32 knots and the spray coming over.[10]

Double disasters: The loss of *Fraser* and *Margaree,* 1940

During the course of 1940, the RCN lost two destroyers, HMC Ships Fraser *and* Margaree, *about a fifth of its modern fleet, in collisions at sea.* Fraser *was cut in half by the British cruiser* Calcutta *on 25 June 1940 and her captain, Commander W.B. Creery, RCN, remembered the moments that immediately followed:*

The upper bridge [of *Fraser*], where eight of us were standing, was neatly picked up by *Calcutta*'s focsle. The shock of the collision sent us flying and it was a moment or two before we recovered our senses sufficiently to realize what had happened. To us, our perch seemed very precarious and we hastily climbed over the front screen of *Fraser*'s erstwhile bridge and dropped some six feet or so onto *Calcutta*'s focsle. So *Fraser*'s bridge personnel – myself, the Officer of the Watch, the Second Officer of the Watch, signalmen and lookouts – were now aboard *Calcutta*. One of the wheelhouse crew was also rescued there – he was in a small cavity between *Calcutta*'s deck and the floor of *Fraser*'s bridge, which had buckled. The man who had been standing beside him had been squashed flat. *Fraser*'s bridge remained on *Calcut-*

On the bridge.

Bridge personnel on the destroyer HMCS *Restigouche* watch a freighter burn in the Atlantic in late 1940 or early 1941. The circular apparatus on the right is the ship's MF/DF (Medium Frequancy/Direction Finding) aerial. (National Archives of Canada, PA 176750)

ta's focsle until it was burned off in Devonport Dockyard by acetylene torch. ……

By now it was pitch dark and I couldn't see any part of *Fraser,* but I had heard shouts from the fore part and then, a little later, the men's voices singing "Roll out the Barrel."[11]

Sub Lieutenant Robert Timbrell, RCN, was in Margaree *when she was cut in half on 21 October by the merchantman* Port Fairy. *He remembers the experiences of the last men on board the destroyer:*

By now, it was two-thirty or three o'clock in the morning. …… Four of us were left on board: Pat

Russell – the First Lieutenant, Bill Landymore – the Gunnery Officer, the L[eading] T[orpedo] O[perator], and myself. ……

By now we had drawn well away from the *Port Fairy.* Pat had the ship checked – there was no one else on board, number one boiler room was filling up and number two was leaking. It was decided we would get a carley float out. We had a float on the torpedo-tubes, so we swung the tubes outboard on the leeward side. The LTO and I got up on the tubes to throw the float over the side but, before doing so, we passed the line over to Bill Landymore, not giving any thought to the length of the line. When you're in such a position and thinking of saving your soul, you seem to get extra adrenalin or super-strength – we *threw* that carley float – the next thing we saw was Landymore hanging on to the rope, going over the side and hitting the cold Atlantic water.

... it must have been four or five o'clock in the morning – it was October and cold, and we were about five hundred miles west of Ireland. There was dead silence on top of the tubes looking down, Pat Russell was at the ship's side looking over. Up came the fluttering, unhappy Gunnery Officer and I can still see this moment of crisis. Pat Russell leaned over and yelled, "Landymore, did I give you permission to leave the ship?"[12]

"I can't get down the ladder:" HMCS *Saguenay*, December 1940

On 1 December, the Italian submarine Argo *torpedoed HMCS* Saguenay *about 400 miles west of Ireland. Lieutenant Louis Audette, RCNVR, never forgot the heroism of a young seaman during the moments that followed:*

There was a strange hush about the ship. I went up to the bridge and [Lieutenant Commander G.W.] Miles [captain of *Saguenay*] told me to go aft and take charge of the after guns. Most of the focsle was blown away and everything around the two forward guns was ablaze. Nobody could man the forward guns, so I went aft. Of course, when your ship's been torpedoed, you don't know who's been killed – you don't know who's been wounded, and you don't know who's available for anything. I had to man X and Y guns. I got Y gun manned and went to X gun, and called for volunteers.

Lots of chaps volunteered, one I'll always remember – a youngster, Clifford McNaught, not a gunnery rating, not skilled in the art of gunnery. I put him on as a supply number, which required him to lift cold, heavy, metal shells and put them in the gun tray. We had to do a bit of firing, because the submarine was on the surface and firing further torpedoes at us. Fortunately they missed. This went on for a while. There's an awful lot to do when a ship is torpedoed, there really is.

Big ship – HMCS *Prince Robert*. At the beginning of the war, the biggest concern was not U-boats but surface raiders. The RCN's six destroyers were supplemented by the conversion of three small liners into armed merchant cruisers. *Prince Robert*, shown in this aerial photograph taken in July 1942, displaced 5,736 tons, carried a complement of 400 officers and men and was armed with ten 4-inch guns, two 3-pdr. guns and eight 20mm guns. In 1943 she was converted to an anti-aircraft ship. (National Archives of Canada, PA 205373)

After a while I had a moment when I could do what I wanted, and went to McNaught and said, "I know you're not familiar with the shells." There were shells spread around X gun, which is one deck up, and I was pointing out to him what was armour-piercing and what was starshell, so that he'd know what to do if he was called upon to produce one or the other. ……

All of a sudden the flames on the forepart of the ship went wildly ablaze and it grew a lot brighter. Then I observed that McNaught was standing in a very unusual position, his elbows flexed above his head and his hands very near his face, an unusual position for any man to adopt. I finally really looked at him. For a moment, when the flames were particularly bright, I was able to observe that his hands and face were hideously burned. How he ever could have handled the shells, I have no idea. Naturally, I immediately told him, "Go below, got to the Doctor in the Wardroom and get the necessary medical care." Then I had to find someone to replace him.

Other things occurred; I can remember the flames were getting near the magazine and the flooding-valve was stuck – that caused a bit of anxiety for a few moments. After a while I found McNaught sitting on the deck – he hadn't gone below. I turned on him angrily and said, "Look! I told you to go below. Go and see the Doctor." Then I realized he was quietly sobbing, just like a child, like a hurt child. Indeed he was a hurt child and those were devastating tears of shock, of course. He looked up at me and really silenced me. He sobbed, "I can't. My hands! I can't go down the ladder." And he couldn't! But he was the fellow who had handled these shells throughout the action, quite cheerfully, no problem. But the

moment the strain was taken away he could no longer do it.

I put a line around him and we lowered him down onto the main deck. He was able to walk, there was no problem there. But the next morning he was in quite bad shape.[13]

"Waves cresting near fifty feet:" One of the first corvettes encounters rough weather on the Atlantic

HMCS Hepatica *was one of the first Canadian-built corvettes to be commissioned. Intended for the Royal Navy, she left Halifax for Britain in December 1940 with a veteran merchant marine captain but a green crew, 6 depth-charges and a wooden gun. As Seaman Lionel Kennedy remembers, it was a difficult voyage:*

Three days out of Halifax the convoy ran into a wicked gale that saw the waves cresting near fifty feet, scattering the merchant ships and forcing us to heave to for three days, bow on to the heavy seas and high winds. Finally, the skipper decided to make a try at swinging the ship about to carry on for the U.K. and at that time I was in the wheelhouse. Seas were far apart and, as the next wave approached, the skipper kept her bow on until part way up the wave, then put the helm hard over to starboard. This brought *Hepatica* broadside on to the crest and still turning, our stern to the sea as we dropped down into the trough. It was a neatly-done manoeuvre, carried out by a skipper who had once sailed the China seas, and we were glad we had a professional to do it. The rest of us had never seen anything bigger than York Lake or the Assiniboine River.[14]

A wet and open deck.
One of the major problems with the original corvette design was that the main deck was open between the bridge structure where the galley was located and the foc'sle where the sailors slept and ate. The result was that in any but the most calm sea, corvettes were very wet ships. This fault was corrected by later modifications that extended the foc'sle back to the bridge. (Canadian Naval Memorial Trust)

TIME OF TRIAL: THE ROYAL CANADIAN NAVY AND THE BATTLE OF THE ATLANTIC, MAY 1941–MAY 1942

*T*he man chosen to command the Newfoundland Escort Force, Commodore Leonard W. Murray, was a professional naval officer who had graduated from the Royal Naval College of Canada in 1912 and served with the RN in the First World War. During the interwar period, he had followed the usual career pattern: shore duty in Canada alternating with sea duty, interspersed with periods of service with the RN. Murray was not a fire-breather but a thoroughly competent officer who always showed empathy for the sailors under his command. He had a somewhat distant personality (he was actually rather shy) but was well known in the RCN as a consummate shiphandler – a captain able to manoeuvre his vessel in all weathers with skill and precision. In the Commonwealth and most other navies, shiphandling rated above all other officer qualities as it was believed with some justification that good shiphandlers were good leaders.

(Facing page) **The Royal Canadian Navy steps onto centre stage, May 1941.** The corvette, designed as a local escort for coastal convoys, became the major escort vessel on the North Atlantic in 1941-1943. Seen from HMCS *Chambly,* the corvettes of the newly-formed Newfoundland Escort Force are on their way to St. John's in May 1941. The creation of this force brought the RCN into the mid-Atlantic and marked the beginning of two years of grim and relentless struggle against not only the U-boats but also the elements. (National Archives of Canada, PA 115350)

Murray would receive strong support from one of his senior subordinates – Commander James Douglas Prentice, RCN. Universally known in the Canadian navy by his nickname, "Chummy", Prentice was a study in contrast. A native of Victoria, B.C., he had joined the RN as an officer cadet in 1912 and had enjoyed a worthy but unspectacular career, mostly in small ships, until he had taken early retirement in 1934 to return to his native British Columbia. At the outbreak of the war, Prentice had accepted NSHQ's offer of a commission in the RCN at his old rank of lieutenant-commander and first came into contact with Murray when stationed at Halifax in 1940. Murray made him "Senior Officer, Canadian Corvettes," a somewhat nebulous appointment that involved Prentice with the working-up problems of the first Canadian corvettes. In March 1941 he was appointed to command of HMCS *Chambly* and sailed for St. John's in May as Senior Officer of the first seven corvettes of the Newfoundland Escort Force. "Chummy" Prentice was an experienced saltwater sailor, a fine shiphandler, an extremely competent officer and a tactical innovator.

He was also a character whose eccentricities made him a popular figure. Prentice wore a monocle, which intrigued his Canadian crew who were unfamiliar with such a device, and one day, during divisions or inspection on *Chambly,* many turned out wearing a similar appurtenance. A more conservative officer might have taken offence but Prentice passed down the ranks without comment. When the inspection was over, he assumed a position in front of the crew, glared at them fiercely and, with the words "Try this," flipped his monocle in the air with a toss of his head, and caught it squarely between the eyebrow and lower lid of his right eye, not once touching it with his hands. After that, Prentice was the only man on *Chambly* to wear a monocle and, not surprisingly, he was much loved by his crew.

The Newfoundland Escort Force

Prentice and *Chambly* arrived in St. John's on 27 May 1941 with the first group of corvettes. The Flower Class corvette was not really a practical warship for the mid-Atlantic because, although very seaworthy, its short length meant it rode the ocean like a cork rather than slicing through the seas – as a result, in anything but a dead calm sea, a corvette was inclined to be very lively. Its deck was open between the bridge structure and foc'sle, which meant that in even moderate seas it was often awash. Furthermore, the foremast was positioned squarely in front of the bridge, hampering visibility from the bridge, which in any case was not a good observation platform because of its relatively low height. The Royal Navy had already taken many of its corvettes in hand for modifications that would make them more suitable for mid-ocean work but Canadian shipyards, overburdened with new construction, were unable to provide such a service. Even worse, Canadian corvettes were equipped with useless minesweeping gear as it had originally been intended that they would function in a dual role. Their armament and other equipment were on a par: almost none had radar, the latest ASDIC or

Commander Leonard W. Murray, 1940.
A graduate of the Royal Naval College of Canada, Murray was a prewar regular officer who took over command of the Newfoundland Escort Force in May 1941. For the remainder of the war, Murray was the senior Canadian officer most directly concerned with the Battle of the Atlantic. A quiet but determined man, Murray strove hard to improve conditions for his crews. This photograph, taken on board HMCS *Saguenay* in 1940, depicts him in a Nelsonian pose that is rather spoiled by the strange headgear. (Canadian Naval Memorial Trust)

radio telephones, and most had unreliable magnetic compasses rather than gyro compasses while their secondary armament consisted of First World War vintage machine guns. In short, they lacked almost every necessity to be effective ASW vessels and this put an undue burden on the destroyers assigned to the NEF.

Their crews were willing but raw. In 1941, it was often the case that only two officers on board a Canadian corvette possessed watchkeeping certificates, the naval "licence" to stand a bridge watch and con a ship. A corvette was fortunate if it had a small cadre of experienced ratings as, by and large, most of the crew were going to sea for the first time and they were going into the North Atlantic, famous for its gales, ice, fog and generally bad conditions. They would sail out of St. John's, Newfoundland, affectionately known as "Newfie John" or "Hole in the Rock," which more aptly describes the small harbour with its narrow entrance. There were few naval facilities in St. John's in 1941 and even fewer recreational facilities for the sailors. Things were no better at the other end as, at the completion of a voyage, Canadian ships would go into Hvalfjord in Iceland, an open, windswept anchorage in barren surroundings.

To control a force that would in the next six months come to include most of the destroyers and corvettes in the RCN, Commodore Murray had a ridiculously small staff. He also came under a cumbersome command structure resulting from an agreement made in March between Britain and the United States which made the United States Navy responsible for the protection of shipping west of a line running between Greenland and Iceland and, in effect, brought the Canadian navy under American control, although neither the Canadian government

Rudimentary – ASDIC equipment on early corvettes.

The ASDIC equipment on the early corvettes was very primitive. It included, on the right, a magnetic compass binnacle with a handwheel to control the direction of the Type 123A ASDIC and, on the left, a primitive recorder with earphone jacks for the ASDIC operator and officer. This equipment was obsolescent when it was installed in 1941 but it remained in Canadian use until 1943. It was difficult to obtain accurate information from the Type 123A and such information as was gained was often transmitted by the ASDIC officer to his captain on the bridge outside by means of loud shouts. (National Archives of Canada, PA 136247)

Old Reliable – the Mark IX 4-inch gun.

The standard main gun on Canadian corvettes was the breech-loading 4-inch gun, either in single or double mount. Although it dated back to the First World War, the 4-inch possessed good range and accuracy. As the war progressed, fewer U-boats attempted surface gun duels with Allied escorts and the 4-inch gun was used less frequently. This photograph illustrates the weapon on HMCS *Arvida* in late 1943 or early 1944 – note the rails mounted on the sides of the turret for illumination rockets. Note also the caps with ear flaps worn by some of the gun crew; these were issue items in the RCN in the later war years. (National Archives of Canada, PA 184185) nor its senior naval officers were consulted about this arrangement. In reality, the commander of Task Group 4, Rear Admiral L. E. Bristol, the senior American officer, whose headquarters were at Argentia, Newfoundland, only exercised "coordinating supervision" over the NEF and left daily operations in the hands of Murray at St. John's.[1] Bristol proved supportive of the RCN's efforts as did many of his staff, who thought their Canadian counterparts "active, capable and good companions."[2] The Americans concentrated on escorting fast convoys while the NEF escorted the slow convoys.

The slow convoys, unfortunately, were the worst. Composed of old and weather-beaten merchantmen prone to breakdown, they were longer in passage and more vulnerable to attack. The fast convoys, composed of newer ships, were less likely to suffer attack because, although the U-boats could keep up with them on the surface, their speed was such that the enemy found it difficult to make concentrated attacks against them. An additional problem with slow convoys was that, in order to receive some protection from the limited air units available in Iceland, they were often routed to the north on a longer and rougher passage than the fast convoys, which took a more direct route across the Atlantic. Although it was planned that the NEF would provide an escort group of six ships for each slow convoy, this strength was rarely attained on operations. The slow convoys sailed from ports in Nova Scotia (and later New York) under local escort to a point off southern Newfoundland designated the WESTOMP (West Operational Meeting Point). Here an NEF escort group took them over and escorted them to the MOMP (Mid Ocean Meeting Point), where they were taken over by British escorts. The Canadian group then went to Hvalfjord in Iceland for refuelling and maintenance before picking up a westbound convoy, which they would take back to the WESTOMP. Theoretically, the ships of the NEF were to get at least a week for rest and maintenance between the inward and outward legs of each voyage but this rarely proved possible.

As if all this was not bad enough, Murray also faced problems finding time and facilities to train his green crews. He had originally hoped that at any given time one of his groups would be exercising under Prentice's supervision to work their crews up to a minimum level of proficiency, but from the outset operational requirements doomed these intentions. It was not until early September, nearly three months after the creation of the NEF, that Murray was able to provide Prentice with this opportunity.

The summer of 1941: The Newfoundland Escort Force commences operations

The problems of the Newfoundland Escort Force were apparent when it fought its first convoy battle a week after Murray assumed command. Convoy HX 133, which consisted of 58 ships escorted by the destroyer HMCS *Ottawa* and the corvettes *Chambly*, *Collingwood* and *Orillia* left Halifax for Britain in mid-June 1941. On the 23rd of that month, it was sighted by a U-boat which reported its position and called in other submarines for a group attack. Efforts by the escort commander, Commander E.R. Mainguy, RCN, to protect the convoy were frustrated by lack of radio telephones on his ships, forcing the escorts to communicate by signal lamp. Many signals were not picked up and it proved impossible to co-ordinate the defence of HX 133, which lost six ships and was only saved from total disaster when the escort was reinforced by several British ships.

It was fortunate for the NEF, given its unready state, that, throughout much of the summer of 1941, Ultra intelligence allowed convoys to be routed around known concentrations of submarines and losses were therefore minimal. This was just as well because the NEF was very inexperienced, as was demonstrated by Convoy SC 41, which left Sydney in the last week of August escorted by the ex-USN "four-stacker" destroyer *St. Croix* under Commander H. Kingsley, RCN, who was also Senior Officer,

(Facing page) **Busy place – the bridge of a corvette, 1941.**
The original bridge design of the corvette was very crowded, as illustrated in this photograph of HMCS *Moncton* taken during her work-ups in May 1942. It was another feature that had to be changed, but in the RCN modernization lagged far behind the RN. Note the 20-inch signal projector and the twin .50 calibre AA machine guns. Also note the proper uniform of officers and sailors – this vessel has not yet seen service. (National Archives of Canada, PA 191631)

and the corvettes *Buctouche*, *Galt* and *Pictou*. The voyage of SC 41 was a dismal record of equipment breakdowns on three of the four escorts, collisions at sea, naval and merchant vessels getting lost and communications failure, all of which were played out against a background of bad weather, fog, storms and ice floes. More by chance than anything else, SC 41 arrived in Britain without loss, but by the time the next slow convoy, SC 42, set off, the Newfoundland Escort Force's luck had run out.

The ordeal of SC 42: August–September 1941

Convoy SC 42 departed Sydney, Nova Scotia, for Britain on 31 August 1941 and two days later was taken over at the WESTOMP by Canadian Escort Group 24 under the command of Lieutenant Commander J.C. Hibbard, RCN, with the destroyer HMCS *Skeena* (Senior Officer or command ship) and the corvettes *Alberni*, *Kenogami* and *Orillia*. For a large convoy of 67 merchant ships, this was rather thin protection and the situation was not improved when SC 42 encountered a gale on 3 September that lasted four days – three ships were forced to turn back, speed was reduced to an absolute crawl of 5 knots while stemming the sea, and fuel consumption increased. Eight days out of Sydney and only just south of Greenland, SC 42 was sighted by *U-85*.

That boat was deployed on Dönitz's orders. After a summer of fairly meagre results, Dönitz had become suspicious that British aircraft were equipped with a secret device that could locate his submarines. At the end of August he therefore concentrated a large force of 14 boats, *Gruppe Markgraf*, westward beyond the range of aircraft from Iceland, and in the first week of September they were in a perfect position to intercept SC 42. Forewarned by Ultra, the Admiralty routed most convoys south of this peril but SC 42, running low on fuel, was ordered to make a diversion up the eastern coast of Greenland to take advantage of the shorter distance on the northern route to the British Isles. On 9 September, just after it had turned eastward for Iceland, SC 42 was sighted and Dönitz guided the other submarines of *Markgraf* into position. The first torpedoes struck after midnight from the port, or northern side of the convoy, and claimed the SS *Muneric*, which sank immediately with no survivors.

The port side escort, HMCS *Kenogami*, commenced an ASDIC search and obtained a contact which turned out to be false but almost immediately sighted a submarine running on the surface. *Kenogami* opened fire with her 4-inch gun, but not being equipped with starshell, was unable to illuminate the target and soon lost it. She was then joined by *Skeena*, which steamed back from her position ahead of the convoy to commence firing starshell but was called away to investigate a report of a surfaced submarine ahead of the convoy. In response, the convoy commodore ordered SC 42 to make an emergency turn to starboard and *Skeena*, taking a shortcut, steamed through the columns of merchant ships to investigate the sighting. Almost as soon as the convoy turned, the leading ships reported a surfaced submarine directly ahead and the commodore, again responding to a visible threat, altered course back to the original heading. Ninety minutes later, another surfaced submarine was reported off the starboard quarter of SC 42 and *Skeena* again moved through the convoy to check this latest sighting.

At this point, the commodore ordered a third course change, now to port, which caught *Skeena* steaming between the columns of ponderous, wallowing, merchant ships. Hibbard (and his crew) had some exciting moments as he steered to avoid collision, and the destroyer was hard over in the middle of a turn when the surfaced *U-81* passed at high speed between the seventh and eighth columns of convoy, totally ignoring the fire it drew from those merchantmen which were armed. It was heading directly toward *Skeena*, now between the seventh and eighth columns on a reciprocal course, but the U-boat commander, *Kapitänleutnant* Friedrich Guggenberger, either brave or foolhardy, opted not to submerge and passed *Skeena* at such close range that the destroyer was unable to depress her main guns to bring them to bear. As Hibbard prepared to reverse course, Guggenberger dived, but *Skeena's* attempts to obtain an ASDIC contact were rendered useless by the turbulence and propeller noise of the nearby merchantmen. Minutes later, two merchant ships, the *Pentland* and *Tahchee*, were hit in succession by *U-652* and the convoy commodore ordered a fourth course change, this time to starboard, bringing the convoy back on its original heading.

Shortly before dawn on 10 September, the *Empire Hudson* on the port side of the convoy was torpedoed, bringing still another course change.

The attacks continued throughout the day of September 10 as *Skeena*, *Alberni* and *Kenogami* prowled around and through the convoy, responding to frequent reports of periscope sightings, and carrying out a series of depth charge attacks on faint echoes or none at all – all of which were accompanied and frustrated by numerous course changes ordered by the convoy commodore. They did manage to damage the Type VII boat *U-85* so severely in one attack that its captain, *Kapitänleutnant* Eberhard Greger, was forced to abort his patrol. *Orillia*, meanwhile, continued to stand by the *Tahchee*, which was still afloat, as her captain, Lieutenant Commander W.E.S. Briggs, RCNR, had failed to receive Hibbard's order for his ship to return. By nightfall, another merchantmen had been sunk and the three remaining escorts could only fear that worse was to follow. And it did – a few hours later the *Bulysse* was hit from the port side bringing *Skeena* over to fire starshell but causing the commodore to commence the by-now-standard alteration of course. Minutes later, the *Gypsum Queen* was torpedoed on the starboard side of SC 42 and *Skeena* immediately steamed to that side to fire starshell in the hope of illuminating a surfaced enemy. The fireworks from this latest attack were observed by newcomers to the battle – two Canadian warships ahead of the convoy – because, fortunately for SC 42, help was on the way.

Enter "Chummy" Prentice, attacking

Prentice had been in St. John's preparing to conduct his first training session when SC 42 sailed from Sydney but he became concerned about the deployment of *Gruppe Markgraf*, whose positions he could follow through the signals received at Murray's headquarters in St. John's. Although he was not planning to put to sea for another four days, Prentice decided to sail in support of SC 42 and, with Murray's blessing, left Newfoundland with his own

Chambly, a relative veteran, and HMCS *Moose Jaw*, a newly-commissioned corvette with a crew so green that most immediately became seasick as soon they hit the open ocean. While at sea, Prentice received signals indicating that SC 42 was under heavy attack and he steamed on a course intended to intercept the convoy after nightfall on its dark side, which would provide the best chance of spotting surfaced submarines silhouetted against the southern sky.

As it turned out, just after midnight on 11 September 1941, Prentice obtained a firm ASDIC contact ahead of the convoy and immediately attacked it with depth charges. Because of technical malfunction and human error this attack at first appeared to have failed but it did have results as almost immediately the sailors on *Moose Jaw*, following in *Chambly*'s wake, were astounded when a U-boat surfaced beside them and began to move away at high speed.

Lieutenant F.E. Grubb, RCN, *Moose Jaw*'s captain, recovered from his surprise and ordered his 4-inch gun crew to open fire but one of the crew, tense in his first action, made a mistake that jammed the weapon. Grubb pursued the enemy and when he saw the German crew preparing to man its after gun, ordered one of his .50 calibre

Commander James D. "Chummy" Prentice, RCNVR, 1941.
An RN officer who had retired to Canada in 1934, Prentice joined the Canadian navy on the outbreak of war in 1939 and quickly proved to be an outstanding leader and trainer. Seen here on the bridge of his corvette, HMCS *Chambly*, in May 1941, he is wearing mittens probably knitted by his wife as they have his initials embroidered on them. A first-class shiphandler and an aggressive commander, "Chummy" Prentice was admired by his crews, who delighted in his many eccentricities, which included the wearing of a monocle. He was also responsible for working out tactics for the early corvettes and was involved in the sinking of a number of U-boats. (National Archives of Canada, PA 151743)

THE IMMORTAL CORVETTE

The corvette was the brainchild of William Reed, a marine architect at Smith's Dock Company in Middlesborough in northeastern England. Asked by the Admiralty in early 1939 to design a small escort for work in the North Sea and English Channel, Reed based the corvette on his design for the whaler *Southern Pride*, increasing its size and making some modifications. The RN was satisfied with the result, which they named the Flower Class corvette, as it was relatively simple in design, construction and power plant and could be built in small shipyards that did not normally undertake naval work. The RN ordered its first corvette in July 1939 and over the next five years 269 of these little warships would be built for the Allied navies and would participate in the destruction of more than 50 German and Italian submarines.

Although Reed designed the corvette for a week's service in the North Sea or English Channel, the exigencies of war forced it to be used in the North Atlantic. Corvettes were lively ships even in relatively calm seas, leading to the oft-stated belief they would roll "on dew" or "wet grass" but they were eminently seaworthy although no one who sailed on one would call them comfortable, as they rode the sea like a cork, pitching and heaving with dizzying motion.

The corvette in Canadian service

When the RCN planned an ambitious construction programme in 1939 it identified the need for a coastal escort/minesweeper. It intended to build Halcyon Class minesweepers to accomplish this role but these vessels required a higher level of expertise than was available in Canadian shipyards and, somewhat reluctantly, the Canadian navy settled on the Flower Class corvette as its auxiliary warship. Orders for 60 corvettes were issued early in 1940 and, over the next four years, a total of 123 corvettes were built in Canada with 111 commissioned in the RCN. There were three major variants:

Programme	Type	Number built
1939-1940	Original, short foc'sle	64
1940-1941	Original, short foc'sle	6
1940-1941	Revised Flower Class	10
1942-1943	Revised Flower Class (Increased Endurance)	15
1943-1944	Revised Flower Class (Increased Endurance)	12

The first 70 Canadian corvettes were based on Reed's original design with a short foc'sle and a foremast in front of the bridge. Beginning in the summer of 1943, these vessels were taken in hand for modifications that lengthened their foc'sles, re-sited their masts and reconstructed their bridges, although HMC Ships *Brantford*, *Nanaimo*, *Rosthern* and *The Pas* served throughout the war in the original configuration.

Beginning with the last 10 corvettes ordered under the 1940-1941 construction programme, Canadian corvettes were built with an extended foc'sle and increased sheer and flare to their bows to improve stability and make them dryer ships in the North Atlantic. The final development of the Flower Class corvette was the "Increased Endurance" type. ■

(Facing page) **Workhorse of the North Atlantic escorts.**
The illustration by Latham B. Jenson opposite illustrates the 70 short foc'sle corvettes of the original design as constructed in Canada from the spring of 1940 to the summer of 1941. The ship is basically divided into three areas: crew space, power plant and an aft space. The main crew space is in the foc'sle area, the forward part of the ship, with the seamen on the upper deck and officers and stokers on the lower deck. The midships is taken up by the propulsion machinery, the two boilers and the triple-expansion engine. At the stern is a smaller space which provided storage and more accommodation that was originally intended for officers but later taken over by the petty officers.

The faults with this design are obvious. The foremast was planted squarely in front of the bridge, which hindered visibility, and the bridge itself was too low and too small. Perhaps the worst feature was the open area of deck immediately aft of the foc'sle which was washed by the sea. The messmen or "mess cooks" had to cross this space to bring hot food from the galley in the lower part of the bridge structure to the messdecks in the foc'sle – the result was that the crew's food often arrived cold and wet.

Despite its faults, the corvette was a sturdy little vessel that became the quintessential Canadian warship of the Battle of the Atlantic. It was immortalized in two films. In 1943 Hollywood produced *Corvette K-225*, starring Randolph Scott as a lantern-jawed Canadian corvette commander, and using much footage taken in wartime Halifax and on board Canadian corvettes at sea. In 1953 Jack Hawkins starred in the British film *The Cruel Sea*, based on Nicholas Monsarrat's novel of the same name. The last surviving Flower Class corvette is HMCS *Sackville*, which is a museum ship in Halifax (see pages 223-228).

About as new as you can get.
Looking suspiciously like a plastic model on a piece of glass, the corvette *Dauphin* awaits commissioning at the Canadian Vickers yard in Montreal in May 1941. She displays the builder's coat of mid-grey paint which will be shortly be covered with the Western Approaches camouflage scheme of a white-grey hull and patches of light sea blue and sea green. Unfortunately, many Canadian shipyards often failed to properly prepare the hulls of corvettes before applying the first coats of paint and the result was that subsequent coats did not adhere well, giving many Canadian corvettes a rust-streaked and rather battered appearance. (Canadian Naval Memorial Trust)

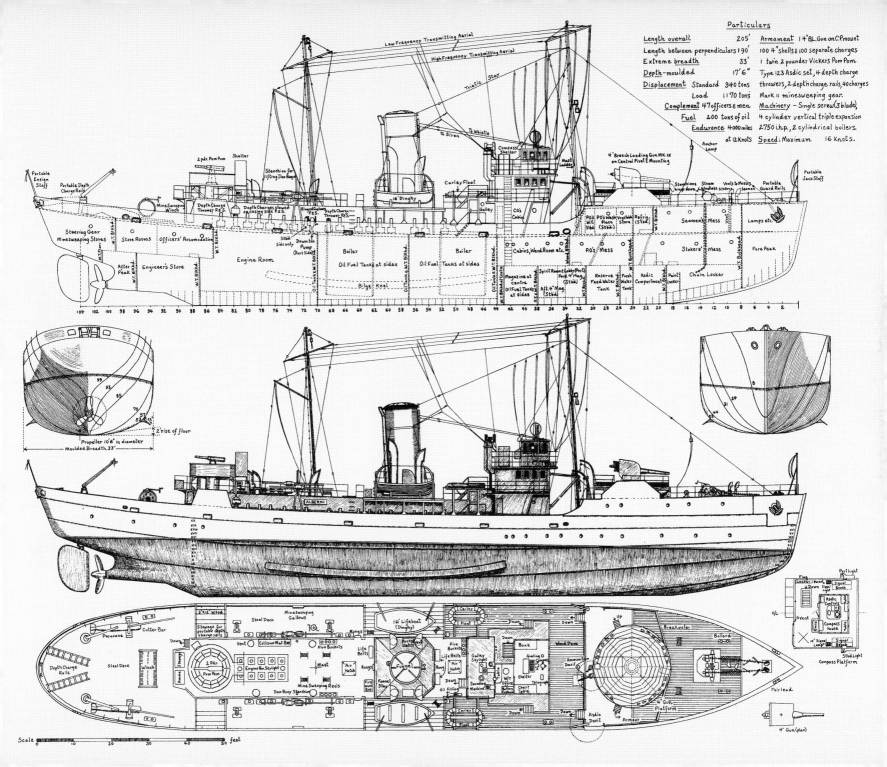

machine guns to fire at them. Nothing happened as the gun crew, in their excitement, had failed to cock their weapon. By this time *Moose Jaw* was close alongside the U-boat on its starboard side and struck it a glancing blow. Grubb called upon the men he could see in its conning tower to surrender – in response, he was astonished to see a German make an athletic leap from the submarine onto his corvette and the man's comrades preparing to do likewise. Not wishing to repel boarders, Grubb sheered off and when the U-boat subsequently altered course across his bows, he rammed it. By this time, his 4-inch gun crew had cleared their weapon and they managed to put a round through the submarine's conning tower, at which point the crew began to jump into the sea.

Prentice, in the meantime, had brought *Chambly* up on the other side of the enemy and cleared away a boarding party in a boat to capture the enemy craft, later identified as *U-501*, a Type IX boat. They got aboard only to find that the crew had opened its scuttling valves and refused, even when urged at gunpoint by the Canadians, to make any attempt to save their vessel. The boarding party was forced to join the German crew in the water when *U-501* sank beneath them and one Canadian was drowned while attempting to swim to *Chambly*'s boat. When it was all over, 35 German survivors were on board the two Canadian corvettes, including the athletic leaper, who turned out to be the captain of *U-501*, *Korvettenkapitän* Hugo Förster. As Grubb later reported, Förster was not one of Dönitz's best and bravest – not only had he abandoned his crew to their fate but his major concern when brought to Grubb on *Moose Jaw*'s bridge was the Canadian ship's use of searchlights to rescue his men because he feared the light would attract other U-boats in the vicinity.

"A sad state of affairs:" The aftermath of SC 42

The sinking of *U-501* was the only bright spot in what was otherwise an unmitigated disaster. Prentice and his two corvettes joined Hibbard but the increased escort was unable to prevent repeated attacks during the night, resulting in the loss of seven ships. The battle finally ended in the late morning of 11 September when SC 42 moved into range of aircraft from Iceland, but by the time Hibbard and Prentice turned it over to a strong British escort group (5 destroyers, 2 sloops and 2 corvettes), it had lost 15 ships, nearly a quarter of its number.

The disastrous passage of SC 42 demonstrated that the Atlantic convoys, particularly the slow convoys, must have stronger escorts and, above all, air cover. It also revealed that Canadian escorts lacked proper training and that their ships were poorly armed and equipped for the tasks they had to carry out. A month after the SC 42, a British officer stationed at St. John's summed up the effectiveness of the NEF with the acid but probably entirely accurate comment that most Canadian escorts were "equipped with one weapon of approximate precision – the ram."[3]

A particular deficiency was the lack of an effective radar that could locate a surfaced submarine at night. Unlike the RCAF, which early appreciated its utility, the RCN had been slow to comprehend the advantages of radar, and it was only in the spring of 1941 that NSHQ asked the National Research Council of Canada to develop a radar that could detect subma-

End of a corvette, HMCS *Lévis*, 1941.
Commissioned in the spring of 1941, *Lévis* escorted only one convoy before she was torpedoed by *U-74* off Greenland in September of that year. Determined efforts by her officers and crew kept the vessel afloat for several hours before she sank. (National Archives of Canada, GM-1463)

rines on the surface in the darkness hours. The NRC was already at work on an airborne version of the Royal Navy's Type 286 and in commendable time produced a naval version, the SW1C (Surface Warning, First Canadian), which performed well under laboratory conditions and which began to be fitted to Canadian warships in late 1941 and early 1942. Unfortunately, the SW1C was a temperamental device that often broke down and, worse still, it was based on an obsolete piece of equipment. Just as the RCN started to receive it, the RN began to equip its escort vessels with the improved Type 271, a much more accurate centimetric radar.

The deficiencies of RCN escorts were also evident during the battle for SC 44 in the following month. This convoy departed Sydney with 60 ships in late September 1942, escorted by a British destroyer, a Free French corvette and three Canadian corvettes, *Agassiz*, *Lévis* and *Mayflower*. Attacked by five U-boats of *Gruppe Brandenburg* after a chance sighting near the tip of Greenland, SC 44 lost five merchantmen and HMCS *Lévis*, which was torpedoed during the night of 19 September. *Lévis* lost her bows during the attack and her inexperienced captain prematurely ordered his crew to abandon ship but his officers and crew, taking a more level-headed approach, managed to keep the vessel afloat. The next day *Lévis* was taken in tow by *Mayflower* but when her damaged bulkheads began to give way – contrary to standard naval practice, there was no timber on board to shore them up – she sank, becoming the first Canadian corvette lost in action.

Pom-pom, pom-pom, pom-pom.
The 2-pdr. (40mm) high angle gun which was the main anti-aircraft armament of the corvettes was nicknamed a "pom-pom" because of the noise it made when firing. Basically an oversized Maxim machine gun adopted by the Royal Navy shortly before the First World War, the 2-pdr. had a cyclic rate of 200 rounds per minute and a maximum range of just under 8,000 yards. It could be elevated to 80 degrees and was trained by handwheels. It took 51 complete revolutions of the traversing handwheel to turn the weapon 360 degrees. (Canadian Naval Memorial Trust)

SC 48, which sailed in mid-October, also came under attack. Her escort, consisting of the four-stacker destroyer HMCS *Columbia*, four Canadian corvettes and a British and a French corvette, was heavily reinforced on 16 October by American and British warships but still lost nine merchant ships to *Gruppe Mordbrenner* southeast of Greenland. Ironically, one of the vessels sunk was the Canadian freighter *Vancouver Island*, the former

German *Weser*, which had been captured the previous year. The one positive event was that *Columbia*, which had only joined the escort that day, spotted *U-553* on the surface and launched a determined depth charge attack that so heavily damaged the Type VII craft that its commander, *Kapitänleutnant* Karl Thurmann, was required to give up contact for 24 hours while he carried out repairs. The poor state of training in the NEF again became evident when the corvette *Shediac* missed a crucial signal advising a nighttime course change because of a defective radio and sailed off on a lone course into the Atlantic, losing all contact. When the escort commander's report on this incident was circulated to the Admiralty, an unknown British naval officer added the terse marginal comment, "a sad state of affairs."[4] And it certainly was.

"Grave danger exists:" The strain begins to take its toll

By October 1941, senior officers of the NEF were becoming worried about the effect the convoy cycle was having on the health, morale and discipline of their crews. When the force had been created, the plan was that each escort group would have up to 12 clear days after each convoy for rest, maintenance and training. Given the inexorable pressure of the cycle, some groups received, at best, a day in harbour before sailing again – Prentice's *Chambly*, for example, spent 72 days at sea in the last three months of 1941. It did not help that the "rest periods" were often spent in windswept Hvalfjord in Iceland, where there were few opportunities for recreation. At the other end, St. John's, the "Newfie John" of the sailors, was somewhat better as the locals, warm-hearted and seagoing folk, were at least friendly, which could not be said of the Icelanders, who resented the occupation of their country by Allied forces.

The unrelenting pressure took a terrible toll on ships and equipment. To make things worse, when ships from the NEF were sent to Halifax for refit and repair, they often lost trained officers and seamen who were transferred to newly-commissioned vessels, as by late 1941 the RCN's first wartime construction programme was at its zenith. Escorts not only lost experienced crew members; they also had to return to the North Atlantic with green replacements, which further reduced their efficiency.

America's spearhead – USS *Kearny*, October 1941.
Three months before Pearl Harbor, American warships began to escort convoys in the western Atlantic. Inevitably, they encountered the U-boats and on 16 October 1941 *U-568* torpedoed a "hostile destroyer" escorting Convoy SC 48, which turned out to be the USS *Kearny*. Eleven sailors, the first American casualties of the Second World War, were killed but the *Kearny* survived to limp into Hvalfjord, where she is shown here. Fifteen days later, the USS *Reuben James* was sunk with the loss of 115 men, including her captain. (US Navy Photograph, author's collection)

"Chummy" Prentice summed up the situation facing the NEF in a uniquely Canadian way: "It is as though we were attempting to play against a professional hockey team with a collection of individuals who had not even learned to skate."[5]

Murray was angry about the constant personnel turmoil in his command, which placed great strain on his few veteran seamen, particularly his ship captains. As he put it, it was "asking a lot of the morale of an inexperienced crew" to expect them "to be happy, and remain fighting fit and aggressive" when they knew that "their safety from marine accident alone," and not from possible enemy action, depended on the ability of their captain to remain awake.[6] One of his staff officers pointed out that the captains of newly commissioned corvettes "have not one other officer on whom they can completely rely; furthermore many of these ships are grossly under manned, which imposes extra duty on men who are already suffering most arduous conditions."[7] Unless some immediate relief was available to relieve the pressure, this same officer warned that "grave danger exists of breakdowns in health, morale and discipline."

At sea, meanwhile, Dönitz began to concentrate his forces off Newfoundland in late October and his U-boats were successful against a number of convoys. On 31 October, while attacking HX 156, under escort by American warships, *U-552* sank the destroyer USS *Reuben James* with the loss of 115 men. In early November, Dönitz had a notable success when he was able to deploy 20 boats from *Gruppe Raubritter* against SC 52, escorted by a patchwork of British, Canadian and Free French warships. Four merchant ships were lost and the Admiralty, concerned that SC 52 would suffer even worse losses, ordered it to turn back to Sydney, making it the only Atlantic convoy during the war to be stopped entirely by the U-boats. Dönitz was unable to maintain the momentum of his attack and capitalize on these successes because, much against his will, he was ordered to redeploy most of his available U-boats out of the Atlantic to the Mediterranean to support German forces fighting in North Africa. This brought a welcome lull in operations for the NEF, which was nearly at the breaking point.

By early December 1941, the complaints of Murray, Prentice and other senior officers had brought some improvement. Murray received enough new corvettes to enable him to form seven escort groups, permitting him to relieve one group for rest and training on a regular basis. His warnings, however, about the problems of raw crews received short shrift at NSHQ which, while it agreed that the situation was "deplorable," felt it was "inevitable" given the RCN's policy of rapid expansion.[8]

And that expansion was at high tide in 1941 – between May and November of that year, 42 corvettes and 12 Bangor minesweepers were commissioned – and there were a further 12 corvettes and 18 Bangors about to leave the builders' yards. This magnificent, but in hindsight, misguided effort exhausted the Canadian navy's small pool of trained seamen and there was literally no choice, as NSHQ saw it, but to continue to rob operational ships of experienced personnel to commission new vessels. At the end of 1941 the Director of Personnel in Ottawa summed up the situation with the statement that the RCN "must still be regarded largely as a 'training' Navy" in 1942.[9]

Ride 'em, mountie!
The gunshield art of HMCS *Dauphin,* a Flower corvette commissioned in 1941, was chosen because her first captain and some of his officers were former members of the RCMP Marine Section. (Canadian Naval Memorial Trust)

Officers on the "Fiddley Deck."
The area immediately abaft the funnel called the "Fiddley Deck" was one of the few sheltered spaces on a corvette deck and a favourite place for off-duty sailors to congregate and pass the time. In this photograph, taken on board HMCS *Dauphin* in the Denmark Strait following a night attack on their convoy, the corvette's officers have gathered to have their photograph taken. From left to right: Petty Officer Lyons, the cox'n; Sub Lieutenant Keeling; Lieutenant Bouchard, first lieutenant; Lieutenant R.A.S. MacNeil, RCNR, commanding officer; Sub Lieutenant Hunt, navigating officer; and Sub Lieutenant Miller. If MacNeil, the captain, looks uncomfortable, it is because he is recovering from three broken ribs sustained while on duty. (Canadian Naval Memorial Trust)

Another "Happy Time" for the U-boats: America enters the war

On 7 December 1941, the Japanese attack on Pearl Harbor brought the United States into the war as an active partner on the Allied side. Unofficially, of course, the United States Navy had been involved in the Battle of the Atlantic for nearly four months and had lost one destroyer, the *Reuben James*, sunk, and another, USS *Kearny*, damaged by German submarines. But Pearl Harbor also brought about a redeployment of much of the USN's force from the Atlantic to the Pacific, and by the first weeks of 1942 the only American warships in the North Atlantic were a few destroyers and two escort groups of Coast Guard vessels.

Dönitz took immediate steps to attack American shipping and insti-

tuted Operation *Paukenschlag*, ("Drumroll" or "Drum Tap"), a series of patrols by individual U-boats against shipping in North American waters. Unfortunately, he was assisted in his efforts by Admiral Ernest King, the commander-in-chief of the USN, who, despite considerable evidence as to its effectiveness, did not fully believe in the convoy system and did not feel that he had the strength available to implement it. The result was a near disaster – between January and June 1942, the U-boats sank 280 merchant ships, totalling 1,650,272 tons, from the Gulf of Mexico to the coast of Nova Scotia, many of them scarce and valuable tankers. For nearly six months, German submarines rampaged in American coastal waters, at first picking off victims in shallow waters that were illuminated by the lights of coastal towns because there was no blackout in the United States. When the USN introduced the convoy system in one area, they moved to a new area where independent ships were still sailing and increased their tonnage scores. It was with good reason that German submarine crews referred to the first half of 1942 as their second "Happy Time" and their morale was high. One U-boat ace, *Kapitän-leutnant* Johann Mohr, who sank 10 vessels (8 of them tankers) off Cape Hatteras in March 1942, submitted his report to Dönitz in the form of a ditty:

More ice.
Lieutenant Miller of HMCS *Dauphin* on the corvette's iced-up bridge when she was operating in the Denmark Strait in the late autumn of 1941. (Canadian Naval Memorial Trust)

The new-moon night is black as ink
Off Hatteras the tankers sink
While sadly Roosevelt counts the score –
Some 50,000 tons – by Mohr.[10]

The German offensive spilled over into Canadian waters. In January 1942, Dönitz sent two groups to patrol around Cape Breton Island and Newfoundland with orders to strike coastal shipping beginning on the 13th of that month. While the RCN would have regarded the awful weather in this area as normal for winter conditions off the coast of Canada, the U-boat crews were appalled:

Blinding blizzards raked the bleak land and seascapes. Thick ice encrusted the exposed superstructures, adding tons of destabilizing weight to the boats. Before diving, the bridge watch had to chip ice from the main air-induction inlet so the valve would seat properly. There was small comfort below; most of the [Type] VIIs had no cold-weather heating systems. One boat recorded inside temperatures of 33 degrees Fahrenheit day after day. Unheated periscopes fogged up to the point of uselessness.[11]

In a concerted effort the two groups sank nearly 30 ships, almost all independents, but aircraft patrols by the RCAF, which was now becoming more effective, and the implementation of local convoys drove those boats that still had fuel farther to the south to look for easier pickings.

Dönitz's offensive resulted in changes in the deployment of Allied naval forces that eased some of the strain on the Newfoundland Escort Force. Slow convoys were now routed farther to the south on a more direct run across the Atlantic that brought better weather. A new Mid-Ocean Escort Force (MOEF) was created, which combined the NEF, American warships operating out of Argentia in Newfoundland, and British warships. A second new command, the Western Local Escort Force or WLEF, was created at Halifax to escort convoys from that port to the WESTOMP just off Newfoundland. There they would be turned over to the MOEF, which would take them to the EASTOMP (Eastern Atlantic Operational Meeting Point) where they would be picked up by the RN. The MOEF escort group would then go into Londonderry, Northern Ireland, to refuel before picking up a westbound convoy. By March there were fewer Canadian warships in the MOEF than in the WLEF, which now assumed responsibility for a new series of convoys between Boston and Halifax. This was the beginning of the "Triangle Run," Boston to Halifax, Halifax to the WESTOMP, and back to Boston. The increasing number of German submarines deployed in American waters during the first part of 1942 thus caused a shift in the RCN's strength from Newfoundland to the south.

Until an interlocking system of convoys was instituted from the West Indies to Britain – and this did not occur until June 1942 – the Admiralty did its best to assist the USN fight off the German attack. Britain sent 34 escort vessels to serve on the American coast, co-ordinated signal and

Ice, grey seas, barren hills.
This photo, taken from the bow of HMCS *Dauphin* in the Denmark Strait in the late autumn of 1941, reveals a depressing view of grey, cold sea and barren hills. Men who were forced into such seas when their ship was torpedoed had little chance of survival. (Canadian Naval Memorial Trust)

A dangerous enemy – ice on HMCS *Saguenay,* January 1942.
As this photograph demonstrates, one of the most hazardous perils faced by escorts on the North Atlantic was ice that formed when near-arctic temperatures caused spray to freeze on the decks and rigging of ships. If it was not immediately removed, there was a danger that its weight would capsize the ship. (Photograph by W.H. Pugsley, National Archives of Canada, PA 139279)

submarine tracking intelligence with Washington, and provided ASW training for American personnel. It was unfortunate that in February 1942 the Allies lost one of their most important weapons when the *Kriegsmarine* made changes both to *Schlüssel M*, its version of the Enigma machine, and the communications procedure for positioning U-boats that frustrated Allied codebreakers and stopped the flow of Ultra from naval sources. What was worse for the Allies was that the German signal intelligence organization, the *B-dienst*, succeeded at the same time in breaking Allied Naval Cypher No. 3, used for operations in the North Atlantic, permitting Dönitz to read 80 per cent of the radio messages transmitted by convoy escorts. At one and the same time, Allied navies lost their most important source of intelligence while Dönitz gained access to valuable new information.

In the spring of 1942, however, although the U-boats were still creating havoc in American waters, the RCN had reason for guarded optimism. Its 16,000 officers and men at sea were serving in 13 destroyers, 67 corvettes and 34 minesweepers which provided escorts for approximately 40 per cent of the convoys on the North Atlantic. As the first great flood of wartime construction had now receded, there were enough ships in service for some to receive rest and training between convoys and the recent re-organization of the convoy system allowed for longer periods of rest and refit. Those sailors who had survived the previous nine months on the Atlantic were becoming seasoned, while facilities had been built on shore to give recruits better training than had been available in the previous two years. Canadian escorts were still poorly equipped compared to their British counterparts but there was reason to believe that, in the near future, their deficiencies might be made up and plans were in hand to modify the early corvettes to make them more fit for mid-ocean work. Finally, designs for a new and more effective escort vessel, the frigate, had been obtained from Britain and the first of these new warships would soon be ordered from Canadian shipyards.

Unfortunately for the Canadian navy, the most cruel time in this most cruel of battles was just about to begin.

1941

"Many men felt strange:" Commissioning with new ships and crews

In the first half of 1941, as the products of the wartime shipbuilding programme began to arrive in numbers, the RCN commissioned dozens of corvettes. Their crews were as new as the vessels and most corvettes which entered service that year were lucky to have an ex-merchant marine officer in command and one or two key warrant officer or ratings who had been to sea before. Lieutenant Commander Alan Easton, RCNR, one of these merchant marine commanders, remembers what it was like to command a new corvette with a crew of fresh recruits, both officers and ratings, on the vessel's first patrol in 1941:

Of the three officers only the navigator had been in a ship before. He had been twenty-five years at sea in all sorts of small vessels. He had started to sea in fishing vessels when he was twelve, and had gone on from schooners to small steamers to become master of a coastal tanker. He was a rough and ready little man and a rule-of-thumb navigator, I suspected; not that I was disinclined to be one myself. Of the fifty men, about five had been professional seamen or fishermen and, below, no more than six were experienced with engines and boilers. So with more than three-quarters of the complement as fresh to the sea as the ship herself, it was hard to perform our simple task; hard to keep steam up, avoid the shoals or even to steer a straight course. Had anything warlike occurred there would have been a shambles.

Thus, while we were on patrol, the few who knew their profession taught the others. The principles had been explained to them ashore and our specialists had been well instructed, but when they came to supply their knowledge in the ship, a place where discomfort alone had a dazing effect on the mind as well as the stomach, it did not always work out as expected.

We went at it systematically. I had been back at sea almost continuously since the beginning of the war. I was, therefore, in a fair position to know what was needed to develop the crew.

Boats were lowered many times and rowed and then hoisted; men swung the hand lead for soundings; they put out fires; they were taught lookout-keeping; they learned to read a swinging compass and compensate with the wheel; to stoke the furnaces without belching smoke; to handle the guns in a choppy sea and to throw a heaving line. But all this was not learned easily. ……

The two new officers, the first lieutenant and the sub, were trying hard to learn their practical seamanship a step ahead of the men. Their initial training ashore had given them the edge but it was all terribly new. They probably felt as strange on the bridge with their duty before them as they had when they first stood on the parade ground in their new uniforms.

So the navigator and I split the watches between us, and gave them the beginnings of what was to be almost a war-long course. They took it well and as the weeks went by they began to feel more comfortable; though we were all tired.

But my mind was never at peace. There was much to do, so little time. I was afraid of going far afield with such inexperience; we had to become more efficient.[1]

"The next thing I knew I was throwing up:" First days at sea

Very few sailors who sailed on corvettes ever forgot their first days at sea. Seaman James Galloway, who served on HMCS Agassiz *of the Newfoundland Escort Force, remembers leaving St. John on his first voyage and his first watch as a look out on the bridge:*

My eyes were aching, as were my hands from holding the binoculars up. It got to the point I could see very little and be sure of it. The motion of the ship climbing up and down each rolling swell got my stomach heaving. The next thing I knew I was throwing up over all that corner of the bridge.

The first lieutenant called me a few choice names and ordered me below to get a bucket and rags to scrub the bridge clean. I fully understood I should clean up the mess I had made, but to scrub all the bridge gratings while at sea seemed more punishment than fit the crime. The other lookout offered to help me, but he was told off and directed to sweep my sector as well as his own. I went below and got two buckets and cleaning equipment. I spent the rest of the dog watch scrubbing with one bucket and throwing up in the other bucket.

On leaving the bridge, I was completely demoralized, cold, and sick. In the messdeck, the smell of food made me sicker. I went back outside to stand at the break of the forecastle, throwing up over the side from time to time. When I returned to the messdeck, I laid down on the footlockers and slept until time to go on watch again. I took a bucket with me. I used it a lot, I might add.[2]

Signalman George Rickard of the corvette Dauphin *had a similar experience:*

I was on the bridge as a standby at the flag locker on leaving port. Soon the quartermaster piped "duty watch to sea stations" and at the same time we hit the land swells. That was it. Down off the bridge over to the lee side to join about a dozen others in spewing our guts into the Atlantic. …… I heaved up until nothing came but green bile. A real salty able seaman heading for the forward messdeck made the comment that it wouldn't do me any harm, but if I brought up a red ring to push it back down my throat as that would be my asshole.[3]

"Every time the doctor took a slice or two:" Air attack, April 1941

If a small warship engaged in combat, there was a chance that its Sick Berth Attendant, or medical orderly, would be called upon to render assistance. Lieutenant Barry O'Brien, RCNVR, of HMCS Trillium *recorded one such instance after that corvette was strafed by a German aircraft in April 1941. One of O'Brien's sailors, Seaman Donald Robertson, was badly wounded and, when the attack was over, O'Brien and another sailor*

(Facing page) **The corvettes arrive, 1941.**
By early 1941, the massive Canadian wartime construction programme was in full flow and new vessels were entering service faster than crews could be found for them. This photo of the naval dockyard at Halifax taken in September 1941 shows ten spanking new corvettes, while in the left foreground is *V 250* (also known as *CMTB 1*), a prototype motor torpedo boat which did not prove rugged enough for service in Canadian waters. (National Archives of Canada, PA 105508)

half-dragged and half-carried Robertson to the forward mess-deck. It was not a pretty sight. There were 11 wounded men. Shrapnel causes blood to flow pretty freely and the messdeck was awash with blood mixed with the collection of sea-water that had come down the companion-way.

Harry Rhoades was our cook, and also doubled as sick berth attendant, having had a first aid course at Ogilvy's department store in Montreal. He and I did our best to make the injured comfortable. I went to the bridge and detailed the situation to the captain. As we had no doctor aboard in those early days, he immediately closed the senior officer, an RN Destroyer. By bosun's chair, they sent their surgeon-lieutenant over, with books and medical equipment in a canvas bag.

He surveyed the scene in the seamen's messdeck and I remember him saying: "There are two too far gone to save, eight probably will survive if they can get hospital treatment ashore soon and I will have to amputate the left arm of one if he is to have any chance of survival." The doctor administered painkillers to the wounded.

We strapped the unconscious Robertson to the messdeck table as the ship was rolling considerably. The doctor took out a book and turned to the chapter on amputations. He then inquired who would administer the anaesthetic. Nobody else volunteered, so I said I would. The patient was stripped to the waist. The operation began, with our cook assisting and I acting as anaesthetist. Every time the doctor took a slice or two, he would turn a page in his book. Every now and then I would be told to squirt a couple more drops of ether on the mask covering the patient's face and the fumes wafting up were making me dizzy and nauseous. As the doctor

cut deeper, you could see how the shrapnel had shattered Robertson's shoulder, imbedding pieces of the grey duffel coat two or three inches into his body.

Robertson was fighting for his life, with his chest giving mighty heaves. The operation took about two hours. Unfortunately, Robertson died on the messdeck almost simultaneously with the final removal of his arm.

The doctor left and went down to the wardroom where I found him later, lying prone on the settee. I told him he had done all he could. He answered that he was fresh out of medical school and this was the first operation he had ever performed. And if it hadn't been for the calming influence of the cook he would have panicked a couple of times, he said.[4]

"Go and start a Naval College:" Meanwhile, back on shore

As the RCN went through a major expansion in 1940-1941, there was a desperate shortage of training facilities on shore, particularly in Halifax. Lieutenant Owen Robertson, RCNR, remembers the genesis of the Canadian naval officers' training academy in 1941:

As I was walking down to the Dockyard, a staff car passed. It was old "Jetty" Jones – Admiral Jones who, I think, was a captain then. [This officer was Captain G.C. Jones, RCN, Commanding Officer, Atlantic Coast] He leaned out the window and yelled, "Robertson! What are you doing?" I told him and he said, "Come and see me."

I went to his office in fear and trembling, because old Jetty had quite a temper, and I figured I'd done something wrong again. When he heard what I was doing, he said, "Forget that. Go and start a Naval College." I asked, "Where, sir?" He yelled at me, "If I knew where, I'd do it myself." I asked, "For how many, sir?" He yelled at me, "If I knew that, I'd do it myself!" So I went off to start a Naval College.

I looked at a couple of universities, Acadia in Wolfville and St. Mary's. Then I heard about King's, an Anglican college on the Dalhousie campus. I met old Canon Walker; he had only about eighteen or twenty students for the coming year for the Anglican Church. So I rented the place on my signature, without any authority from anybody. They moved their students across to Pine Hill and we started a Naval College and named it HMCS *Kings* – without the apostrophe. ......

I think it wasn't more than about three months before we graduated the first 196 engineers, paymasters and executives [executive branch officers].[5]

More bad weather: Hurricane at sea, August 1941

In 1941, newly-constructed corvettes were sent straight to sea, manned by green crews who had never been in the North Atlantic before. Sick Berth Attendant Stanley Mosher remembers his first voyage in the corvette, HMCS Orillia*:*

It was late August, 1941, not a good time of year for a first trip across the North Atlantic. For the first two weeks, I slept little, ate practically nothing and was constantly seasick. Two metal boxes stuffed with assorted bandages, splints, pills and potions served as my sick bay, plus my trusty medical book.

I was still sick as a dog until we hit a hurricane south of Iceland. ...... Sometime during the three day nightmare, I acquired my sealegs. I found out later I wasn't alone in my terror, the crews in the engine room and boiler room had to stay there throughout the storm. It would have been suicide to venture on the upper deck. The Officer of the Watch and the signalman who stood their watch on the open bridge were lashed to their post by the two coming off watch. The bridge and wheelhouse crews could travel internally from their respective messes to their posts. The crews of the engine and boiler rooms couldn't.

We lost sight of the convoy and most of the escort group. The ships were scattered over miles of ocean. I wasn't sure whether they or we were lost. ...... When the storm finally abated the only ship in sight was the corvette *Agassiz*, our senior ship.[6]

An "East Coast Port" full of shipping.
This photograph shows Bedford Basin, the extension of Halifax harbour, one of the best deep-water ports in the world, full of merchant vessels. The first convoy sailed from Halifax for Britain a few days after war began in September 1939 and for the next six years, convoys left at regular intervals from what wartime censors called "an east coast port." Halifax was also the RCN's major wartime base. (Directorate of History and Heritage, HS-1106-15)

"It was hell:" Convoy SC 42, September 1941

SC 42, outward bound to Britain from Sydney, Nova Scotia, was attacked by a U-boat pack over a three-day period in early September and its outnumbered Canadian escorts were unable to prevent the loss of nearly a quarter of its ships.. Ordinary Seaman Leonard Lamb of HMCS Orillia, *one of the escorts, remembered SC 42:*

For the next 72 hours it was hell. Part of our job was picking up survivors and we ended up with an abundance, along with a German shepherd dog and two cats. The dog understood Spanish only, and when we dropped charges he would hide under the table in the forward mess and someone had to clean up.

We rescued survivors from the *Stargard*, which looked like a pre-World War I freighter. As each survivor came over the side, one of us would take him into the messdeck, strip him bare, clean him up and give him dry clothing.

My survivor was a little man, I finally found out after I got him stripped. Now this is hard to believe, but I will list his clothes as I took them off: one life-belt, one duffel coat, one overcoat, one complete suit, two sweaters – out of which jumped a gorgeous orange cat, one flannel shirt and two suits of wool underwear. Many of this crew were dressed this warmly.

This man spoke very little English and I had a hard time convincing him to get in my hammock. We did this to get them out of the way. But every time I went on watch, this man would go with me and roundly curse out the enemy.[7]

One of the few bright moments in the disaster was the sinking of U-501 by the corvettes Chambly *and* Moose Jaw *on 10 September. Lieutenant F.R. Grubb, RCN, commanding* Moose Jaw, *described what happened when the submarine unexpectedly surfaced beside his ship and the German crew emerged onto its deck:*

At one time four of the submarine's crew made a determined move to the after gun. As our own gun was still jammed, no action could be taken except to increase speed and try to ram before they could fire. This I did, although the chance was small, but, fortunately, someone on the conning tower ordered them back. The .5 inch [.50 calibre] machine guns were bearing at the time, but when the trigger was pulled, they failed to fire. A subsequent check showed no defects, so I assume that in the excitement the crew failed to cock them.

I managed to go alongside the submarine, starboard side to, and called on her to surrender. To my surprise, I saw a man make a magnificent leap from the submarine's deck into our waist and the remainder of the crew move to do likewise. Not being prepared to repel boarders at that moment, I sheered off.

The submarine altered course across my bows and I rammed her. ....

The gun being cleared by that time I opened fire again. The crew jumped into the sea as soon as the first round went, and I ordered fire to be stopped. I subsequently learned that the shell had passed low enough over the conning tower to knock down the men who were standing thereon. ......

The man who I had seen jump on board turned out to be the submarine's commanding officer. He was badly shaken and when he was brought to me on the bridge appeared to be worried at the amount of light we were showing in order to pick up survivors.[8]

Hvalfjord – No refuge for man or ship.
In 1941-1942 the ships of the Newfoundland Escort Force went into Hvalfjord in Iceland to refuel before taking over westbound convoys. Hvalfjord was a barren, windswept anchorage famous for its storms as this photograph aptly illustrates. Gale force winds are threatening to blow the merchant vessel off her anchors, putting her in danger of running aground and breaking up. (US Navy Photograph, National Archives of the United States)

The destruction of U-501 was the high point of Convoy SC 42 and, for the next three days, few men in the crews of its beleaguered escorts got much rest – Lieutenant W.H. Willson, RCN, of HMCS Skeena *remembers the effect:*

I was so God damn exhausted I could hardly think straight. …… I'd been up for the first and the middle [watches] and I had to go on the morning and I'd probably have to get up for an alarm, at nine o'clock [that] morning. A series of sinkings and continuous ringing of that *bloody* [alarm] bell. Get out of your cart and come up. People don't realize there is a point at which you cease to function with any rational approach at all. You're just going through the motions and that's what you can do to a crew if you take them and put them at action stations, run them around for an hour, send them below, twenty minutes later, call them to action stations again; and that's how fast ships were going up, one goes up here, one goes up there. By that time you had submarines in the middle of the fleet [convoy], firing out in all directions.[9]

Rolling on wet dew: Life on corvettes

Corvettes had a reputation for being lively vessels that would "roll on wet dew" and this could make the crew's livingspaces or messdecks very uncomfortable. Life on a corvette messdeck in the North Atlantic has been well described by Lieutenant James Lamb, RCNVR:

Into two triangular compartments, about 33 feet by 22 feet at their greatest dimensions, are crammed some sixty-odd men; each has for his living space – eating, sleeping, relaxing – a seat on the cushioned bench which runs around the out-side perimeter of each messdeck. There is a locker beneath the seat for his clothing, and a metal ditty-box – something like an old-fashioned hat-box – holds his personal things in a rack above. The space where he swings his hammock – carefully selected by the older hands and jealously guarded – is 18 inches beneath the deck-head, or another hammock, which were slung in tiers between stanchions and between pipes, wherever there is room. Most of the mess deck space is taken up with scrubbed deal tables, one to each mess, where you eat or write or play interminable games of cards.

Crowded in harbour and stuffy, the messdecks at sea are like some vision of Hades. There is absolutely no fresh air; all the ports [portholes], open in harbour, are dogged down and blanked over at sea, and in heavy weather even the cowl ventilators from the upper deck have to be sealed off. Dim emergency lights, red or blue, provide the only illumination in the dark hours, and around the clock there is always at least one watch trying to catch a few hours of oblivion, while about them the life of the mess goes on: men coming and going from outside, or snatching a meal before going on watch. With the hammocks slung, there is hardly room anywhere to stand up-right, and there is moisture everywhere – water swirling in over the coamings when the outside doors open, sweating from the chilled steel of the ship's side, oozing from the countless pipe joints and deck-welds and rivets and deck openings, and all the other manifold places where water forces an entrance from the gale outside.

Plunging into a head sea, the noise and motion in the fo'csle must be experienced to be believed; a constant roar of turbulence, wind, and water, punctuated by a crashing thud as the bow bites into another great sea, while the whole world is up-lifted – up, up, up – only to come crashing down as the ship plunges her bows over and downward, to land with an impact which hurls anyone and anything not firmly secured down to the forward bulk-head. With a rolling, corkscrew motion, the nightmare world of the fo'csle starts to climb again, up, up, up … in their navel pipes, the twin anchor cables rattle and clank at each movement, a dominant note in the endless, maddening, din.[10]

Rough weather could make life very difficult as Signalman Howard Cousins of HMCS Algoma *remembered:*

The ship was your home and the weather had a direct effect on the degree of comfort that home provided. When the wind and the seas built up, the comforts of your home were virtually nonexistent. As the ship rolled and pitched, you were thrown around continuously, not daring to move without holding fast to something. The bridge was wet with spray, sometimes solid water. ……

A corvette on the crest of a wave could have one-third of the forward portion clear of the water. As the ship rolled and dropped down into the

(*Facing page*) **In Which They Served – HMCS** *Battleford,* **November 1941.**
In this classic photograph, HMCS *Battleford* shows her bottom in a rough sea. Note that her stern is also under water. *Battleford,* commissioned in July 1941, served in the mid-Atlantic from July 1942 to May 1943 before joining the Western Local Escort Force. She shared in the destruction of *U-356* in December 1942, was sold to the Venezuelan Navy in 1946 and wrecked in 1949. (National Archives of Canada, PA 115381)

trough, it was almost a free fall. The poor blokes in the forecastle felt virtually weightless; anything on the lockers, shelves and tables, including your meal, frequently floated off. When the ship smashed back into the next wave, it felt as if the ship had been dropped on concrete. ......[11]

Medical matters on a corvette

The larger warships in the RCN usually had a doctor on board but the smaller vessels only had an SBA (Sick Berth Attendant) a sailor with rudimentary medical training. The SBA, called "Tiffy" in sailor's slang, was not only responsible for the general health of the crew at sea but was also called on to provide medical treatment for combat casualties or survivors. If there was not a doctor present among the warships escorting a convoy, the SBA had to rely on his own training and resources to treat his patients.

SBA Stanley Mosher remembers his duties on board a corvette in 1941 and demonstrates that he had a working knowledge of human psychology:

During the day I'd spend as much time as possible in the messdeck in case I was needed. Since my supplies were there, it seemed the logical place to be. Besides, I could catch up on my sleep after the depth charge watch. As a matter of fact, they didn't come to see me when they cut themselves, unless it was very bad. One such case involved a man who cut his finger while on watch but it had stopped bleeding by the time he came off so he didn't think it was worth bothering me about. About a week later he came to me with a badly infected finger and a sore arm. First, he got a "blast" from me for not reporting sooner, I then told him he had "blood poisoning." His finger was badly swollen, red streaks ran up his arm. The lymph

Bridge of HMCS *Ottawa*, 1941.
This drawing depicts the bridge of the destroyer HMCS *Ottawa* as it might have appeared in the autumn of 1941. Warship bridges were crowded places and they were also open, which made them very cold places to be in most seasons of the year on the Atlantic. (Drawing by L.B. Jenson, courtesy of the artist)

glands in his armpit were tender, swollen and hard. After several days of epsom salts and glycerine poultices along with sulpha drugs he started to improve.

On one trip, a young seaman who was a pain in neck to everyone, was always complaining about something. Nearly every day he would come to see me with something wrong with him. I couldn't just ignore him in the off chance that he did have a good reason. One day he had the complaint I had been waiting for. He was constipated. As before, I followed proper medical procedures, then prescribed two cascara tablets to be taken with a medicine glass full of "jollop," a clear thick liquid that we referred to as "liquid dynamite." The following day he came to me saying he had the "runs" and couldn't get too far away from the "head;" could I give him something to stop it. Acting very serious and professional I told him the same thing that got him started would also stop it, so I repeated the treatment. Probably not a good practice, but I was reasonably sure that he was in good health. I knew he'd be busy for a couple of days, so I had some of the lads keep an eye on him and keep me posted. They told me he had frequent trips to the head for three days after the second treatment. He never came back to me for anything trivial again. To the best of my knowledge, he was never constipated again, not in my ship anyway.[12]

Mosher recalls the time when his corvette rescued fourteen badly-injured survivors from a life boat:

All my previous medical training was put to the test. The survivors were all suffering from exposure, some were seriously injured. How they survived is a mystery.

One man had a badly fractured leg and some small wounds: another had been blown through a space between two bulkheads studded with bolt ends, a space he couldn't possibly go through otherwise. He had huge patches of flesh missing as if some had clawed out handfuls of meat. All I could do for him was to clean the wounds and apply large first field dressings and make him as comfortable as possible. The man with the broken leg was in a lot of pain, so he got morphine. It was a bad break, you could see the jagged ends of the bone under the skin. They hadn't come through so I set the leg using a Thomas splint to pull the bones into normal position and splints at the fracture, supporting the leg its full length using triangular bandages. Another man had broken ribs and possible back injuries. Taping his chest to minimize movement of the ribs and placing him in a Neil-Robertson bamboo stretcher I then had him placed on a locker and had a piece of canvas (someone's spare hammock) nailed in place so he couldn't roll around with the ship's movements.

Another man had a large scalp wound, about five inches long and down to the bone. This was cleaned, hair around the wound removed and the wound sutured in a manner to permit drainage.

At the busiest time I had lots of help until the action bell went, even the officers were running errands for me and getting morphine from the wardroom safe. I couldn't have asked for better cooperation. All the work was done in the seamen's mess using their table to operate on. We had a great crew.[13]

Wrapped up
Lieutenants Boucher (left) and Wennburg of HMCS *Dauphin* pose for the camera while working in near-Arctic conditions in the Denmark Strait in the late autumn of 1941. (Canadian Naval Memorial Trust)

"Few admitted they were often frightened:" Convoy SC 48, November 1941

In November 1941, Convoy SC 48, escorted by a patchwork group of British, Canadian and French vessels lost 9 merchantmen to a concentrated German onslaught. One of the escorts was the corvette HMCS Baddeck, *commanded by Lieutenant Commander Alan Easton, RCNR, which was undertaking her first mid-ocean operation, complete with an unreliable engine prone to failure, an unserviceable asdic set, and a green crew. Easton recalls that it was a stressful time for everyone on board:*

I was gaining confidence in the sub-lieutenants, but not yet to a point where I could go to sleep with an easy mind.

The men too were uneasy, but not for the same reason. It was not the officers. They trusted them completely. It was the ship. The lack of harmony had disappeared, poor behaviour was gone. We seemed a happy and vigorous ship now, but … The ordinary seaman in the crows nest, the gunner's mate, the radio operator, could not fail to know our searching gear was not working all the time. They knew as well as the stoker in number two boiler-room that the engines were cranky and might fold up at any time. They knew we were short of speed – more or less always had been – and repairs had been a failure. Men had lost confidence in the ship, and in her ability to do her work.

Few admitted they were often frightened. They sometimes asked one another guarded questions, nonchalantly put but with vivid and desperate thoughts behind them. "If the captain wanted to go fast he could really. He's only favouring the bloody engines because the chief want him to,

Lieutenant Commander Alan Easton, RCNR.
A prewar merchant marine officer, Alan Easton commanded two corvettes, *Baddeck* and *Sackville,* on the Atlantic in 1941-1943. *Sackville* was the better vessel and Easton participated in a number of hard-fought convoy battles. He later commanded the frigate *Matane* and the destroyer *Saskatchewan* but his active service ended in August 1944 when he was hospitalized for ulcers brought on by stress. Easton's memoir of his wartime service, *50 North: Canada's Atlantic Battleground,* is one of the best of the genre. (Directorate of History and Heritage, DND, CFPU, PMR 90-193)

aint he?" "Ship rolls like hell but she can't turn over. They never turn over. Uh, T…turn over?" "Corvette's too small to be torpedoed." The answers were almost always reassuring, spoken lustily as a rule but sometime flippantly. Confirmation was all that was asked for and this was given gladly by men in equal doubt. Only at night when two men were keeping watch together did they whisper their fears, admit that the precipitous plunge into the black depths between the billows scared them to death; only at night did they confess that they believed one day the ship would fail to climb the vertical face of the next oncoming wave.[14]

Seaman Phillip George of Baddeck *remembered one of the most terrible incidents of a terrible convoy:*

We had a huge gasoline tanker and every morning they would put it on the starboard wing. Every night they would bring it into the middle of the convoy and put an old clunker, a Greek freighter, on the starboard wing. The submarines finally caught up to us. The first night they hit that starboard wing Greek freighter. The second night they hit another freighter.

We were at action stations almost continually for three days and three nights. The third night I went below, lay down on the floor, took my boots off and put them under my head as a pillow. I don't suppose I'd been there 10 minutes when we were called up to action stations again.

When I came up on deck, I saw the flash of the first torpedo hitting this tanker. A little while later, there was another torpedo, then a huge ball of flame went right up through the clouds. There was nothing to be seen where that tanker was.

Amazingly we picked up the captain and the engineering officer in a life raft. Apparently when the first torpedo hit, the captain had called the chief engineer to the bridge to learn what damage had been done. They were talking when the second torpedo hit and the ship blew. They apparently had been blown off the bridge and must have come together with the raft in mid-air, because they had no idea how they got into it. The captain had a broken hip and we had a good deal of trouble picking them up.[15]

When it was all over, Alan Easton was exhausted:

Counting up the sleep I had had since the first ship had been torpedoed fifty-six hours ago, the various snatches amounted to a total of about three and a half hours. Perhaps it was not surprising then, as we straightened away on our last course with the job over, that I could not give the navigator my final instructions before leaving the bridge, without falling asleep. We stood together. He was leaning against the window of the asdic house and I against the bridge rail. I could speak, coherently only about half a sentence and then my words would dwindle off into nonsense. I knew it and struggled against it and by standing erect and moving about a little I thought I eventually conveyed to him what my wishes were. Then I went below and collapsed in my bunk.[16]

"I am gravely concerned:" The strain begins to take its toll, October 1941

Just six months after the creation of the Newfoundland Escort Force, the strain of escorting vulnerable slow convoys in poorly armed and equipped warships manned by green crews who got little rest between operations, was becoming obvious to the senior officers in St. John's. In October, Captain E.B.K. Stevens, RN, responsible for the efficiency of the NEF's ships, felt constrained to warn Ottawa that, having seen the toll taken by recent operations, he was

gravely concerned about the running of the ships of the Newfoundland Escort Force, particularly the amount of sea-time, relative to rest periods, which is being imposed on the corvettes. ......

Recently corvettes have escorted convoys Eastbound for sixteen days and then after between four and eighteen hours in harbour have returned with Westbound convoys, this voyage lasting between fourteen and sixteen days. This is quite unacceptable.

There seems to be a strong tendency to estimate the endurance of these small ships principally on their fuel carrying capacity. This is not only fallacious, but positively dangerous.

The factor which will ultimately control their ability usefully to keep the sea, is that of the endurance of personnel, particularly that of Commanding Officers.

It is essential to remember … that for the most part Commanding Officers have not one other officer on whom they can completely rely; furthermore many of these ships are grossly under manned, which imposes extra duty on men who are already suffering most arduous conditions ……

Unless very urgent steps can be taken … I must report that grave danger exists of breakdowns in health, morale and discipline.[17]

Western Approaches.
Admiral Sir Percy Noble (Commander in Chief, Western Approaches, 1941-1942) greets a group of British and Canadian officers in Liverpool in 1942. Although the RCN's escort operations were under the nominal control of the USN in late 1941 to early 1943, it was the Royal Navy's Western Approaches command which had the most direct control of day-to-day operations in the North Atlantic. Behind Noble (wearing a greatcoat) stands Captain F.J. Walker ("Johnny Walker"), CB, DSO and 3 Bars, the most successful U-boat killer in the Royal Navy. Standing from left to right are Commander Sterkell, RN; Commander Donald Macintyre, RN, another famous ASW officer; Lieutenant Commander Coleman; Lieutenant Commander R.A.S. MacNeil, RCNR; and Lieutenants Mumson and Cooker. (Canadian Naval Memorial Trust)

Merry Christmas 1941

For many Canadian sailors, Christmas 1941 brought little or no joy. Sub Lieutenant R.L. Hennessy, RCN, of HMCS Assiniboine *recalled that his destroyer was immediately ordered to sea after having completed a refit at Halifax. On Christmas Eve,* Assiniboine *left the refit yard and was*

towed across to the Dockyard [to be] ammunitioned from barges all day. The Dockyard wanted to do a normal day's work and then go back at it the next day. We said, "The hell with that! Tomorrow is Christmas. We'll do the whole job." Of course we started with no ammunition on board as all, so we had to do the whole job from scratch and, when you're doing that from barges it's a hell of a slow process. We certainly spent half the night doing that. We'll draw a curtain over some of the activities on Christmas Day, 1941.

On Boxing Day we went up to Bedford Basin and degaussed,* then down to the compass buoy and swung ship to correct the magnetic compass, completed storing, and by 1600 we were sailing to join a convoy. About eighty-five percent of the ship's company had never been to sea in their lives. Most of them couldn't have been more than eighteen years old – just a bunch of babies.

We had heavy weather and it was very nearly twenty-eight days before we set foot on dry land again.[18]

---

* A process by which the magnetic field of a ship's hull was altered by running an electrical charge through it. This made the ship less vulnerable to German mines which detonated by magnetism.

CHAPTER 5

"IF WE LOSE THE WAR AT SEA, WE LOSE THE WAR:"

THE ORDEAL, MAY–NOVEMBER 1942

Arguments in high places

*B*y the late spring of 1942, shipping losses had risen to alarming levels. In December 1941, the U-boats had sunk 56,957 tons in the Atlantic – in July this figure rose to 513,937 tons. The reasons for the German success lay not just with Dönitz's offensive in North American waters and American reluctance to implement the convoy system but also because the Allied navies had lost their ability to read the German navy's Enigma code. Convoys could no longer be routed away from submarines while Dönitz, thanks to Germany's signal intelligence service, could follow his opponents' movements. Worse still for the Allies, Dönitz was receiving new U-boats in greater numbers and he was now able to keep nearly 90 constantly at sea. When he decided in June 1942 to redeploy in the mid-Atlantic, Dönitz therefore possessed definite advantages.

(Facing page) **Topping up at sea.**
A Town Class destroyer (unidentified in the caption but probably *Columbia* or *St. Croix*) refuels at sea from a tanker, 7 November 1942. The introduction of refuelling at sea in 1942 extended the range of "short legged" escorts but was a difficult operation in anything but a calm sea. At this stage, the process was fairly primitive – the tanker simply trailed a line attached to a hose, which was picked up by the vessel waiting to refuel. Refuelling became more effective after the provision of pressurized hoses permitted the use of "along side" refuelling, allowing a tanker to top up two warships at the same time. (Photograph by G.A. Milne, National Archives of Canada, PA 116335)

The entry of the United States into the war gave promise of ultimate victory, but in the meantime the weight of the battle would have to be borne by the British and Canadian navies. American industry would eventually make up and surpass the crippling merchant ship losses of the first half of 1942, and new warships, foremost among them the purpose-designed ASW frigate and the escort carrier, were on the way. Better equipment and weapons were also being introduced into service, including Type 271 centimetric radar, in both sea and airborne versions, which could distinguish smaller objects from the background "clutter" of the sea; seaborne HF/DF apparatus; and Squid and Hedgehog, anti-submarine mortars that could be fired ahead of an attacking warship. But both ships and specialized technical equipment were in short supply in June 1942 when the U-boats returned to the mid-Atlantic.

They headed for the "air gap," that area of the ocean not covered by air patrols from Newfoundland, Iceland or Ireland. Here, they could operate in comparative safety on the surface, using their greater speed to concentrate. The need to eliminate the "air gap" or "black hole" had long been recognized but all efforts by the Admiralty to obtain VLR (Very Long Range) aircraft from the Royal Air Force had been frustrated by that service's Bomber Command, which regarded itself as Britain's major offensive weapon and jealously fought to prevent its aircraft from being used for other purposes – including the preservation of Britain's lifeline. Bomber Command had a lamentable record of ignoring the naval war. When it became known in 1941 that the Germans were starting to construct bomb-proof submarine pens at their bases in France, Bomber Command refused to attack these targets on the grounds that its aircraft were better employed in "the air offensive to which we must look for winning as opposed to not losing the war."[1] As a result, nothing was done and by early 1942 the U-boats were happily encased in shelters that could not be damaged by any weapon in the Allied arsenal. When Bomber Command finally began to attack these targets in late 1942, it lost 198 aircraft and their crews without doing any damage except to create a few very large dents in the reinforced concrete roofs.*

In the spring of 1942, American four-engined aircraft suitable for long-range maritime patrols, particularly the B-24 Liberator, began to enter service with the RAF. Any attempts, however, by the Admiralty to have even a small number of these aircraft placed under its control were frustrated by the RAF, which steadfastly refused to divert them from Bomber Command despite an admonition by Admiral Sir Dudley Pound that "If we lose the war at sea, we lose the war. We lose the war at sea when we can no longer maintain those communication which are essential to us."[2]

This warning had no effect on the RAF, which from March to December 1942 waged an obstinate bureaucratic struggle over the deployment of VLR aircraft. Despite a growing body of evidence that they were absolutely essential in the Atlantic, senior RAF staff remained obdurate and Prime Minister Winston Churchill, while generally agreeing with the naval case, was reluctant to make any decision that would reduce the strength of the offensive bomber force. By November 1942, it appeared as though Bomber Command had won the battle and, thus, come perilously close to losing the war. The VLR Liberators would remain under its control to join, as senior RAF officers exalted, 4,000 to 6,000 other heavy bombers in the task

---

* The RAF had dropped 15,600 tons of bombs on the U-boat bases in France by May 1943 and are thought to have damaged one submarine. Between 1941 and 1945, the RAF and USAAF also dropped 33,000 tons of bombs on submarine construction sites in Germany for the loss of 883 aircraft without appreciably affecting the rate of construction.

Working dress on the North Atlantic.
Sea duty on the North Atlantic required specialized clothing and equipment. At left, an officer is shown dressed for arctic conditions with several layers of underclothing, a parka, life vest, anti-flash face mask and gauntlets, steel helmet, sea boots and thick socks. Originally, sailors were issued a rubber life vest inflated by means of a tube and a mouthpiece – it was nicknamed the "Mae West" after the buxom film star of the period. In 1943, the RCN introduced an improved jacket-type life vest (lower right) fitted with a collar to keep an unconscious man's head out of the water, a groin pad to reduce injury from exploding depth charges, a lanyard and a hook to latch onto a floating object, and a small, blinking red light operated by a battery so that men in the water could be seen. The sailor on the right wears the traditional British naval duffel coat over his other garments and a balaclava, probably provided by his family. Heavy rubber sea boots were necessary on warships but they were the first thing disposed of if a sailor had to abandon ship. (Drawings by L.B. Jenson, courtesy of the artist)

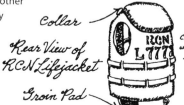

Collar
Rear View of RCN Lifejacket
RCN L 777
Colour was dark blue
Groin Pad

Seamen's mess in HMCS *Gaspé*, July 1942.
Gaspé was one of four Fundy class minesweepers in service in September 1939 and performed minesweeping duties out of Halifax throughout the war. At this time, Canadian sailors ate in their crowded messdecks, as this photograph by W.H. Pugsley illustrates. Note the bottle of Coca-Cola on the table – the Canadian sailor's penchant for mixing this beverage with his rum ration earned the RCN the name of the "Royal Coca-Cola Navy" from their British counterparts. (National Archives of Canada, PA 139294)

that there would be enough fuel to carry out this gigantic aerial offensive. This irrefutable logic finally won the day and VLR aircraft were transferred to Coastal Command, but it was not until the spring of 1943 that enough were deployed to make a difference. In the meantime, convoys would have to sail without air cover in the mid-Atlantic.

"She'll never surface again, sir:" The battle for ON 115, July–August 1942

The re-organization of Allied naval forces resulted in most Canadian warships serving in either the WLEF (Western Local Escort Force) or the MOEF. By June 1942 the greater part of the RCN was in the WLEF although, in the months to follow, the hardest fighting would be borne by the A (American), B (British) or C (Canadian) escort groups of the MOEF. Although nominally organized by nationality, the composition of these groups was often mixed, depending on the ships available. In both the WLEF and MOEF, Canadian warships were theoretically under American control, although in practice they were more concerned with the RN's Western Approaches Command at Liverpool which had overriding authority in the North Atlantic. This unwieldy command structure needed changing, but in the second half of 1942 plans for re-organi-

of the "progressive destruction and dislocation of the enemy's war industrial and economic system, and undermining his morale to a point where his capacity for armed resistance is fatally weakened."[3] The Admiralty immediately seized on this fatuous statement to point out that such a massive air offensive would require four times the current fuel requirements, and since, under prevailing conditions in the North Atlantic, the RN was having trouble providing even the current requirement, it was doubtful

zation were overtaken by events.

In the early summer, Dönitz concentrated in the mid-Atlantic air gap, using a greater number of submarines than on previous operations but with mixed results. In late June and early July, he formed several U-boat groups to intercept convoys but their attacks met with limited success. In late July 1942, however, he was able to concentrate a large number of U-boats against Convoy ON 115, escorted by the RCN.

ON 115 departed Britain in the third week of July and was picked up by C-3 Escort Group off Ireland on the 25th of that month. This group consisted of the destroyers *Saguenay* (Senior Officer) and *Skeena*, and the corvettes *Agassiz*, *Galt*, *Louisbourg*, *Sackville* and *Wetaskiwin*. During its first four days on passage, the escorts obtained a number of MF/DF (Medium Frequency/Direction Finding) radio signals, which they believed to be U-boat sighting reports. The Canadian escorts lacked the more precise HF/DF locating equipment which might have given an estimated distance to the source of the signal, but nonetheless the two destroyers "ran down" the bearings in the direction of the source of these signals. These chases

yielded no results and on the night of 29 July the senior officer, Commander D.C. Wallace, RCNR, of *Saguenay*, stationed his destroyers astern of the convoy to intercept submarines he believed to be closing in on it. As it transpired, the first German sighting report of ON 115 was made only that day by *U-210* and Dönitz ordered six submarines to intercept the convoy.

The German commander's radio transmissions and his submarine commanders' responses were picked up by the MF/DF on the escorts and, throughout 30 July, Wallace deployed his two destroyers and the corvettes *Galt* and *Wetaskiwin* on a number of "bearing sweeps" to locate the origins of these signals. Again, this exercise yielded no results but that night *Skeena* sighted a surfaced submarine on the starboard side of the convoy. She was joined by *Wetaskiwin* and the two ships, having obtained a firm ASDIC contact, carried out a lengthy depth charge attack that lasted until late in the morning of 30 July when a pinpoint launch by *Skeena* resulted in a powerful underwater explosion, as distinct from depth charge detonations. A few minutes later, seagulls were observed circling a patch of ocean and *Skeena* lowered a boat to find that the birds were breakfasting on human remains floating on the surface. First score in the battle of ON 115 went to C-3 Group, which had just sunk *U-588*, a Type VII boat commanded by *Kapitänleutnant* Victor Vogel.

The battle for ON 115, however, was just beginning. The five U-boats shadowing the convoy lost contact on 1 August, but the following day, after Dönitz had positioned a dozen submarines into patrol lines off the coast of Newfoundland, they sighted it again. By this time C-3 Group was operating at reduced strength as the two destroyers were short of fuel and had to make for St. John's. *Wetaskiwin*, meanwhile, lost the convoy in heavy fog and not being equipped with radar that might have allowed her to find it, also sailed for Newfoundland. C-3 Group

"Heart of Oak Are Our Ships, Jolly Tars Are Our Gals."
Led by Wren drummers Joan McMaster and Lorraine McAuley, members of the Women's Royal Canadian Naval Service march at their training establishment, HMCS *Conestoga* at Galt, Ontario. Although there were reservations on the part of conservative male officers, the WRCNS were an instant success and women sailors served at most major shore establishments, releasing men for sea duty, and also worked on ship repair. (Photograph by G.A. Milne, National Archives of Canada, PA 107939)

Pusser rig.
The gun crew of the corvette *Sackville* pose proudly by their 4-inch gun in "pusser rig," or best uniforms. Note the emblem on the gun shield. (Canadian Naval Memorial Trust)

to ram with no success and then carried out what he thought was a very accurate depth charge attack with no apparent result. He was about to order a second attack when one of his officers came to the bridge to tell him not to bother because, from his post at the stern of the corvette, this man had seen that:

> The depth charge from the starboard thrower sank fifty feet and then exploded, as did the others. It must have touched the U-boat's after deck as it went off, for a moment later the bow of the U-boat broke surface a few feet astern. She rose up out of the water to an angle of about forty degrees exposing one-third of her long slender hull. Her momentum was still carrying her forward at right angles to our course. As she hung for an instant poised in this precarious position, a depth charge which had been dropped over the stern rail exploded immediately beneath her and she disappeared in a huge column of water.[4]

Working rig.
Another gun, another gun crew, another corvette and this time the sailors are dressed in working rig for warm weather. There are splinter mats around the bridge structure for protection. Note the rails on the turret, used to fire illuminating rockets, and the perspex dome of the Type 271 radar, both of which indicate that this is a late war photograph. (Canadian Naval Memorial Trust)

now consisted of only four corvettes with command vested in Lieutenant Commander B.D. Johnson, RCNR, of *Agassiz*, although late in the afternoon of 2 August reinforcements arrived in the form of two destroyers, HMS *Witch* and HMCS *Hamilton*. The captain of the *Witch* assumed command of the escort and, as darkness fell, deployed his six vessels around the convoy.

A few minutes after midnight two merchantmen, *Loch Katrine* and *G.S. Waldron*, were torpedoed and, losing way, fell out. *Agassiz* and *Hamilton* closed to take off survivors and were screened in this activity by *Sackville*. A few minutes later, *Sackville*, which possessed a SW1C set, secured a radar contact and, altering course to investigate, found a surfaced U-boat, which immediately dived. Lieutenant Alan Easton, RCNR, of *Sackville* attempted

"She'll never surface again, sir," was the officer's conclusion on the matter. In actual fact, *U-43*, a Type IX commanded by *Oberleutnant zur See* Hans-Joachim Schwantke, had been heavily damaged but survived to limp back to its base at Brest.

About three hours later, *Sackville* obtained a second radar contact – nothing short of a miracle given the unreliability of the SW1C – and set course toward it to sight a surfaced submarine on her beam. Easton altered course to ram, but the submarine dived in time to escape and he then carried out another depth charge attack. No ASDIC contact was made and, after spending a few hours in an unsuccessful search, *Sackville* rejoined the convoy. In doing so, she came upon the freighter *Belgian Soldier*, which had been torpedoed and abandoned by her crew. Easton sent a boarding party to the vessel, which found a survivor still on board, and then, leaving the stricken vessel low in the water, resumed her screening duties.

Heavy fog hampered the efforts of both escorts and attackers the next day, 3 August, but in mid afternoon *Sackville*'s ASDIC operator used his equipment as a hydrophone and obtained a good contact. Easton altered course and, guided by his SW1C set which miraculously continued to operate, saw a U-boat running on the surface. Once again, his attempts to ram were foiled but his 4-inch gun crew managed to put one round into the submarine's conning tower before it dived in the swirling fog.

Sackville's target was *U-552*, a Type VII boat commanded by *Kapitän-leutnant* Erich Topp. Topp had hit the *Belgian Soldier* and expended all but one of his torpedoes and that was the weapon stored in a pressure-resistant container on his submarine's upper deck. He surfaced in the fog and a working party undertook the laborious job of transferring the torpedo from the upper deck down a loading hatch to the forward torpedo room. They had just finished this task and Topp was resting in his bunk when *Sackville* arrived on the scene. As he recalled:

> … there was a shout on the bridge: Emergency! The alarm klaxon shrills out. I rush drowsily into the control room. The bridge watchkeepers tumbled down onto me from the conning-tower hatch, one falling over the other. ……

What's up? …… A glance at the depth gauge shows that the boat is sinking slowly. The Engineer Officer rushes in and jumps to shut one of the vents. I see the horrified face of the warrant navigator, the last one tumbling down the ladder from the bridge. "Destroyer!" he yells.[5]

Unfortunately for Topp's crew, *U-552* had been damaged by *Sackville*'s fire and refused to submerge, causing them some anxious moments, but Topp's *leutnant-ingenieur* finally got control of the situation and the boat descended to 178 metres.

Easton and *Sackville*, meanwhile, were joined by *Agassiz* and the two corvettes carried out an ASDIC search for the *U-552* but sonar conditions were made difficult by the presence of numerous shoals of fish and they were unable to re-acquire their target, and after two hours they gave up the chase. Easton was convinced he had sunk a U-boat although he was sure that the "true story would probably ever remain a mystery, to me at any rate, and my curiosity unsatisfied."[6] In fact, *Sackville*'s single 4-inch round had so badly damaged the air induction and exhaust pipes of *U-552* that Topp was forced to return to his base at Lorient. Topp was a lucky man – while crossing the Bay of Biscay, he was attacked by a British aircraft but escaped with only minor damage.*

The heavy fog which closed in around ON 115 on 3 August made it difficult for the U-boats and Dönitz called off the attack. Although C-3 Group had sunk one submarine and heavily damaged two more for the loss of three ships during the battle, there was some criticism of their tactics. Wallace's use of destroyer sweeps which resulted in fuel shortages was condemned by British but praised by American analysts, a reflection of differing tactical approaches in the two navies. What was clear was that crews of the warships in C-3 were becoming experienced and their defence of the convoy would have been enhanced if their ships had possessed some of the equipment in common service in the RN such as HF/DF. More importantly, Type 271 centimetric radar would have per-

---

* Topp survived the war as the fifth-ranking U-boat commander in terms of tonnage sunk, and later rose to flag rank in the postwar German navy.

"Stand by to ram!" *U-210* **as seen from HMCS** *Assiniboine*, **May 1942.** On 6 May 1942, the destroyer HMCS *Assiniboine* (popularly known as "Bones") fought a gun duel with *U-210* after depth charge attacks brought the submarine to the surface. This dramatic shot, taken from *Assiniboine*, shows her preparing to ram, which was accordingly done, although the destroyer suffered severe damage in the process. (National Archives of Canada, PA 184006))

(Below) **Good shooting – damage on HMCS** *Assiniboine*, **1942.** On 6 May 1942, the destroyer HMCS *Assiniboine* engaged in a running surface battle with *U-210* which ended when the Canadian vessel rammed her opponent. The German gunners were good shots as the damage on *Assiniboine*'s A turret testifies. One round penetrated the hatch, which was open during the action, and made an indentation in the corner of the turret. A second round went through a small service hatch and entered the interior, leaving the square hole on the right. (Directorate of History and Heritage, DND, DHH NF 778)

mitted *Sackville* to accurately locate surfaced submarines in the fog and manoeuvre into the best attacking position prior to visual contact. These deficiencies were noted in the post-action reports but little was done about the problem.

"There was no doubt we had sunk one:" Convoy SC 94, August

At the time *Sackville* and the escorts of ON 115 were battling U-boats in heavy fog, Convoy SC 94, 36 merchant ships, was outward bound for Britain. Escort was provided by C-1 Group consisting of the destroyer HMCS *Assiniboine*, the Canadian corvettes *Battleford*, *Chilliwack* and *Orillia*, and the British corvettes *Dianthus*, *Nasturtium* and *Primrose*, with the Senior Officer being Lieutenant Commander A. Ayer, RNR, of *Primrose*. For the first few days of its voyage, SC 94 was hampered by bad weather and heavy fog which prevented air cover from Newfoundland. It was sighted on 5 August by *U-593*, which reported its position and course and immediately attacked, sinking one merchant ship, but was driven off by the escort. On the next day, 7 August, however, the escorts were very busy investigating multiple radar contacts on all sides of the convoy.

It was during one of these investigations that *Assiniboine* (known in the RCN as "Bones") got a contact on her Type 286 radar and making toward it, came out of a patch of mist to see the Type VII boat *U-210* moving on the surface. As one of the destroyer's officers, Lieutenant R.L. Hennessy, RCN, remembered, the submarine "suddenly swam out of the mist" and "then everyone says, 'Whoops!' and starts pushing buttons and firing guns."[7] *Assiniboine*'s captain, Lieutenant Commander J.H. Stubbs, RCN, accelerated to full speed with the intention of ramming his opponent but the U-boat's commander, *Kapitänleutnant* Rudolf Lemcke, realizing he did not have enough time to dive, opted to fight it out on the surface and manned his deck guns. *Assiniboine* was too close to use her main guns and so, for nearly half an hour, the two vessels exchanged automatic weapons fire from their anti-aircraft armament as they moved in and out of patches of mist. Lieutenant Hennessy recalled that the U-boat's 20mm guns

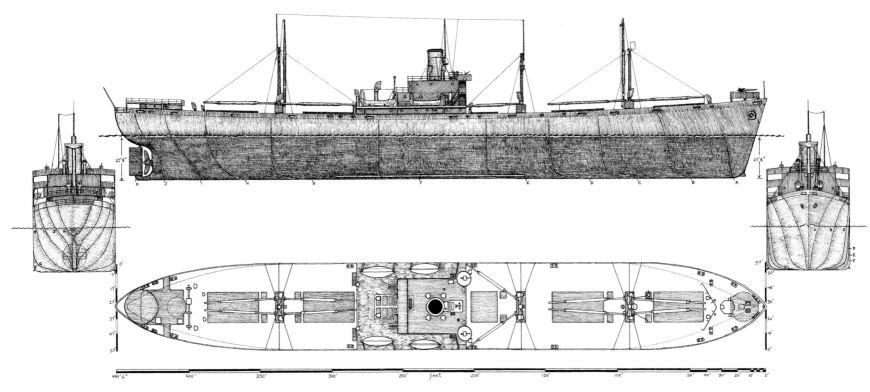

The Liberty ship – a war winner.

The Battle of the Atlantic was also a war of ship construction – the Allies had to replace lost merchant tonnage as quickly as possible. To do so, they began to build standardized types and the most common was the American Liberty ship (and the similar Canadian-built Park and Fort ships) designed for swift completion. The Liberty ship displaced 14,100 tons, could carry about 9,000 tons of cargo, was 441 feet in length and was crewed by 50-60 sailors. American shipyards turned out these vessels in astounding numbers – more than 2,751 were built – and in astounding time, between 40 to 60 days being average. (Drawing by L.B. Jenson, courtesy of the artist)

did a lot of damage around our bridge and set a fire at the back of the bridge, where we had our upper-deck gasoline storage. It was hit and of course started a big fire. The submarine never fired a round out of her main armament. A couple of times, when they tried to get a crew up [to the deck gun], our own boys just shot them off with the half-inch [.50 calibre] machine-gun. That kept the German's heads down.[8]

Assiniboine's captain later reported that "we were so close that I could make out the Commanding Officer [Lemcke] on the conning tower bending down occasionally to pass wheel orders."[9]

Lemcke managed to avoid three or four ramming attempts and was just about to dive when Stubbs hit the U-boat aft of the conning tower, damaging it so severely that it could not submerge, and circled around to find the enemy still on the surface and firing. *Assiniboine* therefore rammed it again and, for good measure, fired a pattern of depth charges over her stern rail before putting several rounds from her 4.7 inch guns into the conning tower which killed the determined Lemcke. This took the fight out of the crew of *U-210* and they abandoned their sinking vessel – 38 prisoners were hauled out of the water. *Assiniboine* suffered one man killed and 13 wounded in the engagement but, with her bow heavily damaged, had to leave for Newfoundland. As one of her crew later commented, everyone on board had behaved well including the destroyer's mascots – her puppy "lay at its moorings throughout the tumult with every hair in place" while the cat "being a cat, found a comfortable hide-out within the vitals of the ship."[10] Lieutenant Hennessy remembered it this way – it "was one time there was no doubt that we had sunk one."[11]

Although the escorts of SC 94 were busy during the remainder of 7 and 8 August investigating evasive ASDIC and radar contacts, there was no further action until the early afternoon of the latter day when two U-boats launched a submerged attack firing spreads of torpedoes. Five merchantmen were hit and the explosions from one stricken ship, SS *Kaimoku*, were so powerful that they frightened the crews of three other merchant vessels into abandoning their vessels. Two of the crews reboarded but the third refused, and their ship, *Redchurch*, dropped astern of the convoy to be sunk later by a U-boat. SC 94 had now lost seven merchant ships although the score was evened somewhat around midnight when HMS *Dianthus* engaged *U-379* with depth charges, blew it to the surface and sank it by ramming. By now, however, no less than 18 German submarines were in contact.

Fortunately, on 9 August 1942, SC 94 came within range of aircraft operating from Iceland and the escort was strengthened by three British destroyers, two of them equipped with HF/DF. Late in the morning of that day, two U-boats carried out a submerged attack from a position ahead of the convoy, firing spreads of torpedoes that sank four merchant ships but this was the last casualty the convoy suffered as air patrols forced the Germans to break contact. The loss of 11 merchantmen in return for two U-boats was regarded by some Allied commentators as an acceptable rate of exchange

MEN of VALOR
They fight for you

Two-man boarding party from the Canadian corvette 'Oakville' subdues crew of German sub in Caribbean

Duel on the deck.
A wartime poster dramatizes an incident that occurred in the Caribbean in August 1942 when a two-man boarding party from the corvette HMCS *Oakville* landed on *U-94* after the corvette had rammed it. Such incidents were rare. (Author's collection)

although the enemy's use of submerged attacks, in contrast to the previous favoured tactic of surface attacks, did not bode well. Dönitz, on the other hand, noting that many of the submarine commanders involved were relatively inexperienced, was satisfied with the results.

Problems increase: The RCN in the autumn of 1942

By the early autumn of 1942, the RCN had some reason to be happy with its recent successes. It had sunk three U-boats in the North Atlantic in August, more than the RN during the same period, and HMCS *Oakville* got a fourth in the West Indies following a boarding operation that more closely resembled the age of sail than the age of steam.* But knowledgeable observers pointed out problems with the Canadian escorts' training, maintenance, efficiency and, above all, their lack of modern equipment. Unfortunately, due to the many and overlapping commands concerned with the Atlantic convoys, its own distance from the theatre of war, and the absence of good technical liaison with the USN and RN, NSHQ in Ottawa did not have a clear picture of the difficulties faced by the escort fleet. When a problem was brought to their attention, they acted upon it, usually slowly, but all too often they remained oblivious to the day-to-day problems at sea.

There was also the attitude of some of the senior naval staff in Ottawa, including Admiral Percy Nelles, who were proponents of a big-ship fleet with aircraft carriers, cruisers and fleet destroyers and regarded the war as a means by which the RCN could acquire the balanced service it had long

---

* Although it was not known until long after the war, the corvette HMCS *Morden* actually sank a fifth U-boat in August 1942 when it engaged with *U-756* while escorting Convoy SC 97.

FINDING U-BOATS: HF/DF, RADAR AND ASDIC

The Allied navies faced the problem of finding U-boats in the vast reaches of the Atlantic and, once their position was located, of closing in to attack them. The solution was provided by three different types of technology: High Frequency Direction Finding (HF/DF or "Huff Duff"), radar and ASDIC.

"Huff Duff" (High Frequency Direction Finding)

Dönitz's command system was based on radio communication between his headquarters at Kerneval near Lorient (subsequently moved to Paris and later to Berlin) and his U-boat commanders at sea. Dönitz knew that radio transmissions could be detected by listening stations on land using High Frequency Direction Finding equipment that could obtain a bearing direction to the transmitter and that two such stations at widely separated locations could provide two different bearings which, if traced out in the direction of the source of the transmission, would provide a "fix" or "cross cut" at the point they intersected. The RN's "Y" Service, or radio intelligence organization, established listening stations in the British Isles, Iceland, Gibraltar, Newfoundland and Bermuda to listen and establish bearings for German radio transmissions. This information was sent to the Operational Intelligence Centre at the Admiralty, which correlated the reports of the various stations and calculated the location of the transmission and, hence, the U-boats.

Dönitz discounted the threat HF/DF posed because he did not believe that a "fix" obtained by this method would be accurate enough for Allied aircraft or surface vessels to find and attack the transmitting U-boat. His commanders were ordered to keep their transmissions short and many signals were in highly abbreviated, standardized formats for that reason. In fact, long-distance HF/DF "fixes" were subject to an error rate of up to 25 miles, but they still permitted the Submarine Tracking Room at the Operational Intelligence Centre in the Admiralty to build up a picture of the deployment of U-boats and to route convoys away from them.

The problem with HF/DF was that the locations it obtained were often too far from Allied warships and aircraft to be of tactical use – to permit U-boats to be attacked in time – and there was also a time lag between locating a U-boat's position and disseminating this information to the relevant naval force at sea. The answer was to fit HF/DF equipment on warships but this proved to be a most difficult task because of the size of the equipment. A technological breakthrough was made, however, in the spring of 1941 and the first British warship was equipped with mobile HF/DF a few months later. In 1942 an effort was made to fit at least two vessels in every escort group with HF/DF to permit them to obtain timely and accurate fixes on U-boats in their immediate vicinity. Two separate escorts, fitted with HF/DF, could obtain a "fix" and then run down the bearing to attack the source of the transmissions. The use of seaborne HF/DF became widespread in 1943 and by the end of the war, most major Allied warships were equipped with it.

Radar (Radio Direction Finding and Ranging)

HF/DF was useful for locating U-boats at a distance, but at closer range radar came into play. Radar is an electronic device that generates a short radio energy pulse which, if it hits

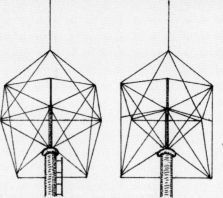

An H/F D/F Aerial

Two views of a major A/S weapon. The aerial did not revolve but it achieved its directional sensitivity by measuring the signal strength received by each of the several loops. A skilled operator could distinguish a "sky wave" from a "ground wave" & even estimate the range of a ground wave!

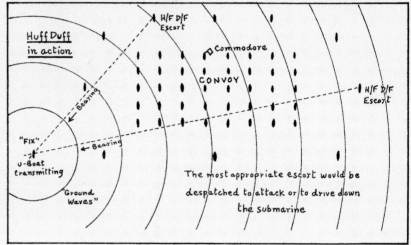

Huff Duff in action

H/F D/F Escort · Commodore · CONVOY · Bearing · Bearing · H/F D/F Escort · "FIX" · U-Boat transmitting · "Ground Waves"

The most appropriate escort would be despatched to attack or to drive down the submarine

a solid object, will return an electronic echo. Invented in Britain in the mid-1930s, it saw widespread naval use for surface searching, fire control and ranging, and navigation. Its utility for ASW was not appreciated until 1940 when the need to counter night attacks by surfaced U-boats led to the introduction of the first British seaborne surface search radar, Type 286. This was an extremely primitive device that transmitted on a broad band of 1.4 metres that could not distinguish the conning tower of a trimmed-down submarine (a submarine with only its conning tower above the surface) from the background "clutter" of the sea. Under optimum conditions, Type 286 had a range between 1,000 and 2,000 yards (not much better than the human eye) and the original model could not be trained through 360 degrees, only about 120 degrees in a forward direction.

The inadequacies of Type 286 radar led to it being replaced by Type 271 in the spring of 1941. Type 271 was a surface search radar that generated its energy pulse on a much more narrow beam than Type 286 – 9.7 cm as opposed to 1.5 metres – which provided a more distinct and accurate echo that could differentiate the conning tower of a trimmed-down submarine from background "clutter." For this reason, it was termed "centimetric" or "10 cm." radar. Type 271 was provided with a full 360-degree sweep capability and under optimum conditions had a range of up to 5,000 yards. Although production was slow, by May 1942, 236 British escorts were equipped with Type 271 and it was followed by a constant procession of improved models (Types 272, 273, 276, 277 and 293).

In terms of radar, the RCN lagged behind the RN throughout the war. This was largely the result of a decision by the government in the spring of 1941 to manufacture a Canadian version of the Type 286 radar just as that equipment was superseded by Type 271. Dubbed "Surface Warning-First Canadian" (SW1C), this Canadian device only differed from Type 286 in having 360-degree sweep capability (albeit by manual power) but it proved unreliable and extremely delicate.* An improved model, SW2C, followed but neither set was as capable as the Type 271, and in the spring of 1942 complaints from the escort fleet led to NSHQ trying to obtain 100 sets of Type 271 from Britain. This proved impossible because of the demand for these sets but the RN did agree to install 10 sets per month on RCN warships when they were in refit in British ports. By the end of 1942, however, just over half of the Canadian warships on the North Atlantic possessed Type 271 radar while most British escorts were fitted with it. Many RCN vessels were forced to use the SW1C and SW2C sets until well into 1943.

At this point, Ottawa compounded the problem by trying to introduce a Canadian version of Type 271 centimetric radar instead of copying the British original. Dubbed RX/C (if manufactured in Canada) or RX/U (if manufactured in the United States), it proved no more reliable than its SW1C and SW2C predecessors and led to much cursing on the Canadian vessels forced to use it. The result was that the RCN was always behind in terms of radar and the problem was never solved.

ASDIC or SONAR

If an escort vessel detected the presence of a submarine by HF/DF and radar, it would attempt to close with the target to attack it. Since U-boats usually submerged to escape, escort vessels used ASDIC to locate them under the water. ASDIC (now known by the American term SONAR from *Sound Navigating and Ranging*) was an apparatus housed in a dome on the underside of a ship's hull that emitted a sound pulse which, if it struck an underwater object, would return an echo giving that object's bearing and range. It could also be used in a passive mode as a hydrophone listening device. ASDIC was by no means perfect: its range was restricted, effective use limited a ship to a speed of less than 18 knots, and it was affected by the noise generated by the propellers of nearby ships, depth charge explosions or heavy weather; the depth and temperature of the water, ocean currents, and the presence of other objects under water such as whales, schools of fish or wrecks. It was also ineffective against surface targets and, finally, ASDIC contact with a target was usually broken when a depth charge attack was carried out.

* For more on the SW1C radar visit the Canadian Heritage Information Network website <www.virtual.ca/~military/remembrances/>, which contains a graphic animation of the working of this equipment.

Type 271 Radar

The 271 Perspex "Lantern."

As was the case with radar, Commonwealth ASDIC equipment experienced continual development and its range and capability were constantly being improved. but, as was also the case with radar, the RCN was generally behind the RN on the development curve. The Canadian corvettes built in 1940-1941 were equipped with Type 123A ASDIC, which was already obsolescent in the RN, and the Canadian navy never quite caught up: when the RCN introduced the improved Type 123D, the RN was using the improved Type 127, 128 and 129 sets. British wartime ASDIC equipment reached its peak of development in 1943 with the introduction of Type 144 and 145, which, with various attachments, could provide accurate information about the range, bearing and depth of an underwater target. Some British ships possessed the Type 147B, which was mated with the Squid mortar to create a fully-automated targeting and firing sequence. Although the RCN tried to procure this equipment, production delays meant that most Canadian escort vessels did not get the Type 144 or 145 ASDIC until late in the war, and many did not receive it at all.

German counter measures

Dönitz , who had been assured by his signals experts that it was impossible for HF/DF to be fitted to warships, never fully comprehended the asset it provided for Allied warships or the danger it represented to his submariners.

Germany was also behind the Allied navies in providing radar and radar detection equipment. From 1941 on, attempts were made to fit U-boats with these devices but generally they were not as effective as their Allied counterparts and were consistently a generation behind Allied models. When many U-boats reported surprise attacks by aircraft and surface vessels, Dönitz realized that the Allies were using radar, and in August 1942 U-boats were fitted with a radar detector. Commonly called *Metox* after the French company that manufactured it, this device was capable of picking up pulses from metric search radars, such as the Type 286, at a safe distance but it entered service, however, just as metric radar was being replaced by the centimetric Type 271, which it could not detect. When the surprise attacks increased in 1942, Dönitz at first believed that the *Metox* device itself was emitting a signal that could be picked up by Allied radar and this delayed the introduction of equipment that could warn against centimetric radar until September 1943 when the *Naxos* equipment entered service. It proved effective but Allied scientists quickly came up with countermeasures that reduced its performance.

To counter ASDIC, German submarine commanders relied on tactics such as accelerating, forcing the escort vessel to undertake a stern chase through the wake of the U-boat and thus interfering with ASDIC contact. Other tactics were to make a sharp, power turn to disturb the water and confuse the ASDIC operator or to dive beneath an ocean thermal layer that would also interfere with ASDIC. Finally, in 1942 the U-boats were issued with *Bold*, the codename for a chemical projectile consisting of 370 grams of calcium and zinc which was ejected from the boat by a special discharge tube. When *Bold* came in contact with the water, it produced hydrogen gas bubbles which simulated the sound of a U-boat and unwary ASDIC operators could be thus decoyed away from the real thing. ∎

Convoy SC 97.
HMCS *Dauphin* of C-2 Escort Group launches a depth charge attack while escorting Convoy SC 97 in September 1942. This convoy was attacked by four U-boats and one was sunk by HMCS *Morden*. (Canadian Naval Memorial Trust)

obliged the Admiralty by detaching 16 Canadian corvettes to take part in Operation TORCH, the invasion of North Africa.

Senior officers in operational commands, particularly the newly-promoted Rear Admiral Len Murray, now stationed at Halifax as Commanding Officer, Atlantic Coast, were fully aware of the problems facing the escorts, particularly the MOEF groups. For nearly a year, Murray had warned his superiors that the policy of building and manning as many ships as possible, and shoving them out to sea without proper training, equipment, maintenance and personnel, would ultimately backfire, and by the late summer of 1942 he and many others in the WLEF and MOEF were convinced that, unless positive steps were taken to improve the efficiency of the Canadian escorts, a disaster would result. Having been forced to deal with the many problems caused by unchecked expansion, Murray could see that a crisis was at hand.

The performance of the poorly-equipped Canadian C-Groups stood in contrast to their British counterparts. An example of what a well-trained and equipped escort group could achieve was demonstrated during the passage of ONS 122 in late August. This convoy was escorted by B-6 Group, consisting of a British destroyer and four Norwegian corvettes. All the escorts were equipped with Type 271 centimetric radar while the destroyer had HF/DF and Hedgehog, a type of mortar that threw its projectiles ahead of the vessel, usually permitting it to retain ASDIC contact during the attack. This group had served together for a long time and its Norwegian crews were composed of experienced seamen regarded as some of the best sailors on the North Atlantic. ONS 122 sailed from Britain in the third week of August and for four days, from 22 to 26 August, came under attack by nine U-boats. The Senior Officer in the destroyer used the corvettes to chase down accurate HF/DF contacts but did not permit them to stray far and their efficient Type 271 radar resulted in 13 submarine contacts which were followed up by depth charge attacks. Two U-boats were heavily damaged and forced to withdraw while, in return, the convoy lost four ships. Allied analysts praised the work of B-6 Group whose success contrasted with that of Canadian escorts carrying out a similar task.

desired. These officers viewed the escort fleet only as a stepping stone to the creation of a "real navy." An additional problem was the seeming willingness on the part of Nelles to try to meet every request for assistance from the Admiralty, without considering the effect it had on his own service. The result was that in mid-1942, while there were grave shortages of trained personnel in the North Atlantic, thousands of Canadian officers and sailors were serving with the Royal Navy, and ironically there were more Canadian radar specialists in the RN, thanks to a British recruiting drive in Canada cheerfully assisted by NSHQ, than in the RCN. As a case in point, in September 1942, when escort strength on the North Atlantic was estimated to be 100 ships short of the necessary figure and German submarines were actively operating in the Gulf of St. Lawrence, Nelles

"Pitiable entreaties … from the voice pipe:" Convoy ON 127, September 1942

By September 1942, Dönitz had enough submarines on station in the North Atlantic to form two patrol lines covering hundreds of miles of the main shipping lanes. Just what this meant was brought home during the battle for Convoy ON 127 which departed from Britain in the first week of September. Its mid-ocean escort was C-4 Group consisting of the Canadian destroyers *Ottawa* and *St. Croix*, the Canadian corvettes *Amherst*, *Arvida* and *Sherbrooke* and the British corvette *Celandine*. Only the British vessel had Type 271 radar and none of the escorts were equipped with HF/DF. C-4 picked up the convoy on 5 September and the first five days were uneventful, but on 10 September, just as ON 127 moved beyond the range of air cover, it was attacked by the 12 submarines of *Gruppe Vorwärts*.

For three days, under constant attack, ON 127 battled its way through the air gap, losing 10 merchantmen (7 sunk and the others so badly damaged they had to drop out) in the process. The escorts obtained multiple visual, ASDIC and radar contacts as numerous submarines attempted to penetrate the defensive screen and get at the columns of merchantmen. The situation was not helped by the fact that, although ON 127 was nominally a fast convoy, the majority of the ships were empty and thus travelling light against prevailing headwinds with the result that their speed was so reduced that the U-boats could maintain contact. The Senior Officer, Lieutenant Commander A.H. Dobson, RCNR, of *St. Croix*, tried desperately to protect his charges and C-4 was happy when air cover from Newfoundland arrived in the morning of Sunday, 13 September, and drove the circling submarines under the surface, damaging three U-boats so severely that they were forced to break contact. At dusk that day reinforcements in the form of the British destroyer *Witch* and the Canadian destroyer *Annapolis* steamed up to help out.

It was at this time that the crew of *Ottawa* buried the young gunner who had been picked up, badly wounded, after his ship was torpedoed the previous Friday. A few hours later, the destroyer was ordered to investigate radar contacts ahead of the convoy. Shortly before midnight, *Ottawa* was torpedoed by *U-91*, a Type VII boat commanded by *Kapitänleutnant*

Keeping up civilian morale, c. 1942.
Wartime poster by Alex Colville depicts a stylized depth charge attack off the stern of a corvette. Note the twin .50 calibre machine guns in the stern AA position. (Author's collection)

Heinz Walkerling. The torpedo blew off the destroyer's bows and at first there was some hope that she could be kept afloat, but Walkerling hit *Ottawa*'s boiler room with a second torpedo and she began to sink. On her bridge, Lieutenant Thomas Pullen, RCN, the first lieutenant, was horrified to hear "pitiable entreaties emanating from the voice pipe" from two young sailors trapped in the ASDIC centre below decks, entreaties

> which became unbearable to those … who were totally helpless to do anything for them. What could, what should, one do other than offer words of encouragement that help was coming when such was manifestly out of the question? What happened at the end is hard to contemplate for the imprisoned pair, as that pitch black, watertight, sound-proofed box rolled first 90 degrees to starboard and then 90 degrees onto its back before sliding into the depths and oblivion.[12]

Nearly two hundred men were now in the water clustered around life rafts and carley floats as the convoy sailed past them – "the huge ships' sides (how could they be so big?) and small people at the top calling down to us," remembered Lieutenant Latham B. Jenson of *Ottawa*.[13] When HMS *Celandine* arrived next morning to pick up survivors, 69 officers and men were rescued, gamely singing to keep up their spirits and their body warmth, but *Ottawa*'s captain, Lieutenant Commander C.A. Rutherford, RCN, was not among them – while in the water he had given his lifejacket to one of his sailors and disappeared in the darkness.

"Fishing boats, coastal ships and luxury yachts:" Deficiencies and distractions

Air cover from Newfoundland provided by RCAF Catalinas flying at extreme range ended the battle for ON 127. Although there was shock at the losses suffered, there was pride in the fact that C-4 Group had fought back effectively. Unfortunately, the loss of *Ottawa* reduced the RCN's modern destroyer strength to just three vessels (*Restigouche*, *Saguenay* and *Skeena*) as *Assiniboine* and *St. Laurent* were in refit or repair. The Town Class destroyers (the old four-stackers) had rendered yeoman service but only two had the range to operate effectively in the North Atlantic and all required constant repair. This reduction in destroyer strength was a major concern because these vessels were the RCN's most effective escorts. More compelling was the lack of modern radar, and although Murray had requested that all MOEF escorts be fitted with the useful Type 271 in place of the nearly useless SW1C, there were simply not enough sets to go around. It was ironic that the 16 Canadian Flower Class corvettes sent to support Operation TORCH included some of the most best examples of the type, with extended forecastles, increased endurance and Type 271. It seemed that the Mid-Ocean Escort Force, tasked with the most important Canadian naval operation, would forever be the poor stepsister of its own service.

In the autumn of 1942, however, the attention of both the government and NSHQ was distracted from the North Atlantic to waters closer to home. The previous May and June, as part of Dönitz's offensive against North America, two U-boats had made a very successful cruise in the Gulf of St. Lawrence, sinking six merchant ships. They reported that the area was poorly defended, and although NSHQ tried to beef up escort forces in the Gulf, the RCN did not have the strength to contain a second onslaught that took place in September and October when five U-boats entered the Gulf area and sank several small coastal vessels, the passenger ferry *Caribou* and the corvette *Charlottetown* with great loss of life. There followed a media frenzy reminiscent of the "Hun Sea Wolf" scare of 1918 but the RCN was stretched far too thin to provide more escorts. Under public pressure to do something, the government took the momentous decision of closing the Gulf of St. Lawrence to shipping and moving freight destined for Atlantic ports by rail. It was a humiliating setback but it resulted from the RCN being asked to do too much with too little for too long.

Although Radio Berlin crowed that "the Canadian navy, which is nine-tenths composed of requisitioned fishing boats, coastal ships, and luxury yachts" was third-class, Dönitz was not enjoying the same success in the North Atlantic.[14] The rate of sinkings continued high, 35 ships in September and October, and his strength increased to 150 U-boats by the end of the latter month (although only one third were usually on patrol, the

Not a winter wonderland.
A Town Class destroyer, either *Niagara* or *St. Croix,* comes alongside so heavily covered in ice that she is almost unrecognizable. Winter conditions in the North Atlantic were brutal and ice accumulation was a serious hazard as the increased weight could cause a vessel to capsize. There was nothing for it but to chip it off by hand. (Canadian Naval Memorial Trust)

others in transit or refit). A combination of poor weather and inexperienced commanders frustrated his attempts to repeat his success against ON 127 until late in October when he managed to concentrate a large number of submarines against a single convoy. That convoy was SC 107 and, unfortunately, it was escorted by Canadian warships.

"Little flickering lights in the water:" SC 107 – Convoy from Hell

Signal intelligence provided by the *B-dienst* reached Dönitz in time for him to station a patrol line in a good location to intercept an eastbound convoy. On 29 October, *U-522* sighted just such a target off Cape Race in Newfoundland and began to track it. Dönitz immediately ordered *Gruppe Veilchen,* 17 U-boats, to concentrate for an attack.

His target was SC 107, 42 merchant ships escorted by C-4 Group consisting of the destroyer *Restigouche* under Lieutenant Commander Desmond W. Piers, RCN, who was the Senior Officer, and the corvettes *Algoma, Amherst, Arvida, Celandine* (RN) and *Moose Jaw.* In terms of equipment, C-4 Group was relatively well off, both *Restigouche* and the convoy rescue ship, *Stockport,* possessed HF/DF equipment and the destroyer and *Celandine* had Type 271 radar. On 1 November, as *Gruppe Veilchen* concentrated, C-4 Group became concerned when they picked up multiple signals as *U-522* guided various submarines into the attack. Piers in *Restigouche* could identify the location of these signals by HF/DF but commanding the only destroyer in the escort, he could not leave the convoy to "run them down" to their source and attack. By midnight six boats from *Gruppe Veilchen* were in position and the battle commenced when three submarines penetrated the escort screen and sank eight merchantmen. One torpedo narrowly missed *Restigouche,* which was only saved when she made a routine course adjustment at the end of a "zig zag." It was a terrible night for C-4 Group as, badly outnumbered, they were nearly swamped by the attackers and the hours of darkness were a kaleidoscope of illuminating rockets, explosions and burning ships.

Lieutenant Commander Louis Audette, RCNVR, known as "Uncle Louis" because he had reached the rather advanced age of 30, commanded *Amherst.* That night, he got a good ASDIC contact about 1,500 yards ahead and was racing in at high speed to launch a depth charge attack when he realized his target was exactly beneath "a lot of little flickering lights in the water" – the small emergency lights on the lifejackets of survivors.[15] Faced with the terrible choice of attacking and killing these people or letting the enemy escape, Audette chose to attack. As *Amherst* bore down on the doomed men, Audette's first lieutenant asked, "Are you going to go ahead?" in a hushed voice. Audette replied "Yes." "I couldn't leave the submarine," he recalled years later, "I held him on asdic. I couldn't leave him free to kill more men, sink more ships and their cargoes – and there were hundreds of other men in the convoy still." Fortunately for Audette and his crew, at that moment *Amherst*'s ASDIC equipment failed and he cancelled the attack.

Bad weather on 2 November hampered the efforts of both escorts and their opponents although *U-522* was able to sink a ninth victim, raising its score to three ships in 24 hours. On 3 November the action was renewed although the British destroyer *Vanessa* arrived to assist *Restigouche*. There were still nine U-boats in contact and they were able to penetrate the escort screen in broad daylight and torpedo more ships. The escorts carried out continuous attacks on their assailants, damaging two submarines so badly that they had to break off contact. On went the battle. By 4 November, the rescue ship *Stockport* was so overloaded with sur-

Christmas dinner, 1942.
Happy to be in port for the festive season, the wardroom of HMCS *Sackville* celebrates with a formal dinner. From left to right: Lieutenant Tony Osborne, RCNR, first lieutenant; Mrs. Alan Easton; Sub Lieutenant Colin Carruthers, RCNVR (standing); Lieutenant Alan Easton, RCNR, commanding officer; Sub Lieutenant Neil Chapman, RCNVR; and Sub Lieutenant John Margison, RCNVR. On the bulkhead behind Easton can be seen the White Ensign. (Canadian Naval Memorial Trust)

Working rig.
Working rig, or dress, as opposed to "Pusser Rig," or best dress, was practical and comfortable and consisted of a blue denim shirt, jacket and trousers worn with dark blue rank badges but no other insignia. The leading seaman illustrated here has added an inflatable "Mae West" type lifejacket and rubber seaboots, the most popular form of footgear on board ship. By regulation, every officer and sailor on board ship was to carry a knife although the regulation "pusser's dirk," a large clasp knife with a folding marlin spike, was not popular. Most Canadian sailors carried knives according to their own personal taste. The traditional naval cap, while smart in full dress, was liable to be carried away by the wind, and was often replaced on the North Atlantic by the more practical tuque or stocking cap. (Drawing by L.B. Jenson, courtesy of the artist)

vivors that she had to be detached for Iceland, as did two American tugs which had joined the convoy to assist her in her important task. Late that day more help arrived in the form of two American destroyers and a Coast Guard cutter, but they were still unable to prevent the loss of another ship. That night, *Amherst* closed a burning freighter, SS *Daleby*, which had supposedly been abandoned only to find three men still on board the blazing wreck and screaming for help. Against standing orders, Audette lowered a boat and called for volunteers to board the fiery hulk – the boat was quickly manned and the three survivors were rescued.

Matters came to an end on 5 November when aircraft from Iceland arrived and Dönitz called off his dogs. The disaster long predicted by Admiral Murray had finally come to pass – 15 merchant ships totalling 88,000 tons, more than a third of the convoy, had been lost – leaving SC 107 with the reputation for having suffered one of the worst convoy loss rates in the Battle of the Atlantic.

"The expansion of the RCN has created a ... problem:" The reckoning

By November 1942 the situation on the Atlantic had become serious. Shipping losses, combined with the ever-increasing strength of the German submarine fleet, the absence of Ultra intelligence, the scarcity of VLR aircraft, and the need to siphon off Allied naval strength to provide escorts for Operation TORCH, had begun to sway the contest in Dönitz's favour.

It was obvious to the British government that the Battle of the Atlantic had to be won before any other major operation, including the bomber offensive against Germany and an invasion of the European continent, could take place. They therefore took important steps to ensure that it would take precedence over all other theatres of war. A special Anti-U-Boat Warfare Committee, consisting of Churchill and senior representatives of all the services concerned, was instituted to supervise its higher direction and prevent a repetition of the bureaucratic "Battle of the Air" which had come close to losing the war. More important was the appointment of Admiral Sir Max Horton to the position of Commander-in-Chief, Western Approaches, the RN command directly concerned with the defence of shipping on the Atlantic. A ruthless ex-submariner, Horton was a good choice to oppose the artful and resolute Dönitz and he immediately began to shake up all aspects of his new command. It was Horton's belief that success in the Atlantic lay in providing proper leadership, training and equipment for the escort groups. Those groups that were not up to his exacting standards would have to be made so and it is not surprising therefore that his gaze fell on the C-Groups which had the worst record in ships lost in the MOEF.

Horton proposed to rectify this problem by removing them from the Atlantic and replacing them with British groups. The C-Groups would be shifted to the UK-Gibraltar convoys but, before that, they would receive "some really thorough training."[16] There is no evidence that Horton knew anything about the reasons for the Canadian escorts' poor record or the background of Canada's participation in the Battle of Atlantic – to him it was a simple matter: the Canadian escorts were the least efficient and had to be replaced. He convinced Churchill that the change was necessary and on 17 December the British leader sent a telegram to Prime Minister Mackenzie King which adroitly but plainly stated that the RCN must be withdrawn from the MOEF:

> A careful analysis of attacks on our transatlantic convoys has clearly shown that in those cases where heavy losses have occurred lack of training of the escorts both individually and as a team, has largely been responsible for these disasters.
>
> I appreciate the grand contribution of the Royal Canadian Navy to the Battle of the Atlantic, but the expansion of the RCN has created a training problem which must take some time to solve.[17]

The problem of unchecked wartime growth, as Murray had long feared, was now steaming directly for NSHQ at high speed.

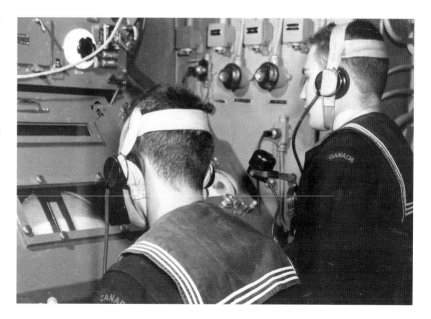

Submarine detectors.
The Battle of the Atlantic was waged not only at sea but also in the laboratory, and technology became increasingly important. The technological level of the Allied navies far surpassed that of the *Kriegsmarine*. Submarine detection equipment had by 1945 become extremely sophisticated and the sailors trained to use it (SDs – Submarine Detectors) were some of the most important members of escort crews. (Photograph by W.H. Pugsley, National Archives of Canada, PA 139273)

1942

The loss of HMCS *Spikenard*, February 1942

The year 1942 began badly for the RCN when the corvette Spikenard *was torpedoed on 10 February while escorting convoy SC 67. Seaman Wilfred Mills, a crew member, recalled that,*

When the torpedo exploded it destroyed the stoker's mess and the wardroom and tore upward through the bridge structure, leaving it in ribbons of steel and setting the well deck on fire. I covered my head with a coat and ran through the flames, sustaining third-degree burns on my hands, only to fall into the hole full of water. From there I climbed to the upper deck over the strips of steel to my abandon ship station, which was the port Carley float. People came up out of the stokehold. I was so stunned I couldn't get the Carley float free and someone else came and cut it loose.

Whether there were other people in the water, I cannot tell you. All was confusion. …… We started out on a port side Carley float from the upper deck, which by this time was level with the water. We caught up with a raft and transferred to it. The convoy steamed on unaware that *Spikenard* had been hit.[1]

Mills was one of only eight survivors from Spikenard *rescued by the British corvette HMS* Gentian *after spending eighteen hours in the North Atlantic.*

"Almost any meal could be an adventure:" Corvette dining

Living conditions on corvettes were primitive and in no matter was this more apparent than in arrangements for cooking and eating. Seaman Murry Laidlaw remembers that new sailors

had to make certain adjustments changing to Navy grub, getting used to things like "red lead and bacon" – lukewarm, watery tomatoes and either raw or overcooked bacon. My first sea draft was to the corvette *Chicoutimi*, one of the ships which had a short forecastle and kept it until the war ended. There I discovered that there was just one cook for about 65 men. He didn't have the time, space, or facilities to make food dishes like my mother did. Then there was a supply department victualling manual which clearly spelled out the menu and quantity which sailors should eat.

The first long trip was from North Sydney to Tobermory, Scotland – some twenty-one days of questionable weather. Our bread turned green after about seven days out, and after paring off the outside mould, we had only a two-inch square that we could eat. When the bread was gone we reverted to hardtack, a biscuit some six inches in diameter and half an inch thick. They were so hard the man has yet to be born who could take a bite from one. You either split them with a knife or dunked them and still came up with a tasteless product. ……

The victualling dry store in the *Chicoutimi* was aft and down under the quarterdeck, with access

The Messman

An essentially tricky job. Canadian warships utilized a messing system to feed sailors. Each mess of about six to eight men sent a "messman" or "mess cook" to the galley to bring back their food to their crewspace where it was eaten. On corvettes, the messman's return journey, laden with hot food for his comrades, could be a tricky business and there were many days when his messmates ate their food cold and laced with seawater after the messman had scraped it off the deck. (Drawing by L.B. Jenson, courtesy of the artist)

through a hatch which the V.A. (victualling assistant [or storesman]) always kept locked tight and dogged down. Sometimes, though, not all the dogs were secured and I recall when a bad storm put four feet of water into the storeroom. The water washed all of the labels off the tins of canned goods. As a consequence it was a surprise with every can we opened. ……

Any seaman who ever sailed in a corvette with an original short forecastle will know the problems that created, whether trying to get from mess to galley or going on watch. You had a stretch of open deck to cross buffeted by high winds, often drenched by waves coming aboard. Many a meal was lost along the way or else was well "salted." Most corvettes later had forecastles extended to as to take in the galley and bridge access.

Crockery was always being broken in rough seas, until it reached a point where we had to eat in shifts. In rough seas, you kept one hand on the plate to be sure it stayed put while you ate, at the same time bracing yourself so that you yourself stayed put. Almost any meal could be an adventure.[2]

Ports of call (1): "Newfie John," spiritual home of the North Atlantic escorts

St John's, Newfoundland (at that time not part of Canada), was established as a base for the trans-Atlantic escort vessels in May 1941 and, over the next four years, hundreds of Canadian warships visited it. "Newfie John," as the Canadians called it, was one of their favourite ports of call because of, as Lieutenant Latham Jenson, RCN, remembered, the friendliness of its people:

The redeeming feature of Newfoundland was the nature of the inhabitants. Kind, friendly, generous and decent, rich and poor alike, they could not have been more supportive of all these strangers who had descended upon them.

The escorts generally berthed near the oil tanks on the other side of the harbour from the city. It was a long walk on a rocky road to St. John's and most people took a bum boat over for a few cents. In the harbour were several merchant ships that had been damaged by the weather or the enemy and were awaiting repair. One ship had a large hole blown through her stern and the bum boat man often took his boat and passengers right through the hole. The one lung engine really echoed while we were in the great hole.[3]

Recreation activities were limited, as Seaman Frank Curry remembers, but "a run ashore" in Newfie John was usually enjoyable:

Many of us set out on the long hike from the South Side, around the end of the harbour, and into the centre of town. The narrow, cobblestoned streets were jammed with sailors, all searching for a break from life aboard ship. The restaurants were packed with hungry sailors, happy for a rest from everyday fare aboard ship. The movie theatre always had a long lineup. Many a sailor was on the lookout for something to drink other than tea or pop. Beer was often in short supply, but it didn't take long for us to discover the joys of Newfoundland's famous Screech, a liquor based on rum, clear and innocent enough to look at, but powerful enough to knock out even the hardiest of drinkers. Bottles of this native drink passed hands in dark alleys in exchange for seaman's precious dollars. Well into the night, sailors crawled back on board after polishing off a bottle of Screech. More important than food, drink and movies was a bit of female companionship, for which we sailors were constantly on the look out. The search often proved to be a tricky business, since sailors vastly outnumbered the girls. There were crowds of seamen pouring ashore; there were soldiers and airmen; and there were our greatest rivals, the Yanks from Fort Pepperall and the American ships. Despite the competition, many a Canadian sailor found romance. Many of them married into St. John's families.

Many of us headed for the hostels which had sprung up with the war, most particularly the YMCA, the Sally Ann (Salvation Army) and the K of C (Knights of Columbus). In these hostels we found a bed for the night; three-tiered bunks,

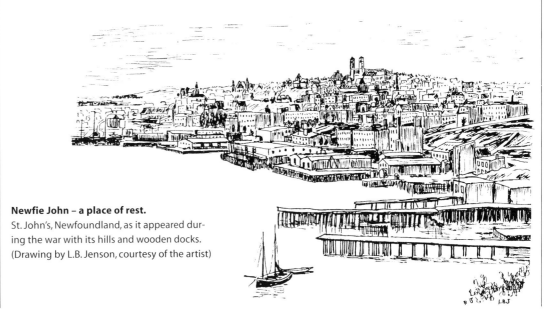

Newfie John – a place of rest.
St. John's, Newfoundland, as it appeared during the war with its hills and wooden docks.
(Drawing by L.B. Jenson, courtesy of the artist)

stacked inches apart in the huge dormitories which reminded me of the Stadacona barracks, except that the beds were real ones. With overnight leave until 0700 hours, it was possible to get a good night's rest, and have supper and breakfast in somewhat more civilized surrounds than the seaman's mess.[4]

For officers, the greatest attraction in St. John's was the famous Crowsnest Club and Lieutenant James Lamb, RCNVR, remembers that,

If any single place could be said to be the heart of the corvette navy, the Crowsnest, officially entitled the Seagoing Officers Club, would be it. Certainly it was home to all of us in the escort ships; a place you could drop into at any time of day or night and be assured of a welcome, a drink, or a simple snack – the hot ersatz eggs and Spam sandwiches were always good – from the assiduous Gordon and his wife, who presided there. Dozens of enormous leather armchairs were scattered about the bare floor, and grouped about the fireplace, with its comfortable padded fender. The walls were resplendent with the crest of every escort ship in the western ocean; original works of art, most of them, and always worth a tour of inspection to see what new ones had been added since the last visit. In a corner, the head of a large spike, "Spikenard's Spike," protruded from the floor; it had been driven in there by Shadforth, commanding officer of the corvette *Spikenard* during a nail-hammering contest on his last night ashore before *Spikenard* sailed. She was torpedoed and lost with all hands, and her spike in the Crowsnest floor was retained as a memento of lost friends.[5]

"U-boat considered sunk:" Convoy ON 115, July–August 1942

Convoy ON 115, which left Britain bound for Halifax in late July 1942 was attacked by two different U-boat wolfpacks during the course of its voyage but fairly effective defence by the Canadian escort group limited losses to three merchant ships. On the plus side, HMC Ships Skeena *and* Wetaskiwin *disposed of U-558 on 31 July following a hunt which lasted more than five hours and involved repeated depth charge attacks as the two vessels worked in concert, conversing by frequent messages, including this final exchange:*

Wetaskiwin: Contact bearing 300 degrees, 1000 yards.
Wetaskiwin: Attacking [with depth charges].
Wetaskiwin: Lost contact.
Skeena: Echo bearing 120 degrees, 700 yards.
Wetaskiwin: O.K. Let me do an attack now.
Skeena: Unable to gain contact.
Wetaskiwin: I will try to help you by directing.
Skeena: Attacking.
Wetaskiwin: Excellent.
Skeena: Did you hear that underwater explosion?
Wetaskiwin: Yes. Definitely.
Skeena: Your turn.
Wetaskiwin: Plenty of wreckage over this way.
Skeena: I am lowering a whaler to pick up the guts.
Skeena: (General Signal) U-boat considered sunk by HMCS *Wetaskiwin* and HMCS *Skeena*. Floating wreckage and human remains recovered.[6]

"He opened fire with all his guns:" Convoy SC 94, August 1942

A second confirmed submarine kill was made by HMCS Assiniboine *on 6 August 1942 when she sank U-210 after a running gun battle on the surface through patches of fog. As* Assiniboine's *captain, Lieutenant Commander J.H. Stubbs, RCN, reported:*

I closed [the] U-boat to ram at full speed. ……

He opened fire with all his guns and for about 35 minutes the action continued at a point blank range of about 100 to 300 yards. A second degree fire broke out on the starboard side of the break of the forecastle and spread almost to the bridge and through the sick bay flat. The enemy took constant evading action and I was forced to go full astern on the inside engine to prevent him from getting inside our turning circle, which he was obviously trying to do.

It was impossible to depress the 4.7" guns sufficiently at this range, but I ordered them to continue firing, more to keep the guns' crews busy while under fire than from any hope of hitting. One hit was gained on the conning tower however.

During most of the action we were so close that I could make out the Commanding Officers on the conning tower bending down occasionally to pass wheel orders. A gun's crew appeared on the deck and attempted to reach the forward gun but our multiple .5's [.50 calibre] successfully prevented this.

I turned as quick as possible to find him surfacing again but slightly down by the stern, still firing and making about 10 knots. After a little manoeuvring, we rammed him again well abaft the conning tower and fired a shallow pattern of depth charges as we passed. Also one 4.7" shell from 'Y' Gun scored a direct hit on his bows. He sank by the head in about two minutes.[7]

"Would you like a cup of tea?" The loss of HMCS *Ottawa*, September 1942

Late in the evening of 13 September 1942, while escorting Convoy ON 127, the destroyer Ottawa *was sunk by U-91. Lieutenant L.B. Jenson, RCN, was on the bridge when the first torpedo hit:*

An amazing geranium-colour flash forward was followed by a great pillar of water which went straight up! All of us took shelter under the overhang at the front of the bridge as the water and all sorts of solid objects tumbled down from the sky. When the downpour stopped, I went back to the compass and we stopped engines. The ship lay still in the water, rocking gently. The forecastle with anchors and cables together with A Gun had vanished, and the forward canopy with B Gun drooped down towards the water. This was visible because the interior lights were all on and shining out all over the ocean. We obviously were a lovely target so the engines were ordered slow astern. ...... Mr. Jones left the bridge and hurried at once to the quarterdeck, where he set all the depth charges to "safe" so that if the ship sank survivors would not be blown up by our own charges.

I asked the captain if I could do a quick inspection and report back. He agreed and I went down the ladders to the starboard passage into the messdecks. The forward messdecks, upper and lower, were gone, and the ocean splashed outside the great open hole, illuminated by the messdeck lights and a calcium flare from a lifebuoy burning in the tossing waters. In the after upper messdeck a group of about 20 men were clustered by a hammock netting. A number were terribly wounded. Men with grotesquely twisted limbs were lying there; it was like a scene from hell. ......

Back on the bridge I found the captain and the first lieutenant engaged in firing a rocket, a signal that we had been torpedoed. At almost that very moment a second torpedo hit us, this time in number 2 boiler room, a huge flash then water deluging downwards on us. It was obvious that the ship was doomed.

She started to settle in the water and the captain called out to "abandon ship!" Men were trapped in the Asdic compartment in the bottom of the ship and called up the voice pipe. I cannot bear to think of it. Others were trapped in the seamen's wash place, where a sliding steel door had jammed shut. If one thinks of war as a policy, also think for a moment what I heard that night and cannot bring myself to describe. ...... Strong men become little children crying for their mothers, not like John Wayne the motion picture hero.[8]

Able Seaman C.R. Skillen was at his action station at one of the destroyer's anti-aircraft guns when he was ordered forward to assist the wounded. As he recalls, he never got there:

As I stepped onto the first rung of the ladder to the upper deck, the second torpedo hit us amidships and split *Ottawa* in two. It hit directly below me, and when I came to, I was lying on the upper

HMCS *Ottawa*, September 1942.
HMCS *Ottawa*, a River Class destroyer, sets out on her last convoy. She was sunk with great loss of life on 13 September 1942. (Drawing by L.B. Jenson, who served as an officer on *Ottawa*, courtesy of the artist)

deck, aft of the stern-most funnel, with my legs, somehow pinned by the guard rail. I struggle to free myself, but to no avail, As I lay there, I knew that the bow of the ship had already sunk and that it was only a matter of time before the stern would follow suit. That is when the thought entered my mind that I was going to die.

However, I wasn't going to give up that easily. I said a little prayer to my Maker, asking him to forgive me, and then I gave it another try. My leg came free and I rolled myself into position and slipped into the cold waters of the North Atlantic.[9]

Lieutenant Jenson, also in the ocean hanging onto a spar, watched his ship sink and then,

Oil started spreading out from where the ship had been. It was all over my face, my head and hands. The smell filled the air and the taste was in my mouth. Gradually it lessened and the waves were now fresh and clean. Three or four Carley floats bobbed around hundreds of yards away. They were crowded with men, some of whom were sitting inside the floats, and the floats kept turning over. Each time there would be fewer men on the float.

Now to my astonishment the ships of the convoy passed through us – the huge ships' sides (how could they be so big?) and small people at the top calling down to us. One voice told us they dare not stop and I hoped they wouldn't because we would still be in the water when they were fished (torpedoed). ……

The night was getting darker, the waves were steeper, the breeze stronger and it seemed to be raining. The men on one of the rafts [floats] were singing. I recognized the cheerfully commanding voice of the gunner's mate, Petty Officer George Grivel, a splendid man. The songs were "Pack up Your Troubles," "It's a Long Way to Tipperary" and "There's a Long Long Trail Awinding to the Land of My Dreams." These were the hit songs of the First World War, sung by our fathers and uncles as they had faced death in the hideous mud and trenches of the Western Front.[10]

In Peril on the Sea – the loss of HMCS *Ottawa*.
On 13 September 1942 HMCS *Ottawa* was torpedoed by *U-91* while escorting Convoy ON-127. Many of her crew perished before the ship sank, while those who abandoned ship had to spend long hours in the water before being rescued. One of the findings of the board of inquiry was that if *Ottawa* had possessed modern Type 271 radar, she probably would have located her attacker before the U-boat fired. Unfortunately, it would be many months after her demise before the RCN began to receive such equipment. (Drawing by L.B. Jenson who served as an officer on HMCS *Ottawa,* courtesy of the artist)

Seaman Skillen, badly wounded, jumped off the sinking destroyer and remembered that,

When I surfaced, I could hear my shipmates yelling and moaning in the distance. I made my way towards the noise, but all the while I watched the stern of *Ottawa* slowly disappear beneath the surface. I was pretty certain that there would not be an explosion from the depth charges, since these had been rendered safe. Soon I came across a carley float, and this would be my lifeline for the next five hours. Although the seas became rougher as time passed and more and more of my shipmates succumbed, one by one, to the cold, slipping silently away, I clung to that float, knowing that one wrong move would spell the end. I wanted to sleep so bad, with the sea lulling me into a false sense of warmth, but I knew that if I shut my eyes, I would suffer the same fate as my shipmates. Therefore I hung on with grim determination.

The sea tossed the carley float about like an old inner tube. I think that there had been originally twenty-two of us clinging to it, but there was only about six of us left, when suddenly out of the dark loomed the outline of a ship. I soon recognized it as one of the escort group and they had found us![11]

The rescue vessel was the British corvette HMS Celandine, *and when Lieutenant Jenson was identified as an officer, he was directed to the wardroom where he encountered a shipmate from* Ottawa:,

Immediately I entered, Barriault, our leading steward, came over and said, as if nothing unusual had happened, "Good evening, sir. Would you like a cup of tea?"

So I replied, "Good evening, Barriault. That would be very nice, thank you," and had a cup of delicious, wonderful hot tea.[12]

Of the Ottawa's *crew of 213 officers and men, 69 survived.*

"The release we sought:" Shore leave

Seaman Frank Curry has left an excellent account of the importance of shore leave to the sailors on the North Atlantic run:

Sometimes, the release we sought was no more complicated than a soccer game. With our ship tied up for a few hours, and no shore leave, the crew got hold of a soccer ball and turned the jetty into a field, for the wildest game. It was no-holds barred soccer, with plenty of kicking and butting, as we released every pent-up feeling, battered each other into bruised submission, and finally climbed back aboard to collapse, exhausted yet restored. In some ports, we managed to gain access to a gymnasium, where we had a two-hour game of floor hockey, a game which must be the most savage sport ever invented, especially the way we played it. But the violent exercise did a lot to relieve the miseries buried deep within us. Others settled for a good meal, a haircut, a night in a hostel bed, a hot shower and a long walk in the English and Irish countryside – another effective way to restore the soul; to try and ready oneself for the return to sea. ……

Sometimes, the release came in a good old-fashioned brawl. Sailors clashed with each other or with civilians; shop windows were smashed; and patrols lugged bleeding and drunken sailors back to their ships, or to lock-up. …… Often,

through the long years of despair, our pent-up feelings found temporary release in man's oldest source of comfort – alcohol ……[13]

Enlisted men were not the only sailors who drank too much. Lieutenant Latham Jenson, RCN, never forgot the night he was ordered to accompany his captain and an infamous officer, "Two Gun" Ryan, on a run ashore:

My captain, "Do" Donald, found a kindred spirit in Two Gun Ryan and ordered me, as his sub-lieutenant, to go ashore with the pair of them, I suppose to bring them home. They conversed in what sounded like grunts, not that it interfered with their consumption. On one occasion when we went to a club, Donald said he was interested to find a glove in the urinal. As he was urinating, he was able to move the glove back and forth. Ryan, who was rather intoxicated, grunted from time to time in response to Donald's story. Then when we left the club, Donald discovered he only had one glove.[14]

"It tore me asunder:" Hard decision on Convoy SC 107, November 1942

In the autumn of 1942, Convoy SC 107 came under ferocious and concentrated submarine attack and lost 15 ships. Lieutenant Commander Louis Audette, RCNVR, commanding HMCS Amherst, *obtained a good asdic contact and moved into the attack, only to be faced with a dilemma:*

This was in the middle of the night – dead black of night – and I mean no lights of any kind. Then all of a sudden ahead of me I saw a lot of little flickering lights in the water. These were, of course, the little flashing lights on the shoulders of the survivors in the water. The submarine was about fifteen hundred yards ahead of me – so were the lights – the submarine was beneath the men. I don't think it was there deliberately, it just happened.

I was struck with the stunning realization that I was going in to attack and that I was going to kill these men or, at the best, maim them … and they were the very men we were trying to protect. And everybody on the bridge realized that at the same time as I, because the lookouts who were supposed to be looking out were looking in at me, obviously thinking, "What's the old blighter ever going to do?" and very glad that the decision was mine to make and not theirs. I wasn't quite as glad but I really had only minutes in which to make the decision.

Number One … asked me in sort of hushed tones, "Are you going to go ahead?" and I said, "Yes." Now I think it was the right decision. I know it was the right decision. I mean, I couldn't leave the submarine. I held him on asdic. …….. But don't think that's an easy decision to make – it would tear any man asunder, and I'm no stronger than the rest – it tore me asunder.

But those men were lucky; one of our guardian angels was out on special duty-watch that night. As I moved, my asdic broke down [and] then the solution was simple. I couldn't drop charges among those men by guess-work. That would have been a criminal thing to do, so I counter-manded the attack. ……

That night was really the nadir of my war experience.[15]

"A huge bubble rose from the surface:" ONS 154, December 1942

For most Canadian sailors on the North Atlantic run in 1942, the enemy remained unseen but there was always the knowledge that the U-boats were there, waiting. Seaman Rod Kendall of HMCS Napanee *spent the entire year on convoy duty in the North Atlantic and never saw his opponent until the night of 27 December 1942 when*

Towards midnight I stepped out on the wings of the bridge for a breath of fresh air. One of the merchantmen fired a star shell and there dead ahead was what I first took for one of our escorts. It turned out to be a sub on the surface, facing the convoy. The captain ordered full ahead to ram. Our 4-inch gun fired a start shell and I could see

Survivors, 1942.
HMCS *Trail* rescues survivors from the American troopship USS *Chatham*, torpedoed in the Gulf of St. Lawrence on 27 August 1942. This oil-covered man had been in a lifeboat for four days and was too weak to climb onto the corvette's deck. The medical facilities on escort vessels were limited and many Sick Berth Attendants were forced to carry out advanced surgical procedures on survivors. (Photo by Lieutenant A.W. Stevens, 31 August 1942, National Archives of Canada, PA 200327)

the sub going into a crash-dive. I ran back to the asdic set, but as the operator had good contact with the sub, I let him operate.

We dropped a full pattern of charges and opened to the customary 1,000 yards before turning back to run another attack. The ratings manning the depth charge throwers on the starboard side could see the disturbed water caused by the sub's crash-dive. That's how close we were.

According to routine, the leading torpedo operator dropped a calcium flare over the side with the last of the charges to mark the spot in the event we lost contact by asdic. It was the leading torpedo operator's job to keep his eyes on the flare and he told us later that after the charges had all gone off, a huge bubble rose from the surface. As we were ordered to maintain our station, we couldn't turn back to investigate. We heard later than an aircraft reported a damaged sub on the surface in our area.[16]

"Some called it sea-fatigue:" Exhaustion takes its toll

For Canadian sailors on the North Atlantic, 1942 was a grim and terrible year. The unrelenting struggle to preserve the sealanes, however, was beginning to exact a human price as Lieutenant Commander Alan Easton of the corvette HMCS Sackville, *who spent the entire year on the North Atlantic, remembered:*

Symptoms of jadedness – some called it sea-fatigue – were beginning to show on the surface. There were always fears, of course. But these fears could be held in check, could be stowed away in the recesses of the mind. Now, and more frequently, they were pushing to the fore. They were vivid pictures of the ship breaking up under stress of weather, of getting in among the ships of the convoy on dark, invisible nights, as had happened, and being run down by a heavily laden merchantman, of being torpedoed and trying to abandon ship on a rough night.

The worst time was dusk, when the dull day was fading and another ominous night was bearing down. I hated the sight of the yellowish-grey light, the dun seascape, the cold, curling waves as the evening dissolved into blackness.

There were times when I had been unjustifiably irritable, intolerant, which made me angry with myself afterwards – and probably angered others more. It was stupid, but there it was! Yet it was hard to tell how acutely I had been affected. I wondered how good my perspective was in judging my own nervous behaviour. I felt certain I had had enough.[17]

Seaman Frank Curry of HMCS Kamsack *felt that service on the North Atlantic was so awful that,*

I don't think anybody can really comprehend it, unless you have been through it. It's not just the one or two, or even sometimes three weeks of this kind of living, but it's that it went on and on and on and on. …… If you spent most of your time at sea, (as I happened to do) the overwhelming feeling was that it would never end! That was the terrible part of it; you thought this was a war that would never end. ……

The ones I feel sorry for were the ones that just didn't have quite enough strength. I don't mean they were weaker than me: I can still remember when I thought I just couldn't take it any longer. I just thought that way for a while, then toughed it through. However, I think there were others that just didn't get over that barrier as I had.[18]

We're not downhearted but we sure are hungry. Before the war, Britain depended on imported foodstuffs to feed her population. The U-boats threatened to cut off that supply, and although every piece of arable land was placed under cultivation, strict rationing was required to ensure that every civilian and member of the armed forces got enough to eat. The operative word is "enough." Civilians could eat unlimited amounts of bread, cereal and potatoes but all other foodstuffs were strictly controlled, and this photograph shows the *weekly ration* of an adult British civilian late in the war. From lower left: 55 grams (2 ounces) of coffee; 1 shilling, 2 penceworth of meat (about 3 small lamb chops and 4-5 thin slices of bacon as shown); 1,185 grams (42 ounces or 5 small glasses) of milk; 225 grams (8 ounces) of sugar; 225 grams (8 ounces) of fat (butter, margarine or lard); 85 grams (3 ounces) of cheese; slightly more than half an egg; and in the centre, 115 grams (4 ounces) of jam or honey. British doctors reported that obesity disappeared as a medical problem, which is not at all surprising. (Photograph by Dianne Graves)

CHAPTER 6

"THE BATTLE OF THE ATLANTIC IS GETTING HARDER:"

VICTORY IN MID-OCEAN, DECEMBER 1942–MAY 1943

"Keep the hell out of it:" Tempers flare in Ottawa

THE tactful language in which Churchill phrased his message did not lessen its impact when it reached Ottawa. Having spent more than three years trying to respond to every British request for assistance, often to its own detriment, the RCN was now being asked to leave the main theatre of operations because the Royal Navy did not regard it as an effective fighting force. Some officers at NSHQ felt that the British were overlooking the fact that the Canadian navy, poorly equipped to do so, had only undertaken mid-ocean escort work in 1941 at the request of the Admiralty and had largely been stuck with escorting the slow convoys – the most vulnerable convoys which usually suffered the highest losses. But these same officers were ignoring the fact that prescient observers such as Murray had, for more than a year, been pointing out the difficulties faced by the escort groups, with little helpful response from either the Admiralty or NSHQ. Ottawa bore a large share of the responsibility for the situation it now found itself in because its insistence on the un-

bridled expansion of the navy had created deficiencies in training, equipment and, ultimately, performance. The snowball of expansion had now landed on Admiral Percy Nelles's desk – and he was not at all happy about it. Captain Eric Brand, RN, the British officer posted to Ottawa, remembered what happened when he entered Nelles's office with an offer to help by using personal contacts at the Admiralty and was abruptly told to "keep the hell out of it."[1]

One of Nelles's subordinates took a more balanced view. When the Chief of the Naval Staff learned that Horton's chief of staff, Commodore J.M. Mansfield, was coming to North America to explain the reasons for the change, he sent one of his senior staff officers, Commander Harry De Wolf, RCN, to attend a joint Allied conference on the trans-Atlantic convoys held in Washington in the last days of December 1942. De Wolf pointed out to the American and British officers present that the root of the RCN's problems was that, for two years, it had made every effort to meet continuous requests from Britain and the United States for more escorts in the North Atlantic, under the premise that "any ship is better than none."[2] He also told them firmly that a decision to remove the C-Groups from the mid-Atlantic would have to be approved by the Canadian government, whose view was that the RCN had "sort of grown up with this North Atlantic problem and feel we have a permanent interest in it." De

(Facing page) **The most constant enemy.**
In the North Atlantic, warship decks were hazardous in anything but a calm sea. In this fine photograph by G.A. Milne, taken on the frigate HMCS *Matane,* in January 1944, a sailor checks the depth charges in his ship's stern racks. The sea is rough but it could be a lot worse. (National Archives of Canada, PA 134326)

Wolf was actually laying the groundwork for a goal long favoured by the RCN – the removal of the complicated command structure in the western Atlantic which placed it under nominal American control. It was time for Canada to secure control of its own waters.

When De Wolf returned to Ottawa, the question of the removal of the C-Groups was still under discussion but any possible Canadian grounds for opposing the transfer were demolished by the sad tale of Convoy ONS 154.

"The sea was dotted with lights:" Convoy ONS 154, December 1942

On 19 December 1942, Escort Group C-1 sailed from Londonderry to pick up ONS 154 coming out of Britain with 45 merchantmen. Consisting of the destroyer *St. Laurent* (Senior Officer) and the corvettes *Battleford*, *Chilliwack*, *Kenogami*, *Napanee* and *Shediac*, half of which were veterans of the MOEF, C-1 was relatively well equipped for a Canadian group. *St. Laurent* had HF/DF and Type 271 radar, while the five corvettes had been fitted with Type 271 just prior to sailing. The Senior Officer, Lieutenant Commander Guy Windeyer, RCN, a former British officer who had joined the Canadian navy at the outbreak of war, was new to the group, however, and had only served as Senior Officer for one convoy. Although Windeyer had planned a group exercise at Londonderry, it was cancelled because of bad weather and there was no time for further training, particularly on the new radar sets, before C-1 sailed. Another problem was that the group's second destroyer, HMS *Burwell*, was forced by mechanical defects to remain behind in Londonderry.

Unfortunately for ONS 154, it was routed south toward the Azores to give it some respite from the stormy winter weather. This not only meant that it had to transit the "air gap" at its broadest point; it also brought the convoy within reach of two U-boat packs with 20 submarines in total. On Boxing Day 1942, *Gruppe Spitz* sighted the ONS 154 and Dönitz guided all available submarines to intercept positions. The first attacks came that night – three merchant ships were sunk and a fourth left drifting and abandoned – but Windeyer did achieve an early success. At 0330 on 27 December, *St. Laurent* sighted the surfaced *U-356*, a Type VII boat com-

Liberty ship *Mark Twain*.
The Liberty ships were one of the Allies' war-winning assets. Designed for quick production using pre-fabricated sections that were transported to construction sites by railway, 2,751 were produced in American shipyards between 1941 and 1945 and more than balanced the heavy wartime losses in merchant tonnage. The cargo capacity of a Liberty ship was 9,140 tons dead weight, equivalent to 300 railway freight cars – one ship could carry 2,840 jeeps or 440 light tanks or 230 million rounds of small-arms ammunition or 3,440,000 daily rations. (National Archives of the United States, NA 80 G84-360)

manded by *Oberleutnant zur See* Günther Ruppelt, and raked it with 20mm Oerlikon fire which drove it down and then delivered a shallow pattern depth charge attack on the surface swirl where the boat had dived. Ten detonations followed, and then an eleventh which was louder, and a large oil slick appeared. *U-356* was no more although its destruction by the RCN was not confirmed until well after the war.

About three hours later *St. Laurent* sighted another surfaced enemy and drove it off with gun fire. After that, there was a near respite for about 30 hours as many of the U-boats lost contact but HF/DF operators in the convoy picked up multiple radio signals and it was clear that the Germans were massing for a major attack. One submarine, *U-225*, did manage to maintain contact and torpedoed the tanker *Scottish Heather* as she was refuelling *Chilliwack* astern of the convoy. Fortunately for the tanker, her cargo did not ignite and, although damaged, she was able to make for a British port. *Chilliwack*, with less than a full load of fuel, returned to her escort tasks and, early on the morning of 28 December, drove a surfaced sub down with gun fire before launching a depth charge attack that produced no results.

As the day wore on, 12 submarines manoeuvred into position and in the early evening the onslaught began. At 1920, *Battleford* gained a distant radar contact and while steaming away from the convoy towards it, sighted no less than four submarines on the surface moving in line abreast, about a mile apart, in the direction of ONS 154. The two nearest boats dived but *Battleford* was able to engage the more distant vessels with her 4-inch gun. Unfortunately, the blast from this weapon knocked out her 271 radar and *Battleford* lost contact

Behind the battle – Plot Room, Naval Service Headquarters, Ottawa.
This photograph, taken on 29 November 1943, shows the Plot Room at NSHQ in Ottawa. On both sides, the Battle of the Atlantic was controlled by headquarters and intelligence from all sources – agents, radio direction finding, prisoner of war interrogations and decoding – was funnelled to Operational Intelligence Centres in London, Ottawa and Washington and then transmitted to the relevant commands. The Plot Room kept track of all friendly and enemy ship movements so that staffs could follow the course of operations. (National Archives of Canada, PA 134337)

in the dark. Even worse, when she tried to regain the convoy, her captain could not find it because Windeyer had not informed him of an important course change. *Battleford* searched all night but only rejoined the next morning.

This was unfortunate because ONS 154 was definitely in harm's way and every escort was needed. Admiral Sir Max Horton, following events from his headquarters in Liverpool, realized this and ordered two British destroyers to proceed at high speed to reinforce the escort. Meanwhile, in the late afternoon of 29 December Windeyer made an attempt to balance the odds. HMS *Fidelity*, the special service ship attached to the convoy,

possessed two float planes and tried to launch one to drive away the surfaced submarines following in the convoy's wake. The sea was so rough that it crashed although, happily, the aircrew were rescued by *St. Laurent*. As darkness fell, it was clear to every sailor on every ship in ONS 154, naval or merchant, that the coming night was going to be a terrible one.

At 2005, a mass attack was launched seemingly from all directions – in the space of less than four hours, nine merchant ships were sunk, including that of the convoy commodore. The escorts fought back gamely but were unable to prevent the slaughter – three of the corvettes sighted and attacked U-boats and at one point *St. Laurent* came close enough to ram a surfaced submarine but Windeyer could not risk damaging the only destroyer in C-1 Group and sheered away at the last moment. The darkness was lit up by the fires of burning wrecks and the continuous firing of illuminating shells – the commanding officer of HMCS *Napanee*, Lieutenant Stuart Henderson, RCNR, later remembered the scene:

> All ships appeared to be firing snowflake [illuminating shells], and tracers crisscrossed in all directions, escorts firing starshells. The sea was dotted with lights from boats and rafts, and two burning wrecks which had hauled to starboard helped the illumination.[3]

The attacks ceased around midnight, bringing a welcome lull.

During the daylight hours of 30 December the enemy finished off the damaged survivors which had fallen behind. Sadly, they also sank *Fidelity*, which was astern of the convoy and she went down with the loss of 334 crew members and survivors. That afternoon, HM Ships *Meteor* and *Milne*, the destroyers sent by Horton, arrived and managed to drive off three submarines shadowing the convoy. However, their fuel state was such that, after a quiet night, they had to be detached to the Azores, along with *Shediac* and *Battleford*, to refuel as C-1 had lost its tanker when *Scottish Heather* had been hit. This reduced the escort to only four vessels (*St. Laurent, Chilliwack, Kenogami* and *Napanee*).

By this time, Windeyer was verging on physical and nervous collapse. He fully expected that the coming night would witness "the final carving" of ONS 154 and advised the captains of the fast steamers, *Adrastus* and *Calgary*, who were carrying many civilian passengers, to use their own judgement about whether or not to stay with the convoy.[4] Both opted to continue with ONS 154 and the night of 30 December was fortunately a quiet one with no attacks. The following day, the destroyer HMS *Fame* arrived and her captain, who was senior to Windeyer, assumed command. This was a good thing as by now Windeyer, "seeing torpedoes at every turn," was in such a state that he had to be sedated by *St. Laurent*'s medical officer.[5] The battle for ONS 154 ended that day when the U-boats broke contact.

"Another real good turn you have done us:" The RCN leaves the mid-Atlantic

There was no doubt that ONS 154, which had lost 14 of its 45 ships, was a catastrophe and it was also clear there had been a failure in the leadership of the convoy escort. The debacle destroyed any opposition that NSHQ could put up against the transfer of the C-Groups and it was now simply a question of arranging the details. This was done when Horton's representative, Mansfield, arrived in Ottawa on 2 January 1943 and, after discussion, it was agreed that the four C-Groups would leave the mid-Atlantic for a period of four months. During that time they would undergo intensive training and have their equipment upgraded before joining the Britain-Gibraltar convoy route, which, compared to the North Atlantic in winter, would seem almost like a tropical cruise. The Canadian Cabinet War Committee agreed to the transfer on 6 January, subject to three conditions: the four groups would be returned to the MOEF not later than May 1943; the RN was to continue its commitment in terms of ships to the Western Local Escort Force; and the Canadian corvettes detached for Operation TORCH were to be returned as soon as possible.

In communicating these conditions to Admiral Sir Dudley Pound, his British opposite number, Nelles stressed the importance of the North Atlantic for Canada and its navy:

> It has been our policy to build up Canadian escort forces for the specific purpose of protecting North Atlantic trade convoys in addition to our coastal communications. Public interest in the Canadian Navy is centred on the part it has taken in this task, which is without question one of the highest and enduring priority upon which the outcome of

(Facing page) **Depth charge attack.**
A depth charge barrage dropped from the stern racks of a Canadian frigate detonates in this photograph by G.A. Lawrence taken in January 1944. Depth charges, either dropped astern or launched sideways, interfered with the operation of the ASDIC and often caused loss of contact with a U-boat. The answer to the problem was ahead-throwing weapons such as Hedgehog and Squid, but these did not enter Canadian service until 1943. (National Archives of Canada, PA 133246)

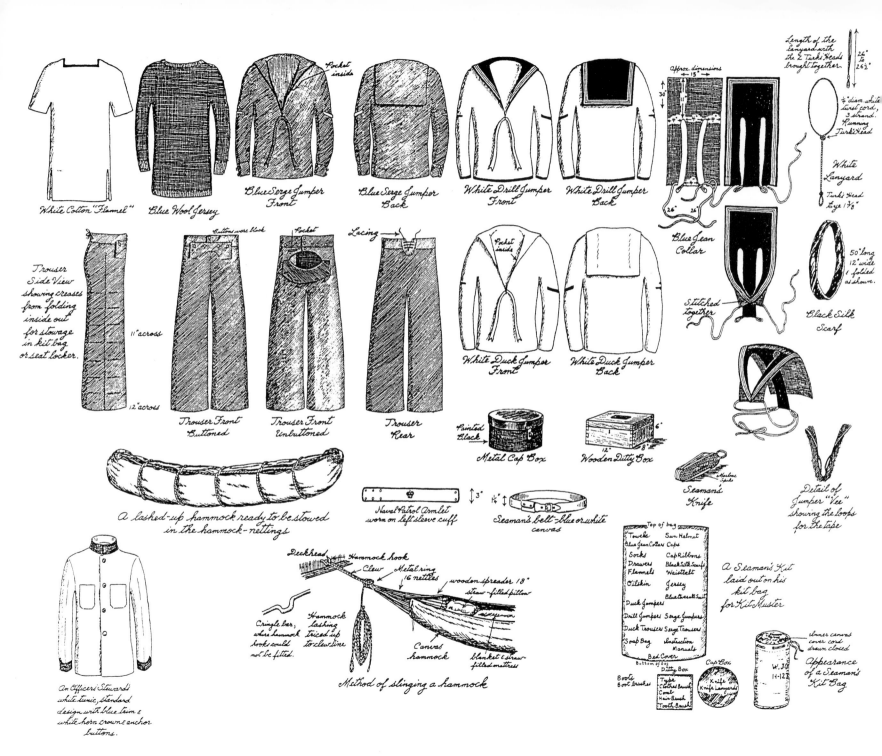

White Cotton "Flannel"

Blue Wool Jersey

Blue Serge Jumper Front

Blue Serge Jumper Back

White Drill Jumper Front

White Drill Jumper Back

Pocket inside

Length of the Lanyard with the 2 Turks Heads brought together. 26" to 26½"

¼" diam. white twist cord, 3 strand Running Turks Head

White Lanyard

Turks Head Eye 1⅜"

Approx. dimensions 15"

30"

26" 26"

Blue Jean Collar

Stitched together

50" long 12" wide & folded as shown.

Black Silk Scarf

Trouser Side View showing creases from folding inside out for stowage in kit bag or seat locker.

11" across

12" across

Buttons were black

Trouser Front Buttoned

Pocket

Trouser Front Unbuttoned

Lacing

Trouser Rear

Pocket inside

White Duck Jumper Front

White Duck Jumper Back

Seaman's Knife

Marline Spike

Detail of Jumper "Vee" showing the loops for the tape

A lashed-up hammock ready to be stowed in the hammock-nettings

Metal Cap Box

Painted Black

Wooden Ditty Box

6"

12" 9"

Naval Patrol Armlet worn on left sleeve cuff

3"

¾"

Seaman's belt - blue or white canvas

An Officers Steward's white tunic, standard design with blue trim & white horn crowns anchor buttons.

Deckhead

Hammock hook

Clew

Metal ring

16 nettles

wooden spreader 18"

straw-filled pillow

Cringle bar, where hammock hooks could not be fitted.

Hammock lashing triced up to clewline

Canvas hammock

blanket & straw filled mattress

Method of slinging a hammock

Top of bag

Towels	Sun Helmet
Blue Jean Collars	Caps
Socks	Cap Ribbons
Drawers	Black Silk Scarfs
Flannels	Waistbelt
Oilskin	Jersey
	Blue Overall Suit
Duck Jumpers	
Drill Jumpers	Serge Jumpers
Duck Trousers	Serge Trousers
Soap Bag	Instruction Manuals
	Bed Cover

Bottom of bag

A Seaman's Kit laid out on his kit bag for Kit Muster

inner canvas cover cord drawn closed

W. JO 14-123

Appearance of a Seaman's Kit Bag

Ditty Box

Boots Boot Brushes

Type Clothes Brush Comb Hair Brush Tooth Brush

Cap Box

Knife Knife Lanyards

the war depends. We are satisfied that the Canadian Navy can serve no higher purpose than to continue to share this task, which we have come to look upon as the natural responsibility for Canada.[6]

There was a certain amount of relief in Britain when this message was received. Senior officers at the Admiralty were aware that Horton had placed them in a very awkward situation with a nation that had done its utmost, despite very inadequate means, to support Britain since the outbreak of the war. Attempting to smooth ruffled feathers, Winston Churchill sent a personal message of thanks to Mackenzie King which concluded with the phrase: "This is another real good turn you have done us."[7]

More to the point, a previous Canadian request for the transfer of modern destroyers from the RN to the RCN, which had been delayed pending the decision on the removal of the C-Groups, was approved and the RCN could look forward to getting a badly-needed increase in destroyer strength in the coming months. In saying farewell to the C-Groups, the Admiralty did acknowledge their contribution in its *Monthly Anti-Submarine Report* for January 1943 by stating that the Canadians had carried "the brunt of the of the U-boat attack in the North Atlantic for the last six months, that is to say, of about half of the German U-boats operating at sea."[8] However the *Report* also warned that "the critical phase of the U-boat war in the Atlantic cannot be long postponed."

Winter battle in the Atlantic, January–February 1943

At the beginning of 1943, Allied naval planners compiled the statistics for the preceding year – 5,471,222 tons or 70 per cent of global Allied shipping losses – had been lost in the North Atlantic. Still worse, of the 1,050 naval escorts estimated to be necessary to successfully defend the Atlantic lifeline, only 445 were available and a quarter of those were obsolescent vessels dating back to the First World War.

There was, nevertheless, guarded reason for optimism. Shipbuilding capacity had expanded tremendously in the previous year, meaning that the loss of much of the merchant tonnage would soon be replaced, while hundreds of new escort vessels were being built in Britain and North America. The other encouraging feature was that new weapons and equipment had passed the prototype stage and would soon be reaching the frontline forces. An airborne version of centimetric radar, accurate enough to pick up the periscope of a submerged submarine at a distance, was now being fitted into aircraft. The USN was building escort carriers, small aircraft carriers that could accompany convoys and provide air cover throughout their passage and, until these entered service in large numbers, Britain had converted a half dozen merchantmen into temporary aircraft carriers that could fly off four aircraft. The lengthy argument over the deployment of VLR aircraft having finally been won, these were on the way, as were new weapons such as Squid and Hedgehog. Finally, the designs of three advanced types of escorts – an improved corvette, the Castle Class, and the River and Loch Class frigates – had been approved and they would soon be entering service. Until that time, however, the war in the North Atlantic would have to be waged with the forces, ships and equipment on hand.

But the enemy was also gathering his strength. On 30 January 1943, Dönitz was named the commander-in-chief of the *Kriegsmarine* and from this point until the end of the war, the *U-Boot-Waffe* would have priority in the German naval war effort. By this time, Germany's construction programme was in full flow and in January 1943 Dönitz had enough strength to keep nearly 200 boats at sea and more than 100 in the North Atlantic alone. His crews also received new equipment, including a radar detector which warned them of Allied detection attempts and a new torpedo that could be preset to change its course after running a certain distance and was therefore almost certain to score a kill among the crowded columns of large convoys. An even more deadly weapon – an acoustic torpedo that could home in on the noise of a ship's propellers – was in the final stages

(Facing page) **Pusser Rig – Dress Uniform.**
This detailed drawing depicts the elements of the traditional RN naval uniform adapted by the RCN. Sailors took great pride in their appearance when going ashore in this distinctive dress and spent much time keeping their kit in order. Also shown are details of the hammock used on Canadian warships – it was surprisingly comfortable and had the added advantage of being easy to stow when not in use, creating more space on the messdecks. (Drawing by L.B. Jenson, courtesy of the artist)

of development. Perhaps the U-boat service's greatest asset in the next phase of the struggle was that Allied codebreakers were still unable to crack the *Kriegsmarine* cyphers introduced in early 1942. Some success had been achieved but it was not consistent, and in the meantime the German *B-dienst* was still able to read much of the Allied signal traffic.

These German assets, however, were not evident during January 1943 when fierce winter gales hampered Dönitz's efforts to concentrate against a major convoy. Only 15 ships were lost in the Atlantic that month and seven of those came from one convoy, TM 1, whose route had been discovered by the *B-dienst* in time for Dönitz to lay an ambush across its path from Trinidad to Gibraltar. Losses continued low in February with 34 ships being sunk but almost all of these were in just two convoys: SC 118 and ONS 166.

Convoy SC 118 of 63 merchantmen was escorted by the British B-1 Group, heavily reinforced to a total of five destroyers, four corvettes and two US coast guard cutters. This was nearly twice the number of warships available for the slow convoys the RCN had escorted in 1942 and, from this strength and the fact that British ships were better equipped than their Canadian counterparts, it was reasonable to expect that SC 118 would suffer fewer losses. This, however, did not turn out to be the case. The convoy left Halifax at the end of January and Dönitz, fore-warned of its existence and route, was able to intercept it on 4 February. Over a period of four days, his U-boats sank 11 ships for the loss of two submarines. These losses prompted Horton to formalize an idea that had

Air power – the deciding factor.
A VLR (Very Long Range) Liberator GR V of the RAF's Coastal Command patrols above a convoy in 1943. The introduction of aircraft, either long-range or carrier-based, into the mid-Atlantic in the spring of 1943 proved to be the decisive factor in winning the battle. Nearly 58 per cent of all Axis submarines destroyed during the Second World War were sunk by aircraft. (National Archives of Canada, PA 107907)

been suggested before – the use of support groups (what the USN called "hunter killer" groups) that could reinforce the escorts of any heavily threatened convoy – and, by taking vessels from British local escort forces and the RN's Home Fleet, five such support groups were formed. Another important decision made after SC 118 was to increase the allotment of VLR aircraft to close the air gap.

These measures were not available for Convoy ONS 166, which was escorted by A-3 group in late February. Consisting of two American coast-guard cutters, two British corvettes and four Canadian corvettes (*Chilliwack, Dauphin, Rosthern* and *Trillium*), A-3 fought a six-day battle against 18 submarines only to lose 14 of 49 merchantmen under its protection. These losses were offset by the destruction of one submarine by ramming but it was clear that MOEF escorts, whatever their nationality, were having problems handling the large numbers of U-boats now operating in the Atlantic. Ironically, British escorts newly assigned to the MOEF were complaining about the weather, short rest periods and lack of numbers – all conditions familiar to the RCN for nearly two years. At the end of February 1943 the situation was such that Horton decided to return the four Canadian C-Groups to the North Atlantic earlier than planned as it was clear that the crisis of the Battle of the Atlantic was fast approaching.

The Northwest Atlantic: Canada's own theatre of war

While the now predominantly British MOEF suffered from the blows of the U-boats, the four Canadian C-Groups experienced a relatively peaceful time. One after another, each group went to Londonderry where, following a long leave for its crews, new equipment was fitted and a period of intensive training, lasting from ten days to two weeks, was undertaken. As a group finished this programme, it was assigned to a Gibraltar convoy which, since these convoys were more heavily escorted and covered by aircraft throughout almost the entire length of their voyage, were far different from their North Atlantic counterparts. While on this duty, the destroyer *St. Croix* sank her second submarine and the corvette *Prescott* got her first. Added to the three German or Italian submarines sunk by the Canadian corvettes assigned to Operation TORCH, this made a respectable total of five submarines killed by the RCN in southern waters in three months. As the C-Groups were enjoying this respite, however, important decisions were taking place on land and at sea.

The first of these had been prompted by the Casablanca Conference of January 1943 at which Churchill and Roosevelt had plotted long-term strategy against Germany. A successful invasion of the European mainland

An unrelenting enemy – U-boat crews.
The crew of *U-190* attends the commissioning ceremony of *U-3021*, a Type XXI boat, at Bremerhaven in January 1945. The *U-Boot-Waffe* or submarine service was the most effective part of the *Kriegsmarine* and represented the most deadly threat to the western Allies. It also suffered very heavy casualties – an estimated 29,000 men of approximately 40,000 who served in U-boats were killed, but their morale, although it sometimes faltered, never broke and U-boat crews were as relentless in 1945 as they had been in 1939. (Courtesy, Werner Hirschmann)

first required a massive build-up of American forces in Britain, but before that could take place, the security of the trans-Atlantic shipping lanes had to be established. One of the problems in the previous 18 months had been the overlapping commands in the Atlantic, a complicated structure that had led to the ultimate irony that much of the RCN was nominally under American control. Britain wanted the appointment of a super commander-in-chief for this vital theatre and, not unnaturally, the Admiralty was pressing for this to be a British officer. Admiral Ernest King, the commander-in-chief of the USN, would have nothing to do with this proposal but did agree that command matters had to be simplified.

Toward this end, he called a conference in Washington in early March 1943 aimed at thrashing out issues relating to the convoy system. Amazingly enough, given the national aspirations and egos involved, it went fairly smoothly and the result was to give the three navies in the Atlantic

ANTI-SUBMARINE WEAPONS

During the Second World War, Canadian escort vessels deployed three major types of weapons against submerged targets: depth charges, Hedgehog and Squid.

Depth charges

These were basically steel drums packed with explosives that detonated at a pre-set depth by means of a hydrostatic pistol, and they were dropped off the stern or fired off the sides of an escort vessel as it passed over a submerged enemy. The standard MK VII charge, used by the RCN throughout the war, contained 300 lbs. of Amatol, Minol or TNT and there were two major types: heavy charges sank at a rate of 16 feet per second while light charges descended at 10 feet per second. To make a depth charge "heavy" or "light," weights were added or removed from the MK VII weapon. In 1939 depth charges had a maximum setting of 150 feet depth but this was constantly increased until by 1943 they could be set for depths in excess of 700 feet. Despite their large explosive load, individual depth charges were not that lethal to a U-boat as their destructive radius was only about 7 yards. As a result, they were usually dropped in numbers, in "barrages," but even so it was calculated that depth charges would only destroy a submarine about 6 per cent of the times they were used.

There were other problems with depth charges. They had to be dropped while the attacking ship was over the target and this often resulted in the surface vessel losing ASDIC contact due to the noise of its propellers passing over the target, or the explosion of the charges. In addition, they had to be launched at fairly high speed, otherwise the attacking vessel would not clear the area in time and might suffer damage from the explosion – and unfortunately ASDIC did not perform well at high speeds. The drawings on the opposite page illustrate the difficulty with depth charges. In A, a frigate has acquired a U-boat using ASDIC pulses generated by the dome on the bottom of its hull, but when it closes in to attack, as shown in B, the turbulence from its own propellers and the explosion of the depth charge makes maintaining ASDIC contact difficult. By trial and error, it was worked out that two ships were needed to make the best use of depth charges – one holding the target in ASDIC contact and directing the second ship which made the actual attack. Although ASDIC contact was still broken at the moment of the attack, it was more easily re-acquired by this method. Later in the war, improved ASDIC sets were introduced which permitted escort vessels to maintain contact with their targets during an attack.

Hedgehog and Squid

The weakness of depth charges – that they often caused loss of ASDIC contact when used – led to the development of Hedgehog and Squid. Both were "ahead throwing" weapons, which meant, as shown in Drawing C opposite, that an attacking warship which had a good contact could fire them up to 1,000 yards ahead of its position and they would detonate before the ship passed over the target, allowing the attacker to either maintain or quickly re-acquire ASDIC contact.

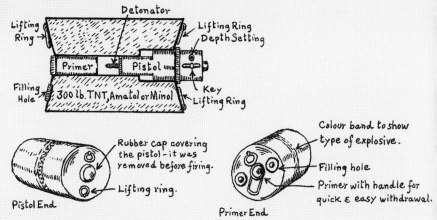

First conceived in 1940, Hedgehog did not come into widespread operational service until mid-1943. Hedgehog was basically a spigot mortar capable of firing up to 24 projectiles, each containing 35 lbs. of Torpex explosive, 200-300 yards ahead of the attacking ship. These projectiles landed in an oval pattern about 120 by 140 feet and then descended onto the target but did not explode unless they actually struck, with the result that there were fewer explosions to interfere with ASDIC contact. Hedgehog projectiles were good to a depth of about 1,300 feet, which made them effective against the deep-diving U-boats of the later war years. Hedgehog did have one disadvantage – it could only be fired directly ahead of the attacking ship, which had to be pointing in the direction of the target. Nonetheless, it was much superior to the depth charge. By 1944 almost all Canadian warships were equipped with Hedgehog and the weapon was often connected with improved types of ASDIC that could provide targeting information.

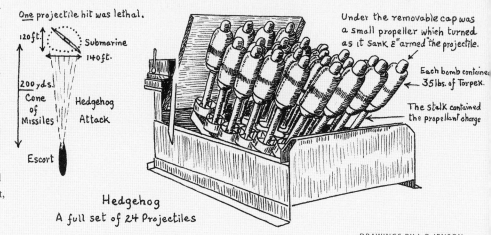

Hedgehog
A full set of 24 Projectiles

DRAWINGS BY L.B JENSON

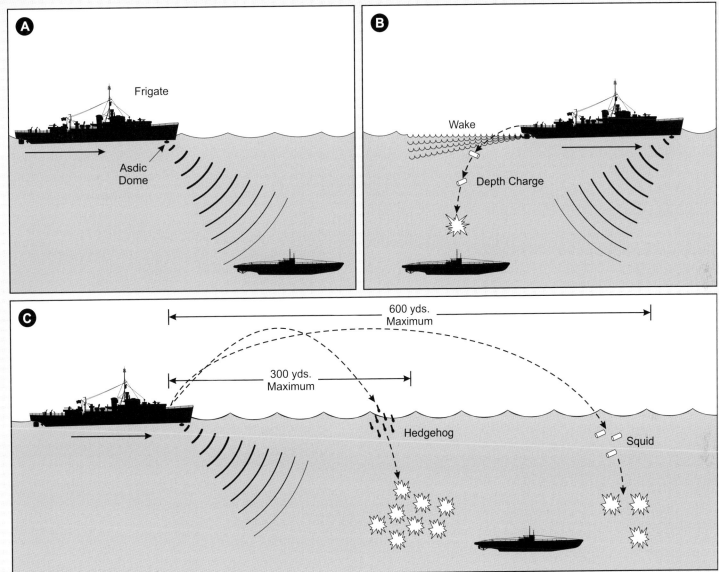

A

Frigate

Asdic
Dome

B

Wake

Depth Charge

C

600 yds.
Maximum

300 yds.
Maximum

Hedgehog

Squid

DRAWINGS BY CHRISTOPHER JOHNSON

Introduced in September 1943, Squid consisted of a three-barrelled mortar that could fire three projectiles at the same time out to a range of about 600 yards. Each projectile contained 200 lbs. of explosive and detonated at the desired depth by means of a hydrostatic pistol. One of the great advantages of Squid was that its mounting permitted it to be traversed to fire in directions other than straight ahead. This weapon was particularly effective when mated with the Type 147B ASDIC with the Q attachment, which entered service in October 1943 and permitted contact to be kept with a deeply-submerged U-boat and the target's depth to be accurately ascertained. Once this was done, the Squid projectiles were automatically set for the proper depth. In the RCN, only the Loch Class frigates were armed with Squid. ■

their own distinct spheres of operations. Britain would assume responsibility for the North Atlantic from a point just east of Newfoundland to British waters, including the MOEF. The United States would assume control of all convoys crossing the Atlantic farther south from American ports to the Mediterranean and Britain. Canada, meanwhile, would assume control of the northwestern Atlantic giving the RCN control over operations in its coastal waters from a point just south of Nova Scotia east to the limit of the British mandate. These changes were implemented almost immediately, and on 30 April 1943 Rear-Admiral Leonard Murray was appointed Commander-in-Chief, Canadian Northwest Atlantic, with complete authority over all Allied naval and air forces operating in his area. Murray would be the only Canadian to command a major theatre of war between 1939 and 1945.

"Ship disintegrated completely in flames:" The scales begin to tip, March–April 1943

While these decisions were being made, the battle moved to its climax. During March 1943, the Allies suffered the worst shipping losses, 108 vessels of 627,377 tons, since the previous November with one convoy alone, SC 121, losing 13 ships to a mass attack by 17 U-boats. The heaviest actions occurred when 38 U-boats, the largest concentration Dönitz had yet achieved, attacked Convoy SC 122 at the very time it was being overtaken by a fast convoy, HX 228. The battle began on 16 March and lasted four desperate days. By the time it was over, despite the appearance of VLR aircraft for the first time in the mid-Atlantic area, 21 merchantmen had been lost, with another 10 heavily damaged, for the loss of one U-boat. The fury of these March battles is captured in the report of *Kapitänleutnant* Hans Trojer of *U-121*, describing his attack on Convoy HX 228:

In a snow squall came up at right angles to course of the enemy, surfaced as soon as latter emerged from the snow squall ...... fired two torpedoes at two large, overlapping merchant ships. First torpedo hit. Ship disintegrated completely in flames and a vast cloud of smoke.

"Pass the mustard."
Corvette sailors enjoying a meal, obviously in calm weather. Note the wide variety of clothing – at sea escort sailors were usually permitted to wear whatever they wanted and hockey sweaters were big favourites. A civilian who crossed the North Atlantic on a corvette in 1943 described the food as "solid and heavy." It had to be, considering the nature of the work done by men like these happy munchers. (Canadian Naval Memorial Trust)

Cod for dinner.
Depending on how you look at it, one of the unfortunate or fortunate results of depth charge attacks was that they killed hundreds of fish. Since there was no sense wasting the sea's bounty, this man from the corvette *Sorel* is collecting fresh Atlantic cod for dinner. (Canadian Naval Memorial Trust)

Hundreds of steel plates flew like sheets of paper through the air. A great deal of ammunition exploded.

Shortly afterwards scored another hit on a freighter, which also exploded. From bows to bridge the ship was under water. Heavy debris crashed against my periscope, which now became difficult to turn. ……

Then I myself heard the noise of the destroyer's propellers where I stood in the conning tower and at once gave the order: "Dive! – full ahead! Both!" Depth charges, two patterns of four, were already falling, and pretty close to us. The conning tower hatch started to leak, and a mass of water came down into the boat. The boat plunged and jumped, but she gained depth steadily.[9]

By the end of the third week in March, Dönitz's commanders had sunk 87 merchant ships totalling more than half a million tons and the U-boats seemed on the verge of cutting off Britain's lifeline.

It was at this moment that the battle turned in the Allies' favour. The codebreakers at Bletchley Park were now able to read more of the *Kriegsmarine*'s improved cyphers at shorter intervals and convoys could be routed away from enemy concentrations, or at least be warned about them. More important was the appearance of the first escort carrier, USS *Bogue*, in the mid-Atlantic and *Bogue* was followed by two British counterparts. For the first time, some convoys had continuous air cover throughout their passage and aircraft flying from them could be sent to check out radar and HF/DF contacts at a distance, sparing the escorts and forcing the U-boats to submerge far from their targets, which made it difficult for them to make contact with their slow underwater speed. Although Dönitz had 120 U-boats available for service in the North Atlantic in April 1943, the escort carriers tipped the balance and, during the first week of that month, the *Bogue* beat off a concentrated attack by 40 submarines against convoy HX 230 with the loss of only one merchantman. In three convoy battles later in the month, three submarines were sunk for the loss of only four merchantmen, a bad rate of exchange for Dönitz. Not surprisingly, the statistics for April showed a marked improvement – the Allies lost 56 ships totalling 327,943 tons but sank 15 U-boats, about 10 per cent of Dönitz's operational strength.

"As if a steel gauntlet had relaxed its grip:" Victory, May 1943

In the end, the crisis point of this seemingly unending struggle was the battle for ONS 5, which departed Britain in the last week of April with 42 merchantmen escorted by eight British warships. The convoy was sighted by a German patrol line and Dönitz attempted to bring no less than 41 submarines, about a third of his strength in the North Atlantic, against it. The shadowers briefly lost contact when the convoy encountered bad weather in the first few days of May, but on 4 May 11 U-boats attacked ONS 5, which itself had been somewhat scattered by gales. During that day two RCAF flying boats from Newfoundland arrived and, while searching ahead of the convoy, managed to sink *U-630*. That night, the Germans

Warm clothing was usually necessary.
A view of the signal bridge of the corvette HMCS *Sorel* while acting as supervising ship for warships in the Pictou Strait, Nova Scotia, in the summer of 1943. Even in sheltered waters in summertime, sea duty could be cold, and warm clothing was a necessity. During work-ups, proper rig was always worn – things changed on escort duty. (Canadian Naval Memorial Trust)

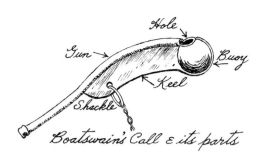

Boatswain's Call & its parts

Holding the boatswain's call

Bosun's call.
The traditional method of communicating orders in a British or Dominion warship was by means of the "bosun's call" or "bosun's whistle," a small whistle held in the palm of the hand by which the frequency of the sound was modulated by opening or closing the fist. Normally, the call was followed by a spoken instruction but some the most important calls ("Pipe down" and "Hands to dinner") were not. When a flag officer or captain came aboard or went ashore, he was "piped" by a single, long note. (Drawing by L.B. Jenson, courtesy of the artist).

closed in and sank five merchantmen, but with dawn on 5 May came a VLR aircraft from Iceland operating at extreme range. It managed to stay with ONS 5 for much of the day although four more ships were lost in return for one enemy submarine.

During the night of 5 May, the convoy was subjected to two dozen separate attacks but the escort, now down to six ships because of the need to detach vessels to refuel, fought back hard and sank four U-boats, one of the kills being made by the destroyer HMS *Vidette*, which was equipped with Hedgehog. Continuous RCAF air patrols arrived on 6 May, as did an RCN group from the WLEF, and Dönitz was forced to call off the attack. The U-boats had sunk 12 ships but had lost 7 of their own (including 3 by aircraft) with 5 boats being badly damaged – more bad news for Dönitz.

The German commander, however, was not a man to be beaten easily. Although Allied codebreakers could read enough of the *Kriegsmarine*'s Enigma messages to divert convoys away from known submarine concen-

trations, the *B-dienst* was still reading enough Allied code for Dönitz to redeploy his packs against Convoys HX-237 and SC 129 in the second week of May. Both convoys enjoyed almost continuous air cover from escort carriers and VLR aircraft. Convoy HX 237 traded 3 merchantmen for 3 U-boats while SC 129 lost 2 ships in return for two submarines. To Dönitz, these losses represented "unbearable heights" because they equalled one submarine for 10,000 tons of merchant shipping – in 1942 the ratio had been one U-boat for 100,000 tons.[10]

Even so, it took two more defeats before he gave up the struggle. Convoy SC 130, proceeding under the protection of continuous air cover, crossed the Atlantic without losing a single ship despite being attacked by 33 submarines – the German losses were five U-boats. By this time, U-boat commanders were understandably getting somewhat twitchy and, faced with many instances where submarines failed to make contact or, having made contact, lost it in good weather, Dönitz's staff recognized that the U-boat commanders were exhibiting a particular "concern for vulnerability to air attack."[11]

On 22 May, just before he ordered an attack on Convoy HX 229, Dönitz therefore sent a stern signal to all his commanders in the North Atlantic:

If there is anyone who thinks that combating convoys is no longer possible, he is a weakling and no true U-boat captain. The battle of the Atlantic is getting harder but it is the determining element in the waging of the war.[12]

Dönitz then concentrated 22 submarines against HX 229, which was accompanied by two escort carriers, USS *Bogue* and HMS *Archer*, throughout its voyage – their aircraft sank two U-boats but the convoy did not lose a ship. A similar phenomenon took place with the next large convoy, SC 130, which crossed the Atlantic without loss under the protection of VLR aircraft, which sank two submarines.

Having lost 33 submarines and nearly 1,500 of his highly-trained personnel (including his own son) in just over three weeks, Dönitz finally admitted defeat on 24 May 1943. That day he recorded that the situation "now forces a temporary shifting of operations to areas less endangered by aircraft" and pulled his submarines out of the mid-ocean area to redeploy them against the Britain-Gibraltar convoy route.[13] The German commander, however, had not entirely given up on the North Atlantic as he knew it was the crucial operational area and he anticipated that, once the equipment of his vessels had been upgraded, the battle "will be completely resumed once more."[14]

To the amazed victors, however, the North Atlantic was suddenly free of the enemy – "as if a steel gauntlet had relaxed its grip on the Allied throat."[15]

Hollow victory for the Royal Canadian Navy

The C-Groups returned to the Atlantic in mid-May just in time to play a small part in the final battles. C-2 Group, consisting of two British warships and four Canadian corvettes, *Chambly*, *Drumheller*, *Morden* and *Primrose*, were part of the escort for HX 237, which beat off continuous attacks with the help of the escort carrier HMS *Biter* and VLR aircraft. In the fight to get this convoy through, *Drumheller* shared in the destruction of *U-456* with the British destroyer *Lagan* and an RCAF aircraft. A few days later, C-1 Group, consisting of a British destroyer and six Canadian warships (the destroyer *Skeena* and the corvettes *Bittersweet*, *Eyebright*, *La Malbaie*, *Mayflower* and *Pictou*), took Convoy HX 238 unharmed across the Atlantic with assistance from the escort carrier USS *Bogue*.

That was the extent of the Canadian navy's participation in the climactic battles of the spring of 1943. The struggle had largely been borne and won by the RN, with assistance from the USN and the Allied air forces, and it had been won by good training, signal intelligence, air power and modern equipment – all assets conspicuously lacking in previous years when the RCN had struggled valiantly to guard the Atlantic sea lanes. While Canadian escort sailors applauded their British comrades, there was a growing resentment that, condemned by the deficiencies of their ships and equipment, they would forever remain the Cinderella of the Allied navies.

Wren signallers, Signal Hill, St. John's, Newfoundland.
Despite doubts on the part of conservative senior officers, the creation of the Women's Royal Canadian Naval Service in 1942 proved to be an instant success and they quickly became an indispensable part of the Canadian naval war effort. (National Archives of Canada)

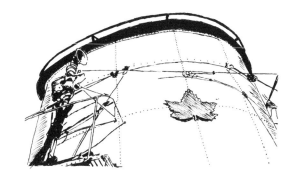

The Maple Leaf Forever.
In the latter years of the war, Canadian warships began to display a green Maple Leaf funnel badge as an emblem of their nationality. Although the RCN started the war more or less as a subdivision of the Royal Navy, it evolved into a national service and the third largest Allied navy. (Drawing by L.B. Jenson, courtesy of the artist)

1943

Ice: An even greater peril

In the North Atlantic in winter, one of the greatest dangers was spray from the waves freezing on the upper surfaces of a ship, increasing its weight and affecting its stability. Lieutenant Latham B. Jenson, RCN, describes the perilous situation that ice caused for HMCS Niagara during a winter voyage from St. John to Halifax in early 1943:

The trouble with freezing spray is that it compounds itself exponentially. The more iced-up the ship is, the greater the area on which the spray freezes and the greater the top weight. Eventually, the weight increases so much that there is a real possibility of rolling over. An ordinary wire rope, say one inch in circumference, starts with a thin film of ice and rapidly grows. Our guard rails had become an icy bulwark. It was a dangerous situation.

There was nothing to be done but to call all hands and get them on deck with whatever they could find to pound off the ice. Soon the pitch darkness was filled with bundled-up people with hammers, baseball bats, shovels, axes, rolling pins and who knows what else, all pounding and banging, seeming to make little progress. By eight o'clock it was getting light and the ship was still covered with ice. The chief boatswain's mate said to me that the hands were going to quit and have some breakfast. I replied in rather a loud voice, "Fine, you tell them to enjoy it because it will probably be the last meal they will have." Every-

one kept right on pounding and within an hour or two the ice was diminished and the ship felt much better. By that evening, we were alongside in Halifax.[1]

"Those guys ain't fooling:" The RCN encounters the glider bomb, August 1943

In late August 1943, Escort Group 5, consisting of HM Ships Nene *and* Tweed *and HMC Ships* Calgary, Edmundston *and* Snowberry, *participated in a series of offensive patrols in the Bay of Biscay intended to make it difficult for U-boats to break out into the open Atlantic. On 25 August, Lieutenant Barry O'Brien, RCNVR, commanding the corvette, HMCS* Snowberry, *remembered that they ran into a new and terrifying German weapon:*

At 1342 they appeared overhead at 4,000 feet, all 21 of them – later identified as fourteen Dornier 17s and seven Ju-88s. They proceeded to split into groups of three and we all fully expected a dive-bombing attack from ahead, but they fooled us and moved over to the starboard side, giving evidence of a low-level job from beam-on. This, too, was not to be.

It was evident that this was not an ordinary high-level attack as each bomb appeared to shoot out from under the planes for a distance of 200 feet or so, leaving behind a trail of white vapour. First the bomb ran on a parallel course to the target ship, then it suddenly made a right-angle turn towards the target and followed any evasive actions of the ship. Each Dornier dropped a bomb, but their homing technique was lousy. They caused damage only by two near misses.

At 1418, *Nene* signalled, "Speed 14 knots" and at 1425, "Flag 1," which means take individual

avoiding action. At 1430, *Tweed* to *Snowberry*, "What is your best speed? Answer, "15 knots." *Tweed* to *Snowberry*, "Don't give us that, we are doing 18 and we can't shake you." The chief ERA [Engine Room Artificer of *Snowberry*] confessed afterwards to urging 10 more revs out of the old ice cream freezer than he ever had before. He claimed that by the time the news of the enemy planes reached the engine-room, there were at least 50 around, so he figured we needed all available juice. Heard from the 4-inch gun platform, "Guess those guys ain't fooling today." And from another, "Come on in you bastards, so we can get a decent crack at you." And on the bridge, "Boy this is the first time *Snowberry* has been in this kind of action." Then came a reply, "Yes, and I had to be here at the time." ......

The Admiralty sent a wireless message that the enemy had used a new weapon which had been nicknamed "Chase Me Charlie" because of its capability of homing in on a ship. You moved and it moved. The Admiralty also suggest two antidotes: Shoot it down with anti-aircraft guns or plug in all your electric razors because they might be on the same wavelength as the radio-controlled glider bombs. This was later tried, without positive result.[2]

"The King – God Bless Him!" In Commonwealth warships, sailors received a daily rum ration. It was often mixed with water in ornamental buckets like this to create grog and then served out to each man. (Drawing by L.B. Jenson)

Up spirits!

The RCN followed the custom of the RN in issuing rum to enlisted personnel on a daily basis. Normally it had to be drunk on the spot, under the watchful eye of an officer, and Lieutenant Latham B. Jenson, RCN, describes this cherished and time-honoured naval tradition:

Whenever the navy is mentioned, in the minds of many people there is a word association: rum. Rum was carried in all ships under the White Ensign in small wooden casks in the spirit room. This was situated in the vicinity of the tiller flat. Wardroom liquor also was stowed there, as was the communion wine. The total daily issue of rum was pumped up by the victualling department with the utmost care as every last drop (except "spillage") had to be accounted for.

At the pipe "up spirits," cooks of messes would gather with their fannies (containers) at the place of issue. They were given grog, [2.5 ounce] tots of [overproof] rum mixed with two parts of water, according to the number entitled in their mess. All men age 21 or over were entitled to rum. Men could decide to be Grog or Temperance (G or T on their papers). If Temperance, they were entitled to an extra shilling or 25 cents a day with their pay. The reason for grog, as opposed to neat rum, was that grog would not keep and had to be consumed the same day. There was a custom called "sippers" (quite illegal) which meant that someone having a birthday or other event of importance might have a sip from each of his messmates' tots. The result often was drunkenness and into the "rattle," the first lieutenant's or captain's report for appropriate punishment. ......

Fog on the sea.
The corvette HMCS *Chambly* emerges from a fog bank while on escort duty in the North Atlantic. Fog was a mixed blessing; it concealed the convoys from the U-boats, which were not equipped with radar in the early days of the battle, but brought the added danger of collision. One of the few things that the Canadian-built SWC radars sets were good for (when they worked) was stationkeeping during times of poor visibility. (National Archives of Canada, PA 115352)

[Sometimes] the odd man cheated and poured the tot into a container tucked inside his jersey. Neaters, two ounces of over-proof neat rum, went straight down to your boots and, I suppose, was a test of manhood. The rum issue was the height of the day for most men and was a major factor in maintaining morale.[3]

The weather again

Life on a corvette was tough enough in rough weather but, in a storm, it was nearly impossible. Seaman Edward O'Connor of the corvette Morden *recalls a bad gale at sea in 1943:*

The weather started out fine that first week or so and we were making good time when …… the first hint of the coming storm appeared on the horizon to the west. It was a few small clouds to begin with but they grew in size and a stiff breeze sprang up, lifting the tops off waves that hit the ship in a fine spray. The sky was now dark and threatening and rain began to fall but failed to calm a rising sea. The crew was called out to secure lifelines and watertight hatches and to run down a depth-charge that had broken loose, threatening everything in its path as it rumbled about. One second we were chasing it and the next we were trying to get out of its way.

Throughout that night the wind and seas increased, the wind tearing our ensign to shreds and playing a tune on the guy wires. Heavy seas were breaking over the bow, tossed clear back over the bridge, officers and lookouts trying to find a bit of shelter behind the canvas dodger. Crashing sounds from the seamen's mess could be heard clear up on the bridge. In the mess, it was like a war zone. Cutlery, dishes and metal hat boxes flew

about like shrapnel to land in a good few inches of water that sloshed about and continued to pour down from an air vent that had its cover torn away by the wind. The anchor cable pounded on the sides of the downpipe to the cable locker, as if some demon inside was trying to get out. Each time we hit bottom in a trough, the men were driven to their knees and a number of lightbulbs popped in their sockets.

By now the convoy was in a real mess. Ships scattered to the four winds. It was a case of every man for himself. Escorts could no longer keep station, let alone continue sweeps. *Morden* had all she could do just to keep bow on to the seas. ……

Life went on though, somehow. The cook lost our dinner one day when a great pot of beans became airborne and painted the galley. Trying to scrub out the messdeck flats, the same thing happened to me. After three slides on the wet deck, I became airborne, ending up head first in the pail of suds. A mate clapped and wanted to know what I planned for an encore. ……

The gale or hurricane blew for some five days before … relative calm [arrived].[4]

"A lot of good men died:" U-boat attack on Convoy SC 163, October 1943

Convoy SC 163 with 60 merchant ships bound for Britain in early October 1943 was escorted by C-2 Group which consisted of two British ships and five Canadian corvettes, among them HMCS Morden. *The convoy escort was reinforced shortly before it was attacked 15 U-boats and Leading Seaman Edward O'Connor of* Morden *remembered that the*

Talk in the mess was mostly speculation on when an attack might come and one of us felt the Ger-

mans would back down, even if they knew about our added fire power and it was very likely they did. When you knew an attack was coming, there didn't seem any point to worrying about it when you couldn't do anything. That doesn't mean we weren't scared but feeling that way came so often out there you came to accept it as just a normal thing and went on with the business at hand. Since I had the morning watch I turned in around 2200 and was soon sawing wood in my mick [hammock]. At around 0315 a hand shook my mick, a voice telling me, "Up and at 'em, O'Connor. There's a pot of kye [hot chocolate] on the table." Only half awake, I muttered, "Anything stirring?" and was told everything was quiet. I dropped to the deck and pulled on my sea boots. Regulations had us sleep fully dressed to cut down on time closing up to actions stations. Telling us a corvette would likely sink in fourteen seconds, if hit, also offered come encouragement to be ready. ……

We were just finishing up when, sea, sky and ship turned a blood red, as if a light had been turned on. We ran for the quarterdeck and got there just in time for the big blast. On *Morden*'s port beam a tanker was ablaze bow to stern, a great mushroom of black smoke and flashing gases hung over and smaller explosions sent dark objects high against the flames that I hoped weren't men. Later I realized it was their deck cargo – drums of aircraft fuel exploding. Our alarm bells now broke in and I started running for the bridge down the port side. …… I was halfway up to the bridge when there was a great white flash of light, followed by one hell of a blast that knocked me down but not off the ladder. Back on my feet I reached the port Oerlikon [20mm anti-aircraft gun] and helped strip the cover off. The ammo hatch opened, Smitty took the gun as I reported us closed up and ready to the bridge.

Minutes later, we learned that the second blast had been from the [Polish destroyer] *Orkan*, obviously taking one in her magazine for there wasn't a sign of her left. We slowed down slightly, passing through the area, but there was nothing, no survivors or even a trace of wreckage. ......

It seemed pretty definite a sub was in the convoy and, if the destroyer flushed him out, the German would probably come out where *Orkan* went down. At least our skipper seemed to be thinking that when *Morden* picked up speed to move ahead. It proved a good move. Minutes later, asdic picked up a contact moving out of the convoy and it was a good one. At least to judge by the bridge speaker. The sharp "ping" had changed to something like "ping-guh."

The [engine] telegraph [on the bridge] rang and *Morden* leaped ahead, swinging to port to get between the sub and the convoy. We then came on the sub from behind for a nail-biting time of expecting the German to let loose a torpedo. For some reason, he didn't. ...... Right over him now and a ten-charge pattern went over the side of *Morden*, the fifty foot setting lifting our own stern. A sharp turn then and another ten charges dropped in the same spot. We slowed on the third pass, looking for any sign of wreckage. There was none but one of the seamen yelled and pointed to a spot where oil bubbled up and spread in a great stain. Asdic reported a "lost contact" and, at the same time, the S[enior] O[fficer]'s destroyer came on us from the stern of the convoy, her signal light flashing, "GOOD SHOW, MORDEN, YOU MIGHT GIVE OWEN SOUND A HAND WITH SURVIVORS."

The sun had not yet got over the horizon, we could make out the thin spiral of smoke from the burning tanker and made for it. The smoke disappeared before we got halfway and the burning ship must have gone down at that point. ......

A lot of good men died out there and I still think about them.[5]

Ports of call (2): Halifax – the depised "Slackers"

If Newfie John was high on the list of favourite ports of call, Halifax was at the bottom. Lieutenant James Lamb, RCNVR, explains why:

For men on the lower deck, Halifax was a virtual desert. Swarming ashore from crowded messdecks at the end of a long voyage, they found little to entertain them there, apart from the handful of crowded movies, seedy cafés, and the wet canteen. In later years there were games on the sporting-grounds ashore and film showings for the duty watch on board, organized by base sports and recreation officers, but Halifax, perhaps because of its size and the numbers of men cooped up in barracks and ships, never got around to providing the range of activities laid on for ships' crews in other ports, particularly Newfyjohn. Boredom in barracks and frustration in the messdecks of ships alongside bred a growing anger and tension in Halifax, a feeling intensified by the base's "9 to 5" and "long weekend" mentality, which left the dockyard virtually deserted except for thousands of men cooped up in berthed ships.[6]

The most dangerous cargo.
A torpedoed tanker sinks as her flammable cargo burns in a fiery inferno. Tankers were the most vulnerable and the most important merchant vessels – they received extra protection in convoys and, not surprisingly, merchant seamen received bounty pay for serving on board them. (United States National Archives, NA 242 PKAZ 103)

Halifax, as seen from the harbour.
Halifax in 1960 but little changed from the wartime era. Halifax was disliked by the wartime navy because of limited leave activities, the perceived unfriendliness of the civilian population, and the rigid attitudes of the many shore-based officers. (Drawing by L.B. Jenson, courtesy of the artist)

As the wartime navy used to sing about Halifax:

You're a little bit of Hades, rose from out the sea one day,
And it settled across from Dartmouth on a dark and dreary day,
And when the government saw it, sure it looked so bleak and bare,
They said, "Suppose we grab it, we can send the Navy there!"

So they sprinkled it with barracks and matelots then dropped in,
And here and there a jukebox added to the awful din,
And then they had a Shore Patrol so the boys could not relax,
And when they had it finished, sure they called it Halifax![1]

"Queen of the Sea protect us:" A civilian in the North Atlantic, October 1943

In the autumn of 1943, John Connolly, executive assistant to Angus Macdonald, minister of the Naval Service, travelled across the North Atlantic on the corvette Orillia *to carry out a fact-finding mission. Connolly kept a diary of his voyage which, because he was seasick for most of its duration, was brief in detail but does portray the nature of the war in the North Atlantic with compelling immediacy.*

Beautiful – but eerie. Watch standing around in their hoods. – Always looking, It is monotonous. Zig zagging. No time [have] these men for great policy thinking. They live from watch to watch and carry on regardless [of] weather or subs ......

No school boy enthusiasm here. Just a job to be done. Maybe leave to London. ......

I just don't think about Subs. But carry lifebelt always and wear it on deck. Not much point worrying about Subs. I wouldn't be much at a job like this – even in command. The monotony would get me down. But I am lost in admiration at these young Canadians – giving up so much at home to do this.

[At] Times [it is] rough – others smooth. This ship rides everything. It doesn't cut into the waves so its up and down hill all the time – and pitching. ......

What a war effort! No home comforts. Rolling and pitching – keeping station Thinking out Navigation Guarding the convoy Threatened by torpedoes every minute.

Heavy food – no exercise. Dependent on weather – engines – other ships ......

How brave these young men are ...... running a ship with complete confidence Joking laughing. They are the stuff. ......

One can't go through this thing without a deep emotional reaction. The sea at night – the slender ship the clouds the moon ...... the foam the roar, the whistling winds – What a power of the elements – and the God that *made* them

Oct 13 ...... We are now in the gap ...... Saw the last of Newfy planes this a.m. Lots of talk of subs. Two said to be on our path moving south some officers pessimistic about ability to deal [with acoustic torpedoes] and take a dim view because of [the loss of] *St. Croix.*

When you see the waves and the rain and the pitching of the ship you realize that fair equipment is not good enough. They need the best. ......

(Facing page) **The true heroes – merchant sailor survivors arriving in Halifax.**
Seamen from sunken merchant ships arrive in Halifax on 21 April 1943 on the rescue trawler HMS *Northern Gift.* An effort was made to provide for each convoy a rescue vessel or vessels equipped for the task of saving and caring for survivors. The presence of such ships was a tremendous boost to the morale of the merchant seamen, whose chances of surviving a torpedoing in the North Atlantic were usually poor. (Photograph by G.A. Milne, National Archives of Canada, PA 153052)

Unwarned – Action stations bells I was not happy. I shook. Out of bed fast – into Life Belt, coat and hat and up. Drama and Death – I thought I was sent for. Silent hooded figures on the Oerlikons. Gun crew active on the 4" Officers at post Gunnery Officer calling the routine enemy in sight Fire – the half black, half blue sky, the moon ……

Oct 14 Partly cloudy. Rather rough – heavy swell – not sickly but nearly so. Planes in A.M. from Iceland. Support group now with us …

Captn at supper says to-night's the night. The X-O [executive officer] says before midnight. Well its midnight now, but I don't feel any more secure. It doesn't worry these young lads ….

Stood on bridge tonight for an hour – in rain. There is brilliant moonlight – Heavy clouds – danger is close. God help us. Queen of the Sea protect us. ……[8]

The enemy below – U-boat officers, 1943.
Young, dedicated and professional, two U-boat officers relax on the "Winter Garden" at the rear of the conning tower of *U-612*, a Type VII boat, while training in the Baltic. On the left is *Leutnant zur See* Pieper and on the right *Leutnant (Ing)* Werner Hirschmann, age 20, the chief engineer. Although they suffered horrendous casualties, the U-boat crews remained undaunted until the end of the war. (Courtesy, Werner Hirschmann)

True heroes – the Merchant Marine

The Battle of the Atlantic, Rear Admiral Leonard Murray stated, "was won by the courage, fortitude and determination of the British and Allied Merchant Navy." As the senior Canadian naval officer in the theatre, Murray was in a good position to know just how important the contribution of the merchant marine sailors was to the Allied victory but there is also the grim evidence of the statistics. During the Second World War, German U-boats sank 4800 merchant vessels totalling more than 21 million gross tons, killing at least (the figures are not complete) 40,000 merchant marine sailors. About 75% of these losses occurred in the North Atlantic and the Battle of the Atlantic could not have been fought – and certainly could not have been won – without the Allied merchant mariners. Unfortunately, their vital role is all too often overlooked.

Many of the Canadian merchant sailors were young teenagers who were rejected by the RCN because of their age. Earle Wagner of Lunenburg, Nova Scotia, recalls that,

The war broke out just a few months after I finished school, I was fifteen. When I was sixteen I went to go into the Royal Canadian Navy as a boy seaman and they wouldn't take me, didn't need me. So a few months later when I turned seventeen I went in the merchant navy. It was usually sixteen [before] you could get in, but people lied about their age and got in at fourteen and fifteen. Things weren't too strict. If you looked able and willing and had reasonably good health, they took you.[9]

Wagner remembered that, contrary to popular belief, the pay was not that good in the Merchant Marine:

I got $45 a month and they put a 35 percent war bonus on top of that. Comparisons of wages between the Royal Canadian Navy and the Canadian merchant navy overall, invariably wound up that they were all making more than we were. That can be proven out. But the myth was that we were overpaid. They thought we were all mercenaries, that we would go wherever the biggest money was. That was one of the things the navy always threw at us. Whenever we got in port sometimes it could end up in a drunken brawl.[10]

Discussions of pay, of course, do take into account the element of risk – merchant vessels, not warships, were the prime targets and that was particularly true of tankers and ammunition carriers. As Clarence Purcell of Musquodoboit, Nova Scotia, comments, the shipping companies had ways of reducing the bonuses paid for dangerous cargo:

We left Manchester and come back and the ship went in dry dock in New York 'cause she was carryin' gasoline before and her plates were all gone. I guess a ship can only carry gasoline so long 'cause it rots the tanks. You change either to a crude [oil], or a light and heavy cycle [of fuel]. You don't carry the same cargo on every trip. …… So I got off there in New York and I got on another Norwegian ship called the *Tercero* as an ordinary seaman. She was carryin' half cargo, half ammunition. See, they'd load them half with half, than they wouldn't have to pay the bonus. You got to carryin' a full load of ammunition before you get paid extra money, danger pay. That's what they done.[11]

Whatever the merchant sailors were paid, it was not enough for the hazards they faced. Jim Boutilier was on the tanker Montrolite *when it was torpedoed off the east coast of the United States in February 1942 and remembered that, when the torpedo struck,*

It was a sort of blinding flash. For a few minutes I didn't know anything. It just knocked me right away from the wheel over in the flag locker at the side of the wheelhouse. I scrambled to my feet. The way I look at it, I must have been out for a few minutes because when I came out on the boat deck, one of the boats had been launched and was gone. So then we saw one of the lifeboats from aft – we had a following wind at sea from the stern – and the boat was launched and was drifting up along side the ship towards the bow, so I jumped and they pulled me into the boat. ......

We were dead in the water and we knew that we were going to get another one, so the best thing was to get out of the way, abandon ship. About fifteen or twenty minutes later, they hit her on the other side with another torpedo, but we were all clear of it by then. It hit, we figure, between the fuel tanks and cargo tanks. You take, with diesel oil mixing with the Venezuelan crude – it was a good grade of light crude – boy, she just went, everything went. She caught fire and all you could see was the flames and the smoke. The first thing, she was gone.[12]

Percy Lambert was on the modern freighter Loch Katrine, *sailing as part of Convoy ON 115, when she was torpedoed in the evening of 2 August 1942:*

It's an awful bang when a torpedo hits a ship; you go about twenty feet in the air, or I did. It's hard to describe the noise, it's such a racket. Right in

A dangerous weapon – the acoustic torpedo.
In 1943, the U-boats were equipped with acoustic torpedoes which homed in on the propeller noise of their targets. Countermeasures were quickly introduced but the acoustic torpedo remained a threat for the remainder of the war. In September 1944, *U-1227* hit the frigate HMCS *Magog* with an acoustic torpedo and the resulting damage shows clearly in this photograph taken by R.G. Arless when *Magog* was in dry dock for repairs. (National Archives of Canada, PA 153486)

the engine room. Everything went black, everything went out. …… I jumped and I knew right where to go for boat stations. ……

I started to put the lifeboats in the water. I said to hell with this, I'm going on the next one. Instead of going down the ladder, I jumped and grabbed the halyards or falls and went down. We hauled some people out of the water and that's how I learned my hands were burnt. I reached down to haul a fellow out and salt water hits my fingers. I burnt my fingers, I imagine, lowering them in the water with the rope and then grabbing the falls and going down. You know, you're nervous, you want to get in there too. Panic is an awful thing. I never knew panic till I seen that. I was never one like that. People just dove in. If you haven't seen panic, you don't know it, how people react. Even in the dark you could see it.[13]

Even if the sailors got safely off a torpedoed ship, there remained long voyages in lifeboats in the Atlantic. George Evans of St. John's, Newfoundland, was on one of two lifeboats that got away from the Norwegian freighter Einvik *when it was torpedoed in the North Atlantic:*

It started to get cold and it was blowin' and snowin'. Three or four days later my feet started to get numb and [we would] rub one another's legs to keep the circulation goin' because you were cramped up in a small boat – eleven of us in one boat and twelve in the other. We started to get mountains of sea then and we put out a sea anchor and that'd keep you from goin' back. The other boat was a motor boat and had towed us, it got rough, it broke clear and they went one way and we went another way. We had a sail and put

the sail up. It was about 450 miles south of Iceland. ……

That was my home for eight and a half days, out in a lifeboat. We had to ration. We were only allowed about an ounce or two of water, two or three times a day. We had hard biscuits and meatballs and gravy, that's all we had. Then we got to the Icelandic fishermen and they gave us their lunch – coffee, hot chocolate and their grub. I'll tell you, it was some great to have hot chocolate and food, it really was wonderful.[14]

Seaman Jim Boutilier was in one of three lifeboats that got away from the tanker Montrolite:

We were in the lifeboat about three days, rough weather all the time. We managed to keep her afloat; if she'd swamped, there wouldn't have been a chance at all. It was just like a nightmare. We had everything, even sleet. You take where we were sunk, it was pretty well around the edge of the Gulf Stream, but [we were] … driven north in a gale for three days. We had to use our sail for a sea anchor; tie it to a rope and put it over. Tried to keep the lifeboat up into the wind and sea, but there was times we had to take to the oars. But you had to have a rest too, you couldn't do it all the time. We bailed steady all the time, just a couple of buckets, whatever we could, and spell one another off. We tried everything we could [to keep] from filling with water. At one point we had to take the sea anchor in, and take the sail and try to lash it around the boat because we were tired of bailing.

I don't think they put on too much a search to look for anybody. It was an old British merchantman who got astray from a convoy [that rescued them].[15]

More than 12,000 Canadians served in the merchant marine during the war and 1,600 lost their lives, a higher proportional loss rate than that suffered by the Royal Canadian Navy, the Royal Canadian Air Force or the Canadian army. Their valour must never be forgotten.

The enemy below: A U-boat officer remembers

Werner Hirschmann began his career in the Kriegsmarine as a 17-year-old officer cadet in the autumn of 1940 and ended it in on 12 May 1945 as a 22-year-old Oberleutnant (Ingenieur) *on board U-190 when it surrendered to the RCN in 1945. In 1952 he he emigrated to Canada and worked as a computer engineer up to the time of his retirement. Mr. Hirschmann is a member of a number of Canadian naval associations and has frequently spoken to Canadian audiences on the subject of his wartime service. The following passages, which deal with his decision to join the navy, life on a U-boat and the morale of German submarine crews, were extracted from his unpublished memoirs and appear with his permission.*

My father participated in the battle of Jutland in 1916. Through him I became interested in all matters maritime. As a kid I read every book about naval history I could get hold of and as a kid I never dreamed of a career as a fireman or a pilot – I wanted to be a sailor.

When I finally had to choose a career, other factors entered into my decision to join the Navy. I wanted to save my parents the costs of a university education, I hoped to play soccer against the British in Hong Kong, and I suffered terribly from hay fever! I also had this theory that a sailor's marriage would never suffer from that deadly enemy of romance called boredom. After long absences there would always be the renewal, the starting all over again. Having had my navy career terminated rather prematurely I was never able to test this theory.

I chose the engineering branch, because it accommodated my technical inclinations and also, because I wanted to have a profession other than to find places, to which the ship was expected to go. Guns and torpedoes were of no interest to me.

When your country is at war, as a young man you can't just sit home and let the others fight, and worse, come home in chic uniforms and impress all the girls. And the challenge of adventure was irresistible. ....

After graduation from the Naval Officer's Academy at Flensburg, I wasn't asked where I would like to serve. I was told to report to submarine training. The time was January 1942.

When I was finally involved in front-line missions, the "Happy Times" were over. In my time in the U-Boat service in 1943-1945, we only came to the surface to charge our batteries and to get some fresh air to breathe. In 1944 we were cautioned not to surface during the daylight hours anywhere north of 15 degrees south. Due to the coverage of the Atlantic by small carrier taskforces, there was no place left where we were safe from sudden attacks from the air. Only the snorkel, which enabled us to draw fresh air into the boat while running the diesel engines submerged, enabled us to survive on operations. ......

Some of the readers may have seen the German movie, "Das Boot." Movies have to be entertaining but, in reality, life on a submarine is visually as interesting as watching paint dry. You

Cold day in Newfie John – three veteran corvettes, November 1943.
From left to right, the corvettes *Orillia*, *Trillium* and *Calgary* take a welcome break from the North Atlantic. Commissioned in late 1940, *Orillia* and *Trillium* were veterans of the North Atlantic run while *Calgary*, which entered service in early 1942, had just participated in Operation TORCH. *Orillia* and *Calgary* were paid off in 1945 and broken up in 1951 but *Trillium* enjoyed a postwar career as a whale-catcher and ended up as a Japanese vessel. (Photograph by G.A. Milne, National Archives of Canada, PA 107932)

can't sell a movie that shows submarine life as it actually was. In a movie, when depth charges explode, people inside the boat must be falling all over each other, if not desperately hanging onto something to keep them upright, while the boat rolls through thirty-degree arcs. In reality that submarine isn't moving a fraction of an inch because it is a mass of a thousand tons, surrounded by an almost solid mass of water. In my experience, a depth charge feels like a blow with a giant hammer on an immovable object – valve shafts break, fuses blow, light fixtures shatter, but the boat doesn't move. One may have the understandable inclination to duck, but one has to wonder why. The chaos, the panic, the screaming in "Das Boot" was interesting to watch but has no connection with reality. But let me be generous, in many aspects the movie was incredibly true to reality and this applies particularly to the everyday life and conditions aboard a submarine. I surely must have met, at one time or other during my service, people very like those officers and enlisted men portrayed in the movie.

Back to reality. The moments of listening to the splash of a depth charge entering the water and the seemingly endless seconds of waiting for it to explode, are truly terrifying. Cold sweat breaks out and I myself always had a terrible urge to go for a bowel movement, but of course I couldn't. With everybody watching you, there is this necessity as an officer to stay cool and put a up a brave face, even make a joke. Then the charge explodes and just as you realize you are still alive, the next charge is already on its way. During all this time the utmost silence must be maintained throughout the boat. All conversation is reduced to a minimum and then only in the form of whis-

pering. Shoes are replaced with specially made socks to avoid any noise when moving through the boat. Coughing or sneezing is considered more criminal than high treason and has to be avoided at any cost. Between depth charges the operator of the hydrophone listening device is attempting to analyze the ship movements above, while the pinging sounds of asdic indicate that the enemy is still in contact. But when another explosion reverberates through the boat and something breaks, there is no time for fear as one is far too busy taking care of the damage to worry any longer. This can go from four to six to ten hours before your boat is finally able to slink away with the hope that the enemy have lost you.

Except for the occasional bursts of action, generally life on a submarine was full of boredom. I remember the countless hours of reading books and playing in chess tournaments. We had competitions for inventing the most stupid joke…… Philosophical contemplations about anything and everything were geared to compensate for the somewhat stupefying effects of the endless periods of nothing happening in a closed environment 60 meters below the surface. Atrophy of the brain was one of our biggest problems. Some things, however, that we did not discuss were politics, war aims, or the reason for being out there in the first place.

If you lie down you use less oxygen than when you stand up. If you sleep, you use less oxygen than when you are awake. So, during the last year of the war we were often required to sleep about 20 hours a day to save oxygen and electricity.

There were compensations for the dangers we faced. During the entire mission we were happy to have three normal meals and to have a warm

bunk, kept warm by the guy who had just gone on watch. When we came back after a three to four month-long patrol, the boat was usually in need of extensive overhaul and so the crew had weeks of leave-of-absence, far more than any other branch of the German armed forces. We also got favoured treatment with respect to goods in short supply, whether alcohol, coffee, butter, silk stockings, etc., to take home to our families and we probably ate better than anybody else in the country. After every mission there was the ceremony of receiving medals, which boosted our already sizeable egos. ……

Let me make a few remarks with respect to the state of our morale during the last years of the war with its unprecedented attrition for our submarine crews. It has been said and said truly that our morale never faltered and I don't think that uneasiness about the future dominated our lives. We learned to put up a good front and I think we approached everything with the same casualness one has when one does one's job in peacetime, whatever it may be.

I believe that the vast majority of us had to fight the fear that threatened to overcome us. But much worse and more immediate was the fear of being considered to be a coward and therefore there was always an internal imperative to do what was necessary or desirable, if not always rational. You simply acted, almost automatically in ways, which, when you thought about it later, seem utterly impossible.

The chances of coming back from a mission were very slim during the last years as many boats never even survived their very first mission. The fact that we could lose our lives was only a rather unfortunate and unavoidable side effect of our own choice of profession and we just kept on doing our job.

Time and time again, however, we had to accept the fact that one after the other of our close
friends would never come back. The shock lasted
a few seconds and then, over another drink, we
switched the conversation to more mundane matters. It was quite astonishing how we lost all sensitivity to the occurrence of death. We considered it
quite natural, that before embarking on another
mission, we had to pack and lock all our private
belongings into a special wooden box and label it
with the address of our nearest relative. If we did
not come back, the flotilla simply sent the box off.
Case closed.

Although the odds against us were well known
to us, it never became a subject of discussion. In
our minds it would always be the other boat that
wouldn't make it. Immediately after leaving port
we were, just like any sailor, looking forward to
the moment of returning to base. But today I find
it almost beyond belief, that after a few weeks at
home with our families or in specially dedicated
recreation centres, we became very edgy, got ants
in our pants and couldn't wait for the moment of
departure for the next mission. Such is the foolishness of youth.

Rarely did we become aware of the human suffering we caused. In fact, during the entire war I
did not see one single dead person, or any blood.
As far as we were concerned, we either came
home, happy and healthy, or we didn't come back
at all. With a few exceptions, there wasn't anything in between.

Upgraded: HMCS *Sorel* in July 1943.
Commissioned in August 1941, *Sorel* served in the Western Local Escort Force and the MOEF and was one of the first
Canadian short foc'sle corvettes to be taken in hand for much-needed modifications, which were completed in early
1943. She later served primarily as a training ship, which is why she appears so trim in this picture taken at Pictou in
the summer of 1943. *Sorel* is painted in the Western Approaches camouflage scheme of very light grey overlaid with
patches of light green and blue in a "wave" sequence. (Canadian Naval Memorial Trust)

CHAPTER 7

THE ROYAL CANADIAN NAVY COMES OF AGE:

JUNE 1943–APRIL 1944

The navy at mid-war: Problems and possibilities

By the middle of 1943, although it still faced many problems, the Royal Canadian Navy was beginning to mature as a fighting service. Fortunately, manpower was no longer an issue as there were about 50,000 officers and sailors in service.* Contrary to popular myth, the region of Canada that contributed the greatest percentage of recruits to the RCN was not the prairie provinces, but Prince Edward Island and British Columbia, followed closely by Nova Scotia. Expressed as a percentage of males of military age in the prime 18-45 age group, the wartime enlistment in the RCN by province was as follows: Prince Edward Island (7.3 per cent); British Columbia (6.9 per cent); Nova Scotia (5.6 per cent); Ontario (4.9 per cent); Manitoba (4.9 per cent); Alberta (4.2 per cent); Saskatchewan (3.4 per cent); New Brunswick (2.9 per cent); and Quebec (1.8 per

cent). RCN standards regarding age, health and education were high, more so than for the army, and many a would-be sailor was turned away from a naval recruiting centre with directions to the nearest army equivalent. Shore-based training, which had been minimal during the first two or so years of the war, was now fairly extensive and no longer were raw crews thrown into brand-new ships and sent to the North Atlantic to do battle with Dönitz's submariners. There was time for newly-commissioned vessels to do some basic training or "working up" in Canadian coastal waters before being assigned to escort duties – it was not much but it was a big improvement over 1941 and 1942.

The RCN's troubles lay with the state of its ships and their equipment. The workhorse of the mid-ocean escort groups was still the Flower Class corvette and would remain so until the new frigates began to enter service. Originally christened the "twin screw corvette," the frigate was another brainchild of William Reed, the designer of the corvette. The shortcomings of the Flower Class vessels had quickly become obvious to the RN after they began to enter service in early 1940 and, at the suggestion of the Admiralty, Reed had designed the frigate, an improved ASW vessel with better speed and armament. The RN ordered its first frigates from British yards in the spring of 1941 and the advantages of the new design were so readily apparent to NSHQ that it decided in 1942, after the current orders

---

* This figure does not include the Women's Royal Canadian Naval Service formed in 1942 and which, by 1945, had reached a strength of nearly 6,000.

(Facing page) **HMCS *Swansea* in a rough sea, January 1944.**
A nice study of the frigate *Swansea* off the Flemish Cap in January 1944. *Swansea* entered service in October 1943 and became one of the RCN's most successful escorts, accounting for three U-boats. In this photograph she is shown with Type 271 radar in its perspex dome behind the bridge but only a single 4-inch gun in her forward, and a 12-pdr. gun in her stern position. (Photograph by G.A. Milne, National Archives of Canada, PA 107941)

for Flower Class corvettes were completed, that only frigates would be constructed in Canada. Unfortunately, the size of the vessel meant that it could not be built in yards on the Great Lakes as it could not pass through the narrow locks on the St. Lawrence to gain the open sea. It was also a more sophisticated and expensive vessel than the corvette and required a level of technical expertise that was not common in wartime Canada. Nonetheless, in early 1942, orders for 30 frigates, later increased to 70, were issued to Canadian yards but their construction and commissioning were delayed, and in any case the first 10 vessels built in Canada were destined for the RN. The RCN did not receive its first frigate until June 1943 and the last was not commissioned until the end of 1944.

In the meantime, in 1943, the RCN had to work with what it had. In June of that year, the escort fleet consisted of 5 prewar destroyers (soon to be increased by the transfer from Britain of six sister ships), 8 ex-American "four-stackers" (of which only 2 really had the range to serve in the North Atlantic) and 65 corvettes. The large fleet of 60 Bangor and Algerine Class minesweepers were utilized mainly for local escort in coastal waters. The corvette, designed as a stopgap vessel for coastal escort, remained the largest single class of Canadian warship available for mid-ocean work, and by mid-1943 Canadian corvettes lagged far behind their British counterparts in terms of modernization and equipment. In June 1943, few of the RCN's corvettes had undergone the very necessary refit – which included a larger bridge, increased armament, extension of the foc's'le, resiting of the masts and the installation of gyro compasses, as well as other upgrades – while only two of the RN's 60 Flower Class corvettes had *not* been modernized. There were not enough facilities in Canada to upgrade its corvette fleet, and in any case NSHQ's attention was distracted by the frigate and its long-term ambition to acquire larger warships.

The backward state of the RCN's escorts compared to their British counterparts was obvious to their crews and it affected their performance. In the first six months of 1943, at the height of the battle for the sea lanes, the RN sank 110 submarines in the North Atlantic while the RCN, al-

Lieutenant Commander D. W. Piers, DSC, RCN. A prewar regular officer, Piers commanded the destroyer HMCS *Restigouche* in the North Atlantic from 1941 to 1943. In the early summer of 1943 Piers wrote a memorandum to his superiors about the backward state of the equipment on Canadian escort vessels which later came, with a growing body of other evidence on the technical deficiencies of the Canadian warships, to the attention of the naval minister, who removed Admiral P.W. Nelles from his position as Chief of the Naval Staff. Piers's action did not affect his career – in February 1944, he assumed command of the V Class destroyer HMCS *Algonquin*, a prime assignment, and later reached flag rank. Note that he has left the top right button on his jacket undone – an affectation common among British and Canadian destroyer officers, who quite naturally regarded themselves as the elite of their respective navies. (Canadian Naval Memorial Trust)

though it provided nearly half the escorts in this theatre, shared only a third of a kill. This striking disparity and the reasons for it were touched on in a lengthy and detailed report dated 1 June 1943 written by Lieutenant Commander Desmond W. Piers, RCN, captain of HMCS *Restigouche*. It contained a precise summary of the Canadian navy's strengths and weaknesses including a

blunt statement of fact that R.C.N. Ships are outdated in the matter of A/S Equipment by 12 to 18 months, compared to R.N. Ships doing the same job of convoy escort. Unfortunately this gross disparity is not taken into consideration when comparisons of U-boat sinkings and merchant shipping losses are made between British and Canadian [Escort] Groups.[1]

Piers's report was passed on to NSHQ with approving comments from his immediate superiors but, as regards ship modernization, nothing came of it. A more scathing criticism and one that could not be ignored resulted from the visit to Ottawa of the Anti-Submarine Board, a panel of senior Allied naval officers, tasked with co-ordinating the war against the submarines. The Board, while acknowledging the constraints under which the RCN had expanded and was operating, was highly critical of the backwardness of the Canadian navy. This did cause NSHQ to make some changes, albeit, as usual, very slowly. The problem, however, was not going to go away.

ASW begins to change, May–August 1943

The inefficient state of the Canadian mid-ocean escorts was all the more troublesome because the nature of anti-submarine warfare was beginning to change. Prior to 1943, the overriding concern had been the "safe and timely arrival of shipping" – it did not matter if U-boats were sunk; the important thing was that no merchant ships were sunk. With the introduction of VLR aircraft, ship and airborne centimetric radar, "ahead-throwing" weapons such as Hedgehog and Squid, HF/DF and, above all, with the advent of large numbers of new and modern ASW vessels, this outlook changed. The Allied navies now began to think in offensive terms, of killing the enemy whether he attacked convoys or not. The traditional defence of merchant shipping would remain the concern of the close escort groups, but the offensive would now be taken to the enemy by the new support groups, which would have the best commanding officers, vessels and equipment. These support groups would not be tied to a single convoy but would have a roving commission to attach themselves to any convoy that came under heavy attack. Their value had been demonstrated in the convoy battles of the spring of 1943 and if the RCN wanted to achieve a position as a major participant in the offensive against the U-boats, it was clear that it would have to gain membership in these new and elite forces.

Given the state of the Canadian escort force in mid-1943, this would be difficult. After several false tries, two Canadian support groups, Escort Groups 5 and 9, were formed, but they were commanded by British officers and built around British frigates. The best that Canada could do was contribute a single four-stacker destroyer and a few modernized corvettes. Escort Group 5 was created in June 1943, and, after a period of training in the UK, was assigned to the Bay of Biscay area, where an air and surface offensive was underway.

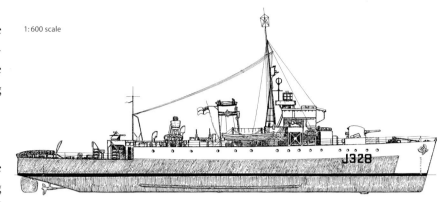

HMCS Kapuskasing, Algerine Class minesweeper
Twelve Algerine Class minesweepers were commissioned in the RCN in 1943-1944. Somewhat larger than the Flower Class corvettes, they were not as seaworthy and were used as coastal escorts, particularly as Senior Officer's ships. Vessels of this class displaced 990 tons, were 225 feet long, had a top speed of 16 knots, carried a complement of 107 and were armed with one 4-inch gun, four 20mm AA guns and Hedgehog. In this drawing, *Kapuskasing* is equipped with Type 271 radar (the dome on top of the bridge) and HF/DF antenna on her foremast. Note the maple leaf on her funnel. (Drawing by L.B. Jenson, courtesy Directorate of History and Heritage, DND)

This was bringing the war to Dönitz's doorstep and it gave him some uncomfortable moments. When he had ordered his submarines out of the North Atlantic in May 1943, Dönitz believed he had lost only a battle, not the campaign he had been waging since September 1939. "We have succumbed to a technical problem," he stated, referring to the efficient radar now mounted on Allied aircraft and escort vessels, "but we shall find a solution."[2]

As he contemplated the strategic situation, Dönitz was fully aware that, although he commanded Germany's most powerful offensive weapon, his future operations would be increasingly defensive in nature. It was clear to him that it would be impossible to starve Britain into submission and that the objective of his operations had to be to sink enough Allied shipping to prevent the build-up in Britain of the troops and supplies necessary to mount an invasion of the European mainland in 1944. And there was no doubt that this invasion would come as, while his submarine crews had been battling at sea, the war had been going badly for Hitler's Third Reich. The German invasion of the Soviet Union in June 1941 had opened a vast

Grey warrior – HMCS *Athabaskan,* March 1944.
Possessing large warships such as the big, fast, powerful Tribal Class destroyers was the ambition of the prewar regular Canadian navy. Unfortunately, by the time the Tribals entered service in 1943, the RCN's primary task was anti-submarine warfare, which required smaller and more specialized vessels. *Athabaskan* was sunk in action in the spring of 1944. She displaced 1,917 tons, carried a complement of 259, and was armed with six 4.7-inch guns, two 4-inch High Angle guns, four 21-inch torpedo tubes, four 2-pdr anti-aircraft guns and six 20mm AA guns. (National Archives of Canada, PA 115361)

new theatre that ultimately engulfed most of Germany's land forces and by the summer of 1943 they were being pushed steadily back. The Allies had eliminated the German and Italian armies in North Africa the previous spring and, following their invasion of Sicily in late July, Mussolini's Fascist dictatorship collapsed and Italy had surrendered. Germany's only hope for victory lay in bringing the Soviet armies to a standstill and preventing, or defeating, a major invasion of the European mainland.

After withdrawing from the North Atlantic, Dönitz had redeployed his submarines against the Britain-Gibraltar and central Atlantic convoy routes but the power of the US Navy, which guarded the middle Atlantic and the ever-increasing numbers of Allied aircraft, whether carrier-borne or operating from land bases, blunted his attempts to maintain a threat. No longer could his submarines take advantage, as they had previously, of resupplying at sea from the large Type XIV "milk cows" or supply boats, in areas not patrolled by Allied aircraft. The number of radar-equipped aircraft, either VLR or shipborne, in service and the formation of support or "hunter-killer" groups resulted in these supply boats being tracked down and destroyed throughout 1943.

Even worse for Dönitz, the Commonwealth navies now brought the fight to the Bay of Biscay, which the U-boats had to cross to reach the open seas. For much of the war, they had been able to sail through this area on the surface but, beginning in 1942, British air and naval forces mounted offensive patrols in the Biscay to prevent the enemy from gaining the wider ocean. Attempts by German submarine commanders to use their AA armament to ward off air attacks often resulted in their boats being sunk or heavily damaged and Dönitz's "wolves of the sea" were forced to cross the Biscay submerged or to creep along the north coast of Spain, which consumed time and fuel with the result that both their range and time on patrol were severely restricted.

In late August, the RCN's Escort Group 5, consisting of the British frigates *Nene* and *Tweed* and the Canadian corvettes *Calgary*, *Edmundston* and *Snowberry*, participated in the latter stages of the bay offensive, carrying out sweeps near the border between France and Spain. The group was backed up by two larger warships, the British destroyer *Grenville* and the Canadian Tribal Class destroyer *Athabaskan*, the second of these large, fast and powerfully armed warships to join the RCN and the pride of the regular Canadian navy. Unfortunately, it became the first target of a new German weapon – the aircraft-launched and controlled guided missile – which sailors, with good reason, nicknamed "Chase Me Charlies." On two successive days, German aircraft attacked EG 5 with this weapon, sinking the sloop HMS *Egret* with the loss of most of her crew and heavily damaging the *Athabaskan*. Soon afterward, operations in the Biscay, which had been garnering fewer results all the time, were ended.

"Dying struggle of a caged tiger:" The U-boats return to the Atlantic, autumn 1943

Both Dönitz and his opponents knew that ultimately the U-boats would have to return to the North Atlantic. It was not only the main shipping route from America to Britain, it was also the area closest to his bases in western France and this proximity, given the recent Allied restrictions imposed on his operations, had becoming increasingly important. On 30 July, the situation was summed up by Commander Rodger Winn, RN, who supervised the Submarine Tracking Room at the Admiralty:

It is common knowledge both to ourselves and the enemy that the only vital issue in the U-Boat war is whether or not we are able to bring to England such supplies of food, oil and raw material and other necessaries, as will enable us, (a) to survive and (b) to mount a military offensive adequate to crush enemy land resistance. Knowing this is so, the enemy in withdrawing from the North Atlantic must have intended an ultimate return to this area, so soon as he might be able, by conceiving new measures and devising new techniques, to resist the offensive which we might be able to bring to bear upon there ...... but it might be the last dying struggle of a caged tiger for the enemy to send back in September or October into the North Western Approaches his main U-Boat forces unless in the meantime, he acquires by sheer luck, or the brilliance of some unknown inventor, the antidote and the panacea to all those well proven weapons which our armoury contains.[3]

The enemy is listening.
Oberleutnant zur See Hans-Edwin Reith, captain of *U-190*, listens on a lead to his boat's hydrophone as Allied warships hunt for his submarine in British waters during the summer of 1944. *Funkobergefreiter* Kurt Petereit, the hydrophone operator, mans the wheel which can turn the hydrophone a full 360 degrees. (Courtesy, Werner Hirschmann)

Winn's assessment proved to be entirely accurate as by the late summer Dönitz felt that he did possess the antidote to the Allied navies' "well proven weapons." It had long been obvious to Dönitz that the Type VII and Type IX boats were at the limit of their development and needed to be replaced by more modern craft. In early 1943, he had chosen two designs, the Type XXI and Type XXIII, based on research by a German naval engineer, Helmut Walter, which incorporated many innovations, including increased numbers of electric batteries that gave these craft an impressive underwater speed. The Type XXI also possessed extremely long range – a boat of this type could journey to the Cape of Good Hope and back without refuelling. In April 1943 Dönitz ordered 450 of the ocean-going Type XXI and 250 of the smaller, coastal Type XXIII from German shipyards and he expected these new vessels would be entering service by the summer of 1944.

Type XXI U-boats under construction.
In 1943, Dönitz instituted a massive construction programme of new submarines but shortages of labour and raw materials and the Allied air forces' disruption of the German transportation system doomed his plan to commission hundreds of the new Type XXI U-boats in 1944, and only one of these craft reached operational status by May 1945. Shown here are unfinished Type XXI boats in a Bremen shipyard. (National Archives of the United States, NA 80G 705573)

For the time being, the Type VII and Type IX would have to fight on, but during the summer of 1943 Dönitz ordered their anti-aircraft armament upgraded so that, if attacked by Allied aircraft on the surface, his commanders had a chance of defending themselves. Boats operating in the Atlantic now carried as many as eight 20mm AA guns although this increased armament still proved inadequate when they tried to fight off Allied aircraft. The U-boats also received radar search detectors to warn if they had been detected by shipborne and aerial radars, allowing them to dive to safety in time. Finally, the first T-5 *Zaunkönig* acoustic torpedoes, which the Allies termed the GNAT (German Naval Acoustic Torpedo), had now entered service. The T-5 did not have to be fired directly at its target and a submarine commander therefore did not have to manoeuvre into the best firing position, often a lengthy and risky operation. He simply let a T5 loose and it homed in on the target ship's propellers to accomplish its purpose.

In September Dönitz decided that, with this new equipment and weaponry, he would resume operations in the North Atlantic. During the first days of that month, 29 U-boats, most equipped with radar detectors and acoustic torpedoes, sailed into the Atlantic to form *Gruppe Leuthen* with the objective of intercepting a major westbound convoy. The *gruppe* was to remain unseen both during passage and while formed in a patrol line but Dönitz emphasized that once a convoy was sighted *Leuthen* was "to make full use of the surprise blow," by attacking the convoy escort with acoustic torpedoes:

> The decimation of the escort must be the first objective. The destruction of a few destroyers will have considerable moral effect upon the enemy and will greatly facilitate the attack on ships of the convoy in addition. ...... I expect of all commanding officers that each chance of a shot at a destroyer will be utilized. From now on, the U-boat is the attacker – fire first and then submerge.[4]

The stage was now set for the last of the great Atlantic convoy battles.

"Beasts of prey were gathering:" The battle for ONS 18 and ON 202, September 1943

Bletchley Park was able to provide timely intelligence of the German commander's intentions and deployment. At risk were two westbound convoys, slow convoy ONS 18 with 27 merchant ships and, coming up astern, fast convoy ON 202 with 40 ships. The escort for ONS 18 was provided by B-3 Group with two destroyers, a frigate and five corvettes assisted by a MAC (Merchant Aircraft Carrier) ship, *Empire MacAlpine*, which carried eight obsolescent Swordfish biplanes. ON 202 was under the guard of C-2 Group which comprised the destroyers HMCS *Gatineau* (Senior Officer) and HMS *Icarus*, the Canadian corvettes *Drumheller* and *Kamloops* and the British corvette *Polyanthus*. Available to reinforce either convoy was Canadian Escort Group 9 with the frigate HMS *Itchen*, the destroyer HMCS *St. Croix* and three Canadian corvettes, *Chambly*, *Morden* and *Sackville*. The

The chiefs and petty officers had it no better.
The chiefs and petty officers' messdeck on a corvette was no more spacious than that of the ordinary sailors – as this photograph demonstrates. (Canadian Naval Memorial Trust)

The pleasures of dining at sea.
In a time when Canadian warships had only rudimentary refrigeration facilities, fresh food, particularly bread, quickly became stale. Here, Able Seaman C.G. Walker of HMCS *Georgian* demonstrates how to cut rock-hard bread with a saw. Note the crowded quarters and the off-duty sailor sleeping in his "mick" or hammock behind Walker. (Photograph by W.H. Pugsley, National Archives of Canada, PA 134351)

commanding officers and crews of all three groups were experienced and they were backed up by no less than 73 VLR aircraft flying from Ireland, Iceland and Newfoundland.

It was a Canadian aircraft that got first blood. At 0855 on 19 September a VLR Liberator of 10 RCAF Squadron was covering ONS 18 when it sighted a submarine on the surface 160 miles ahead of the convoy but moving toward it. The Liberator attacked but the U-boat commander,

On both sides, the forces employed in the Battle of the Atlantic were subject to highly centralized command from shore-based headquarters. The Allied convoy system depended on rigid control of sailing schedules and routes, while Dönitz's employment of wolfpack tactics depended on frequent radio communication between his headquarters and U-boats at sea. The result was that both combatants generated a tremendous amount of radio communications that provided an important source of intelligence for their opponent.

Ultra intelligence

The Allied codebreakers' success in unravelling the mysteries of cyphers generated by the Enigma machine was a war-winning asset. Information derived in this manner, termed "special intelligence" or Ultra, was not the most important weapon possessed by Allied naval intelligence, and perhaps too much emphasis can be put on the effect of Ultra in the Battle of the Atlantic as it did have weaknesses. It was subject to a delay and might not reach the relevant command in time, and there was always great concern about security – if the Germans learned that their Enigma-generated cyphers had been broken by the Allies, they would switch to a completely different system and this valuable asset, which affected land and air as well as naval operations, would be lost. For this reason, circulation of Ultra was restricted to a very few senior officers.

Ultra was also sensitive to procedural changes on the part of the *Kriegsmarine*. Most simply put, Allied codebreakers were able to read the German *Heimisch* or "Dolphin" traffic, the code used for *Kriegsmarine* surface vessels and U-boats in home waters, without delay from the summer of 1941 to early 1942. At that point, changes made to U-boat coding systems and the introduction of the M4 Enigma machine led to the creation of a new cypher, called *Triton* by the Germans and "Shark" by the Allies, which baffled codebreakers until late 1942 when they were able to read it intermittently but with considerable delay. *Triton* was completely broken in March 1943, just in time for the high point of the battle, but it was still subject to delays. From September 1943 to the end of the war, however, advances in codebreaking technology led to *Shark* being read within 24 hours.

It should be remembered that both sides were involved in codebreaking. The German signals intelligence organization, the *B-dienst*, had broken the major British naval cypher before the war and were able to read it until the late summer of 1940 when Naval Cypher No. 3 was introduced. The Germans broke Cypher No. 3, used for the routing of convoys and escorts, in the first part of 1942, and from July 1942 to June 1943 were able to read almost all communications in this cypher with little delay, which offset the Allies' possession of Ultra. *B-dienst* lost this powerful asset in June 1943 when Cypher No. 5 was introduced and never regained it during the war.

Other intelligence

As discussed above, HF/DF, "Huff Duff," or High Frequency Direction Finding, was another crucial weapon for Allied intelligence. Land-based HF/DF stations that picked up a U-boat's signal could provide an approximate location although with some degree or error. Those signals would then become the subject of traffic analysis, the rigorous appraisal of the characteristics, frequency and form of the transmission that might give some clue as to its contents. Traffic analysis was made simpler by the fact that many U-boat transmissions were highly stylized. Weather, position, and sighting reports were often prefixed with a "Beta-Beta" code, giving them priority over other communications on the same radio frequency. Termed "B-bar" signals by Allied intelligence organizations, such transmissions hinted at their contents and a B-bar signal from a U-boat in the known vicinity of a convoy, for example, was an indication that it had been sighted and might be attacked.

Information provided by Ultra, HF/DF and traffic analysis was combined with other intelligence, such as U-boat siting reports made by vessels and aircraft or information provided by agents (the many French civilian staff employed at U-boat bases in France proved very useful in this regard). No matter what its source, all information relating to the U-boats ultimately arrived at the Operational Intelligence Centre at the Admiralty in London.

Collection, analysis and dissemination of operational intelligence

The OIC and its component, the Submarine Tracking Room, correlated and analyzed all this information and then disseminated it to the relevant naval and air commands. Up to 1943, the major use of operational intelligence was to re-route convoys around the known or estimated positions of U-boat packs, and, if at all possible, an attempt was made to provide accurate information about possible U-boat locations before a convoy sailed. From 1943 onward, it was also used offensively in providing Allied "hunter-killer" groups with locations for U-boats that would then be attacked. The OIC in London most often dealt with the headquarters of Western Approaches Command in Liverpool, which assumed responsibility for operations in much of the North Atlantic and the RAF's Coastal Command but, if relevant, it would also share information with the OICs in Ottawa and Washington (known as Op-20-G to the USN), which would then warn any threatened naval or air force commands in their areas of responsibility.

If a situation developed where recent intelligence revealed a shift in German dispositions, an attempt was made to actually divert convoys at sea. On many occasions, however, this information did not arrive in time to prevent a convoy being attacked and in other cases Dönitz received timely information from the *B-dienst* to counter such a move.

Convoy SC 42, September 1941

The map opposite provides an illustration of how operational intelligence was used in September 1941 to frustrate German attacks on a number of convoys, but unfortunately not the luckless Convoy SC 42, which suffered heavy losses.

On 4 September 1941 Dönitz, having failed to intercept a number of convoys which had been routed around his patrol lines because of timely information, ordered 14 U-boats to form *Gruppe Markgraf* to patrol a large area off the southeast coast of Greenland (shaded area on map). This order was decoded by Bletchley Park on 6 September, and although the

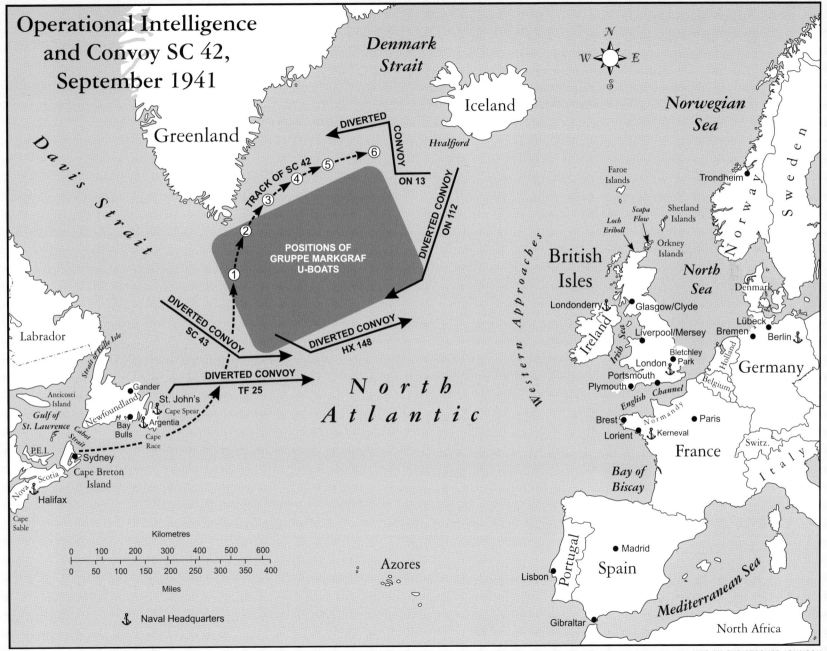

Operational Intelligence
and Convoy SC 42,
September 1941

Denmark
Strait

*Norwegian
Sea*

Iceland

Greenland

Hvalfjord

DIVERTED

CONVOY

TRACK OF SC 42

ON 13

DIVERTED CONVOY

ON 112

POSITIONS OF
GRUPPE MARKGRAF
U-BOATS

Davis Strait

DIVERTED CONVOY

SC 43

DIVERTED CONVOY

HX 148

DIVERTED CONVOY

TF 25

Labrador

Gander

Strait of Belle Isle

Anticosti
Island

*Gulf of
St. Lawrence*

Newfoundland

St. John's

Cape Spear

*Cabot
Strait*

Bay
Bulls

Argentia

Cape
Race

P.E.I.

Sydney

Cape Breton
Island

Nova Scotia

Halifax

Cape
Sable

*North
Atlantic*

Faroe
Islands

*Scapa
Flow*

*Loch
Eriboll*

Shetland
Islands

Orkney
Islands

British
Isles

*North
Sea*

Western Approaches

Londonderry

Glasgow/Clyde

Norway

Sweden

Trondheim

Denmark

Lübeck

Bremen

Berlin

Liverpool/Mersey

Ireland

Irish Sea

London

Bletchley
Park

Portsmouth

Plymouth

English Channel

Normandy

Brest

Lorient

Kerneval

Paris

France

Germany

Holland

Belgium

Switz.

Italy

*Bay of
Biscay*

Portugal

Lisbon

Madrid

Spain

Mediterranean Sea

Gibraltar

North Africa

Azores

Kilometres

0 100 200 300 400 500 600

0 50 100 150 200 250 300 350 400

Miles

⚓ Naval Headquarters

N
W   E
S

MAP BY CHRISTOPHER JOHNSON

area to be patrolled by *Markgraf* was not exactly clear to the Allied intelligence, four convoys were routed north or south of the suspected German locations (lines on map). Convoy SC 42, 64 merchant ships escorted by a Canadian destroyer and three corvettes, had been battling headwinds, rough weather and heavy seas since it had left Sydney, Nova Scotia, on 4 September. The escort vessels were too short on fuel for SC 42 to be re-routed to the south so it was diverted north up the coast of Greenland in an attempt to make an end run around the location of *Markgraf*.

Unfortunately for SC 42, a straggler from the convoy was sighted and sunk by *U-81* on 8 September (1 on the map) and the following day the convoy was sighted (2 on map) by *U-85*, which sent a sighting report and began to track it. Dönitz's response was to order all boats in *Markgraf* to concentrate and attack. At this point, the situation favoured the Germans because SC 42 was beyond air cover from either Newfoundland or Iceland and the U-boats could therefore proceed on the surface using their superior speed to catch the convoy. The German transmissions were decoded by Bletchley Park but there was little that the OIC in London could do to prevent what was about to happen.

During the night of 9-10 September, at least five U-boats came into contact with SC 42 (at 3), sinking five merchantmen despite the best efforts of the escort. The score was evened somewhat when two Canadian corvettes, HMC Ships *Chambly* and *Moose Jaw*, under the command of Lieutenant Commander J.D. Prentice, arrived from Newfoundland. Prentice, who had been watching the situation develop around SC 42 on the naval plot at St. John's, had asked for and received permission to put to sea to reinforce the escort and had fortuitously appeared just in time to sink *U-501* ahead of the convoy.

The U-boats reported their victories to Dönitz by radio during the day of 10 September, and since it was clear that they were in good contact with a slow convoy, he ordered them to attack without mercy. The escort, however, was assisted on that day by a Catalina aircraft flying from Iceland at extreme range (4 on map), which patrolled briefly over the convoy and made it difficult for the attackers to manoeuvre into the best positions. Over the next two days, 10-11 September, SC 42 would enjoy intermittent air cover (5 on map) but not in strength enough to prevent the U-boats mounting further attacks which resulted in the loss of 11 more merchantmen. In all, 11 U-boats made 25 separate recorded attacks on SC 42 before the arrival of escort reinforcements and continuous daylight air cover forced Dönitz to call off the attack at this position (6 on map).

As the experience of SC 42 demonstrates, although operational intelligence could prevent or reduce losses, it was not always successful in doing so when other factors such as weather, seas, availability of air cover, strength of escort and fuel states affected convoys. Operational Intelligence was a means to an end – and an important means – but the outcome of the tactical battle was often resolved by the skill and determination of the escorts and their German opponents. ∎

Kriegsmarine *Schlüssel* M4 Enigma machine, 1942.
The Enigma machine was an electronic coding machine that was adopted by the German armed forces in the 1930s. The *Kriegsmarine* introduced an upgraded model, the *Schlüssel M4*, in late 1941. Up to that time, thanks to the efforts of the codebreaking organization at Bletchley Park in England, the Allies had been able to read much of Dönitz's signal traffic, but *Schlüssel M4*, which possessed a more complicated enciphering mechanism, produced a sophisticated code called "Triton" that baffled Allied codebreakers from early 1942 to March 1943. "Triton" was broken just in time to have a major effect on the highpoint of the Battle of the Atlantic in the spring of 1943. (Courtesy, Steve Fahie)

Oberleutnant zur See Dietrich Epp, elected to stay on the surface and use his heavy AA armament to defend himself – that proved to be a mistake as well-placed depth charges blew his vessel's bows out of the water and *U-341* was no more. Just before midnight, *U-402* of *Gruppe Leuthen* sighted ONS 18 and, at 0155, 20 September, *Oberleutnant zur See* Paul-Friedrich Otto of *U-270* sent a Beta-Beta, what Allied codebreakers called a "B-Bar signal" or sighting report giving the convoy's location and heading: "beta/beta. Convoy square 1944, AL, 270 degrees, Otto."[5] Almost immediately, the reply came back from Dönitz's headquarters: "Leuthen at 'em. Otto report contact. Manseck [commander of U-758] report weather at once." The battle was joined.

Otto's signal was picked up by the HF/DF equipment on board the vessels of C-2 Group, which was with ON 202 coming up behind the slow convoy. The group's Senior Officer, Commander P.W. Burnett, RN, obtained a fix for *U-270* and dispatched the frigate HMS *Langan* to investigate, and when *Langan* acquired a firm radar contact, reinforced her with HMCS *Gatineau*. The target was Otto's *U-270* but at 0259 Otto fired an acoustic torpedo at *Langan* which blew the frigate's stern off and killed 29 of her crew – a spectacular debut for the new weapon. *Gatineau*, coming on the scene, responded with a depth charge attack that damaged *U-270* and forced Otto to withdraw from the attack. The tug *Destiny* took the shattered *Langan* in tow and got her safely back to a friendly port but the frigate's career was finished.

Unfortunately, while the escort group was diverted by this incident, *U-238*, commanded by *Oberleutnant zur See* Horst Hepp, made contact with ONS 18 and, maintaining strict radio silence, manoeuvred into a position ahead of the convoy. At 0732, as the lead ships were approaching his position, Hepp sank the merchantmen *Frederick Douglas* and *Theodore Dwight Weld* before diving deep and passing under the convoy. C-2 Group carried out ASDIC searches and attacked suspected contacts but *U-238* escaped unharmed and remained in touch. The escorts, however, were assisted in their work by the arrival of VLR aircraft, which stayed over the convoy the entire day.

The loss of three ships in a few hours prompted Admiral Max Horton to order the two convoys to merge and their escort to be reinforced by the RCN's Escort Group 9. On receipt of this signal, Commander M.B. Evans, RN, the Senior Officer of B-3 Group with the slow convoy, later recalled that, although the fast convoy astern of him "was the centre of attraction around which the beasts of prey were gathering," he "felt rather a brute in leading my poor little ONS 18 into the turmoil," although his crews expressed "delight at a chance of activity – with handsome escort – after months of dreary ocean plodding."[6] However, combining 65 merchant ships and three escort groups into a new and defensible formation proved to be a very difficult task and, as the commander of C-2 group later commented, throughout most of 20 September ONS 18 and ON 202 "gyrated majestically about the ocean, never appearing to get much closer, and watched appreciatively by a growing swarm of U-boats."[7]

As this cumbersome elephant dance took place on the face of a calm sea, VLR aircraft and the convoy escorts were keeping the prowling enemy at bay. Several attempted attacks were foiled and in the early evening an RAF Liberator sank *U-338*. When another aircraft reported a surfaced U-boat a few minutes later, HMCS *St. Croix* of Escort Group 9 steamed toward the area, right into the periscope sights of *Kapitänleutnant* Rudolf Bahr of *U-305* who fired an acoustic torpedo that blew off her stern. While his crew struggled to keep *St. Croix* afloat, her captain, Lieutenant Commander A.H. Dobson, RCN, ordered her boats lowered and the wounded placed in them as a safety measure and then signalled HMS *Itchen*, which was coming to his rescue, that he was "leaving the office."[8]

Almost at that same moment, *U-305* fired a second, standard torpedo at *St. Croix* that cut the vessel in half. When *Itchen* arrived on the scene, she found only the destroyer's bow above water and the sea around it dotted with the heads of survivors. Presented with a new target, Bahr fired an acoustic torpedo at *Itchen* which detonated in the frigate's wake and her captain wisely decided to wait for support from the corvette HMS *Polyanthus* before attempting to pick up survivors.

Unfortunately, *Polyanthus* never made it. While she was standing by *St. Croix's* survivors, *Itchen* fired starshells that drew no less than four U-boats toward her. *Polyanthus* had just carried out an attack on one of these

Four-stacker – ill-fated HMCS *St. Croix*.
One of six ex-USN destroyers taken over by the RCN in late 1940 and one of the few that had the range to operate in the North Atlantic, *St. Croix* served with the Newfoundland Escort Force and MOEF in 1941-1943. She was a relatively successful ship, sinking *U-90* in July 1942 and assisting in the destruction of *U-87* in April 1943 – but her luck ran out in September 1943 when she was sunk by *U-305*. Eighty-one members of her crew were rescued by HMS *Itchen* but only one survived the subsequent loss of that vessel. (Directorate of History and Heritage, DND, PA 104474)

had spent a long and cold night in the oil-soaked Atlantic. Many had drowned or succumbed to hypothermia, but through the diligent efforts of Dobson, just over half the destroyer's complement of 147 men were plucked from the sea.

The fog continued throughout 21 September and into the next day. In such weather, the radar-equipped escorts had the advantage over the U-boats that were trying to manoeuvre into positions to attack the combined convoy, which now consisted of 18 columns of ships spread out over 30 square miles of ocean. Time and time again, they beat off the enemy but the only escort to score a kill was the destroyer HMS *Keppel*, which ran down a HF/DF fix during the early hours of 22 September and surprised *Oberleutnant zur See* Robert Schetelig's *U-229* running on the surface – *Keppel* promptly rammed and sank it. Despite hazardous flying conditions, the *Empire MacAlpine* launched one of her rickety Swordfish biplanes and VLR aircraft patrols were kept constantly overhead.

The fog finally lifted during the afternoon of 22 September and Commander Evans, who had assumed command of all the escorts recorded that, after "living under a blanket for so long …… it was very nice to come into the open air and find it filled with Liberators."[9] Those aircraft were from 10 Squadron RCAF based in Newfoundland and over the next few hours they made three separate attacks on surfaced submarines prowling around the convoy. Liberator L/10 flown by Warrant Officer J. Billings attacked Otto's *U-270* with depth charges in the face of anti-aircraft fire so accurate that it knocked out one of his engines and hit the cockpit of the aircraft. Having expended his depth charges, Billings requested assistance from Liberator X/10, another 10 Squadron aircraft, only to receive the reply: "I have a U-boat of my own on my hands."[10] Billings was forced to break off the attack after he expended his ammunition but Otto's submarine was so badly damaged he had to return to base. Meanwhile, Liberator X/10, having dropped all its depth charges, severely raked *U-377* with its machine guns,

opponents when another submarine, *U-952* commanded by *Oberleutnant zur See* Oskar Curio, fired an acoustic torpedo that immediately sank the corvette, taking down her entire crew except one survivor who was rescued the next day. It was now quite dark and the night that followed degenerated into a confused series of separate actions as the escorts tracked down and attacked several U-boats, which responded by firing acoustic torpedoes without success.

Just before dawn on 21 September, a thick blanket of fog descended on the two convoys which had finally managed, more by luck than skill, to position themselves abeam of each other. Thirteen hours after *St. Croix* had sunk, *Itchen* finally found time to return and rescue her survivors who seriously wounding its captain, *Oberleutnant zur See* Gerhard Kluth. His second-in-command submerged and withdrew from the battle to seek medical assistance. A few minutes later, Liberator X/10 attacked another surfaced submarine only to lose it in a fog bank. Elsewhere, two Swordfish from *Empire MacAlpine* sighted another surfaced submarine but, being no match for its heavy AA armament, contented themselves with circling out of range and calling in the escorts to deal with it. The U-boat dived deep before surface vessels came up and escaped. Finally, at dusk Liberator N/10 from 10 Squadron RCAF arrived and mounted a patrol around the convoy until darkness fell.

But there were still 10 boats from *Gruppe Leuthen* in contact and they were not yet finished. At 2130 hours, *Itchen* got a good radar contact ahead of the convoy and steamed to investigate, beginning a confusing but very lively night as the U-boats tried to penetrate the escort screen only to be foiled by the warships. The enemy responded with acoustic torpedoes which, fortunately, either missed their targets or exploded prematurely. Tragically, at one minute before midnight, *Itchen* was hit by a T5 fired by *Kapitänleutnant* Herbert Engel in *U-666* and sank so fast that only three men were rescued: a sailor from her own crew, a survivor from *St. Croix* and the sole survivor from *Polyanthus*. At about 0200, the intrepid *Kapitänleutnant* Hepp of *U-238* managed to slip on the surface through a gap in the escort screen and sink three merchantmen. At 0615, while it was still dark, *Kapitänleutnant* Oskar Curio, commanding *U-952*, recorded "At last, shadows to starboard," as he sighted the convoy and fired a spread of standard torpedoes that hit and sank a sixth merchant ship.[11] That was the last casualty because, when dawn came on 23 September, the Liberators of 10 Squadron from Newfoundland returned in strength to drive the U-boats under and Dönitz ended the attack.

"We cannot stand these losses:" The U-boats leave the North Atlantic
Both sides claimed victory. Dönitz, working from the radio reports of the commanders of *Gruppe Leuthen* believed that, for the loss of 3 submarines, his crews had used the new torpedoes to sink no less than 12 destroyers and 7 merchant ships, and damage 3 more destroyers and 3 merchant

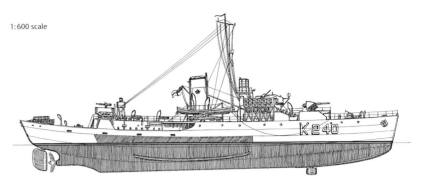

1:600 scale

HMCS *Vancouver*, Flower Class corvette, as modified.
Commissioned in early 1942, *Vancouver* was later modified to the configurations shown here. Her bridge has been rebuilt and enlarged, new bridge wings have been installed to bear the weight of heavier AA armament and her foc'sle has been extended. *Vancouver* carries Type 271 radar in the dome at the base of her foremast. (Drawing by L.B. Jenson, courtesy of Directorate of History and Heritage, DND)

ships. He also believed that the new radar search detectors mounted on many of the submarines in *Leuthen* had worked satisfactorily and would go some way to eliminating the threat of Allied aircraft. In actual fact, his commanders had sunk 3 escorts and 6 merchant ships while, as for the new German T5 torpedo, an effective Canadian countermeasure was introduced within a matter of days. Dubbed the CAT (Canadian Anti-Acoustical Torpedo) gear, it was basically a noisemaker, an arrangement of loosely connected pipes which, if towed behind a ship, produced a louder noise than her propellers, causing the torpedo to explode harmlessly against it. The battle for ONS 18 and ON 202, however, cost the lives of about 400 British and Canadian sailors from *Itchen*, *Polyanthus* and *St. Croix* and more or less eliminated Escort Group 9 in the process. It was formally disbanded a few weeks later.*

Believing wrongly that the new weapons had turned the balance in his favour, Dönitz continued group operations in the North Atlantic with disastrous results. In early October, 15 U-boats attacked Convoy SC 143 and sank one escort and one merchant ship for the loss of three of their

---

* The designation Escort Group 9 was given to a new support group formed later in the war.

number. Operations in late October and early November were even worse – one merchant ship sunk against four submarines lost. By this time, there were even more aircraft above the Atlantic as Portugal had finally permitted the Allies to fly from the Azores Islands, thus closing the southern part of the Atlantic air gap. On 1 November, the daily log of the U-boat Headquarters complained: "We cannot stand these losses particularly with no successes to counterbalance them" and a week later Dönitz redeployed his remaining submarines from the mid-ocean to the eastern Atlantic.[12] His plan was to continue offensive operations as long as possible until the new and more effective Type XXI and XXIII submarines appeared the following year.

The magnitude of the German defeat in this last attempt to operate in strength in the North Atlantic is revealed in the statistics – between June and December 1943, the Allies lost 87 merchant ships, although 47 of these vessels were either sailing independently or stragglers from convoys. Of the 41,000 ships convoyed across the Atlantic during the same period, 40 were sunk, a loss rate of just under 1 in a 1000. Balanced against this was the loss during the same period of about 150 U-boats. Dönitz's bid to return to the Atlantic had utterly failed.

"War is not won by valour alone:" Crisis in Ottawa, December 1943

Unfortunately, very few of the German submarine kills in the last half of 1943 were made by the RCN – HMC Ships *Snowberry* and *Calgary* joined a British vessel in sinking *Kapitänleutnant* Rolph Schauenburg's Type IX boat, *U-536*, on 20 November – and that was the sole success. This did not please Prime Minister Mackenzie King's Liberal cabinet which had been under considerable criticism throughout 1943 for its ham-fisted management of the Canadian war effort. The Minister of the Navy, Angus L. Macdonald, who was not noted for having any real knowledge of naval warfare, was embarrassed in front of his cabinet colleagues and wanted to know why the RCN, which was absorbing a considerable portion of that war effort, was not more successful, and he began to suspect a cover-up by Nelles and his senior staff of the RCN's technical backwardness. Throughout the summer and autumn of 1943, Macdonald had collected informa-

Angus L. Macdonald (1890-1954).

Angus L. Macdonald, shown here with Rear Admiral G.C. Jones and (on the right) Commander E.R. Mainguy, was the Minister of Defence for Naval Service from 1940-1945. Macdonald presided over the wartime expansion of the RCN but he did not take much interest in the navy until 1943 when its poor record of submarine victories caused the Liberal government some political embarrassment. The result was an investigation into the backwardness of the escort fleet that ultimately led to the replacement of Admiral P.W. Nelles. (Directorate of History and Heritage, DND, DHH-H115)

tion from various British and Canadian sources, some of it accurate and some not, about the state of the Canadian navy and its equipment. Since, in Macdonald's eyes, German submarines killed translated into Liberal votes gained, he began to look for a scapegoat and his sights became firmly fixed on Rear Admiral Percy Nelles, the Chief of the Naval Staff.

In October 1943, Macdonald sent his executive assistant, John Connolly, on a fact-finding mission to Britain. Connolly crossed the Atlantic in the corvette *Orillia* to meet with Horton and other British officers concerned with Canadian operations in the Atlantic and gained valuable information, particularly about the slow rate of modernization of the Flower Class corvettes. After his return to Ottawa, he submitted a long memorandum to Macdonald detailing the deficiencies in the RCN, which was prefaced with the remark that

> My personal views cannot count in this business. I must admit they are prejudiced – because I know what men in Corvettes at sea have to face from the elements – because I have been told what they must face at the hands of a desperate, scientifically armed enemy – because I doubt the ability of some of our ships to deal with submarines.
>
> A war is not won by valour alone, or by the keenness of the individual fighter.[13]

Macdonald used information provided by Connolly and from other sources to begin an exchange of increasingly acrimonious correspondence with Nelles that ultimately led to the admiral's dismissal as Chief of the Naval Staff in late December 1943. The firing was sweetened by the appointment of Nelles as Senior Canadian Flag Officer Overseas, the pretext being that the build-up of Canadian naval forces for the forthcoming invasion of the European mainland required such an appointment, but it was essentially an empty position as all Canadian warships operating in British waters were under the operational control of the Admiralty. Nelles had served as CNS for ten years, and although it was clear that he found it difficult to assimilate the highly technological nature of ASW, he had done an honest if rather plodding job of overseeing the expansion of the RCN since 1939.

His replacement was Rear Admiral George C. Jones, an intelligent and ambitious officer, but not a man liked or respected by his peers – his service nickname was "Jetty Jones" because his record of minor collisions had kept the vessels he commanded in dockyards for long periods. In 1941-1942, Jones held the appointment of Commanding Officer, Atlantic Coast, at Halifax while Murray was commanding the Newfoundland Escort Force – the two officers had never particularly liked each other and Murray

suspected, with some reason, that Jones had not fully backed up the NEF during its very difficult first year of operations. This was the closest Jones ever came to the Battle of the Atlantic – essentially a desk officer and a political animal, he had transferred to NSHQ in 1942 and had adroitly manoeuvred himself into a position of being the best candidate to replace Nelles.

Jones was fortunate to take over command of the RCN just as that service, having suffered through awful growing pains brought on by unbridled expansion, was about to reach maturity. The autumn 1943 successes in the North Atlantic had convinced Allied naval staffs that the sea lanes were nearly secure and all three English-speaking navies cut back plans to build more ASW escorts. At the same time, the construction of merchant shipping reached unprecedented levels – in the previous 12 months, the United States alone had produced 1,949 merchantmen totalling 13 million tons of gross weight, which compared very well to the 420,000 tons that had been lost that year in Atlantic. By the end of 1943, 16 of the new frigates had joined the RCN and at long last Canadian corvettes were being taken in hand for modernization. The state of equipment on warships, particularly radar, ASDIC and "ahead throwing" weapons such as Hedgehog and Squid, still lagged behind the RN and USN but it was beginning to catch up and there were plans to send a technical liaison team to Britain to keep abreast of the latest developments.

Vice Admiral G.C. Jones, RCN, (1895-1946), second wartime commander of the RCN.

A prewar regular, Jones served as COAC (Commanding Officer, Atlantic Coast) from 1940 to 1942 while his longtime rival, Commodore L.W. Murray, was commanding the Newfoundland Escort Force. He later moved to NSHQ and replaced Rear Admiral Percy Nelles as senior officer of the RCN in January 1944. An ambitious man, Jones excelled at staff work but did not have a good reputation as a shiphandler – his nickname, "Jetty Jones," derived from the amount of time ships under his command spent in dock for repairs following minor collisions. (National Archives of Canada, PA 200116)

The RCN's "Happy Time:" January to April 1944

On 1 January 1944, Dönitz had 436 U-boats in commission but only about 160 were available for deployment and a significant proportion of these were usually in transit to and from their area of operations. The remainder were new boats working up, or boats being refitted or repaired. Most were Type VII and Type IX craft but Dönitz still hoped that, by the spring of 1944, the first of the new submarines would be ready to thwart a possible invasion of Europe. In the meantime, he was forced to change his tactics. On Hitler's orders, Dönitz reinforced the submarine flotillas in Norway operating against the Allied convoys to the Soviet Union and those in the Mediterranean, leaving him 121 boats available for the Atlantic and Indian Oceans. He sent most of the Atlantic boats to operate in two large groups in the eastern part of that ocean, but such was the strength of Allied airpower that they were forced to remain submerged during much of their time at sea and were unable to concentrate against convoys. Dönitz simply placed them in the best intercept positions on the major shipping lanes where they waited for the targets to come to them.

Their locations, of course, were known to the Allies through Ultra and the change in German tactics played right into the hands of their opponents, who were shifting emphasis from the defensive protection of shipping to the offensive task of killing German submarines. This was to be the main role of the hunter-killer groups formed in the three Allied navies.

Although the RCN had enjoyed indifferent success in 1943, things changed in the first part of 1944 as, with increased experience, new ships and better equipment, the Canadian ASW forces enjoyed a very successful period. The first kill was registered by Escort Group 6, consisting of two British frigates and three Canadian corvettes, *Camrose*, *Edmundston* and *Snowberry*, which reinforced the escort of Convoys KMS 38 and OS 64 off Ireland in early 1944. On 8 January, the group obtained a surface radar contact which turned out to be *U-757*, a Type VII craft commanded by *Korvettenkapitän* Friedrich Deetz, and after the warships drove it under, they attacked it continuously for 12 hours until a depth charge launched by *Camrose* resulted in "a pool of oil, some bits of wreckage and a uniform cap" floating on the surface.[14]

The next success was gained by the frigates HMS *Nene* and HMCS *Waskesiu*, which picked up an ASDIC contact on 24 February while serving as part of the escort for an eastward-bound convoy. They commenced an attack which drove the contact deep and kept attacking until *Nene*, becoming impatient, broke off the hunt and returned to the convoy. *Waskesiu* remained and, soon after the British vessel left, obtained a firm contact which she blew to the surface with a depth charge attack. When the crew of *Kapitänleutnant* Heinz Rahe's Type VII boat, *U-257*, attempted to man

1:600 scale

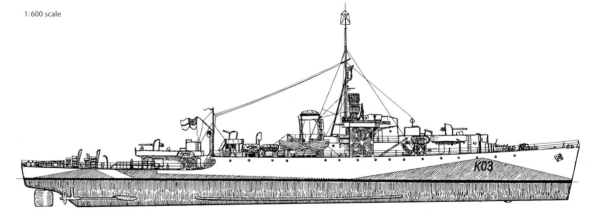

HMCS *Dunver*, River Class frigate.
The frigate, or "twin-screw corvette," was an improved ASW vessel intended for mid-ocean escort work that entered Canadian service in 1943 and 67 River Class frigates were commissioned by the RCN. A vessel of this class displaced 1,445 tons, was 301 feet long, carried a complement of 141, had a top speed of 19 knots, twice the range of a Flower Class corvette, and was armed with two 4-inch guns, four 20mm AA guns and the Hedgehog ASW weapon (mounted on the main deck ahead of the forward gun) as well as depth charges. *Dunver* is shown here with HF/DF antenna and Type 272 radar. The main armament of the first 15 Canadian River Class frigates was one 4-inch gun and one 12-pdr. gun. (Drawing by L.B. Jenson, courtesy Directorate of History and Heritage, DND)

their guns, they were cut down by a hail of fire from the Canadian ship and abandoned their sinking boat. *Waskesiu* recovered 19 survivors but Rahe was not among them as he had thrown his lifejacket to one of his crew and chose to go down with his command. *Waskesiu* became the first Canadian frigate to score a kill.

One of the most notable victories in this period was gained by C-2 Group while escorting Convoy HX 280. Late in the evening of 5 March 1944 HMCS *Gatineau* picked up a contact which was attacked by five British and Canadian warships. The submarine, *U-744*, a Type VII commanded by *Oberleutnant zur See* Heinz Blischke, dived deep and executed a series of turning manoeuvres which frustrated the attackers for nearly 15 hours. In mid-afternoon, new submarine contacts caused the larger warships to depart, leaving HMC Ships *St. Catharines*, *Chilliwack* and *Fennel* in place. They were later joined by HMS *Kenilworth Castle*, equipped with the new Squid mortar, which made a series of attacks on *U-744* until darkness fell on 6 March. At dawn the next day, two British destroyers arrived to carry out a further series of attacks that lasted for nearly three hours but, frustrated with the lack of results, the British left the three Canadian vessels to simply wait out Blischke, who had not been able to surface to recharge his batteries.

At 1520 hours, the two corvettes were about to commence a new attack when *U-744* rose to the surface directly ahead of *Chilliwack*. The corvette opened up with everything it had, scoring several hits on the conning tower, killing Blischke and blowing one of the U-boat's AA guns off its mount. The German crew, who were in no condition to fight, indicated that they wished to surrender, and as the heavily damaged *U-744* lay wallowing on the surface, a race began between the three Canadian ships to launch boats and get aboard the prize. The sea was so rough that some of the boats capsized but eventually all the Canadians and 39 German survivors were safe, although the U-boat was too badly damaged to be taken in tow

and had to be sunk. The hunt for *U-744*, which had lasted 36 hours, was the second longest U-boat hunt of the war and a signal success for the ships involved.

The RCN's good fortune continued in March 1944. Four days after the destruction of *U-744*, another submarine was sunk while shadowing Convoy SC 154, which was strongly protected by C-1 Group and the Canadian Escort Group 9. HMCS *St. Laurent* had dropped astern of the convoy to assist a merchantman put out a fire when she picked up radio transmission which, with HF/DF, she was able to locate as having originated between her position and the convoy. These signals were from *Korvettenkapitän* Werner Weber's Type IX boat, *U-845*, which had been sent on a

The capture of *U-744*, March 1944.
On the morning of 5 March 1944, British and Canadian escort vessels obtained an ASDIC contact that initiated the second-longest U-boat hunt of the war. After 32 hours and constant attacks, *U-744* surfaced directly ahead of HMCS *Chilliwack*, and promptly came under heavy fire that hit its conning tower repeatedly, as is evident from this photograph. Boarding parties were sent to capture *U-744* but it was heavily damaged and sank. (National Archives of Canada, PA 112996)

The frigate HMCS *Saint John*, 1944.
In the last half of 1943, the first frigates began to enter Canadian service. Commissioned in December 1943, *Saint John* joined Escort Group 9 in April 1944 and shared with HMCS *Swansea* the destruction of *U-247* in September 1944 and, in February 1945, destroyed *U-309*. *Saint John* was sold for scrap in 1947. Note the HF/DF antenna on her foremast and the Type 271 radar in its perspex dome. (Photograph by E.W. Dinsmore, National Archives of Canada, PA 134503)

long patrol into Canadian waters the previous month. Weber was an aggressive officer. On 1 February he had run aground while trying to tail a freighter entering the narrow harbour of St. John's but had got his badly damaged boat off and encountered SC 154 during his return voyage.

In mid-afternoon on 10 March, *St. Laurent* and the corvette *Owen Sound* came upon Weber when he was running on the surface to recharge *U-845*'s batteries and drove him under. Over the next several hours, the two Canadian ships and the British destroyer *Forester* made a series of depth charge and Hedgehog attacks but Weber went deep, about 700 feet, and escaped damage. By early evening the three ships were about give up when *U-845* suddenly surfaced about 400 yards away, manned her guns and moved at high speed on the surface. Weber had been forced to take this dangerous action because of the need to recharge his batteries, and when the escorts recovered from their surprise, they immediately closed and smothered *U-845* with gunfire blowing away half its bridge and killing Weber and his first officer. *St. Laurent* alone expended 119 rounds of 4.7-inch ammunition, 1,440 rounds of 20mm ammunition and 1,400 rounds of small arms ammunition in this action. The German scuttled their craft and jumped in the water – 45 were rescued by the victors.

On 13 March, the frigate *Prince Rupert* assisted aircraft from the escort carrier USS *Bogue,*and two American destroyers to sink *U-575,* a Type VII boat commanded by *Oberleutnant zur See* Wolfgang Boehmer, which had sunk the British corvette *Asphodel* four days earlier. A British aircraft had spotted Boehmer on the surface and transmitted homing signals that had brought up the American task group and *Prince Rupert,* which just happened to be passing by. Badly damaged and forced to surface, *U-575* was finished off by gunfire from the warships and rockets from aircraft. Boehmer and 37 of his crew were rescued.

April 1944 was also a good month. Escort Group 9, consisting of the frigates HMC Ships *Matane, Stormont* and *Swansea,* and the corvette *Owen Sound* joined the British escort carrier HMS *Biter* and three RN sloops to attack *Oberleutnant zur See* Helmut Dauter's *U-448* on 14 April. Driven to the surface, the Type VII was riddled with gunfire and sank but the Canadian ships picked up Dauter and 41 of his crew. Two weeks later, *Matane* and *Swansea* co-operated to kill *U-311,** a Type VII boat commanded by *Kapitänleutnant* Joachim Zander, who was one of the few U-boat commanders during this period to actually sink a merchant vessel.

This action concluded the Canadian navy's string of successes. During a six-month period, they had sunk 6 of the 31 U-boats destroyed in the North Atlantic as opposed to 19 for the RN and 6 for the USN. This Canadian "Happy Time" was an indication that at long last the RCN had come of age as a professional fighting force.

---

* This victory was at first attributed to RCAF aircraft but a postwar re-appraisal caused it be awarded to Escort Group 9.

Triumphant – the escort carrier USS *Guadalcanal*, 1944.
In the spring of 1943, the introduction of escort carriers providing immediate air cover for convoys turned the conflict decisively against the U-boats. One of the first such vessels to enter battle, and certainly one of the most successful, was the USS *Bogue,* which sank, or helped to sink, nine U-boats and two Japanese submarines during the war. On 27 May 1944, an American "hunter-killer" group centred on the escort carrier USS *Guadalcanal* attacked and captured *U-505* as shown in this photograph. (USN photograph)

Ship's company.
The crew of HMCS *Wallaceburg* pose for a photograph in 1944 shortly after the vessel was commissioned. By this time the RCN had nearly overcome the problems caused by the unprecedented expansion it had undergone from 1940 to 1943 and had matured as a professional fighting service. It is doubtful that more than five of the officers and sailors in this photo had ever been to sea before 1939. The RCN was a wartime creation and it learned its business the hard way, at sea in the North Atlantic. (Canadian Naval Memorial Trust)

1944

"Shall I ram?" The death of U-845, March 1944

On 10 March, the destroyers HMS Forester *and HMCS* St Laurent, *together with the frigate HMCS Swansea, forced U-845 to the surface after a series of heavy attacks. The U-Boat attempted to escape at high speed on the surface using her AA armament to keep her pursuers at bay but the three warships gave chase and scored several direct hits which forced the submarine to stop and ultimately surrender. A few miles away, the fascinated crew of HMCS* Matane *listened as a blow-by-blow description of the action was transmitted throughout their ship by her loudspeaker system. Among the fascinated audience was Lieutenant Commander Alan Easton, RCNR,* Matane's *captain, who was resting in his cabin:*

Suddenly a voice said: "Submarine breaking surface – two miles to port." ……

A moment later I heard another announcement; this time the voice was obviously English.

"Submarine surface to starboard of me – am closing."

There was a lapse of about three minutes, then the same English voice. "General chase – sub getting away on surface – am too distant for accurate fire control." ……

The Canadian destroyer [HMCS *St Laurent*] came on the air again: "Enemy drawing away – am using what guns will bear."

Immediately after this came a voice yet unheard: "Am engaging submarine ahead of me with gunfire."

It was our frigate [HMCS *Swansea*], who had evidently arrived on the scene as the chase reached its height.

Then from the senior officer in the British ship [HMS *Forester*]. "Am barely closing – enemy has amazing speed." ……

After a brief interval of silence the voices came on the air again in quick succession. It seemed as though each was waiting for a chance to speak.

British Destroyer [*Forester*]: "Am closing now – report situation."

Canadian Destroyer [*St Laurent*]: Range decreasing – now 2800 yards – am making 24 knots."

Frigate [*Swansea*]: "Maintaining distance – have enemy ahead."

Canadian Destroyer: "Cannot see fall of shot but have his mark."

British Destroyer: "Beware of diving."

British Destroyer: "Report range."

Canadian Destroyer: "2400 yards."

Frigate: "3000 yards – holding my own."

I sat up in my bunk; I could rest no longer. I filled my pipe unconsciously, hesitating to strike the match in case I missed something.

Canadian Destroyer: "Believe scored direct hit – range 1900 yards – enemy fire fairly accurate, if meant for me."

Frigate: "Assume direct hits also."

Suspense for several minutes.

British destroyer: "Closing more rapidly – keep star shell up."

Canadian destroyer: "Sub's speed has diminished – am gaining fast now."

Canadian destroyer: "Another hit – sub slowing down."

Canadian destroyer: "Shall I ram?"

British destroyer: "If he is stopping no."

Evidently the Canadian destroyer was a good deal closer than the British ship, probably had been throughout the engagement, and was now almost upon his prey. Another message from him convinced his listeners that the U-Boat's game was up. "Sub stopped – crew abandoning boat – sending boarding party."[1]

A lucky German.
In April 1943 U-boats attacked Convoy HX 233, escorted by American, British and Canadian warships. In the ensuing battle, *U-175* was forced to the surface by depth charge attack and hit by heavy gunfire. Her crew abandoned their boat and 41 were rescued by the warships, including this man, shown being hauled on board a US Coast Guard cutter. Dangling near his cheek is his Draeger life-saving device. (US Coast Guard Photo)

"I feel suicidal with shame:" Escort Group 9 gets a kill but does not know it

In April 1944, Escort Group 9, consisting of the frigates HMC Ships Matane, Swansea *and* Stormont *and the corvette, HMCS* Owen Sound, *were on an independent patrol near Ireland when they got an firm asdic contact. The Senior Officer, Commander A.F.C. Layard, RN, a very conscientious man, recorded what happened in his diary:*

Saturday, 22nd April – at sea

Not a very nice day with S[outh].W[ester]'ly wind force 6. We got an H/F D/F bearing at 5.15 [AM] and although we weren't certain of distance I turned the group to the bearing and steamed along it till 11 o'clock but saw and heard nothing. …… We were just about in the middle of the area spread out in line abreast when at 2000 we got an A/S [asdic] contact to port. It was a cracking echo and very soon it became obvious that this really was a U boat. I went slow meaning to take my time but the range closed very rapidly and I found myself in to about 300 yds with the bearing going rapidly right and the ship's head swinging as fast as possible to the St[arboar]d to keep pointed. Suddenly ahead appeared the swirl of the thing which must have been very shallow. I was still worried lest I was going to get so close as to lose contact before ready to attack when the periscope was reported just off the Std. bow. I then got thoroughly rattled and in case he should fire a torpedo or Gnat [acoustic torpedo], I reckoned I must go for him. Went full ahead and forgetting we were still in A/S [asdic] contact I dropped a pattern by eye, which as it turned out was a good deal too early. However, we picked him up astern and the other ships were now on the scene. *Swansea* then attacked and although we held him and so did *Stormont* for a time, the A/S [asdic] conditions, which were never good, suddenly became awful and we simply couldn't get our [illegible] out at all and that was the last we heard of him. I started Observant patrols and then a parallel sweep but it was dark soon after losing contact and if he got away he could make off on the surface. I went through agonies of suspense and worry. What I've always dreaded has happened. We find a U boat and then I make a balls and lose it. It must be admitted the lack of daylight, the bad A's [asdic] conditions and the periscope all made it v[ery]. difficult but I feel I've let the ship and group down and I feel suicidal with shame.[2]

Although they did not know it at the time, Commander Layard's Escort Group 9 had just sunk U-311 although the victory was not confirmed until the early 1980s. Commander Layard had no reason to feel ashamed of his efforts.

Officers' country: The wardroom

Naval officers on a warship had their own area called the wardroom which was their combined dining room, bar and kitchen. In a corvette, the wardroom was a tiny compartment crowded with furniture, in larger warships it was much more sizeable and even a little elegant. In the wardroom, officers relaxed and, although it was not the custom to drink while at sea (except for medicinal purposes), wardroom parties on Canadian warships on "the first night in" after a convoy were raucous occasions when everyone relaxed – perhaps too much. Normally the wardrooms were more sedate and Lieutenant Commander Alan Easton, RCNR, has left a charming word portrait of that on HMCS Saskatchewan, *the destroyer he commanded, during a stay in port in the summer of 1944:*

There was an atmosphere of conviviality and visitors. It looked cheerful and bright in the glow of the lamps and the more austere aspects of the place were softened by the green carpet covering the hard steel deck. Although it extended across the width of the ship the room was hazy; the wet air outside seemed incapable of drawing the smoky warmth out through the open scuttles and absorbing it.

The place was crowded, all in the everlasting monotony of blue, relieved only by white collars and cuffs and splashes of gold. A group was sitting at the end of the mahogany dining table leaning across it, talking earnestly, the pack of cards

---

(Facing page) **"Slackers:" The RCN's major base, Halifax, 1944.**
This view from Jetty No. 3 looks north in HMC Dockyard on 3 August 1944. In the foreground, with her side to the camera, is HMCS *Reo II*, a prohibition rum-runner commissioned in 1941 as an auxiliary minesweeper and examination vessel. To her left, at the end of the same jetty, are from left to right: probably the towing vessel HMCS *Standard Coaster*; an unidentified vessel; and the replenishment ship HMCS *Provider*. Immediately behind are three Flower Class corvettes while to the right, across the jetty, is another Flower corvette. Immediately in front of that vessel are two Fairmile B Type motor launches used for harbour defence. In the background are, left to right, River Class frigates *Charlottetown* (K 244), *Kokanee* (K 419) and *Lasalle* (K 519). Two other River Class frigates are secured behind *Lasalle* and a third is in the right background, immediately in front of the large dock building. There are more ships in the dockyard on this day in 1944 than there were in the entire Canadian navy in 1939. (Photograph by Walter S. Legget, National Archives of Canada, PA 115367)

and dice discarded. Some were sitting on the bench around the fire-place laughing; two leaning against the mantlepiece. Others were standing in groups in the middle of the room talking and sipping their drinks, and behind them at the piano several were singing "Roll out the Barrel." ......

I found Peters with the chief engineer and first lieutenant of a neighbouring destroyer, talking to Bimson and our M.O. [Medical Officer] ...... Behind us on the bench, beside the [electric] fire, Jason was using his hands to illustrate a tactical theory. He was always keen to convince.

From what I could hear of the snatches of conversation going on among those standing near the forward open scuttle, Everleigh was telling his friends from other ships how it was they saw at our bow the open-mouthed muzzle of a pompom leaning out over the water like a figurehead. It had been an old ordnance friend who had got it for him, as well as the rockets for the gun-shield of the forward four-seven – all contrary to regulations and not in the books. ......

The torpedo officer hammered out something fast on the piano, and Larose, with one of the subs and several visitors standing around him in the brave attitude of those who are not going to let lack of talent prevent them from singing, launched into another song. Windram's fingers flew over the keys and his head moved slightly as his eyes watched his hands. The glass on the end of the keyboard vibrated and its contents bubbled.

A quartermaster came to the wardroom door to make a report and two more visitors arrived. But several left and, with the exchange of two guests, the piano and singing stopped.

Unobtrusively the piano began again, quietly, then grew, but songs were not being played. ......

The sea was always the worst enemy.
The caption of this photograph, taken on board a Canadian destroyer, states that the ship was being buffeted by 100 mile per hour winds. This might be an exaggeration but winds of that velocity were not unknown in the North Atlantic. In any case, the vessel is heeling strongly to port. (National Archives of Canada, PA 200128)

Presently the piano went back to a song. Windram played a few bars of "Road to the Isles," then stopped. It was the signal! When the lilting tune began again every voice in the wardroom started to sing what had now become almost a shanty in the Canadian ships, written by a surgeon-lieutenant who had been in the Barber Pole Group:

It's away! Outward the swing fo'c'sles reel
From the smoking sea's white glare upon the
strand.
It's the grey miles that are slipping under the keel
When we're rolling outward-bound from New-
foundland.[3]

Ports of call (3): Derry of the Emerald Isle

At the other side of the Atlantic, most Canadian escort vessels sailed into Londonderry in Northern Ireland, always a tranquil oasis of verdant scenery and a relief from the North Atlantic, as Lieutenant Allan Stevens, RCNVR, recalls:

When at the end of our run eastwards we had turned over the convoy to the local escort force and headed for Londonderry, the green hills of Ireland would appear out of the morning mist as we made our landfall.

It is impossible to describe how we felt on seeing that beautiful, green, verdant part of the world and to realize that, thank God, we had come through up to thirty-one days of hell and were still alive to fight another day.[4]

Stevens also remembered that when the Canadian warships passed up and down the Foyle, one landmark was always watched for in passage:

Down stream from town was a former Irish estate we called "Boom Hall" [actually Broome Hall]. It had been taken over by the Navy for use as a residence for female Naval personnel. As we sailed past, our way up the stream, it was customary for everybody to try to get to the bridge, and with our binoculars, have a good look at the girls as we swept by. They were usually in various stages of civilian dress or undress in many cases, and the exchange of waves and shouts was a pleasant event after a long gruelling trip across the Atlantic.[5]

The weather never improved: HMCS *Restigouche* in a hurricane, September 1944

Occasionally, sailors encountered weather so bad that they never forgot it. This was the case when HMCS Restigouche, *escorting a westbound convoy in September 1944, ran into a hurricane. Lieutenant Alan W. Stevens, RCNVR, the destroyer's Anti-Submarine Control Officer, recalled that,*

As we left St. John's, the barometer had started to fall, and Davey's [his captain] comment was, "There's some dirty weather around." He ordered lifelines rigged, and everything top side battened down, and in particular one hundred depth charges we still carried. Food was cached after in case the lookouts couldn't be replaced due to heavy seas.

We thought we were ready. ......

The waves grew steadily larger. The wind began converting their crests into fine mist. Soon we were enveloped in what seemed like a white smoke cloud. It was impossible to see anything through it, except from the height of the bridge. All that was visible of our convoy was the tops of the masts of the smaller ships and the funnels of the larger ones – eventually they also disappeared from view. ......

My last entry in the log at the end of the first dog [watch] read, I think – "Barometer falling rapidly. Wind force 6, racked by waves, some rivets have popped."

The howling of the wind increased until it sounded like a banshee. The flying spume began to freeze in our rigging. To add to our problems a fire started in one of the boiler rooms and the stokers were unable to extinguish it. Our engineer officer, Leslie Simms, was called to the bridge where he caught a blast from the captain, who was a worried man.

Simms advised him the only way he could put out the fire was to seal off the boiler room to stop air from getting in and he would have to shut down the boiler for a few hours. We could still make revolutions for 20 knots on the other boiler so the order was given.

The fire was extinguished and the boiler fired up so we had extra steam pressure in case it was needed.

A few hours later the fire broke out again and the whole process had to be repeated. The fire was caused by oil that had leaked into the bilges due to popped rivets in the fuel tanks. In addition to this problem, we had popped so many rivets that the sea was pouring in and soon the boiler room pumps were no longer able to keep it under control. We were going to sink, unless something was done.

Restigouche had survived a hurricane in 1941 almost as bad and had limped into Gourock [Scotland] a wreck. Many of the repairs carried out then [now] started to let go. A rupture in the fuel tank at the break of the forecastle opened and closed as we pitched.

The storm continued to increase in intensity during the night. The needle on our wind speed indicator, which was calibrated to a maximum of 120 knots, had a stop at the high end. The needle reached this and broke off. As we discovered later, the wind reached 180 miles an hour, making it the worst hurricane ever recorded in the Atlantic.

Restigouche began to suffer serious damage.

Below decks it was chaos. In the forward mess decks it was impossible to serve a hot meal. At least the crew had no trouble sleeping in their hammocks, the problem was getting into them. However, as usual they were soaking wet twenty-four hours a day. In the officer's quarters things were as bad. Our wardroom furniture was tied down but if one tried to sit in a chair, there was no way to prevent yourself from being forcibly ejected and thrown across the room when a large wave hit. It was easy to break an arm or a leg. To move around it was necessary to hang onto something solid with one hand. Hot meals were impossible, but our stewards, God bless them, found ways to make thick sandwiches with Spam or bully beef. Coffee and tea were replaced with beer.

Although we had on revolutions for 20 knots, at the end of the storm, we were four hundred miles astern of our position when the storm began. Meanwhile the water level in the boiler rooms was steadily rising and we must have lost ten percent of the rivets which held the ship together, including many in the fuel tanks. The engineer officer had over three inches of oily salt water in his cabin. We finally staggered into Halifax and the shore staff took over the pumping.[6]

"There was one Christless explosion:" *Chebogue* gets hit, October 1944

In October 1944, the frigate HMCS Chebogue *was part of Escort Group 2 which was escorting a small convoy when it encountered U-1227. Leading Seaman Richard Aldhelm-White of* Chebogue *remembered that she*

had all the latest equipment on board, and suddenly we got into an engagement which lasted eight hours. We went over the submarine, attacking it repeatedly, going back and forth, dropping charges, and I had the brilliant job (at Action Stations) being a communication number of the quarterdeck, converting all the ABCD codes to depths; screaming them out to the crew members who physically set the depth charge pistols.

We'd go running for an attack, but there were a few whales in the area and that sort of screwed it up for a while, but we finally got on, and we kept after this son-of-a-gun until about 2200 at night.

I guess the U-boat commander finally got fed up with our nonsense and decided to come to the surface. That was great! They then went into surface action. At this particular time, of course, we opened fire with the four inch. I left my position and got as far as the forecastle break, when all of a sudden there was one Christless explosion, and I bounced off the funnel! …… Luckily nothing happened to me, other than bruises. Apparently the submarine which was on the surface, and since we were running in on him, had decided that they'd fire acoustic torpedoes. ……

So we came to a grinding halt in the moonlight, wondering what to do next?

The Damage Control parties then began shoring up the bulkhead at station 133 and we didn't

know whether she was going to sink or not, or whether the Admiralty wanted to sink her, as she did have a lot of good equipment still aboard.

Arnprior came sneaking up behind us, after all this had transpired, and immediately thought we were the submarine! They lit us up beautifully, with a starshell, and then found out who we were. They then came alongside us with a beautiful piece of seamanship, and took most of us off, where we then operated in *Arnprior* for a while.[7]

Chebogue survived and was towed to Britain but was so badly damaged that she was never repaired. The submarine, U-1227, was destroyed by bombing at Kiel in 1945.

But sailors still got ill: Late war medical practice

Leading Sick Berth Attendant Ray Burrell recalls his duties aboard the corvette HMCS Huntsville, *which served on the North Alantic in the last months of 1944:*

The life of an SBA at sea is not a hard one, but as to the rest of the crew, he must be constantly alert. On him depends the well-being of very member. The ship I was in, a Castle Class corvette, carried a crew of one hundred and twenty-six. Situated on the port side and forward of the After Gangway, the Sick Bay formed the nucleus of all medical facilities aboard. At strategic points First Aid kits were placed, ten in all. Two other emergency posts, one in the Wardroom Flats and one in the Officer's Accommodation Lobby acted as emergency centres. Packed in a chest in the Sick Bay and ready for use at all times were sterile instruments, intravenous glucose, blood plasma, apparatus for taking and giving blood, containers of sterile dressing of all kinds, and various sterile trays. This chest, if necessary, in case of action, would be taken to the Wardroom.

A patient admitted to Sick Bay slept in one of two swinging bunks, and should the occasion arise, as it once did, when we had two cases of Scarlet Fever and four contacts, the port gangway was closed off and micks (hammocks) slung there. ......

On occasion, the Medical Officer of the Group could be contacted over TBS (Telephone Broadcasting System). ...... Generally, based on information provided by the SBA, the MO's opinion on the prognosis and treatment of the case was all that was necessary. Only once did a patient have to be transferred from our ship to the Senior Ship while at sea and this only because the condition required the continued close observation of the Medical Officer.

Daily sick parades ran no more than ten or twelve ratings and generally the simplest kind of treatment sufficed. Our most common ailment, infection of the upper respiratory tract requiring bed care, I put in the bunks. Once I had a case of chronic seasickness to look after until we reached port. There wasn't much one could do except feed him RCN Seasick Tablets, but he could never keep them down long enough to take effect.

On the whole, the SBA seldom runs into a case which requires him to put into use his full training, knowledge and skills. Nevertheless, the sound of the next "Action Stations" could just be the occasion to do so. [8]

Member of the Women's Royal Canadian Naval Service.
During the war, more than 6,000 Canadian women served in the WRCNS, taking over shore duties that released their male counterparts for service at sea. The artist has illustrated this member of the Service in her light blue summer uniform. (Painting by Ron Volstad, courtesy of the Directorate of History and Heritage, DND)

They also served: The Women's Royal Canadian Naval Service

Prior to 1939, the Royal Canadian Navy showed little interest in recruiting women to serve in any other capacity than as nurses. Even in that respect, the RCN was very traditional – a Royal Canadian Navy Nursing Service was not formed until late 1941 when the expansion of the navy resulted in a demand for medical personnel. It was only in 1942 when, faced with a personnel shortage, NSHQ seriously began to contemplate recruiting women and, in July of that year a Women's Royal Canadian Naval Service was created, modelled on its British counterpart.

The purpose of the WRCNS (commonly called "Wrens") was to relieve men for sea duty as stated in the words of their song: "Carry On! Carry On! Sailor boys must sail!" They certainly fulfilled that purpose as, by 1945, there were nearly 6,000 women in the WRCNS, serving in shore stations in such trades as stenographers, cooks, dieticians, telegraphers, signallers, dental assistants, supply assistants, postal clerks, mess stewards, coders, pay writers, drivers, teletype operators and laundry personnel. They were supervised by female WRCNS officers who held the King's Commission and had the same authority and power of command as their male counterparts. The WRCNS was disbanded in 1946 but its value and the exemplary conduct of its personnel had been so obvious to even most conservative male naval officer that it was re-created in 1951.

Recruits to the WRCNS were sent to the training establishment HMCS Conestoga at Galt, Ontario, for a three-week basic training course, followed by specialized trade courses. A former provincial training school (or reformatory) for girls, Conestoga was commanded by Lieutenant Commander Isabel J. MacNeill, WRCNS, the only woman during the

Second World War to have an independent command in the British Commonwealth. The new Wrens experienced the usual difficult adjustment period to service life, made worse in their opinion, by the requirement to wear uniform when "going ashore" because, as one of their songs explained,

> *In my sweet little pusser blue gown,*
> *That I wore that first night into town.*
> *But what good does it do when you wear pusser blue,*
> *And your figure looks best in a light, frilly dress?*
>
> *Cotton stocking just don't seem to be,*
> *What a young sailor lad wants to see.*
> *You're sharp as a thistle, but can't raise a whistle,*
> *In your sweet little pusser blue gown.[9]*

Even "getting ashore" could be difficult, as Wren Rosamond Greer discovered at HMCS Stadacona *in Halifax:*

When we went ashore she [their commanding officer] knew our appearance was a credit to the WRCNS because the only way we could get through the Stadacona Wren Gate without a special pass was in a "Liberty Boat." Liberty Boats, like Duty Boats, were not vessels that floated upon the water, but a group of Wrens marching from the Wren Block to the gate to go ashore, and were at the top of our list of "things about the navy we do not particularly care fore." They "sailed" on the hour and half hour, and if we were late for one, or failed to pass Liberty Boat inspection (it was never easy) depended upon which O.O.D [Officer of the Day] happened to be on duty at the time. We lined up and were examined from top to toe: shoes must be issue oxfords and well polished,

black hose not too sheer and their seams straight, hemlines regulation length, uniforms clean and pressed, white collars stiff and spotless, black ties in a perfect knot, hats worn at the proper angle, no dark nail polish, not too much lipstick, hair neat and one inch above the collar. Many a Liberty Boat sailed without me when I was ordered to, "Go and get that hair off your collars," and no pleading of mine ever softened the heart of an O.O.D. as I endeavoured to convince her that it was not that my hair was too long, but that my neck was too short.[10]

Once through basic training, the new Wrens were sent to various shore stations across Canada. Most ended up in Nova Scotia, where the greater part of the navy's administrative and training establishments were located. Wren Audrey Hill was posted to HMCS Cornwallis, *the large new training camp located near Digby, Nova Scotia. She did not have the most exciting job but she explains the devotion of the Wrens to their work:*

I was a Writer, and could type or take shorthand, but in *Cornwallis*, I went to work in the Gunnery School, and I worked out of the Instructional Production Section. Here, they drew diagrams of the guns on great big sheets of paper and these were very precise. Then in the section that I worked in, I had to run off the instructions on how to fire these guns, on a Gestetner, and assemble them into pamphlets.

After a while I went to the book store, which was in the Gunnery School, and from there I distributed those pamphlets that had been produced upstairs, as well as hard-cover books like BR-159 handbook of gunner drill. There were always classes of seamen coming into the Gunnery

School for training, and it was my responsibility to hand these groups of book out to each different class as needed for their instruction.

We also had to amend the books. They would change the gun drill to make it more efficient, and in doing that, you had all these tons of strips of paper that you had to glue into a hundred books, making sure they all got in there for each class. This ensured that everybody was doing the same thing at the same time. ……

However, we were acutely dedicated to the work we did. We were always very aware that we were seen as just pasting strips of paper in the books, but that had an extenuating effect, because what we did affected how those boys would fire the guns.[11]

Surrounded and outnumbered by men, the WRCNS had a very active social life. Rosamond Greer recalls the pluses and minuses when servicemen and servicewomen are involved with each other:

Our dates were boys we met at dances and movies, while walking or shopping, in cafes or at work. Some were boys from home … everybody turned up in Halifax sooner or later during those years. Sometimes they were soldiers or airmen, but Wrens were usually seen with sailors, and on Saturday nights downtown Halifax became a mass of navy blue uniforms. Sailors had a certain protectiveness and possessiveness towards Wrens … we belonged to them and they did not approve of our dating anyone else (particularly officers, even if they were in the navy). ……

At the Wren Gate on Gottingen Street [in Halifax], through which portal no male could pass (unless he was an officer … the navy paid no heed to democracy) we lined up once again, this time along a rock wall where on warm, balmy evenings, in the pouring rain, and even during blizzards, dozens of couples said their lingering "goodnights." The Shore Patrol dutifully did their part to cool the ardour of the cuddling couples by parading back and forth along the wall and, when they spied a pair becoming a mite too friendly, tapping the fellow on the shoulder (with a billy club) and issuing the order to "Move along." It was very effective, I had early discovered that my mother's admonition to "be careful" had been entirely unnecessary. All I had to do was "be visible." The Shore Patrol took care of the rest.[12]

Wren Hill remembered that, at **Cornwallis,**

The relations between the WRCNS and all the sailors coming through was a relaxed, easy atmosphere, somewhat like a big high school. By 1943 they treated us like we were their sisters, but we weren't any different from them. I know one of my ex-WRCNS in the Association has written a paper, and she said they didn't know, at first, whether to treat us as ladies of easy virtue, or Madonnas. But we had an easy relationship.

At Galt, Lt.-Cdr. McNeill had always instilled in us the view that we were ladies first, and that kind of prevailed. We had good relations with the sailors, and let's face it, I think there must have been at least ten sailors for every girl. I can remember one time, I had three dates in one afternoon![13]

Although members of the WRCNS received less pay than their male counterparts and were tasked with some of the most tedious – but necessary – jobs in the shore stations, they were proud to be doing their bit. As Wren Audrey Hill explains:

At no time did I think of myself as a second class citizen in the Navy. At the time I went in, I guess I got $.95 a day because I remember receiving $30.00 a month at pay parade. But I never had that feeling, because what each person did was different, and I was glad to be able to be there, doing whatever I could to help, which was what most of us were seeking. There was never any discussion about us only being paid three-quarters of what the sailors got. We didn't go to sea, so it just never entered into our discussions. ......

At $.95 a day, I was paid less than the sailors, and certainly less than the civilian I replaced, but that didn't enter into it. We were so fired up that we could do something to help end the terrible war that had been going on forever by 1943.[14]

As Wren Greer recalls, her female comrades were proud to be serving as,

we did consider ourselves to be a very important part of a very important mission. We did not particularly want to carry guns, or sail aboard ships that rocked and rolled and bounced and bucked as they plodded the course across the stormy Atlantic – although we certainly would have, had it been deemed necessary. We had no ambition to do battle with *all* men; Hitler, Mussolini and Hirohito were quite enough for us to handle. Nor did we feel it necessary to burn our bras, or act and swear like men. On the contrary, we tried desperately to be feminine despite the uniform. We wore perfume and makeup, and (against regulations) bracelets on our ankles. ......

We were girls and glad of it.[15]

Women in pants – a source of puzzlement.
Although the WRCNS played a major role in taking over shore jobs and releasing men for sea duty, the idea of women in uniform was a novel one in the Canada of the 1940s. Photographers therefore delighted in taking shots like this one that emphasized that novelty. (National Archives of Canada, PA 134330)

CHAPTER 8

VICTORY: MAY 1944–MAY 1945

The fifth wartime spring: The Atlantic secured

By May 1944 it was clear that the Allies were triumphant on the oceans. If Allied warships made contact with German submarines, there were enough escorts to detach ships for "hunts to the death" and the statistics were impressive – 50 U-boats were sunk between January and May 1944 while the Allies lost only 25 escorted merchant ships in all waters. Convoy after convoy crossed to Britain carrying troops, weapons, vehicles, fuel and supplies to complete the build up in Britain of the invasion forces. To some senior Canadian naval officers, the Battle of the Atlantic appeared to have been won and they looked forward to moving beyond the necessary, but not very glorious, task of ASW into more exciting naval operations.

One of the major responsibilities of the Allied navies in 1944 was the planned invasion of Normandy. The naval side of this massive undertaking, codenamed Operation NEPTUNE, required hundreds of warships, large and small, and the RCN was tasked to provide a considerable number of all types. There would be two Canadian flotillas of fast attack craft (Motor Torpedo Boats) serving in the Channel to fight off their counterparts, the German E-Boats. Two of the "Prince" ships, *Prince David* and *Prince Henry*, formerly armed merchant cruisers, had been converted to landing ships for amphibious operations and would carry 16 landing craft to take troops into the assault beaches. There would also be three independent flotillas of Canadian landing craft on hand to carry 4,600 troops, and their way into the beaches would be cleared by an RCN minesweeping flotilla of 16 Bangor minesweepers hastily reconverted to their original role from their service as escorts. Finally, 39 Canadian ASW vessels – destroyers, frigates and corvettes – would ensure the safe and timely arrival of shipping from British ports to the invasion area.

These vessels would be supported by larger warships. Four Tribal Class destroyers (*Athabaskan*, *Haida*, *Huron* and *Iroquois*) were now in commission and these big, powerful and fast vessels had already participated in a number of actions in the English Channel. Late in the spring of 1944, they were joined by two new fleet destroyers transferred from the RN, HMC Ships *Algonquin* and *Sioux*, and were stationed in the Channel to prevent German surface ships interfering with the invasion forces. Two escort carriers, manned by Canadians but commissioned as HM Ships *Nabob* and *Puncher*, had also been acquired and discussions were under way for the

(Facing page) **A "green one" – the corvette HMCS *Barrie* in 1945.**
A fine study of a corvette in a heavy sea, HMCS *Barrie* ships a "green one" in 1945. The veteran *Barrie*, commissioned in May 1941, served throughout the war and was later sold to the Argentine navy and broken up in 1972. (National Archives of Canada, PA 115357)

The escort carrier – HMS *Puncher*.
The introduction of escort carriers into the Battle of the Atlantic in 1943 was crucial to the Allied victory and "hunter killer" groups based on small escort carriers such as HMS *Puncher* carried the war to the enemy. *Puncher* was manned by Canadians but commissioned as a British ship because she was a Lend-Lease vessel and Canada did not accept materiel through this programme. Laid down as a merchant ship, *Puncher* displaced 14,170 tons, was 492 feet in length and 69 in beam, had a top speed of 18 knots, carried a complement of 1,000 and about 20 aircraft, and was armed with two 5-inch guns, sixteen 40mm guns and twenty 20mm guns. (Author's collection)

transfer of a light fleet carrier. Finally, Britain had agreed to turn over two light cruisers to the RCN. The plan was that these large warships would serve as the basis of the postwar Canadian navy, giving Canada, for the first time in its history, a proper fleet.

Triumph of seapower: Operation NEPTUNE, June–August 1944

Admiral Karl Dönitz, of course, was less concerned with Canadian naval aspirations than with defeating the forthcoming invasion. He had hoped to employ the first Type XXI and XXIII boats in the summer of 1944 but technical delays had frustrated the construction of these new craft and he was forced to carry on with his increasingly obsolescent Type VII and Type IX boats. The major weaknesses of these craft was their slow submerged speed and their requirement to surface at frequent intervals to recharge the batteries that powered their electric motors, which made them vulnerable

to radar mounted on Allied aircraft and warships. Late in 1943, however, German naval engineers introduced a device which made these older submarines much more difficult for Allied warships to find and kill.

This was the *Schnorckel* or snorkel (literally "snorter"). Originally conceived by the Dutch navy, it was a breathing tube that permitted a submarine to operate its diesel engines while submerged. The snorkel consisted of two tubes, an intake tube that drew fresh air into the submarine and an exhaust tube that expelled gases from it. U-boats equipped with the snorkel could come to periscope depth and recharge their batteries, extending their underwater range, without exposing themselves to Allied radar. At the same time the *Kriegsmarine* produced radar detectors which could be mounted on the snorkel, warning a submarine commander if Allied sea or air units were present before he employed the device or attempted to surface. There were many problems with the snorkel, it was difficult to use and interfered with the operation of a U-boat's periscope and hydrophones, and it could only be operated in relatively calm seas, but its utility was so manifest that in April 1944 Dönitz ordered all operational boats to be fitted with the device. At the same time, he withdrew his Type VII boats from the Atlantic to redeploy them for operations in the English Channel.

The invasion of Normandy on 6 June 1944 occurred before Dönitz had time to properly position his forces. Despite the dire predictions of Allied naval planners that as many as 120 U-boats would attack the invasion beaches, only 36 German submarines managed to penetrate the English Channel or its approaches during the summer of 1944 and the odds against them were tremendous as Admiral Bertram Ramsay, the Allied Naval Commander-in-Chief, had at his disposal 286 ASW vessels and hundreds of aircraft. The anti-submarine forces deployed for NEPTUNE were the best available and included the British groups from the MOEF, which throughout the summer of 1944 was entirely a Canadian affair. There were

(Facing page) **Triumph of sea power: Operation NEPTUNE, 6 June 1944.**
Canadian landing craft proceed to France protected overhead by mobile barrage balloons. NEPTUNE, the naval component of Operation OVERLORD, the invasion of Normandy, was the largest naval operation in history, involving hundreds of ships, many of them Canadian. (Photograph by G.A. Milne, National Archives of Canada, PA 116339)

also four RCN support groups with the largest and best-equipped ASW vessels in the Canadian navy, commanded by the most experienced officers. Escort Groups 6 and 9 had six frigates each, Escort Group 11 (under the redoubtable "Chummy" Prentice) consisted of five destroyers and Escort Group 12 had four destroyers.

The four Canadian groups arrived in Britain in May and, after some intensive last-minute training, participated in three months of very successful operations in the English Channel and its approaches as the *Kriegsmarine* tried desperately to cut off supplies to the beachheads. Allied naval forces came under attack by coast artillery, destroyers, E-Boats, smaller attack craft, human torpedoes, miniature submarines and aircraft but beat off these opponents, which suffered heavy losses. The most potent German weapons were the U-boats and Dönitz ordered his commanders to attack "without consideration for anything else whatsoever …… even at risk of losing your own U-boat."[1] Despite the fact that the shallow waters of the Channel with its wrecks, reefs and currents were difficult for ASW operations, the submarines failed completely. Of the 36 boats which operated against the beachhead area from June until August 1944, 22 were sunk, against an Allied loss of 12 ships of all types. Five of these victories were scored by RCN warships. Prentice's Escort Group 11 got three and Commander A.F.C. Layard's Escort Group 9 had one while a fifth surprise success was scored by the fleet destroyer HMCS *Haida*. Assisted by a British sister ship and Coastal Command aircraft, *Haida* sank *U-971* on 24 June. The last patrol of this Type VII boat commanded by *Oberleutnant zur See* Walter Zeplien was typical of U-boat operations in the summer of 1944 – *U-971* was attacked on five separate occasions by Allied aircraft and so badly damaged that Zeplien was on his way back to

HMCS *Haida* picks up survivors from *U-971*, 24 June 1944.
A series of successful surface actions made the Tribal Class destroyer HMCS *Haida* one of the most famous ships in the RCN. Her string of victories continued in late June 1944 when, in company with HMS *Eskimo*, she encountered *U-971* and drove it to the surface with repeated depth charge attacks. The U-boat crew abandoned their boat and swam to *Haida*, as shown in this photograph. *Haida*, one of two surviving ships of the wartime RCN, is now berthed in Hamilton, Canada. (Courtesy, HMCS *Cornwallis* Museum)

base when he encountered *Haida*. Operation NEPTUNE was an unqualified victory and at the end of August 1944, when the advance of the Allied land armies forced Dönitz to withdraw his U-boats from their bases in western France, the Allied navies had safely transported to the European mainland 2,052,000 soldiers, 438,461 armoured and other vehicles, and 3,098,259 tons of supplies.

On the North Atlantic that summer, it seemed as though the war was already won. Escorted by the Canadian navy, convoy after convoy arrived on time and without loss, and the high point was Convoy HXS 300, the largest single convoy of the war, which departed New York on 17 July and anchored safely at Liverpool on 3 August 1944. It comprised 167 merchant ships carrying 1,019,829 tons of cargo, including 307,874 tons of oil and 53,490 tons of tanks and military vehicles. Formed in 19 columns, it covered 30 square miles of ocean but was only escorted by one Canadian frigate and six corvettes.

"Goot Vasser Bomb!" The inshore campaign, September–December 1944

Unfortunately for those who predicted that the war would be over by Christmas, the Allied land offensive began to slow in the autumn of 1944. In the west, supply shortages brought about by the failure to clear the approaches to Antwerp, the largest port in Europe, forced the American, British and Canadian armies to halt on the Rhine, while in the east the Soviet armies, facing similar difficulties, had stopped on the eastern borders of the Third Reich. Despite heavy air bombardment, German industrial production actually rose in the last months of 1944 to a wartime high, and it included the Type XXI submarines which Dönitz hoped would allow him to resume operations in the mid-Atlantic.

In the meantime, he decided to undertake a new campaign in North American and British coastal waters. Despite recent losses, increased German industrial efficiency allowed Dönitz to keep up his strength and these craft were equipped with the snorkel, which partly offset Allied maritime airpower. Most of the U-boats that had operated from French bases and were not destroyed in the Channel during the summer managed to escape to either Norway or Germany and were now available for fresh operations. Dönitz's intention was to buy time by tying up his opponents' naval and air forces until enough of the new submarines came into service, and from then to the end of the war, the U-boats operated singly, staying submerged as much as possible and attacking only when the advantage was clearly on their side. Since Dönitz no longer used group tactics, which required frequent radio traffic, Allied signal intelligence became less useful. It could still provide the information that a U-boat was going to be deployed in a certain area, but as submarine commanders no longer made daily position reports, it became difficult to pinpoint their exact location, which was often revealed only after the submarine had made a successful attack. An additional problem was that the U-boats now operated in shallow coastal waters which presented difficult ASDIC conditions.

The danger of the new German tactics was demonstrated in September 1944 when *U-482*, a Type VII boat which had sailed from

The snorkel.
The snorkel, a Dutch invention adopted by the *U-Boot-Waffe* in late 1943, was a breathing device that permitted a submarine to operate its diesel engines while submerged. It consisted of two tubes, an intake that drew fresh air into the boat and an exhaust that expelled gases from it. U-boats equipped with snorkels could recharge their batteries without surfacing and exposing themselves to Allied radar and aircraft. The snorkel dramatically improved the range and survivability of the U-boats but it was a difficult apparatus to use properly. This example is mounted on the *U-889*, a Type IX boat that surrendered to the RCN in May 1945 – note the salt erosion on the front of the conning tower. (Directorate of History and Heritage, DND, DHH HS-1377-13n)

Finally I can see something while snorkelling !

Snorkel problems.
The snorkel improved the survivability and effectiveness of the U-boat but it was a difficult device to use properly and sometimes caused severe pressure changes in the interiors of submarines. It also restricted vision from the periscope, as illustrated in this cartoon drawn by *Oberleutnant zur See* Herbert Rogge of *U-190*. (Courtesy, Werner Hirschmann)

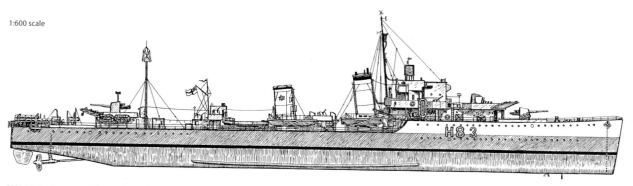

HMCS *St. Laurent*, River Class destroyer, 1945.
During the war, nine destroyers of the standard prewar Admiralty types (which the RCN called the River Class) were acquired to join the six similar vessels in commission in 1939 and all vessels of this type were modified after 1943 to make them more effective ASW escorts. Their guns were reduced to two or three 4.7 inch guns and their torpedo armament cut back to four 21-inch tubes but their AA weapons were upgraded to six 20mm AA guns. In addition to depth charges, they were also equipped with Hedgehog (shown here in the former B Gun position). *St. Laurent* is shown with Type 271 radar (in the dome aft of the bridge) and HF/DF (on her shorter main mast). (Drawing by L.B. Jenson, courtesy Directorate of History and Heritage, DND)

Norway, commenced a two-week operation in the Irish Sea. Using its snorkel, *U-482* surfaced only once during a very successful patrol in which it sank two tankers, two freighters and a British corvette before returning to its base. For the RCN, even more troubling were the operations of three submarines in Canadian coastal area during that month. One boat was sunk by aircraft from the escort carrier USS *Bogue*, but the other two managed to penetrate the Gulf of St. Lawrence and sink a small unescorted freighter before returning to their Norwegian base.

These operations heralded the opening of Dönitz's new offensive and a scramble immediately began to form more support groups to hunt down and kill single intruders. For Admiral Murray, commanding the Northwest Atlantic, a theatre directly affected, the vessels to form these groups were available – by September 1944 the RCN had 63 frigates in service and the last seven were to be commissioned before the end of the year – but he was forced to respond to requests from the Admiralty for Canadian warships to serve in British waters. By October 1944, five of the seven support groups in the Canadian navy were under the command of Admiral Sir Max Horton, the Commander-in-Chief, Western Approaches, and only two, Groups 16 and 27, were available for the defence of Canadian waters,

fleshed out by the ships of the Western Escort Force.* The four groups in British waters (Escort Groups 6, 9, 11 and 12) were worked very hard during this period – the veteran "Chummy" Prentice became exhausted and asked to be relieved of command, and he was not the only sailor worn out by the pace of the inshore campaign.

C-5 Group of the MOEF scored the first Canadian success in this new chapter when the frigate *Dunver* and the corvette *Hespeler* sank the Type VII *U-484* in the Irish Sea on 9 September. About five weeks later, on 16 October, Escort Group 6 was carrying out a patrol off the Shetland Islands, as part of Horton's policy of establishing a defensive line between Norway and the northern British Isles, when the frigate HMCS *Annan* under Lieutenant Commander C.P. Balfrey, RCNR, got a contact and attacked it, so badly damaging *Oberleutnant zur See* Horst Voigt's *U-1006* that it was forced to surface during the night that followed. Voigt might have escaped as Escort Group 6 had given up the hunt but *U-1006* was discovered by the new Type 272 radar on the Canadian frigate HMCS *Loch Achanalt*. She turned back to investigate and her captain deployed his CAT gear, the foil for GNAT, which proved to be a wise move as Voigt immediately fired an acoustic torpedo that missed. As the frigate closed, *U-1006* opened fire with its deck armament and hit *Annan*'s communication masts, rendering them inoperable, and wounding several crew members. The frigate replied with gun fire and a depth charge barrage that sank the submarine, although most of the German crew, including Voigt, were rescued.

---

* This was the former Western Local Escort Force, which changed its name in 1944.

It was more than two months before the next victory in British waters. It came on 27 December when a Castle Class corvette of C-3 Group, HMCS *St. Thomas*, commanded by Lieutenant Commander L.P. Denny, RCNR, which was equipped with Squid, fired one round from that accurate weapon and so badly damaged *Kapitänleutnant* Eberhard Findeisen's Type IX *U-877* that it flooded and dived out of control to a depth of nearly 1000 feet. Findeisen blew his ballast tanks in desperation, *U-877* surfaced violently and the crew abandoned their boat. As the German survivors were being brought on board Denny's ship, one praised his Canadian captors by pointing upward and shouting "*Vasser Bomb, goot Vasser Bomb!!!*"[2]

The RCN had less luck in its own backyard. Informed by the captains of the two boats that had penetrated the Canadian coastal area during September that the defences appeared to be uncoordinated, Dönitz dispatched no less than eight submarines to the Northwest Atlantic in October and November 1944. The thermal conditions in the Gulf of St. Lawrence, comprising different layers of water of varying temperature and salinity, made ASDIC searches in this area very difficult while the snorkel baffled detection by aircraft of the RCAF.

The result was that the U-boats gained a number of individual successes. On 14 October, *U-1223*, a Type IX boat commanded by *Oberleutnant zur See* Friedrich Altmeier carried out a very aggressive night surface attack in the Gulf of St. Lawrence against Convoy ONS 33, 52 merchantmen escorted by six Canadian warships. Not surprisingly, the Canadians responded just as aggressively and mounted a chase which ended when Altmeier blew the stern off the frigate HMCS *Magog* with a GNAT and then escaped without harm. Nearly a month later, after being harassed for several days by a USN hunter-killer group, Altmeier made another attack on a convoy and sank the Canadian freighter *Fort Thompson* before returning safely to his base. This achievement was paralleled by another Type IX craft, *U-1228* commanded by *Oberleutnant zur See* Friedrich-

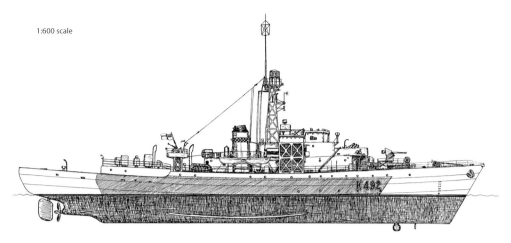

1:600 scale

HMCS *Leaside*, Castle Class corvette.
The Castle Class was the last incarnation of the wartime corvette and was larger, more comfortable and better armed than its Flower Class predecessor. In 1944, the RCN acquired 12 Castle Class corvettes from the RN and they served in the last year of the war. Displacing 1,060 tons, Castle Class corvettes were 251 feet in length, had a top speed of 16 knots, were manned by a complement of 122 and armed with one 4-inch gun, six 20mm AA guns and Squid, as well as depth charges. *Leaside* is shown equipped with HF/DF on her foremast and Type 272 radar atop the lattice structure aft of her bridge. (Drawing by L.B. Jenson, courtesy Directorate of History and Heritage, DND)

Wilhelm Marienfeld, which on 24 November ventured into the Cabot Strait and sank the corvette *Shawinigan* with the loss of her entire crew of 85 men.

Worse things lay ahead. On 21 December *Kapitänleutnant* Klaus Hornbostel, under orders to patrol the approaches of Halifax with his Type IX boat, *U-806*, torpedoed the steamer *Samtucky* just at the mouth of the harbour. Her captain beached his vessel and it was at first thought that she had hit a mine but examination turned up torpedo remnants, confirming the presence of a submarine. As a troopship was scheduled to leave Halifax a few days later, naval and air patrols were stepped up, but on Christmas Eve 1944 Hornbostel struck again to sink the Bangor Class minesweeper HMCS *Clayoquot* three miles off the Sambro Light. A massive task force of 14 ASW ships and 7 smaller vessels assembled to find *Clayoquot*'s killer but *U-806* lay on the bottom for 24 hours before sneaking away without harm.

Hedgehog.
Hedgehog, the "ahead throwing" ASW weapon, is shown above mounted on the corvette HMCS *Moose Jaw* in 1944. Hedgehog fired 24 projectiles, each filled with 35 lbs. of Torpex explosive, ahead of the attacking vessel. Hedgehog possessed tremendous advantages over standard depth charges as it allowed the attacking vessel to maintain contact with the target during the attack and only those bombs that actually hit a submarine exploded, which caused less ASDIC interference. In the photo at right, HMCS *Ottawa II* fires her Hedgehog in the English Channel on a hot day in July 1944. While the bridge personnel check their watches for the time of explosion, the projectiles hit the water ahead of the ship, covering a target area of some 1,600 square yards. (National Archives of Canada, PA 112918, PA 190084)

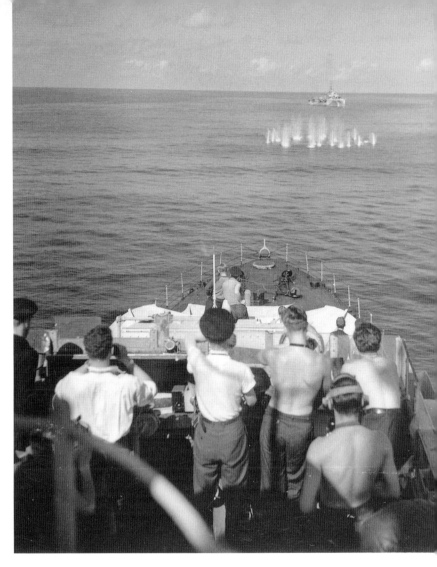

A "real navy:" The RCN at high tide

NSHQ in Ottawa could be forgiven for not taking problems on its own doorstep more seriously as it was distracted by greater thoughts in late 1944. Its long-cherished ambition of becoming a "real navy" had finally been achieved. In September 1939 the Canadian navy had consisted of 3,252 officers and sailors manning 6 destroyers, 5 minesweepers and 2 auxiliary vessels – by late 1944, it consisted of 92,441 officers and sailors,

both male and female, manning more than 400 vessels of all types. The problems caused by this expansion, so evident in 1941-1943, had disappeared and the Royal Canadian Navy was now one of the six largest navies in the world and a force to be reckoned with.

While *U-806* was causing excitement around Halifax, senior officers at NSHQ were finalizing plans to dispatch a Canadian naval force to the Pacific theatre. It would consist of two light fleet carriers to be obtained from the RN, two light cruisers just commissioned in Canadian service, 10 fleet destroyers and 40 of the RCN's most modern frigates and corvettes. Even this was a scaled-back version of the staff's original plan, which would have added an additional 58 warships to this force – making a total of 110 Canadian warships operating against the Japanese Empire. Impressive as this naval contribution looks, when compared to the RCN's strength in 1939, it was not even the major part of the national war effort as the RCN was the smallest of Canada's three fighting services. By late 1944, of a population of 11 million, just under one million Canadian men and women were in uniform, including 41 per cent of the males of military age (18-45). More impressive was the fact that almost all were volunteers because Canada never had a wartime conscription programme for overseas service and only 16,000 of the nearly 100,000 men (popularly known as "Zombies") drafted for home defence were ever sent to serve in Europe.

"Our watchword remains the same!"
Last Battles in European Waters, 1945

The staff's ambitious plans for distant theatres and a postwar fleet, however, overlooked the fact that Dönitz's submarine crews were still fighting hard. On 1 January 1945, the staff of the U-boat high command sent a New Year's Day Message to all its boats at sea: "Our watchword remains the same! Attack, let 'em have it, sink ships. Sieg Heil!."[3] To this, Dönitz added a personal message of encouragement: "The striking power of our Service will be strengthened in the New Year by new Boats" – a reference to the Types XXI and XXIII which were now starting to be commissioned.[4] As the War Diary of the U-boat service summed up the situation:

Advanced – ASDIC equipment in the last year of the war.
This photograph, taken on the corvette HMCS *Cobourg* in July 1944, shows the technical progression of anti-submarine technology during the war. This is a Type 144 ASDIC, which, with various attachments, permitted escorts to obtain and maintain accurate contacts in different water conditions out to 2,500 yards. The attack was actually controlled by the ASDIC officer, seen here standing behind the HSD ratings manning the set, who communicated information to the captain on the bridge of the vessel. The Type 144 was mounted on British escorts beginning in late 1942 but Canadian warships did not receive it until early 1944. (Photograph by W.H. Pugsley, National Archives of Canada, PA 139273)

the loss of the western waters [French bases] would have been disastrous if our future U-boat operations depended on using the same types of boats as before. But the new boats of Type XXI ... will be able to break through to the Atlantic despite concentrated opposition and to operate with success in the North Atlantic and in the remote operational areas.[5]

The widespread deployment of these new submarines was a source of anxiety to the Allied naval forces and it was fortunate that in late 1944 the massive bombing of the German railway network seriously delayed their introduction. Dönitz had hoped to be receiving 23 Type XXIII and 33 Type XXI boats per month by late 1944 but these figures were never met and only one Type XXI was close to being operational in February 1945 when the supreme Allied command issued a directive making any aspect of the production of Type XXI U-boats a priority target for the Allied air forces. In the end, however, it was Allied land forces that put an end to the threat when they overran the shipyards building these new weapon systems.

Norway – the U-boats' last refuge.
As the Soviet and Allied armies advanced to the German borders in late 1944, U-boat operations were increasingly conducted from Norway. In this photo, taken in the autumn of 1944, *U-190* enters the base at Kristiansand astern of another submarine. (Courtesy, Werner Hirschmann)

In January 1945, when signal intelligence revealed that the Germans themselves did not expect to have large numbers of the U-boats in service before July, the objective became to destroy as many of the older craft as possible to reduce overall enemy numbers. It was known that, as the disruptions caused by the transfer of the U-boat fleet from France to Germany and Norway had ended, more craft were at sea and the morale of their crews, as exemplified by the number of determined attacks made, was getting better as they mastered the snorkel. The Admiralty feared a renewed offensive in eastern Atlantic coastal waters that would disrupt the flow of supplies to the armies on the European mainland, and large naval and maritime air forces were concentrated to prevent this – 426 escort vessels and 389 aircraft. The result was that, between January and April 1945, 25 U-boats were sunk in British waters for the loss of 48 merchant ships, mostly small vessels.

Three of these successes were gained by the RCN. On 16 February Escort Group 9 sank *U-309*, a Type VII, off the coast of Scotland (although the kill was not confirmed for nearly 40 years after the event). During the

evening of 7 March, Escort Group 25 (formed in September 1944), operating in the Irish Sea, picked up a good radar and ASDIC contact and illuminated a snorkel by searchlight. The group attacked with Hedgehog, bringing *Kapitänleutnant* Wolfgang Herwartz's *U-1302* briefly to the surface, but the Type VII dived again. At that moment, Lieutenant Commander Howard Quinn, RCNVR, captain of the frigate *Strathadam* and Senior Officer, received a radio message from the commander of a nearby British support group telling him to hold off attacking as the Briton was coming to take charge of the operation. Although the arrogant "Juicer"* officer outranked Quinn, the Canadian was having none of it and firmly replied that, if the Royal Navy intended to rob his group of their kill, they had better be prepared to "come in shooting!"[6] Nothing more was heard of the matter and the operation concluded successfully when further attacks brought convincing evidence that *U-1302* had been destroyed.

The sinking of *Oberleutnant zur See* Werner Strübing's Type VII *U-1003* was even more dramatic. In the evening of 20 March Escort Group 26, consisting of the frigates *Beacon Hill*, *New Glasgow*, *Ribble* and *Sussexvale*, had just left Londonderry when a lookout on *New Glasgow* saw a snorkel trailing smoke moving through the water directly toward his ship. Before anyone on the frigate's bridge could react, *New Glasgow*

---

* "Juicer" was the Canadian sailor's term of endearment for his British counterpart. Canadian sailors used "juicer" or "limey" for the British navy and its sailors because at one time the RN issued lime juice to its personnel to prevent scurvy. Another affectionate Canadian term for their British counterparts was "kipper," supposedly derived from the fish that was a staple food item on British warships. In turn, the Royal Navy fondly referred to the RCN as the "Royal Coca-Cola Navy" because of its penchant for mixing that beverage with its daily rum ration, the "Royal Colonial Navy" (obvious) or the "Royal Colliding Navy" because of its record for ship collisions.

became the first Canadian warship (and possibly the only Allied warship) to be rammed by a U-boat during the Second World War. Badly damaged, *U-1003* settled on the bottom while, not as badly damaged but just as surprised, *New Glasgow* joined her comrades of EG 25 in carrying out an ASDIC search, which failed to obtain a firm contact. As the Canadian warships receded in the distance, *U-1003* limped slowly away but two days later Strübing ordered his crew to abandon their craft and take to their life rafts, where they spent about eight hours in the water before being rescued by HMCS *Thetford Mines* of Escort Group 25. Although the evidence appeared to show that *U-1003* had more or less committed submarine suicide, the Admiralty graciously approved the award of a kill to *New Glasgow*, the last of 33 Axis submarines sunk by the RCN during the Second World War.

The U-boat's most dangerous enemy. Aircraft, land-based or shipborne, proved crucial to winning the Battle of the Atlantic. Land-based aircraft are credited with destroying 209 Axis submarines and Royal Canadian Air Force units accounted for 21 of those kills. Here a Catalina of 116 (Bomber Reconnaissance) Squadron, RCAF, drops a stick of Mark XI aerial depth charges on a training exercise in 1943. The Catalina flew in Canadian service from 1941 onward, and although its range was less than that of Liberator and Sunderland VLR aircraft, it performed well. (Canadian Forces Photo Unit, RE 64-1044)

"The typical noises of a sinking ship:" Final actions in Canadian waters

Ironically, the RCN was not as successful in its own waters. Admiral Leonard Murray had nowhere near the forces available in the Northwest Atlantic that Sir Max Horton had in British waters – Murray possessed 89 escort vessels in his theatre in early 1945 but many were newly-commissioned vessels still working up to full efficiency. The RCAF's Eastern Air Command had seven squadrons with 94 aircraft but the advent of the snorkel and U-boat radar detectors had counterbalanced the effectiveness of aircraft. The worst problems affecting operations in Murray's theatre stemmed from the weather, which was at best variable, and normally foul in the winter months; and the incredibly bad ASDIC conditions. When an American hunter-killer group based on USS *Bogue* – the most successful wartime escort carrier in terms of submarine kills – operated briefly off Nova Scotia in the autumn of 1944 they got a taste of the conditions that Canadian sailors had always endured and considered that their short northern tour was probably the group's "most frustrating time of the war."[7]

There were three U-boats in Murray's theatre when Dönitz sent his New Year's Day Message and they soon went into action. On 4 January 1945, *U-1232* ambushed a small convoy sailing from Sydney to Halifax, just east of the entrance to the latter port. In the space of 20 minutes, it sank two ships but escaped detection despite a determined four-day search by the Canadian Escort Group 16 and two American hunter-killer groups.

The commander of *U-1232, Kapitän zur See* Kurt Dobratz (who had the unusual background of having served eight years in *Luftwaffe*), was not at all dismayed by this show of strength. He stayed in place at the harbour mouth watching the traffic until 14 January when he found himself in a good position to attack the Boston to Halifax convoy BX 141, which was protected by two minesweepers and Escort Group 27 with four frigates. The convoy was strung out in a long line to enter the harbour when the third ship in the column, *British Freedom*, was torpedoed at 2241 hours. There was only a minor explosion and it took some time for the escort vessels to realize what was happening. Before they recovered, Dobratz torpedoed two more merchantmen including the *Athelviking*, the flagship of the convoy commodore. By this time Escort Group 27 was wide awake but the shallow waters being poor for ASDIC, the warships began to make depth charge attacks on likely firing positions in an attempt to scare off the

MARITIME AIR – A POWERFUL WEAPON

Land-based maritime air

Although the submarine threat was largely discounted by western navies during the inter-war period, Britain did create Coastal Command, the maritime air component of the RAF, in 1938 and it came under the operational control of the RN at the outbreak of war. In September 1939, Coastal Command possessed 298 aircraft, of which just over half were operational, and although it did its best in the first 18 months of the war, it suffered from a lack of VLR (Very Long Range) patrol aircraft and effective weapons. The bomb in service at this time was not only useless against submarines; it would often bounce upward and damage or destroy the aircraft that dropped it. Coastal Command aircraft proved most successful in the "scarecrow" role and their presence in British waters forced Dönitz to constantly shift his U-boats westward beyond air range until by the spring of 1941 German submarines were well out into the mid-Atlantic.

Britain and Canada countered by establishing airbases in Northern Ireland, Iceland and Newfoundland. Given the range of the aircraft in service at this time, however, there remained an "air gap" or "black hole" in the middle Atlantic where U-boats could operate with impunity on the surface. Attempts by Coastal Command to obtain Liberator VLR aircraft from RAF's Bomber Command to seal this gap were unavailing until late 1942 and it was only in the spring of 1943 that enough Liberators entered service to eliminate it. In the meantime, new weapons and equipment increased the lethality of aircraft. The Mark VIII, later Mark XI, aerial depth charges, smaller than their naval equivalent and fitted with nose cones and fins, came into service in 1941-1942 as did the first ASV (Air Surface Vessel) radar sets. The results were immediate – between September 1939 and July 1942, maritime aircraft made 327 attacks on U-boats, sinking two and sharing in the sinking of four. but between July and December 1942, 299 attacks resulted in 34 Axis submarine kills as compared to 31 by surface ships.

In 1941 the Royal Canadian Air Force became a major player in the maritime air war when that service's Eastern Air Command started flying from bases in Newfoundland. The command's strength increased steadily until by the spring of 1943 – the time of the climactic convoy battles in the Atlantic which broke the back of Dönitz's *U-Boot-Waffe* – it had 11 squadrons with about 150 aircraft in service. As illustrated on the map opposite, new airbases and better aircraft gradually decreased the size of the "air gap," and when it was finally closed in mid-1943, the RAF, RCAF, USN and US Army Air Force had more than 700 aircraft available for service in the North Atlantic.

Thereafter, land-based maritime air declined in numbers but increased in power as late war aircraft were much better than their predecessors. By 1945, the RAF and RCAF deployed just under 500 modern aircraft equipped with centimetric radar and lethal anti-submarine weapons including sono buoys (a sonar canister dropped into the sea that could detect a submerged U-boat and transmit information about its location back to the aircraft) and homing torpedoes.

Carrier-based maritime air

Early in the Battle of the Atlantic it was recognized that the provision of carrier-based close air support was absolutely essential. Large fleet carriers were not useful for this work and were required for more conventional naval operations, and in any case their construction was a lengthy business. As the need was immediate, a decision was made to convert merchant hulls into small escort or "jeep" carriers that would carry fewer aircraft. A shortage of suitable ships and aircraft delayed the introduction of this type of vessel until 1941 when a captured German merchantman was converted into the first escort carrier, HMS *Audacity*. Although the intention was that she would provide air cover against land-based German aircraft, *Audacity* immediately proved her usefulness in ASW while escorting a convoy from Britain to Gibraltar in September 1941 when her aircraft assisted in the sinking of four U-boats. Unfortunately, *Audacity* was a prime target and was torpedoed during the same convoy. Her success, however, validated the concept of the escort carrier, and in 1942 the RN and USN commissioned 14 of these vessels but they were deployed, not in the North Atlantic, but in European waters to protect Arctic and Gibraltar convoys from enemy aircraft.

In the meantime, air cover for Atlantic convoys was provided by Merchant Aircraft Carriers, merchant vessels with a superimposed flying deck that could operate three or four Swordfish biplanes and still carry cargo. The first of the MAC ships entered service in October 1942 and, in all, 19 vessels of this type served on the Atlantic. It was quickly discovered that the Swordfish was not capable of destroying U-boats and its most useful role was to serve as a spotter for convoy escorts.

The perilous situation on the Atlantic in the first quarter of 1943 required the use of the much more effective escort carrier. In March 1943, the USS *Bogue* became the first such vessel to accompany a trans-Atlantic convoy and she was shortly followed by HM Ships *Biter* and *Archer*. At first, these carriers were made part of the convoy escort, but it was found that their best use was as part of hunter-killer support groups which operated independently but could reinforce the escort of any heavily-threatened convoy. Carrier aircraft were not only directly effective against U-boats; they provided powerful assistance to surface escorts and soon proved their worth. Between April and December 1943, American and British escort carriers sank, or helped surface vessels to sink, 25 U-boats.

Ironically, although the RCN manned two escort carriers, *Nabob* and *Puncher*, during the latter years of the war, neither ship was ever used in ASW and they were deployed in more traditional carrier roles.

The bottom line

The possession of powerful maritime air forces was crucial in winning the Battle of the Atlantic against the U-boats and the evidence for this statement is found in the statistics. During the Second World War, land-based maritime aircraft sank 209 Axis submarines by their own efforts and assisted surface vessels to sink 30, while carrier-base aircraft sank 30 submarines by their own efforts and assisted in the sinking of 12 submarines. For its part, the RCAF accounted for the destruction of 21 submarines, either by aircraft alone or in co-operation with surface vessels. ∎

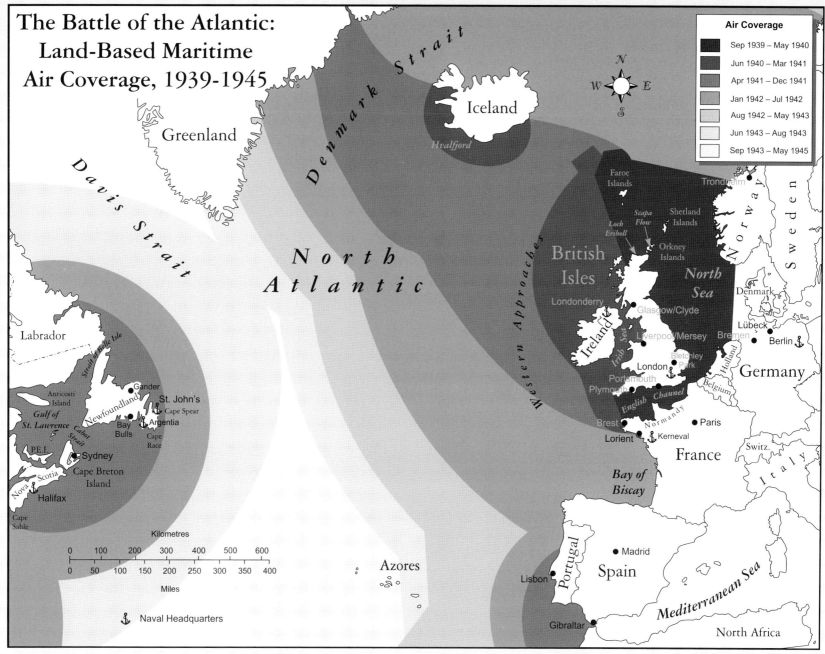

The Battle of the Atlantic: Land-Based Maritime Air Coverage, 1939-1945

Air Coverage

- Sep 1939 – May 1940
- Jun 1940 – Mar 1941
- Apr 1941 – Dec 1941
- Jan 1942 – Jul 1942
- Aug 1942 – May 1943
- Jun 1943 – Aug 1943
- Sep 1943 – May 1945

Greenland

Iceland

Hvalfjord

Denmark Strait

Davis Strait

North Atlantic

Western Approaches

Faroe Islands

Trondheim

Scapa Flow

Shetland Islands

Loch Eriboll

Orkney Islands

British Isles

North Sea

Norway

Sweden

Londonderry

Glasgow/Clyde

Denmark

Lübeck

Berlin

Ireland

Irish Sea

Liverpool/Mersey

Bremen

Bletchley Park

London

Holland

Portsmouth

Germany

Plymouth

Belgium

English Channel

Labrador

Strait of Belle Isle

Gander

St. John's

Newfoundland

Cape Spear

Anticosti Island

Brest

Normandy

Paris

Gulf of St. Laurence

Bay Bulls

Argentia

Lorient

Kerneval

France

Cabot Strait

Cape Race

Switz.

P.E.I.

Sydney

Cape Breton Island

Bay of Biscay

Italy

Nova Scotia

Halifax

Cape Sable

Portugal

Madrid

Spain

Kilometres

0 100 200 300 400 500 600

0 50 100 150 200 250 300 350 400

Miles

Azores

Lisbon

Mediterranean Sea

⚓ Naval Headquarters

Gibraltar

North Africa

MAP BY CHRISTOPHER JOHNSON

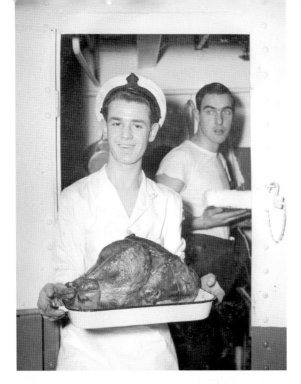

Christmas dinner, 1944. The cook of HMCS *Wallaceburg*, an Algerine Class minesweeper, proudly displays his art on Christmas Day 1944. Meals like this were very rare at sea but *Wallaceburg* was in Halifax on that Happy Day and her cook took due advantage of the occasion. (Canadian Naval Memorial Trust)

attacker. Dobratz ignored the fireworks and was lining up his fourth shot when, through his periscope, he observed the frigate HMCS *Ettrick* bearing down on him. He fired and dived at the last moment but almost left it too late as *Ettrick* struck his submarine a glancing blow, smashing its periscope and tearing up its bridge structure. Unaware he had struck a U-boat, *Ettrick*'s captain, Lieutenant Commander E.M. More, RCNR, thought he had scraped against an underwater rock. American and Canadian warships carried out a three-day hunt for *U-1232* but Dobratz was able to escape and return safely to his base in Norway.

Dobratz's highly successful cruise convinced Dönitz that good pickings were to be had in the Northwest Atlantic. Incredibly enough, given the fact that Allied armies were now closing in on Berlin, between February and early April 1945, he dispatched at least 12 and possibly as many as 14 U-boats to this area in a final throw of the dice. Ultra intelligence warned American and Canadian naval commanders of the planned onslaught and they were able to take timely measures to defeat it. Six of the U-boats formed *Gruppe Seewolf* to operate in waters adjacent to the United States but four were almost immediately sunk by two powerful American "barrier forces," each consisting of two escort carriers and 20 destroyers. Two others, *U-879* and *U-881*, fell victim to American hunter-killer groups off the Grand Banks.

"Hands to muster for grog!"

The high point of a sailor's day was the free 2.5 ounce tot of overproof Demerara rum he received with the thanks of his grateful Majesty, King George VI. It had to be mixed with water or Coca-Cola in the ratio of 1 rum to 2 other liquid and had to consumed immediately. In this photograph taken on a corvette, the cox'n (the senior petty officer on board) has mixed the rum and water and is now dispensing it into the cups of the waiting sailors. Meanwhile, as required by regulations, an officer observes the procedure to make sure that each man drinks his tot immediately. Chiefs and petty officers, as befitting their august status, were permitted to drink their tot undiluted. The custom of providing a daily issue of rum began in the Royal Navy in 1687 and, after 1740, it was mixed with water to make grog. Originally each sailor received a pint, half at noon and half at 6 PM, but this was progressively reduced. The issue of rum ended in the Royal and Royal Canadian Navies about 1970. (Canadian Naval Memorial Trust)

"Being in all respects ready for sea:" HMCS _La Hulloise,_ 1944.
A fine study of the River Class frigate _La Hulloise_ entering Liverpool late in the war. Commissioned in May 1944, she served mainly with Escort Group 25 in British waters and participated in the sinking of _U-1302_ in March 1945. Ordered back to Canada for tropicalization for Pacific service, she was paid off in December 1945. Recommissioned in 1949, _La Hulloise_ was converted to a Prestonian Class frigate and was in commission until 1965 when she was sold for breaking up.
(Imperial War Museum, A-28098)

At least five of the U-boats (the evidence is contradictory), however, operated in Murray's theatre in March and April 1945. The most successful was *U-190*, a Type IX boat which left Germany in February 1945 to carry out a lengthy patrol off the Canadian coast. During this operation *U-190* did not once surface, but used its snorkel to recharge its batteries. The commanding officer, *Oberleutnant zur See* Hans-Edwin Reith, was aware that there was a massive search on to find him but was determined to carry out his mission, which was basically to tie up Allied air and naval forces and *U-190* accomplished this objective with great success.

On 16 April, Reith was off the mouth of Halifax harbour when he heard ASDIC pulses on his hull. Taking a hurried look through his periscope, he sighted the Bangor Class minesweeper HMCS *Esquimalt* on a routine patrol and fired off an acoustic torpedo which sank the Canadian warship in less than four minutes. According to *Oberleutnant (Ingenieur)* Werner Hirschmann, the submarine's engineer officer, the crew of *U-190* knew they had scored a victory when, after the explosion of their torpedo, they heard "the typical noises of a sinking ship."[8] Most of *Esquimalt*'s crew managed to abandon their ship but, due to a tragic series of errors, it was nearly seven hours before a rescue ship arrived to pick up the survivors – by that time only 26 men of 70 were still alive. A massive search for *U-190* was immediately mounted by all available Canadian naval forces but it slipped away.

"Full of respect and fairness:" The enemy surrenders, May 1945

On 30 April 1945, as Soviet troops approached to within yards of his bunker in Berlin, Adolf Hitler committed suicide. One of his last acts was to name Dönitz to succeed him as leader of the Third Reich but, by this time, most of the U-boat bases in Germany were in Allied hands and only Norway remained as a refuge. On 4 May, Germany surrendered unconditionally and on 8 May the Admiralty broadcast a message in plain language to all U-boats at sea or at their bases to sail immediately to designated Allied ports and surrender. This was followed by a similar message from Dönitz. Most of the U-boat crews, 221 out of 371 boats in service, chose to scuttle their craft but 150 obeyed the order to surrender. The final act had not

come a moment too soon – there were 83 Type XXI and 37 Type XXIII U-boats working up, although only one Type XXI and a few Type XXIIIs actually entered service before the war ended.

U-190 was on its way back to Germany on 10 May when it received instructions to surrender and immediately complied by surfacing and transmitting its position in clear language. The next day the frigate HMCS *Victoriaville* and the corvette HMCS *Thorlock* arrived and removed most of the crew, leaving only *Oberleutnant (Ingenieur)* Hirschmann and a few of his engine-room personnel to run the submarine as it headed for Bay Bulls in Newfoundland. A Canadian prize crew was put on board and Hirschmann recalled that relations between the former enemies were "full of respect and fairness" and particularly remembered "being on the conning tower at night, listening to piped-up Strauss waltzes and discussing with my Canadian captors, family, war, and other problems of the world."[9] On board *Thorlock* relations between the Canadians and Germans were also cordial – Seaman James Haigh remembered that "Old sea boots, streetcar tickets, pictures and coins were traded to the Germans for German money, buttons, badges, etc."[10]

A more elaborate and impressive ceremony occurred at Loch Eriboll in Scotland when Escort Group 9, consisting of the frigates *Matane* (Senior Officer), *Loch Alvie*, *Monnow*, *Nene* and *St. Pierre*, escorted 13 U-boats on a 500-mile journey into this remote anchorage. As the convoy, with Canadian warships ahead and astern of the U-boats, which were formed in two columns, approached the loch on 16 May, they were surrounded by dashing fast attack craft and small boats full of press photographers, while aircraft circled overhead, just in case the U-boats decided to go out with a bang. The British press made a great event out of this surrender but, as usual, got it wrong by stating that the escorts were British ships, which, as the Senior Officer of Escort Group 9, Commander A.F.C. Layard, RN, remembered, made his Canadian crews "awfully sore."[11] Layard was later criticized for allowing his men to fraternize with their prisoners, but at that point having just completed nearly 15 months of continuous service at sea, Layard did not really care what shore-based officers thought of him – he was just glad the whole thing was over.

The battle ends

The surrender of the U-boats was the last act in the Battle of the Atlantic, which had lasted 2,075 days from 3 September 1939 when the liner *Athenia* was sunk, to 8 May 1945 when Germany surrendered. During that time, Dönitz had commanded 1,181 submarines, although only just over 800 reached operational service. He had lost 756 of them and 28,000 of the 40,000 men who served in the U-boat arm. It was an incredibly high casualty rate, but, as stated earlier, although the morale of the German submarine crews sometimes wavered, it never broke and they did not stop fighting until ordered to stop.

In doing so, they inflicted grievous losses on the Allied powers. It has been estimated that the Battle of the Atlantic cost the lives of 50,000 Allied sailors and merchant seamen and the loss of 2,603 merchant vessels and 175 warships. The Royal Canadian Navy's share of this loss was 24 warships and nearly 1,800 men while the Canadian merchant marine lost 30 ships and 1,064 sailors.

The Battle of the Atlantic was the longest, most desperately fought, and most important campaign of the Second World War. The preservation of the sea lanes from North America to Britain was the foundation for the western Allies' victory over Germany and all other operations on land, sea and air depended on it (including the maintenance of Soviet fighting power on the Eastern Front). If it had been lost, the war in Europe would have been lost. That it was won is a tribute to the courage and determination of the men of the merchant marine and the Allied navies who served at sea and the many others, both men and women, who supported them on land and in the air.

The Royal Canadian Navy, which had started the war as a tiny service and grown to become the third largest Allied navy, played a major role in this lengthy and costly but very necessary struggle. In the end, victory in the Atlantic would not have been achieved without the sacrifices made by those Canadians who placed themselves in peril on the sea between 1939 and 1945.

"At the going down of the sun and in the morning, we will remember them."
With the corvette *Sackville* in the background, members of the Royal Canadian Navy Sea Cadet Corps perform a memorial service to those who served in the North Atlantic – but did not return. (Canadian Naval Memorial Trust)

1945

"I proceeded to drink too much rum and ginger ale:" Escort Group 9 gets a U-boat, February 1945

In early 1945, Escort Group 9, operating off the Shetland Islands under the command of Commander A.F.C. Layard, RN, sank a U-boat after going for nearly six months without a kill. As Layard noted in his diary, this success came as a surprise:

Friday, February 16 – at sea
Just before midnight the 3 other ships all passed in H/F D/F bearings thought to be near ground wave and so I turned to the bearing which was 060 degrees and swept back for 25 miles but without result and so round we went back for Cape Wrath. We made Radar contact with our convoy N[orth]. of C[ape]. Wrath at about 0400 and took station in each quarter till daylight after which we took station ahead. It was misty and blowing a bit from the S[outh].E[ast]. as we went through the Pentland Firth. At about 2.30 when between No. 34 and 33 buoys we got an A/S [asdic] contact while screening on the starboard bow of the convoy. We altered towards, ran over and got an E/S [echo sounder] trace and as by Q.H.* 3 [navigational charts] there was no plotted wreck in the vicinity I decided to give it a pattern and so we dropped 5 [depth charges] which immediately

---

* Q.H. was the codename for a radio-navigation device fitted on warships in the late war period that provided accurate plotting in inshore waters. The use of this system permitted wrecks and unusual bottom features to be accurately located, an invaluable aid to inshore ASW.

The same view for more than five years.
Day after day, week after week, month after month, year after year, it was the same view – water, sky and ships. The first trans-Atlantic convoy left Britain on 7 September 1939 and the last crossed in early May 1945. (National Archives of Canada, PA 200127)

brought quite a bit of oil to the surface so rather unwillingly, as I wanted to get on with the convoy, I returned and attacked again. After the 3rd attack I was just saying "I don't think this is anything, do you?" when on steaming through the oil and explosion cafuffle we saw a lot of splintered wood work and some paper which, on fishing out of the water, proved to be bits of a German signal log!!!! We lowered a boat and also picked up an aluminium flask and a tube of sorts marked in German "Medical [illegible] Keil". All this was most exciting and seemed to indicate that we were on a U boat. Hoisted the whaler and carried out 2 or 3 more attacks before dark but nothing more came up except a great deal of diesel oil and splintered wood. I recalled *Nene* from the convoy and the two of us held contact all night. The whole thing seems such a complete fluke but at last one of the hundreds of contacts we've obtained and investigated and attacked in coastal waters has proved to be the thing we've been looking for.

Saturday, February 17 – at sea – Scapa
At daylight we started in to renew our attacks on the submarine but in spite of pattern after pattern of D/C [depth charges] and H/H [Hedge Hog] the only thing we could bring up except oil and wood was some torn bits of French charts of the Caribbean with the German Kriegsmarine stamp on them. I can't believe that after about 70 D/Cs and 5 H/H salvos it is possible that the S/M [submarine] is still alive but all the same the lack of more evidence is disappointing. E/S traces latterly suggested that the object had broken up a bit. C.in C. Rosyth told us to turn the contact over to *Monnow* and *Loch Alvie* and proceed to Scapa with our evidence. *Monnow* and *L[och]. A[lvie].* arrived on the scene at about 5 and after some de-

lay in getting contact I pushed off for Scapa at 5.30 arriving about 2000. Went right alongside the oiler *Danmark* and when secured I proceeded to drink too much rum and ginger ale in the W[ard]. R[oom]. before turning in. But still it was a bit of an occasion. I don't know what the experts will say but I don't see that it can be but a U/Boat and I think we killed it.

Although the group was only credited with a "probable," postwar records revealed they had sunk U-309.

"Another died in a similar manner:" HMCS *Esquimalt* is sunk, March 1945

On 30 March 1945, U-190 torpedoed the Bangor Class minesweeper HMCS Esquimalt *off the mouth of Halifax harbour. Able Seaman Joseph Wilson was manning the ASDIC set on* Esquimalt *when the torpedo hit and recalled that*

The ship immediately started to go under, rolling over to starboard and sinking stern-first. She disappeared within four minutes.

The Captain, who was in his cabin, had a hard time coming up the ladders, but finally gained the bridge. With one look he took in the situation and immediately ordered, "Abandon Ship." With this, I left the ASDIC hut, went down off the bridge, and across onto the funnel and into the water, where I came up near a Carley float. I clambered in, but the after mast caught me across the back, pressing me back under the surface. However, I had my lifejacket on and I rolled from under the mast, shooting back to the surface.

When I clambered back into the life raft, there were other friends around, all trying to come over the side of the life raft, or simply hanging on the side ropes.[1]

Seaman Terence Manuel, the Esquimalt's *writer or clerk, remembered that he was still on the deck when the ship went under and,*

After what seemed an eternity and with bursting lungs I surfaced to the oil slick swell of the Atlantic above, having exited *Esquimalt* under water, the last one out of her, my feet coming to rest on the submerged and rolled over bulkhead of *Esquimalt*. I was at nose level to the sea, gasping for air and drinking in sea water and fuel oil, flapping my arms to keep my head above it for I was not a swimmer. A quick look to the left of me revealed approximately ten feet of *Esquimalt's* overturned bow out of the water beyond, rising five-six feet in the air – she began to roll again under my touching feet and suddenly the support was no longer there – a voice carried across the rolling water "Swim, damn it, – swim, she's going."

Rousing myself to that call I endeavoured to do just that but my efforts were impeded by a desperate sailor floundering in the water clutching at me and pushing me under. We struggled and I managed to break his hold just as my eyes caught the movement of an object in the water, it was a sailor's sea-bag. I grabbed my companion's disappearing head by the hair and attacked the water to get a hand hold on it. We held onto it until it became water logged and began to settle under water. An anxious shout from me to a float drifting away from us brought the response "Hang on, Scribe" and Carl Jacques, a P.[etty] O.[fficer] Motor Mechanic from Truro, Nova Scotia, swam out to us and pulled us to the float where we grasped the hand-hold ropes along its rounded sides.

Jacques claimed his perch on the float, after a short interval of time he slumped over and was thought to be sleeping from his extra exertion in

The last casualty – the Bangor minesweeper HMCS *Esquimalt,* 1945.
The work carried out by the RCN's 56 Bangor class and 12 Algerine class minesweepers is often overlooked. They served as coastal and local escorts, although 16 Bangors reverted to their original role during the Normandy invasion. Ten of the Bangors, including *Esquimalt,* were powered by diesel engines and were somewhat smaller than the rest of the class. *Esquimalt* displaced 592 tons, had a complement of 83, a top speed of 16 knots and was armed with one 12-pdr and two 20mm AA guns. Sunk in the approaches of Halifax by *U-190* on 16 April 1945, she was the last RCN casualty of the war. The triangular antenna on her foremast is for the Canadian SW2C radar. (National Archives of Canada, PA 116954)

the water, however, investigation by his immediate companion revealed he was dead as all efforts to rouse him failed. Another died in a similar manner and two others drowned "in the hole of the donut," the bottom of the float covered with rope netting.[2]

Seaman Wilson remembered that, on his raft, his shipmates

spent about six and a half hours in the water, during which time we could see the Sambro Lightship at all times. We tried to row towards it by paddling with our hands, and we were the only raft that actually made the lightship. The rest of the survivors were picked up by HMCS *Sarnia*, which also recovered us.

Seaman Manuel never forgot the long hours on the face of the ocean:

Such was the cold rolling water and the slipperiness of the float's rounded sides that grip was near impossible to hold and in addition to this the clamour of other sailors seeking a purchase too. Shock as well with its terrible body shaking and shivering in tightly clenched self-embrace, or just sheer exhaustion from the struggle and enormity of it all took their toll that morning. Coiled in a foetal position I too had a difficult time of controlling my own shaking and shivering once a place opened up for me on the carley-float. I was clad only in undershorts and the First Lieutenant's life jacket, identified in white stencil markings, which I obtained from the floating debris in the water.

Forty-four men out of Esquimalt's *complement of seventy died that morning in March, most in the long hours they spent waiting for rescue.*

The last patrol of U-190, February–May 1945

Oberleutnant (Ing.) *Werner Hirschmann describes the last war patrol of U-190 in the spring of 1945 and his experiences as a prisoner of war in Canada:*

On February 10 we departed from Kiel for our last patrol across the Atlantic, with a stopover in Horten in Norway to top up our fuel. On entering that harbour we had to witness another submarine following us being blown up by a mine with a total loss of crew.

In December 1944 another boat had been quite successful in attacking convoys leaving Halifax and to our High Command it seemed to be a promising area of operations. With spending about two hours surfaced at night to charge the batteries and otherwise crawling along at less than pedestrian speed, when submerged, it took about six weeks to cross the Atlantic. Under attack a few times by surface vessels we managed to escape each time. I remember how we admired the crews on the surface vessels for their tenacity in staying with us in absolutely horrifying storm conditions with mountainous waves.

When we approached the Canadian coast, we no longer surfaced during the night and started a period of fifty days submerged prowling around the approaches of Halifax. As Chief Engineer I wasn't too involved in tactical matters, but it seemed that all commercial traffic in the area had come to a halt. On the other hand we must have been suspected of being in the area, because there was a never-ending search for us with asdic and depth charges dropped on imagined targets. Any time the situation became too uncomfortable we snuck close in shore and spent some hours on the bottom, where we felt relatively safe. Few of the

A young man's war.
The Battle of the North Atlantic was hard on ships and men and many sailors were broken by the physical and nervous strain. As the war progressed, the personnel on both sides became progressively younger, as is evident of these pictures of Lieutenant Commander W.H. Willson, captain of the corvette *Kootenay*, and his officers taken in 1944 (above) and *Leutnants zur See* Werner Müller (age 22) and Ernst Glenk (age 21) of *U-190* taken in 1945 (below). On his cap, Müller is wearing the badge of the 2nd U-boat Flotilla, a submarine transfixed by a lightning bolt. (National Archives of Canada, PA 179887, PA 191077)

U-boat farewell party, 1944.
Contrary to popular myth, parties for U-boat crews departing on patrol were fairly staid affairs, as shown in the photo at left from 9 March 1944. The officers of *U-66* and *U-190* (wearing their grey service uniforms) are saying goodbye to their comrades in the flotilla mess at Lorient. *U-66* never returned from patrol. (Courtesy, Werner Hirschmann)

depth charges came close enough to cause more than minimal damage and even fewer to present a real danger.

In the middle of April once again we heard the pinging of asdic and then noticed a small warship rapidly approaching from astern. We were sure that she had discovered us and prepared for an attack. We fired an acoustic torpedo from one of our stern tubes and went deep. We heard an explosion, followed by the typical noises of a sinking ship. We had not been able to identify our target, but were told later that it was the Bangor minesweeper, HMCS *Esquimalt*. Since the loss of the minesweeper was not discovered until many hours later, we were able to sneak once more close inshore and to avoid any direct retaliation.

At the end of April, the state of our fuel and food supplies indicated the need to embark on return to our home port and we turned east to begin the long journey. A few days later, to lift our sagging spirits, we staged a somewhat rather unmilitary interlude. May 1 was Germany's National Holiday and we realized that the year being 1945, this was most likely the last opportunity to celebrate that occasion in style.

I must mention here, that in normal times each member of the crew of our subs received a generous ration of alcoholic drinks in form of several bottles of liquor. In normal times these bottles were left in port to be taken home after return from a mission. When we left Germany in February 1945, we were not altogether certain that we would ever come back to that particular harbour, and to prevent the falling of these bottles into undesirable hands, we just loaded them aboard and took them along, just as we did with our dress uniforms. On May 1 the outlook for future parties to enjoy our liquid cargo was rather dim and we decided to live up to our duties and have a rousing National Holiday party right then and there, at a depth of 60 metres somewhere between Halifax and the south of Newfoundland.
……

On May 12, somewhere southeast of Newfoundland, Germany requested us to surface and radio our position in open language. The war was over and looking back – my proudest achievement of the war was that, at the end, the 57 members of our crew were still alive.

Soon after we were asked to change course to Newfoundland and during the following night we were picked up by two Canadian warships, HMCS *Victoriaville* and HMCS *Thorlock*. With the excep-

tion of eight engine room personnel and myself, our crew was transferred to the Canadian warships and Canadian crew took over to complete our final journey.

On the next day I became aware of a commotion going on in our bow torpedo room. There I observed a Canadian petty officer berating a group of his sailors who were highly inebriated, very happy and just having a whale of a time. When looking into the matter, the Canadian officers and myself pieced together the sequence of events: our sailors, justifiably concerned about the fate of their nicely labelled bottles, had had time enough to hide their precious property by pouring the contents into their military issue canteens which were then left lying around all over the

Wardroom of *U-190*, 1944
This grainy photo from September 1944 shows officers of *U-190* in the cramped wardroom of their Type IX boat. Left to right: *Oberleutnant (Ing)* Hirschmann and *Oberleutnants zur See* Reith and Schmidt. *U-190* sank HMCS *Esquimalt* in April 1945 but surrendered to the RCN after VE Day. Reith and Hirschmann spent a year in the officers' camp at Gravenhurst, Ontario, before returning to Germany. They were lucky – most of their comrades never came back. (Courtesy, Werner Hirschmann)

place. Obviously they had not counted on the acute sense of smell of their Canadian colleagues who forthwith made the best of their discovery. When the situation was back under control, the canteens were only half full at best.

The relationship between the Canadian officers and our crew was full of respect and fairness. I remember being on the conning tower at night, listening to piped-up Strauss waltzes and discussing with my Canadian guests family, war and other problems of the world. I will always remember their names and sorely regret that I never met anyone of them again. I had one final triumph – I beat one of my guests in a chess game!

We entered Bay Bulls a day later where we were reunited with our captain and the rest of the crew. We were then transferred to the Canadian frigate, HMCS *Prestonian*, which took us to Halifax. On this trip we had long discussions with the Canadian officers. They demonstrated how they chased us, and we explained how we escaped – a meeting of former enemies, full of respect for each other.

After a warm farewell at Halifax, we officers were then separated from the crew of U-190 and began the long train trip to Gravenhurst in Ontario. Eating in the dining car, in full dress uniform among the passengers of the train, lightly supervised by two Canadian naval officers, was certainly a welcome first step in our transition to a more civilized life.

At the Gateway Hotel in Gravenhurst, which served as prisoner-of-war camp No. 20, we had all the comforts of life with the exception of female company. We were treated like guests of the country. We had our own dance band, playing mainly big band swing, our symphony orchestra, our internal university, six first-run American movies a week, in summer time under the trees. We had a

tennis court inside the barbed wire and outside, there were two hockey rinks and our own fenced-off swimming area in Lake Muskoka with diving tower and water-polo basin. The latter facilities we could use after giving our word of honour not to escape. Further away we had our own farm with chicken, pigs, horses, potato fields and maple trees that supplied us with maple syrup. Eaton's catalogue challenged us to splurge our money, $20 a month. Beer was officially delivered, spirits were distilled illegally and protected through an elaborate alarm system……

With pride and humility, I have now accepted an honorary membership in the HMCS *Esquimalt* Memorial Association. As recognized by the Esquimalt veterans and myself: all of us only did our duty.

"Am I thankful it has come:" VE Day, 8 May 1945

On VE Day, 8 May 1945, the RCN's 9th Escort Group was at sea. As the ever-conscientious and ever-worried Senior Officer of the group, Commander A.F.C. Layard, RN, recorded in his diary, it was a very special day:

Tuesday, May 8 – at sea – Lissahally

…… We got a signal shortly after leaving saying today the 8th was V day and at about 0100 a signal from Com[modore] (D[estroyers]) telling us to return to Moville and so we turned back and anchored at about 0330, very nearly hitting the wreck off Dunagree Point as we came in. …… After we were alongside and secured the Captain cleared lower deck and read prayers - very badly I thought - and then I addressed the ship's company also rather badly. I was having a V[ictory]

day glass of beer in the W[ard].R[oom]. before lunch when we got a signal to embark pilots and proceed up to Lissahally and give leave to one watch. …… At 1500 Churchill broadcast to the nation that the war with Germany was over and the Admiralty ordered "Splice the Main Brace". From then on most everyone in the ships was tight. After that I went ashore for a walk. It was a lovely hot sunny day but my walk was spoilt by worrying about the drunks. As I came on board I passed 3 men carrying jugs to the Canteen with the intention of bringing beer back on board for the watch on board. I found Skinner half tight in my cabin but he gave me some good advice and calmed me down just as I was thinking of putting sentries and patrols everywhere. Really there was nothing for it but to permit booze coming on board and otherwise let them be. Our Ward Room in the evening was full of Wrens who had bicycled over. I had a good many drinks but didn't enjoy myself. Thank God V[ictory]. day only comes once in a lifetime but oh am I thankful it has come.

Lieutenant Commander Louis Audette, RCNVR, remembers the end of the war:

When the European war ended I was in the middle of the ocean. Thank God I was not in Halifax. I was Senior Officer of EG 27 and had four ships in company. One of them was Phil Evans in *Lévis*, another frigate. We were given orders to patrol a line of latitude. …… We patrolled the line, which meant steering west for so many hours and then altering 180 degrees and steaming east for so many hours – and back and forth. It was a pretty dull affair. One morning when I came up to the bridge a signal came in from *Lévis*. It said, "Thirteen Hebrews verse eight." I dragged my bible out and the verse in question was "Jesus Christ. The same yesterday, today and forever."[3]

"This made the Canadians awfully sore:" EG 9 rounds up the U-boats, May 1945

In mid-May Escort Group 9 was ordered to intercept a German convoy of surface ships and submarines in the North Sea and bring the U-boats to Loch Eriboll in Scotland for an elaborate surrender ceremony during which Commander Layard, RN, managed to dodge the media:

Thursday, May 17 – at sea

…… at about 0530 we sighted the convoy on our Port Bow and so all was well. We went to actions stations as we approached. It consisted of a couple of large armed yachts and 3 Submarine Depot ships and auxiliaries and 15 U boats. We closed the leading yacht obviously the S[enior].O[fficer]. and the others closed the U boats and the whole convoy was ordered to stop. I tried to give my orders by hailing but that was hopeless and so I lowered a boat and sent No. 1 over who found a Captain on board who called himself S[enior].O[fficer]. Arctic and Barents Sea. When he heard his U boats had to go to England he was inclined to refuse as it was contrary to the orders for his High Command but No. 1 was v[ery]. firm and he soon saw he had to do as he was told. The chief thing was to get him to tell the U boats how to form up, to find out if the surrender terms had been carried out and such details as amount of fuel, numbers of the boats etc. …… The U/B[oat]s were in 2 columns, *Matane* ahead and 2 escorts either side. My troubles weren't over then,

Loch Eriboll, 1945 – a Canadian frigate escorts a surrendered U-boat.
In May 1945, the RCN Escort Group 9 under the command of Commander A.F.C. Layard, RN, brought fifteen U-boats and four German surface vessels into Loch Eriboll in Scotland to surrender. It was the largest single capitulation of German submarines at the end of the war and the British media waxed enthusiastic about this signal triumph of the "Royal Navy," ignoring the fact that it was the work of Canadian warships. During the war, the British people knew little about the contribution made by the RCN toward the preservation of their seaborne lifeline and the Royal Navy never showed much interest in informing them. (National Archives of Canada, PA 191027)

however, for they started to straggle and develop engine trouble and eventually I made a signal saying this was not in keeping with the known efficiency of the U/B service and on arrival if there was any negligence, C[ommanding].O[fficer]s and any others concerned would be punished and would not return to Germany. …… I don't think they looked like giving any real trouble but it was a most exhausting and worrying day. If we get all [of] them in anybody else can have all the rest of the surrendering they want.

Friday, May 18 – at sea

…… Still rather worried about my boats and thought of all the awful things that *might* happen and wondered what on earth I would do. It is no good I can't be Prussian enough on these occasions. *Nene* has a German interpreter and they in-

tercepted a W/T [radio] signal from the S[enior].O[fficer]. to the other U boats saying it was all over, they had to bite the bitter apple and there was only one thing left to do - to give up their boats. …… however I signalled the S[enior].O[fficer]. and told him we were reading what he [had] made and told him no more signals on W/T without permission.

Saturday, May 19 – at sea – Loch Eriboll

…… Having made elaborate arrangements to get into single line before arriving, S[enior].O[fficer]. Loch Eriboll …… to get them all inside the shelter before stopping and so I quickly had to alter my orders and we approached in 2 columns. …… As we approached we had aircraft overhead and press photographers. It was announced on the news that 15 U boats were being escorted in by the Royal

Navy. This made the Canadians awfully sore. I must say they might have found out or have been told that we were an R.C.N. group. When we got into the entrance at about 1915 I stopped the whole outfit and H[arbour].L[aunche]'s went alongside and put guards on board the U boats and took the whole thing out of my hands, and we proceeded up the Loch to anchor. I must say it a great relief to have got them in without incident. I had a late supper and a v[ery]. good whisky and soda with Jonas. A Canadian press photographer came on board. As I am an R.N. officer and of no news value to him I was able thank God to avoid any personal photography and I suggested it would be far more suitable if he featured Skinner heavily.

The end, 1945.
U-889, a Type IX boat, at Shelburne, Nova Scotia, May 1945. U-889 left Germany on 6 April 1945 but by the time it reached Canadian waters, the war was over and it surrendered to HMCS *Dunvegan* at sea off Sable Island. U-889 was escorted to Shelburne, N.S. Its captain (wearing a white cap cover) is seen talking to RCN officers while a Catalina aircraft of the RCAF flies overhead. Note the air intake for the snorkel attached to the conning tower. (National Archives of Canada, PA 116720)

(Below) **North Atlantic convoy.**
During the Second World War, 7,358 merchant ships loaded at Canadian ports for overseas destinations, most of which were on the other side of the Atlantic. Between September 1939 and May 1945 more than 1,468 convoys crossed that ocean under the escort of Allied warships. The Battle of the Atlantic had to be fought and won before the war in Europe could be brought to successful conclusion. (Drawing by L.B. Jenson, courtesy of the artist)

TRIUMPH AND TRAGEDY: THE LEGACY
OF THE BATTLE OF THE ATLANTIC

The navy's shame: The VE Day riot, May 1945

There had never been any love lost between Canadian sailors and the overcrowded, expensive and rather grim port of Halifax, the despised "Slackers" in the sailors' vocabulary. Between 1939 and 1945 the city's population had risen from 68,000 to 99,000, swollen by service personnel and their families and there were shortages of everything – accommodation, restaurants, entertainment, recreational facilities, cinemas, cabs – and many unscrupulous civilians had made themselves wealthy by extorting service personnel. Particularly galling in sailors' eyes was that the city was officially "dry," and there were no bars or night clubs although alcohol could be purchased at government liquor stores. The stringent drinking laws, intended to keep intoxication to the minimum, actually created a booming trade in bootlegging. Sailors on shore leave from convoy duty, finding nothing to do in Halifax and nowhere to go, too often ended up purchasing liquor at exorbitant prices from bootleggers and then drinking it

(Facing page) **The Allied navies triumphant, 1945.**
By the last months of the war, the U-boats had been swept off the mid-ocean and convoy after convoy completed its journey without incident. While Signalman Jack Scott of HMCS *Sherbrooke* mans his signal projector in the foreground, the corvette HMCS *Barrie* refuels from a tanker. *Barrie*, commissioned in May 1941, was a veteran of the North Atlantic. She was sold to the Argentine navy in 1947 and broken up in 1972. (Photograph by G.P. Boydell, National Archives of Canada, PA 115354)

in public places because they had nowhere to consume it in private. The city's small police force was overwhelmed, and although the navy's shore patrols assisted, the sight of drunken men in uniform weaving through the downtown area was all too common in the latter years of the war.

The tension between service personnel, particularly sailors, and civilians increased as the conflict in Europe began to wind down and there were muttered threats that the navy would "take Halifax apart" on VE Day. Senior naval officers were aware of the potential for violence but their attempts to head it off suffered from the fact that there was no single coordinating commander for the many shore establishments in the city. Admiral Leonard Murray was the senior commander but his attention, particularly in the last days of the war, was directed toward operations intended to defeat Dönitz's final offensive in Canadian waters. The commanding officer of each shore establishment therefore made his own arrangements and no overall authority was in place to head off what was to be a tragedy.

On 7 May 1945, when news of the German surrender reached the city, there were 18,000 sailors, 3,500 airmen, 3,000 soldiers and an estimated 2,000 merchant mariners in Halifax. Many went into the downtown area but finding nothing to do and the government liquor stores closed as a precaution, they drifted up and down the streets. Toward evening a crowd of sailors, egged on by civilians, burned a streetcar and, thus encouraged, spectators broke into two liquor stores and distributed the contents to those gathered to watch the fun. The city police were helpless in the face of the crowd's numbers but, in any event, the participants were in a good mood, helped by the free refreshments, and what followed was a rather happy street party.

At this point, the senior officers of the armed forces and municipal authorities had been given a warning and they might have taken steps to prevent what occurred the next day by confining service personnel to their quarters and beefing up military and naval police patrols. Instead, half the sailors in the port were permitted to return to the city on 8 May and many were roaming the streets during the afternoon as a large civic celebration, complete with bands and politicians, took place on the Garrison Grounds behind Citadel Hill. When it concluded, those who had attended moved into the business section and joined thousands of people wandering aimlessly up and down the streets. Eventually, some uniformed personnel, again encouraged by watching civilians, began to smash store windows and once started, this activity increased – shops were looted and some set on fire, a police car was overturned, a third liquor store and a brewery were invaded – providing free drinks for all and sundry. It was noted that, although servicemen made many of the initial break-ins, the waiting civilians did most of the looting.

By early evening King Mob ruled downtown Halifax in an orgy of drink and destruction. Admiral Murray drove through the streets in a loudspeaker car, appealing to his men to return to their bases and ships, but thousands of sailors continue to reel through the streets and the riot only wound down after a curfew was proclaimed that night and military and naval police began to make numerous arrests. On the following day, 9 May 1945, armed soldiers from a nearby military camp arrived and the city was quiet. In the end, 19 airmen, 34 sailors, 41 soldiers and 117 civilians were charged with criminal acts and 152 people convicted of public drunkenness.

The Halifax Riot provoked outrage across Canada. Vice Admiral G.C. Jones, the Chief of the Naval Staff, flew to Halifax to assume command of all naval personnel in the city and the government appointed a Supreme Court justice to conduct an inquiry, which focused on the navy's role in this miserable event. Murray, believing that a senior officer is responsible for the actions of those under his command, refused to implicate any of his subordinates and took entire responsibility upon himself. He accepted the blame and resigned his commission to go into voluntary exile in Britain, where he died, almost forgotten, in 1971. It was a tragic end to the career of Canada's foremost wartime naval commander, who has been summed up as an officer

> deeply and deservedly respected by the seagoing navy. He was neither colourful nor brilliant, yet he was a hero, a dogged hero, though Canadians resist that word. His name should never be forgotten. The irony of his life was that his downfall came the very day his arch-enemies, the U-boats, surfaced to surrender.[1]

Many in the RCN believed that Murray was made a scapegoat and the true culprit was the government of Canada which, although it compensated property owners for the losses they sustained in the riot, had refused throughout the war to spend a cent more than necessary to ease the strained conditions in Halifax.

The navy's glory: The Bedford Magazine fire, July 1945

Responsibility for the Halifax Riot is still a matter of debate but there is little disagreement over who was to blame for the Bedford Magazine fire which began on 18 July 1945. By this time, the demobilization of the wartime fleet was in full flood and dozens of ships were decommissioning at Halifax and unloading their weapons, ammunition and equipment for storage. Thousands of rounds were placed in the RCN magazine at Bedford near Dartmouth across the harbour from Halifax. Naval regulations wisely prohibited more than one warship at a time unloading its ammunition on a single dock – only when that load had been safely dispensed in the magazines, could another vessel de-ammunition. These safety measures, however, slowed demobilization of the wartime fleet and the Liberal government (whose record on naval affairs was not its brightest feature) wanted the process of converting naval personnel into civilians (and potential voters) accelerated.

The government therefore insisted that, in the name of expediency, the safety regulations be set aside and on 18 July 1945 the ammunition of three warships was sitting on the south jetty of the Bedford Magazine in blazing hot summer weather. Even worse, since there hadn't been time to properly store previous loads in sealed structures, thousands of shells were dispersed in open dumps around the magazine area. At about 1800 that evening, a worker noticed that a pyrotechnic flare on the jetty had caught fire and went to put it out but before he could do so, there was a massive explosion that shook Halifax and Dartmouth and shattered windows in both cities and the south jetty simply disappeared.

Captain Owen Robertson, RCN, the officer responsible for fire safety in the naval base, was having dinner with his wife in the Nova Scotian Hotel in Halifax when he heard a "thump" and observed dust coming out of the ventilators. He immediately took an elevator to the top floor of the hotel and peering out over the harbour, was horrified to see a large mushroom cloud, a malignant toadstool in the sky, hanging over the Bedford Magazine. Proceeding quickly across the harbour in a naval speedboat, Robertson assumed command at the magazine and assessed the situation.

The jetty explosion had set off sympathetic detonations in some of the

Rear Admiral L.W. Murray, CB, CBE (1896-1971).

In the spring of 1943, Rear Admiral Leonard Murray was appointed commander-in-chief, Canadian Northwest Atlantic, becoming the only Canadian to command a major theatre of operations during the Second World War. From 1941 to 1945, Murray was the senior Canadian naval commander most directly concerned with the Battle of the Atlantic. Forced into early retirement by the Halifax Riot, Murray went to England, where he died, almost forgotten, in 1971. In the background are representative vessels of the North Atlantic escort fleet.. (Painting by David McIntosh, courtesy of the Maritime Command Museum)

open dumps and there was a possibility that a deadly chain reaction would start that, ultimately, would detonate the main magazines which contained enough explosives to flatten half of Halifax. As Robertson looked on, ammunition, starshells, flares and rockets were constantly exploding, starting grass fires near the main storage areas and outside the magazine. The situation was perilously close to being a repeat of the tragic 1917 explosion and, with this in mind, Robertson advised his superiors to evacuate that part of Halifax nearest the magazine. Fortunately, there was a well-organized emergency organization in place that ensured that this procedure, which began less than three hours after the initial blast, proceeded smoothly.

Under Robertson's direction, squads of volunteer naval firefighters entered the magazine and managed to put out the worst fires in the compound. As they worked, they were bombarded by projectiles of all kinds and showers of debris from the larger detonations but, labouring through the night, they managed to extinguish the most dangerous fires within the magazine compound and then turned to the tricky job of removing unexploded live ammunition from the open storage dumps. This task preoccupied them throughout 19 July and by the evening of that day the threat of a major explosion had receded and the population were permitted to return to their homes. It took another three days to contain the brush fires raging outside the magazine, a task done by sailor volunteers, many only a day or two from leaving the service but by 22 July all fires were out and the peril had ended.

By efforts that can justly be termed heroic, the RCN had averted a major disaster and the people of Halifax knew it. If the city had come to loathe the navy after the VE Day riot, it now came to admire it.

HMCS *Sackville*: An enduring memorial

On 14 August 1945 Japan surrendered and the Second World War, the most bloody and devastating conflict in history, ended. The wartime Canadian escort fleet, always regarded as a temporary and somewhat embarrassing emergency force by the regular navy, was paid off and hundreds of frigates and corvettes sent to the scrapyard or sold for surplus. On VJ Day, the RCN was, as stated earlier, the third largest navy in the world – a year later it had fewer ships in commission than in September 1939. As the escorts disappeared, so did the Canadian sailors who had served in them as most were wartime volunteers only too happy to return to civilian life.

The years, and then the decades, passed and, as the lean young men of the 1940s became portly and grey, many would gather on a Sunday in early May – Battle of the Atlantic Sunday – to honour their fallen and remember the courage and sacrifice of the war years. Each year they are older and, sadly, fewer in number. Eventually they will exist only as names and photographs in books written about the battle, but when they are gone, the world will be a poorer place because these men represent a generation that paid a very high price for the preservation of freedom. There are many memorials to their sacrifice, but for those who served on the North Atlantic, perhaps the most important can be seen in Halifax during the summer months at a jetty in front of the Maritime Museum of the Atlantic.

That memorial is the corvette HMCS *Sackville*. Commissioned in late 1941, *Sackville* joined "Chummy" Prentice's C-3 Group and fought in the desperate battle for Convoy ON 115 the following summer. After a refit, she went back to the Mid-Ocean Escort Force in April 1943 as a member of C-1 Group and completed six trans-Atlantic convoys. In July *Sackville* joined one of the first RCN support groups and participated in the last great convoy battle of the war, the struggle for ONS 18/ON 202 in September 1943. She served the remainder of 1943 in C-2 Escort Group and, following an extended refit in Texas in early 1944, rejoined the Mid-Ocean Escort Force only to be sidelined because of a boiler defect which caused her transfer to the reserve fleet. This defect actually saved *Sackville* as most of her wartime contemporaries disappeared into the scrapyards, and in 1952 she returned to the sea to begin a long and worthy career as an oceanographic research vessel.

By the time *Sackville* was paid off in 1982, she had claimed the interest of a volunteer group later formalized as the Canadian Naval Memorial Trust. With the assistance of various levels of government, the Canadian Forces and many other supportive institutions, organizations and individuals, the Trust raised the funds to restore the old Atlantic warhorse to her 1944 configuration and appearance. It took nearly two years but, on the day before the Battle of the Atlantic Sunday, 4 May 1985, *Sackville* was officially dedicated as the Canadian Naval Memorial. In the winter, *Sackville* is laid up at the Naval Dockyard, where her short and stumpy profile looks incongruous moored near the big, streamlined frigates and destroyers of the modern Canadian navy. Each spring she moves to her place of honour, a jetty in front of the Maritime Museum, where she is boarded by thousands of fascinated visitors.

Sackville looks better today than she ever did during her wartime career. Freshly painted and well maintained, she is a far cry from the rust-streaked little ship that battled the U-boats and the elements on the North Atlantic. *Sackville*, however, is more than a floating museum, she is a living ship and her decks and crewspaces often resound with the laughter of young sea cadets – some the grandchildren or great-grandchildren of the veterans of the Atlantic – who use her as a training vessel.[*]

It is very fitting that HMCS *Sackville* is the Canadian Naval Memorial because she is a perpetual reminder of what was Canada's greatest contribution to Allied victory during the Second World War – the Royal Canadian Navy's participation in the Battle of the Atlantic. *Sackville* is the last wartime corvette, the sole survivor of all those "far flung, storm tossed little ships on which the German Fuehrer had never looked and yet which ... stood between him and the conquest of the world."[2]

---

[*] The reader is invited to take a pictorial tour of HMCS *Sackville* on pages 224-229.

Sackville is dedicated, May 1985.
The official dedication of Sackville as the Canadian Naval Memorial took place on 4 May 1985 at the same dockyard where she secured many times during the war. At this point in her restoration, Sackville is still missing items (note the absence of rails around the 4-inch gun and the missing AA gun) but they would eventually be acquired. In the background can be seen the Angus L. Macdonald Bridge, named after the wartime minister of the naval service, which connects Halifax and Dartmouth. (Canadian Forces, Photograph HSC 85-2775-6)

THE AFTERMATH

The navy's shame: The VE Day riot, May 1945

There had never been any love lost between the RCN and the overcrowded port of Halifax. As the war in Europe wound down, many naval officers became concerned about the mood of their sailors, who were muttering about "taking the town apart" on the day victory was announced. During the evening of 7 May 1945, the day before the war in Europe officially ended, a crowd, headed by service personnel including soldiers and airmen but mainly sailors, broke into a brewery in downtown Halifax and touched off what would become known as the "Halifax Riot." Lieutenant Commander Anthony Griffin, RCNVR, was in Halifax that evening.

I had changed into civilian clothes and gone out to dinner with a fellow officer. When we came out on the street, the first thing we sighted was a car overturned and on fire. Then a streetcar blazing and a big crowd of naval ratings throwing large stones through a plate glass window. There was an atmosphere of total chaos.

I stopped one of them without identifying myself and asked him what possessed these men to indulge in such an orgy of destruction. He naturally assumed I was a native Haligonian and said, "We're going to repay you bastards for the way you've treated us over six years." Then came a group of three staff cars, all blowing their horns, the leading one carrying the flag of Admiral Murray, addressing the rioters through loud-hailer, telling them they should recover their

senses and go back to their ships or barracks immediately. He was totally ignored. After a while, seeing the downtown section of the city laid waste, and having no authority or connection with the Admiral's staff, I went back to my hotel and slept fitfully, feeling quite sick.[1]

Wren Rosamond Greer recalled that the situation got worse the following day:

Several of us [Wrens] wandered down to Waverly House, a YWCA Hostel which was always open, thanks to dedicated volunteers, and there listened to the King's victory message on the radio and had tea and cake. It was late afternoon as we started back to *Stadacona*.

We thought things were not quite as they should be when we met sailors, soldiers and civilians loaded down with cases of beer and bottles of liquor. And we were sure of it when a soldier invited us to have a drink at the well-stocked bar he had set up on a tombstone in St. Paul's Cemetery. But we did not realize we were in the midst of a riot until we found ourselves surrounded by a mob of servicemen and civilians smashing windows, rushing into stores and carrying away all their arms could hold. Clothing, furniture, dishes, bedding, everything sold in the stores lining Barrington Street, was being carried out and loaded into waiting cars and trucks. A sailor, his arms wrapped around a naked mannequin, slumbered peacefully away upon the bed in an Eaton's display window. A typewriter flew out a third-storey window, missing us by inches. We passed people vomiting in doorways and lying on the sidewalk, cut and bleeding, some unconscious.

In the streets the mob was out of control, shouting, drunken, hostile and ugly.

We did not need the announcement blaring over the police car loudspeaker to tell us it was time to "return to quarters immediately." We ran just as fast as we could, through streets covered by shattered glass, over piles of broken bottles and prostrate bodies, back to the sanctity of the Wren Block.[2]

The riot finally ended early on 9 May when a thousand armed soldiers were brought into the city from nearby Debert Camp. Downtown Halifax was devastated, two hundred people were under arrest, including 34 sailors, and three people were dead. Despite the fact that more civilians than servicemen were convicted of criminal charges arising from the disturbances, most Haligonians held the Navy primarily responsible – at one point there were nearly 9,000 sailors rampaging through the business area of the city – and a subsequent federal government inquiry blamed the disturbances on Rear Admiral Murray, the senior naval officer present. Murray refused to implicate any of his subordinates and took full responsibility for the riot and retired prematurely, bringing a very successful 35-year career to a sad end.

The navy's shame – VE Day riot in Halifax, 8 May 1945.
This photograph of the downtown business section of Halifax, taken from the intersection of Barrington and Salter Streets, looks north on 8 May 1945. Mobs of civilians and servicemen are roaming Barrington Street in search of trouble, and although there are a number of soldiers present, it is unfortunate that the majority of the service personnel are sailors. (Photograph by R. Harvey, National Archives of Canada, PA 79585)

The navy's glory: The Bedford Magazine fire, July 1945

The responsibility for the Halifax Riot is still being debated but there is very little disagreement over responsibility for the Bedford Magazine fire which began on 18 July 1945. Naval regulations wisely forbid more than one warship's ammunition to be unloaded and present on a dock at one time. These safety measures, however, delayed the process of demobilizing the RCN. Mackenzie King's Liberal government wanted the process of converting naval personnel back into civilians – and potential Liberal voters – expedited and insisted the ammunition regulations be set aside. On 18 July 1945, as Captain Owen Robertson, RCNVR, recorded,

there were three ships' outfits on that South Jetty [the jetty at the Bedford Magazine]. Later on, we found one crater about three hundred and sixty five feet across, where about three hundred depth charges had been piled up. Further on, we had stored some very large bombs out in the open. We had broken all bloody regulations there, because of Ottawa's insistence.

As far as we could [later] trace from reports made by ships in the area, we think a pyrotechnic must have leaked and flared and set off some ammunition. AB [Able Seaman] Craig, one of the naval guards at the magazine, spotted it and shouted to his mate, "I'm going down to see if I can put it out." He just got to the end of the jetty when the whole jetty blew up. It was not until the third day of fighting the fire that we found Craig's body about two hundred yards inland.[3]

Captain Robertson, RCNVR, the Commanding Officer of HMCS Scotian, *the Halifax dockyard, was also the King's Harbour Master responsible for naval firefighting. In November 1943, Robertson had won the George Medal for leading a small firefighting team onto the burning merchant ship* **Volunteer**, *lying in Halifax harbour loaded with smallarms ammunition and highly flammable barrels of magnesium, and putting out her fire before the vessel exploded. When the South Jetty blew up at about 1900 on Wednesday, 17 July 1945, he was having dinner with his wife at the Nova Scotian Hotel.*

We had just sat down when there was a *bang* and all the dust came out of the ventilators. I rushed out to the front desk: "What was that?" "I don't know, sir." "Give me the keys for a room at the top overlooking the harbour." A bellboy followed me into the elevator and let me into a room and *Christ*, there was a mushroom cloud *over the magazine!*[4]

That same evening Seaman Edward O'Connor was on duty at HMCS **Stadacona** *where he was awaiting demobilization after eighteen months service on the North Atlantic in the corvette, HMCS* **Morden**. *O'Connor*

mustered with the others at 1900 hours to be given "clean up for rounds" duties. We were still fallen in on the parade ground when several popping sounds were heard, followed soon after by explosions. Word was that an ammo barge had blown up at Bedford and there followed considerable panic as more explosions followed. Our cleaning jobs never materialized and, instead, I was sent to the rear of the Administration Building as a guard to keep any people out. This was because windows and inside partitions were being blown out by the concussion of every blast. I was kept busy dodging falling glass myself and re-

mained on duty here until sometime around 0100 hours. Finally my relief turned up – but what to do now? I joined a crowd trying to get some sleep on the parade ground and learned that all women had been sent out from the base, that civilians in that part of town were rushing off with whatever possessions they could quickly gather. It seemed sleep was to be impossible here. At 0200 the call came for us to make for the basement of the Torpedo building, a big blast being expected at any moment. We never quite made it, being knocked down like ten-pins as we crossed the square.[5]

While Seaman O'Connor and his comrades were being blown around the parade square at **Stadacona**, *Captain Robertson had entered the magazine with the three foremen and a fire-fighter named Emerson who, Robertson recalled, had the job*

to keep track of me. I climbed up over a little hill and sheltered behind a small brick house. Shells up to 4-inch calibre would [explode and] separate, with the bullet going one way and the shell-case the other way – very slowly. Some of the smaller ones were going so slowly that you could catch a 20-millimetre round in your hand – but gracefully. Unfortunately, the cartridges were setting fires behind us on the grass. The Magazine Foreman crawled up and yelled, "For Christ's sake, sir, get out of there." I said, "I'm all right, I'm all right." Then he really scared me [by shouting]: "*This building* [behind which Robertson was sheltering] *is the detonator shack!*"

So I started following him over the hill, when something let go and blew me into a small pond surrounded by alder bushes. I flew through the bushes and landed in the pond, so I didn't hurt myself too badly. But I was shocked and I guess I

didn't know what I was doing. I was wandering up the road, when the Doctor, Len Prowse – a hell of a good guy – saw me from up by the North Gate hill. Len grabbed a fire engine and came through all the cordite all over the place and scooped me up. Apparently I was just stumbling down the road, babbling, and all he could get out of me was: "Mackenzie King, the bastard, won't give my wife a pension!"

Thankfully, Robertson was able to clear his head and organize the naval firefighting parties who were to spend four days struggling to prevent the many small fires from reaching the main ammunition magazines or from setting off brush fires in the nearby area. The worst of the danger was over within the first twenty-four hours although it took nearly four days for all the fires to be extinguished.

"It was time go home:" After it ended

When it was all over, thousands of men and women in the RCN returned to civilian life and their reactions to peacetime varied. Lieutenant Commander Alan Easton, RCNVR, suffering from ulcers brought on by four years of service on the North Atlantic, remembered when he docked his destroyer, HMCS **Saskatchewan**, *at Halifax for the last time:*

When a seaman sails from his native shore and he is young, he is embarking on adventure; if he is neither young nor old he will have an ache in his heart; if he is old he is used to both. But when his ship is homeward bound he is happy no matter what his age. ....

At sunset the shrill call of the bosun's pipe sounded. Those of us who were on deck faced aft and saluted. As the white ensign slowly fluttered down, I knew that it had been lowered for the last time in a ship of mine.

Seeing my distress, the first lieutenant, who was standing beside me, asked, "Do you really think you will not come back with us?"

"I'm afraid not, Bimson," I answered after a long pause during which I saw many things. "I'm destined for the big house on the hill tomorrow," I added, nodding towards the tall hospital building above the dockyard. "I shall be able to sleep there without a voice-pipe at my ear. No, I shall never go to sea again – and I'm not sorry, fond as I am of ships and men."[6]

As he recorded in his diary, for Commander A. Layard, RN, the end of the war was the end of the pressures of command:

Saturday, May 26 – Heysham – Prinsted
...... Liverpool train left at 0830 and we changed at Preston and on arrival at Exchange Station I had to cloak room all my stuff and I had a considerable amount. From there I walked to Derby House and in due course had an interview with [Admiral] Sir Max [Horton] who was v[ery]. nice and told me to insist on a long bit of leave. ...... An uncomfortable journey but the train was pretty punctual at Euston at 1830. I had thought of spending the night in town but changed my mind and trundled all my stuff to Waterloo in a taxi and caught the 7.26 slow to Havant. Got an Army officer, who got out at Guildford, to telephone J[oan, his wife]. and ask her to fix a taxi which was waiting and I was home at about 2145. My God it's wonderful to be home on some really worth while leave and is it a relief to have finished with all that worry and responsibility.

Although almost all the wartime volunteers wanted to return to civilian life, they knew they would miss their comrades. Wren Rosamond Greer, whose exit from the RCN was delayed by illness, was one of the last to be demobilized:

At the end of the sixth day at *Peregrine* I was completely "processed." All of my documents had been found and gathered together, the required signatures secured; my transportation to Vancouver, where I would obtain my final discharge at HMCS *Discovery* ..... arranged; my bags packed.

Although it was a time I had looked forward to eagerly for a long time, it was also the loneliest of any I spent in the WRCNS. All of my friends were gone. Girls I had lived and worked with for almost three years were back home in cities and towns spread all across Canada ... and I did not know if I would ever see them again.

Our lives took different paths once we shed His Majesty's uniform; but the friendships formed would never forgotten, and the *esprit de corps* would remain with us for the rest of our lives.

On Monday, March 4, 1946, there were no parades ... no brass bands. But when I heard the call to "Wakey-wakey – rise and shine!" I knew my job was done.

It was time to go home.[7]

Leading Seaman Frank Curry remembered his last days in the service and the train voyage back to Manitoba:

My last night in naval barracks brought an appropriate final task: duty watch. I found myself in charge of fire patrols, and once again, but for the last time, I got through the long hours between midnight and 0400. Then, later that day, it was

back to the Halifax train station, packed with sailors, soldiers and airmen waiting to head off across Canada to their home towns. We caught the old D.A.R. Railway across Nova Scotia to Digby, crossed the Bay of Fundy on the *Princess Louise*, and then came the biggest shock of our naval careers.

Sitting in the railway station in Saint John, all arranged and waiting for us, was a special train, all sleeper coaches, each with berths made up with crisp white sheets and pillowcases; each with porters, ready to show us to our berths. For us veterans it was the most luxurious train trip imaginable: sleeping in clean, quiet surroundings after the turmoil of mess decks; eating full-course meals served on white table cloths in the dining car; travelling in a style we never knew existed during the long years of war. It was as if the navy had decided to make up for what we had endured with this small taste of luxury. We enjoyed our moment. ......

Then came the sad part: the final stretch into Winnipeg and my stammered farewells to old shipmates continuing across the Prairies and on to the West Coast. I knew few of us would ever meet again. A last wave; a last goodbye and I descended the train steps.

Winnipeg. I was home.

There was no band, no welcoming committee; but it was still a wonderful moment: to return to the old home town after a terrible war, to return in one piece, with many memories to share and tales to tell; and to think about a boundless future, full of possibility.[8]

"Civilian life was hard to cope with:" Picking up the pieces

Many found the adjustment to the peacetime world difficult, including Lieutenant Commander Alan Stevens, RCNVR:

At first civilian life was hard to cope with. Five years of Navy discipline – being in charge of hundreds of seamen, – accustomed to having my orders obeyed instantly and without argument had became so engraved that I made myself unpopular because of the way I reacted to my co-workers. Trouble was, it didn't bother me, but in time, I came to accept that the war was over. I was merely a retired Lieutenant Commander RCN and no one gave a damn.

At home the war was far from over. I had nightmares constantly. If my ship wasn't being torpedoed, we were being dive bombed. I usually ended up on the floor beside the bed – screaming I was drowning in oil. This would wake up my wife who got so fed up she would stick a leg out of bed – give me a kick and tell me to wake up.[9]

Reunions with old shipmates were always welcome occasions in the postwar lives of many former naval personnel but one RCN veteran, Able Seaman John Isbister, had a reunion with his old ship that was not so happy:

Immediately after the war, I returned to my job at Stelco. Some time later, word got around that the plant was cutting up naval ships for scrap. One day in 1947, I finally mustered enough courage to walk down to the yard where this operation was taking place. Secretly, I was hoping *Sherbrooke* would not be among them. She was literally my home for the greater part of my war. Never once

did she let us down. The pounding and the beating we took on the North Atlantic was a testament to the excellent workmanship and quality of Canadian steelworkers and shipbuilders.

I discovered that some corvettes and minesweepers had been attacked by cutting torches. I recognized the pennant numbers of ships with which we had sailed. I stopped dead in my tracks as emotion overcame me. *Sherbrooke* was there. K-152 had followed me home. She was still intact. She still looked trim and seaworthy as I remembered her. I stood for several minutes and fondly recalled the better days spent aboard her.

It would have been very easy for me to go aboard *Sherbrooke*, but I could not bring myself to do it this time. I would be the only person aboard and somehow it would not be as I really remember her. *Sherbrooke* was a ship, yes, but what really made her was her crew and the comradeship we had with each other. The crew was now scattered, God knows where. Finally, I turned and walked away.[10]

"We Remember:" In later years

In the years, and then the decades that followed, the veterans of the Battle of the Atlantic would gather on Remembrance Day and on Battle of the Atlantic Sunday to honour their absent friends. Lieutenant Commander James Lamb, RCNVR, tells us what they think about:

We remember when the world was an exciting place in which to be young and when, with a thousand others, we were likely to be sent halfway around the earth and back again, without a care for tomorrow. One had a sense of destiny in those days; of being a part of historic events, of helping

to mould a new and better world. How innocent, how naive, how pathetic it all seems now.

But we remember only the pleasant times, the high-spirited times. ......

We who are left are young no more; the eager boys' faces of yesterday are creased by time and pouched with civilian living. Yet still, across the widening gulf that yawns between that age and the present, the memory of our shared youth brings a pang to our heart, and moisture to our eyes.

It is not for the dead that we mourn, those bright hearts we have been revisiting in memory. Rather it is for the passing of our lost youth, and for the spirit of adventure and high endeavour which passed with it.[11]

Home is the sailor, home from the sea.
In May 1945, the Royal Canadian Navy had good claim to being the third largest navy in the world, based on the number of ships in commission fit for sea service – a total of 418 vessels of all sizes. A year later, it had exactly eight vessels, fewer than it had in 1939 – and one was a former U-boat.

HMCS *SACKVILLE*
"THE SOUL OF THE NAVY"

Visit the Canadian Naval Memorial Trust's educational website
<www.hmcssackville-cnmt.ca> to learn about the work of the Trust, its
current projects, gift items and how to become a member. This website
also contains more information on the ship and a virtual tour of the
last surviving Flower Class corvette.

The Canadian Naval Memorial Trust and HMCS *Sackville* form an
important part of Heritage Canada's Virtual Military Museum Tour, an
important component of the Canadian Heritage Information Network
(go to <www.virtual.ca/~military/remembrances/>). This tour includes
the narrated story of Convoy ON 115 in August 1942 when *Sackville*
engaged three U-boats, complete with the sounds of the battle. The
viewer can take other virtual tours, learn how ASW weapons systems
worked between 1939 and 1945, examine wartime U-boats and view the
workings of the Canadian SW1C radar produced by the National
Research Council of Canada.

HMCS *Sackville*, the last corvette. Commissioned in December 1941, *Sackville* served on the North Atlantic until late 1944 and fought in some of the hardest convoy battles. After post-war service as a naval research vessel, she was restored to her wartime appearance and dedicated in 1985 as the Canadian Naval Memorial. *Sackville* is painted in the Western Approaches camouflage scheme of grey-white overlaid with patches of light blue or green and looks much better than she did when she last wore those colours. (Canadian Naval Memorial Trust)

(Right and below) **Dressed overall:** *Sackville* **in the summer.**
Each summer, thousands of fascinated visitors tour Canada's little warship at her summer berth at Sackville Landing. Americans often comment on her small size while Britons express surprise that Canada had a wartime navy. In the background is the skyline of modern Halifax, much changed from the grim wartime city. The custom of "dressing overall" or displaying a continuous array of flags in a set sequence from stem to stern is an old and hallowed naval tradition. The Blue Ensign flying from *Sackville's* jackstaff on her stem was worn by all Dominion navies in time of peace. (Both courtesy, Lyncan Photographic, Halifax)

An official visit.
Sackville attends the opening ceremonies of Convoy Quay in Bedford Basin in Halifax as naval veterans parade. Across the jetty from *Sackville* is HMCS *St. John's*, a Halifax Class patrol frigate of the modern Canadian navy. Vessels of this type displace 5,200 tons, are 442 feet in length and 54 in beam, are capable of 30 knots and are armed with Bofors and Phalanx AA weapons, Harpoon anti-submarine torpedoes and Sea Sparrow surface-to-air missiles. *St. John's* is about twice as large as *Sackville*, much more destructive and twice as fast. On the other hand, *Sackville* has seen a lot more action. (Canadian Naval Memorial Trust)

(Above) **Welcome to HMCS _Sackville_.**
The brow, or entry port, where visitors board. Note the 2-pdr. (40mm) AA gun in its tub and the Carley floats or life rafts which, during the war, were cut loose if the crew had to abandon ship, as it often proved impossible to launch the boats. (Canadian Naval Memorial Trust)

(Right) **The 4-inch gun.**
A view of the Mark IX 4-inch main gun with its shield hatches open. Note the primitive sights in the port hatch and the rails for illuminating rockets fixed to the shield. Behind can be seen the bridge and the perspex dome for the Type 271 radar. (Canadian Naval Memorial Trust)

(Right) **The galley.**
Located on the main deck at the rear of the bridge superstructure, the galley was one of the warmest places on a corvette, apart from the engine room. Here the cook prepared meals for 80-90 men, including such traditional naval dishes as "chicken on a raft" (egg on toast) and "red lead and cap tallies" (a mixture of watery canned tomatoes and strips of pale, undercooked bacon). The messmen or "mess cooks" would pick up the food from the galley and take it back to the crew spaces where it was consumed – if it reached there without incident. (Canadian Naval Memorial Trust)

(Left) **View aft from port bridge wing.**
Note the "barber pole" stripes on _Sackville_'s funnel, the 1942 emblem of C-3 Escort Group. When that group was broken up in 1943, the stripes were taken over by C-5 Group and are still worn today by all vessels of the 5th Maritime Operations Group of Maritime Forces Atlantic (the east coast force of the modern Canadian navy). Note too the green Maple Leaf on the funnel. Aft of the ventilators around the funnel can be seen the skylights of the engine room and, aft of that, the raised platform of the 2-pdr. anti-aircraft mount. The Carley floats are clearly visible in this photo. In the background are vessels of the modern Canadian navy. (Canadian Naval Memorial Trust)

Engine room.

A view of the four-cylinder, vertical triple-expansion engine which could produce 2,750 horsepower that would move *Sackville* up to 16 knots. The engine room compartment rose from the keel plate to the skylights aft of the funnel and was separated from the sea by only a few inches of steel – very few engine room personnel survived a torpedo hit in this compartment or in the adjacent boiler rooms. (Canadian Naval Memorial Trust)

Throttle.

A view of *Sackville*'s throttle machinery. Even by the standards of the 1940s, corvette machinery was rudimentary but it was simple to maintain and operate and it was also robust – *Sackville*'s engine ran for four decades. (Canadian Naval Memorial Trust)

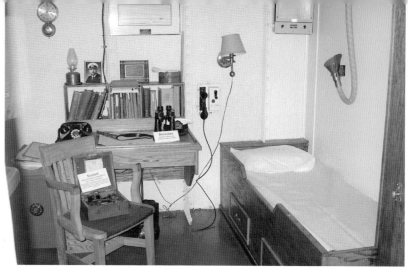

The most luxurious accommodation on board.

The captain's cabin and office on *Sackville* – the most spacious and comfortable accommodation on a corvette. Note the barometer on the bulkhead and the ship's safe below it. Also note the voice pipe beside the bunk for communication with the bridge. At sea, this device was not often used because wartime corvette captains rarely spent much time in their cabins but usually rested in a bunk built in the bridge area. (Canadian Naval Memorial Trust)

(Below) **Forward seaman's messdeck.**

The forward messdeck located in the bow of the ship showing the massive "navel" pipes through which ran the anchor cables and which were a constant source of noise in rough weather. The iron rails fixed to the deckhead are hammock bars, from which the hammocks were suspended – each man had a space about two feet wide. Personal kit was stored in the racks along the bulkhead or in the locker benches below. (Canadian Naval Memorial Trust)

Grown older but not bolder.
Two veterans of the Battle of the North Alantic tour *Sackville*. On the left is Lieutenant Commander Murray Knowles, RCN (Retd.), who commanded the corvette *Louisbourg* in 1945 and on the right is Lieutenant Commander A.W. Murray, RCN (Retd.), who served as first lieutenant on *Sackville* in 1944. Both men wear the Atlantic Star, the theatre medal for wartime service on that ocean. (Canadian Naval Memorial Trust)

Battle of the Atlantic dinner.
An annual event on *Sackville* is the Battle of the Atlantic dinner held each May in the crowded confines of the forward messdeck. It is a well-attended and lively affair and the participants provide their own entertainment. Here, Lieutenant (N) Ian Urquhart, RCN (Ret.), the executive officer of *Sackville*, sings to the accompaniment of Alison MacNeil's accordion and Rear Admiral Desmond Piers's mouth organ. Admiral D.W. Piers, DSC, RCN (Retd.) spent three years on the North Atlantic as a young officer. (Canadian Naval Memorial Trust)

Hanging over the rail but not because they're seasick.
Sea cadets have spotted something interesting and are hanging over the rail to look at it. During the war corvette sailors hanging over the rail like this were most likely being seasick as corvettes were notoriously lively ships. Note the MK II depth charge launcher. (Canadian Naval Memorial Trust)

Staying warm is still a priority.
Young sea cadets on an overnight visit discover that wartime duffel coats make cozy sleeping bags. *Sackville* hosts Royal Canadian Sea Cadet detachments on a regular basis. (Canadian Naval Memorial Trust)

THE ROYAL CANADIAN NAVY IN 1939 AND 1945

STRENGTH OF THE CANADIAN NAVY IN 1939

Personnel[1]

	Officers	Enlisted	Total
Royal Canadian Navy	191	1,799	1,990
Royal Canadian Navy Reserve	74	71	145
Royal Canadian Navy Volunteer Reserve	132	406	538
Additional Personnel Mobilized	18	200	218
Total Personnel	**415**	**2,476**	**2,891**

Vessels[2]

Destroyers, River Class	6
Minesweepers, Fundy Class	4
Trawlers, Battle Class	1
Training Vessels	2
Total Vessels in Commission	**13**

STRENGTH OF THE CANADIAN NAVY IN 1945

Personnel (Officers and Enlisted)[3]

Royal Canadian Navy	4,834
Royal Canadian Navy Reserve	5,300
Royal Canadian Navy Volunteer Reserve	78,000
Women's Royal Canadian Navy Service	5,300
Total Personnel	**92,441**

Vessels[4]

Major Vessels

Escort Carriers		1
Light Cruisers		2
Landing Ship, Infantry (Medium)		2
AA Ship		1
Destroyers		14
River Class	9	
Tribal Class	3	
V Class	2	
Frigates		70
River Class	67	
Loch Class	3	
Corvettes		113
Flower Class	101	
Castle Class	12	
Minesweepers (Used as Escorts)		61
Algerine Class	12	
Bangor Class	49	
Total of Major Vessels		**264**

Major Vessels Used for Training

River Class Destroyer	1
Town Class Destroyers	6
Total of Training Vessels	**7**

Minor Vessels

Anti-Submarine Trawlers		6
Minesweepers		14
Fundy Class	4	
Llewellyn Class	10	
Motor Craft		91
Motor Torpedo Boats	14	
Motor Launches	77	
Armed Yachts		10
Auxiliary Vessels		42
Total of Minor Vessels		**163**

Total Vessels in Commission in May 1945	**434**

[1.] Strength figures are as of 23 September 1939.

[2.] Only includes vessels in commission on 10 September 1939, the date of Canada's declaration of war against Germany.

[3.] Strength figures are for January 1945, when the RCN reached its maximum wartime strength.

[4.] Includes only vessels in commission or manned by the RCN on 8 May 1945, VE Day, and excludes those that may have been in commission but were constructive losses from damage.

From 1939 to 1945 the Royal Canadian Navy expanded 32 to 1 in terms of personnel and 33 to 1 in terms of total number of ships in commission. In terms of major ships in commission (above 600 tons displacement), expansion was 44 to 1.

COMPARISON OF THE SIZE OF THE RCN TO OTHER ALLIED NAVIES

By May 1945 the RCN was the third Allied navy after the USN and RN. The only Allied navy that came close to it in size was the Soviet Navy. In May 1945 the Soviet fleet had 260 vessels of greater than 500 tons displacement in commission comprising: 4 battleships, 9 cruisers, 51 destroyers, 20 torpedo boats (small destroyers), 10 gun boats, 31 minesweepers, 25 minelayers and 110 submarines. The Soviet Navy also included great numbers of small craft but the overriding question is how many Soviet warships, nominally in commission in May 1945, were actually fit for service. Throughout the war, the greater part of the personnel of the Soviet Navy served as soldiers, not sailors, and this had an adverse effect on the efficiency of the wartime fleet. In contrast, all of the larger vessels in commission in the RCN in May 1945 were crewed by trained personnel and ready for service.

In 1945 the Royal Australian, Royal New Zealand, Royal Indian and South African Navies were much smaller than the RCN, as were the French and Italian navies.

It is interesting to speculate how the RCN compared to the *Kriegsmarine* and Imperial Japanese Navy in May 1945. Both enemy navies may have had more ships in commission (certainly the *Kriegsmarine* had more U-Boats) but it is doubtful that they had as many ships ready for service.

Sources

DHH Memorandum, "Relative Naval Strength in 1945," c. 1993 by Robert C. Fisher; John Burgess and Ken Macpherson, *The Ships of Canada's Naval Forces 1910-1985* (Toronto, 1985); Gilbert Tucker, *The Naval Service of Canada. Volume II. Activities on Shore During the Second World War* (Ottawa, 1952).

VESSELS OF THE ROYAL CANADIAN NAVY IN COMMISSION, 10 SEPTEMBER 1939 TO 8 MAY 1945

The following list provides details on every major vessel (excluding minor harbour craft) commissioned in the Royal Canadian Navy between 10 September 1939, the day Canada declared war on Germany, and 8 May 1945, VE-Day. The names of vessels that were lost, for whatever reason, or were decommissioned because they became constructive losses, are marked †.

Key to Abbreviations

A = Gun and torpedo armament
AAS = Armament Anti-submarine
C = Complement (officers and sailors)
D = Displacement in tons
DC = Depth charges
L = Length in feet
S = Top speed in knots
TT = Torpedo tubes

ESCORT CARRIERS[1]

(D = 15,390 L = 495 S = 18 C = 1,000 A = 2 x 5-in; 16 x 40mm; 20 x 20mm 20 aircraft)

	Commissioned	Comments or Transfer
HMS *Nabob*	7 Sep 43	British ship, manned by RCN
HMS *Puncher* †	5 Feb 44	British ship, manned by RCN, torpedoed 22 Oct 44, declared a constructive loss and paid off

LIGHT CRUISERS

(D = 8,800 L = 555 S = 30 C = 730 A = 9 x 6-in; 10 x 4-in (*Ontario*); 8 x 4-in. (*Uganda*); 6 x 21-inch TT

HMCS *Ontario*	26 Apr 45	
HMCS *Uganda*	21 Oct 44	

LANDING SHIP, INFANTRY (MEDIUM)[2]

(D = 5,736 L = 385 S = 22 C = 417)

HMCS *Prince David*	28 Dec 40	Originally an armed merchant cruiser, converted to LSI (M) in 1943
HMCS *Prince Henry*	4 Dec 40	Originally an armed merchant cruiser, converted to LSI (M) in 1943

ANTI-AIRCRAFT SHIP

(D = 5,675 L = 385 S = 22 C = 438)

HMCS *Prince Robert*	31 Jul 40	Originally an armed merchant cruiser, converted to AA Ship in 1943

DESTROYERS

River Class

(D = 1,337 to 1,405 L = 320 to 329 S = 31 C = 181 A (to 43) = 4 x 4.7 in.; 2 x 2 pdr.; 8 x 21-inch TT A (after 43) = 2 or 3 x 4.7 in.; 6 x 20 mm; 4 x 21-inch TT AAS (to 43) = DC AAS (after 43) = DC and Hedgehog

HMCS *Saguenay*	22 May 31	Torpedoed 1 Dec 40, repaired, damaged in collision, 15 Nov 42, made a training ship
HMCS *Skeena* †	10 Jun 31	*U-588* (31 Jul 42), wrecked in Iceland, 25 Oct 44
HMCS *Fraser* †	17 Feb 37	ex-HMS *Crescent*, sunk in collision, 25 Jun 40
HMCS *Ottawa* †	15 Jun 38	ex-HMS *Crusader*, Italian *Faá di Bruno* (6 Nov 40), torpedoed 13 Sep 42
HMCS *Restigouche*	15 Jun 38	ex-HMS *Comet*
HMCS *St. Laurent*	17 Feb 37	ex-HMS *Cygnet*, sank *U-356* (27 Dec 42), *U-845* (10 Mar 44)
HMCS *Assiniboine*	19 Oct 39	ex-HMS *Kempenfelt*, *U-210* (6 Aug 42)
HMCS *Margaree* †	6 Sep 40	ex-HMS *Diana*, sunk in collision, 22 Oct 40
HMCS *Chaudière*	15 Nov 43	ex-HMS *Hero*, sank *U-744* (6 Mar 44), *U-984* (20 Aug 44), *U-621* (28 Aug 44)
HMCS *Gatineau*	3 Jun 43	ex-HMS *Express*, *U-744* (6 Mar 44)

[1.] These two carriers were provided by the USA to Britain under lend-lease agreements but were taken over by Canada. As Canada had no lend-lease agreements with the USA, they were commissioned as HM Ships but had a Canadian crew except for the air squadrons which were Fleet Air Arm but composed of mixed British and Canadian personnel.

[2.] The three Prince ships were originally commissioned as armed merchant cruisers in 1940 but were converted to more specialized roles in 1943 and 1944.

HMCS *Kootenay*	12 Apr 43	ex-HMS *Decoy*, *U-678* (6 Jul 44), *U-621* (18 Aug 44), *U-984* (20 Aug 44)
HMCS *Ottawa II*	20 Mar 43	ex-HMS *Griffin*, *U-678* (6 Jul 44), *U-621* (18 Aug 44), *U-984* (20 Aug 44)
HMCS *Qu'Appelle*	8 Feb 44	ex-HMS *Foxhound*, under which name sank *U-138* (18 Jun 41)
HMCS *Saskatchewan*	31 May 43	ex-HMS *Fortune*, under which name sank *U-27*, *U-44* and Vichy French *Ajax*

Town Class (ex-USN)
(D = 1,069 to 1,190 L = 314 S = 28 C = 153 A (1940) = 4 x 4-in.; 12 x 21-inch TT A(from 1941) = 1 x 4-in.; 1 x 12-pdr.; 4 x 20mm; 3 x 21-inch TT AAS = DC, later Hedgehog)

HMCS *Annapolis*	24 Sep 40	ex-USS *Mackenzie*, made a training vessel in 1944
HMCS *Buxton*[3]	4 Nov 43	ex-USS *Edwards*, ex-HMS *Buxton*, used only for training
HMCS *Columbia*	24 Sep 40	ex-USS *Haraden*, damaged in 1944, used thereafter as an ammunition hulk
HMCS *Hamilton*[4]	6 Jul 41	ex-USS *Kalk*, ex-HMS *Hamilton*, damaged in collision, transferred to RCN as a training ship
HMCS *Niagara*	24 Sep 40	ex-USS *Thatcher*, a training vessel after 1944
HMCS *St. Clair*	24 Sep 40	ex-USS *Williams*, used for training after 1943, paid off in 1944 and used as a fire-fighting hulk
HMCS *St. Croix* †	24 Sep 40	ex-USS *McCook*, *U-90* (24 Jul 42), *U-87* (4 Mar 43), torpedoed 20 Sep 43
HMCS *St. Francis*	24 Sep 40	ex-USS *Bancroft*, training ship after 1944

Tribal Class
(D = 1,927 L = 377 S = 36 C = 259 S = 36 A = 6 x 4.7 in.; 2 x 4-in; 4 x 21-inch TT; 4 x 2-pdr.; 6 x 20mm. AAS = DC)

HMCS *Athabaskan* †	3 Feb 43	Hit by glider bomb 27 Aug 43, repaired, sank *Torpedo Boat T-24* (26 Apr 44), sunk in surface action, 29 Apr 44
HMCS *Haida*	30 Aug 43	Sank *Torpedo Boat T-29* (26 Apr 44), *T-27* (29 Apr 44), *Destroyer Z-32* (9 Jun 44), *U-971* (24 Jun 44), *Minesweeper M-486* (6 Aug 44), currently a museum ship in Hamilton, Ont.
HMCS *Huron*	19 Jul 43	*Torpedo Boat T-29* (26 Apr 44), *Destroyer Z-32* (9 Jun 44)
HMCS *Iroquois*	30 Nov 42	

V Class
(D = 1,710 L = 362 S = 36 C = 244 A = 4 x 4.7 in.; 8 x 21-in. TT; 4 x 40mm; 4 x 20mm. AAS = Hedgehog, DC

HMCS *Algonquin*	17 Feb 44	ex-HMS *Valentine*
HMCS *Sioux*	21 Feb 44	ex-HMS *Vixen*

FRIGATES

River Class[5]
(D = 1,445 L-301 S = 19 C = 141 A = 2 x 4 in. (first 15 of class had 1 x 4-in and 1 x 12-pdr.); 4 x 20mm AAS = Hedgehog, DC

HMCS *Annan*	13 Jun 44	Ex-RN, sank *U-1006 (16 Oct 44)*, returned Jun 45
HMCS *Antigonish*	4 Jul 44	
HMCS *Beacon Hill*	16 May 44	
HMCS *Buckingham*	2 Nov 44	
HMCS *Cap de la Madeleine*	30 Sep 44	
HMCS *Cape Breton*	25 Oct 43	
HMCS *Capilano*	25 Aug 44	
HMCS *Carlplace*	13 Dec 44	
HMCS *Charlottetown II*	28 Apr 44	
HMCS *Chebogue* †	22 Feb 44	Torpedoed 4 Oct 44, constructive loss
HMCS *Coaticook*	25 Jul 44	
HMCS *Dunver*	11 Sep 43	*U-484* (9 Sep 44)
HMCS *Eastview*	3 Jun 44	
HMCS *Ettrick*	29 Jan 44	Ex-RN, returned 1945
HMCS *Fort Erie*	27 Oct 44	
HMCS *Glace Bay*	2 Sept 44	
HMCS *Grou*	4 Dec 43	
HMCS *Hallowell*	8 Aug 44	
HMCS *Inch Arran*	18 Nov 44	
HMCS *Joliette*	14 Jun 44	
HMCS *Jonquière*	10 May 44	
HMCS *Kirkland Lake*	21 Aug 44	
HMCS *Kokanee*	6 Jun 44	
HMCS *La Hulloise*	20 May 44	*U-1302* (7 Mar 45)
HMCS *Lanark*	6 Jul 44	
HMCS *Lasalle*	29 Jun 44	
HMCS *Lauzon*	30 Aug 44	
HMCS *Lévis II*	21 Jul 44	
HMCS *Longueil*	18 May 44	
HMCS *Magog* †	7 May 44	Torpedoed 14 Oct 44, constructive loss

---

[3.] Originally commissioned as HM Ship in 1940, transferred to RCN in 1943.
[4.] Originally commissioned as HM Ship in 1940, transferred to RCN in 1941.

[5.] HMC Ships *Annan*, *Ettrick*, *Meon*, *Monnow*, *Nene*, *Ribble* and *Teme* were originally commissioned as HM Ships but were transferred to the RCN because of the RN's inability to man them.

HMCS *Matane*	22 Oct 43	*U-311* (22 Apr 44), hit by glider bomb 20 Jul 44, badly damaged
HMCS *Meon*	7 Feb 44	Ex-RN, returned 1945
HMCS *Monnow*	8 Mar 44	Ex-RN, returned 1945
HMCS *Montreal*	12 Nov 43	
HMCS *Nene*	6 Apr 44	Ex-RN, while HMS, sank *U-536* (20 Nov 43), returned to RN, 1945
HMCS *New Glasgow*	23 Dec 43	*U-1003* (21 Mar 45)
HMCS *New Waterford*	21 Jan 44	
HMCS *Orkney*	18 Apr 44	
HMCS *Outremont*	27 Nov 43	
HMCS *Penetang*	19 Oct 44	
HMCS *Port Colborne*	15 Nov 43	
HMCS *Poundmaker*	17 Sept 44	
HMCS *Prestonian*	13 Sept 44	
HMCS *Prince Rupert*	30 Aug 43	*U-575* (13 Mar 44)
HMCS *Ribble*	24 Jul 44	Ex-RN, returned 1945
HMCS *Royal Mount*	25 Aug 44	
HMCS *Runnymede*	14 Jun 44	
HMCS *St. Catharines*	31 Jul 43	*U-744* (6 Mar 44)
HMCS *Saint John*	13 Dec 43	*U-247* (1 Sep 44), *U-309* (16 Feb 45)
HMCS *St. Pierre*	22 Aug 44	
HMCS *St. Stephen*	28 Jul 44	
HMCS *Ste. Thérèse*	28 May 44	
HMCS *Sea Cliff*	26 Sept 44	
HMCS *Springhill*	21 Mar 44	
HMCS *Stettler*	7 May 44	
HMCS *Stonetown*	21 Jul 44	
HMCS *Stormont*	27 Nov 43	
HMCS *Strathadam*	29 Sep 44	*U-1302* (7 Mar 45)
HMCS *Sussexvale*	29 Nov 44	
HMCS *Swansea*	4 Oct 43	*U-845* (10 Mar 44), *U-448* (14 Apr 44), *U-311* (22 Apr 44), *U-247* (1 Sep 44)
HMCS *Teme* †	28 Feb 44	Ex-RN, damaged in collision 10 Jun 44, repaired, torpedoed 29 Mar 45, declared a constructive loss
HMCS *Thetford Mines*	24 May 44	*U-1302* (7 Mar 45)
HMCS *Toronto*	6 May 44	
HMCS *Valleyfield* †	7 Dec 43	Torpedoed, c. 7 May 45
HMCS *Victoriaville*	11 Nov 44	
HMCS *Waskesiu*	16 Jun 43	*U-257* (24 Feb 44)
HMCS *Wentworth*	7 Dec 43	

Loch Class[6]
(D = 1,435 L = 307 S = 19 C = 141 A = 1 x 4-in; 6 x 20mm AAS = Squid, DC

HMCS *Loch Achanalt*	31 Jul 44
HMCS *Loch Alvie*	10 Aug 44
HMCS *Loch Morlich*	17 Jul 44

CORVETTES

Flower Class (Original Design Ordered 1939-1941)[7]
(These vessels were constructed with the short focsle and most were later modified, the date being shown below.)
(D = 950 L = 205 S = 16 C = 86 A = 1 x 4 in.; 1 x 2-pdr.; 2 x 20 mm AAS = DC, later Hedgehog on many vessels)

HMCS *Agassiz*	23 Jan 41	Modified Mar 44
HMCS *Alberni* †	4 Feb 41	Torpedoed 21 Aug 44
HMCS *Algoma*	11 Jul 41	Modified Apr 44
HMCS *Amherst*	5 Aug 41	Modified Nov 43
HMCS *Arrowhead*	15 May 41	Modified May 44
HMCS *Arvida*	22 May 41	Modified Apr 44
HMCS *Baddeck*	18 May 41	Modified Nov 43
HMCS *Barrie*	12 May 41	Modified Apr 44
HMCS *Battleford*	31 Jul 41	*U-356* (27 Dec 43), modified Jul 44
HMCS *Bittersweet*	15 May 41	Modified Nov 43
HMCS *Brandon*	22 Jul 41	Modified Oct 43
HMCS *Brantford*	15 May 42	Never modified
HMCS *Buctouche*	5 Jun 41	Modified Jan 44
HMCS *Camrose*	30 Jun 41	Modified Oct 43, *U-757* (8 Jan 44)
HMCS *Chambly*	18 Dec 40	*U-501* (10 Sep 41), modified Mar 44
HMCS *Chicoutimi*	12 May 41	Never modified
HMCS *Chilliwack*	8 Apr 41	*U-356* (27 Dec 42), modified Oct 43, *U-744* (6 Mar 44)
HMCS *Cobalt*	25 Nov 40	Modified Jul 44
HMCS *Collingwood*	9 Nov 40	Modified Dec 43
HMCS *Dauphin*	17 May 41	Modified Sep 43
HMCS *Dawson*	6 Oct 41	Modified Jan 44
HMCS *Drumheller*	13 Sep 41	*U-456* (13 May 43), modified Jan 44
HMCS *Dundas*	1 Apr 42	Modified Nov 43
HMCS *Dunvegan*	9 Sept 41	Modified Dec 43

[6] Originally commissioned as HM Ships but transferred to the RCN due to Britain's inability to man them.

[7] The corvettes *Arrowhead, Bittersweet, Eyebright, Fennel, Hepatica, Mayflower, Snowberry, Spikenard, Trillium* and *Windflower* were built in Canada for the Royal Navy and, following British practice, were given flower names. They were later taken over by the RCN at the request of Britain but retained their original names.

HMCS *Edmundston*	21 Oct 41	Modified Jun 43
HMCS *Eyebright*	15 May 41	Modified Aug 43
HMCS *Fennel*	15 May 41	Modified Sep 43, *U-744* (6 Mar 44)
HMCS *Galt*	15 May 41	Modified May 44
HMCS *Hepatica*	15 May 41	Modified Jun 44
HMCS *Kamloops*	17 Apr 41	Modified Apr 44
HMCS *Kamsack*	4 Oct 41	Modified Mar 44
HMCS *Kenogami*	29 Jun 41	Modified Oct 44
HMCS *Lethbridge*	25 Jun 41	Modified Mar 44
HMCS *Lévis* †	16 May 41	Torpedoed 19 Sep 41
HMCS *Louisbourg* †	2 Oct 41	Sunk by aircraft, 6 Feb 43
HMCS *Lunenburg*	4 Dec 41	Modified Aug 43
HMCS *Matapedia*	9 May 41	Modified Feb 44
HMCS *Mayflower*	15 May 41	Modified Feb 44
HMCS *Midland*	17 Nov 41	Modified Dec 43
HMCS *Moncton*	24 Apr 42	Modified Jul 44
HMCS *Moose Jaw*	19 Jun 41	*U-501* (10 Sep 41), modified March 44
HMCS *Morden*	6 Sep 41	*U-756* (1 Sep 42), modified Jan 44
HMCS *Nanaimo*	26 Apr 41	Never modified
HMCS *Napanee*	12 May 41	*U-356* (27 Dec 42), *U-163* (13 Mar 43), modified Oct 43
HMCS *New Westminister*	31 Jan 42	Modified Dec 43
HMCS *Oakville*	18 Nov 41	*U-94* (28 Aug 42), modified Mar 44
HMCS *Orillia*	24 Nov 40	Modified May 44
HMCS *Pictou*	29 Apr 41	Modified Mar 44
HMCS *Prescott*	26 Jun 41	*U-163* (13 Mar 43), modified Oct 44
HMCS *Quesnel*	23 May 41	Modified Dec 43
HMCS *Rimouski*	26 Apr 41	Modified Aug 43
HMCS *Rosthern*	17 Jun 41	Never modified
HMCS *Sackville*	30 Dec 41	Modified May 44, currently a museum ship in Halifax, NS
HMCS *Saskatoon*	9 Jun 41	Modified Apr 44
HMCS *Shawinigan* †	19 Sep 41	Torpedoed, 25 Nov 44
HMCS *Shediac*	8 Jul 41	*U-87* (4 Mar 43), modified Aug 44
HMCS *Sherbrooke*	5 Jun 41	Modified Aug 44
HMCS *Snowberry*	15 May 41	Modified May 43, *U-536* (20 Nov 43)
HMCS *Sorel*	19 Aug 41	Modified Dec 42
HMCS *Spikenard* †	15 May 41	Torpedoed, 10 Feb 42
HMCS *Sudbury*	19 Oct 41	Modified May 44
HMCS *Summerside*	11 Sep 41	Modified Sep 43
HMCS *The Pas*	21 Oct 41	Never modified
HMCS *Timmins*	10 Feb 42	Modified Oct 44
HMCS *Trail*	30 Apr 41	Modified Oct 44
HMCS *Trillium*	15 May 41	Modified Jun 43
HMCS *Vancouver*	20 Mar 42	Modified Sep 43
HMCS *Wetaskiwin*	17 Dec 40	*U-588* (31 Jul 42), modified Apr 44
HMCS *Weyburn* †	26 Nov 41	Sunk by mine, 22 Feb 43
HMCS *Windflower* †	20 Oct 40	Sunk in collision, 7 Dec 41

Revised Flower Class (Ordered 1941)
(First corvettes constructed with extended foc'sle, slightly larger than the original design)

HMCS *Calgary*	26 Dec 41	*U-536* (20 Nov 43)
HMCS *Charlottetown* †	13 Dec 41	Torpedoed, 11 Sep 42
HMCS *Fredericton*	8 Dec 41	
HMCS *Halifax*	26 Nov 41	
HMCS *Kitchener*	28 Jun 42	
HMCS *La Malbaie*	28 Apr 42	
HMCS *Port Arthur*	26 May 42	Sank Italian sub *Tritone* (19 Jan 43)
HMCS *Regina* †	22 Jan 42	Italian sub *Avorio* (12 Feb 43), torpedoed 8 Aug 44
HMCS *Ville de Québec*	24 May 42	*U-224* (13 Jan 43)
HMCS *Woodstock*	1 May 42	

Revised Flower Class, Increased Endurance (Ordered 1942-1944)
(Possessed twice the range of the original design)

HMCS *Asbestos*	16 Jun 44	
HMCS *Atholl*	14 Oct 43	
HMCS *Beauharnois*	25 Sep 44	
HMCS *Belleville*	19 Oct 44	
HMCS *Cobourg*	11 May 44	
HMCS *Fergus*	18 Nov 44	
HMCS *Forest Hill*	1 Dec 43	
HMCS *Frontenac*	26 Oct 43	
HMCS *Giffard*	10 Nov 43	
HMCS *Guelph*	9 May 44	
HMCS *Hawkesbury*	14 Jun 44	
HMCS *Lachute*	26 Oct 44	
HMCS *Lindsay*	15 Nov 43	
HMCS *Long Branch*	5 Jan 44	
HMCS *Louisbourg II*	13 Dec 43	
HMCS *Merittonia*	10 Nov 44	
HMCS *Mimico*	8 Feb 44	
HMCS *Norsyd*	22 Dec 43	
HMCS *North Bay*	25 Oct 43	
HMCS *Owen Sound*	17 Nov 43	*U-845* (10 Mar 44)
HMCS *Parry Sound*	30 Aug 44	
HMCS *Peterborough*	1 Jun 44	
HMCS *Rivière du Loup*	21 Nov 43	
HMCS *St. Lambert*	27 May 44	

HMCS *Smith Falls*	28 Nov 44	
HMCS *Stellarton*	29 Sep 44	
HMCS *Strathroy*	20 Nov 44	
HMCS *Thorlock*	13 Nov 44	
HMCS *Trentonian*	1 Dec 42	Torpedoed, 22 Feb 45
HMCS *West York*	13 Nov 44	
HMCS *Whitby*	6 Jun 44	

Castle Class[8]

(D = 1.060 L = 251 S = 16 C = 112 A = 1 x 4 in.; 6 x 20mm. AAS = Squid, DC)

HMCS *Arnprior*	8 Jun 44	Ex-HMS *Rising Castle*
HMCS *Bowmanville*	28 Sep 44	Ex-HMS *Nunney Castle*
HMCS *Copper Cliff*	25 Jul 44	Ex-HMS *Hever Castle*
HMCS *Hespeler*	28 Feb 44	Ex-HMS *Guildford Castle*, U-484 (9 Sep 44)
HMCS *Humberstone*	6 Sep 44	Ex-HMS *Norham Castle*
HMCS *Huntsville*	6 Jun 44	Ex-HMS *Woolvesy Castle*
HMCS *Kincardine*	19 Jun 44	Ex-HMS *Tamworth Castle*
HMCS *Leaside*	21 Aug 44	Ex-HMS *Walmer Castle*
HMCS *Orangeville*	24 Apr 44	Ex-HMS *Hedingham Castle*
HMCS *Petrolia*	29 Jun 44	Ex-HMS *Sherborne Castle*
HMCS *St. Thomas*	4 May 44	Ex-HMS *Sandgate Castle*, U-877 (27 Dec 44)
HMCS *Tillsonburg*	23 Jun 44	Ex-HMS *Pembroke Castle*

MINESWEEPERS

Algerine Class

(D = 990 L = 225 C = 107 S = 16 A = 1 x 4 in.; 4 x 20mm AAS = DC, Hedgehog)

HMCS *Border Cities*	18 May 44
HMCS *Fort Frances*	28 Oct 44
HMCS *Kapuskasing*	7 Aug 44
HMCS *Middlesex*	8 Jun 44
HMCS *New Liskeard*	21 Nov 44
HMCS *Oshawa*	6 Jul 44
HMCS *Portage*	22 Oct 44
HMCS *Rockcliffe*	30 Sep 44
HMCS *Sault Ste. Marie*	24 Jun 44
HMCS *St. Boniface*	10 Sep 43
HMCS *Wallaceburg*	18 Nov 43
HMCS *Winnipeg*	29 Jul 43

Bangor Class (Steam, 1939-1942 Programs)

(D = 672 L = 180 S = 16 C = 83 A = 1 x 4 in. or 1 x 3-in.. or 1 x 12-pdr. or 2 x 20mm AAS = DC

HMCS *Bayfield*	26 Feb 42	
HMCS *Bellechase*	13 Dec 41	
HMCS *Blairmore*	17 Apr 42	
HMCS *Burlington*	23 Nov 40	
HMCS *Canso*	6 Mar 42	
HMCS *Caraquet*	2 Apr 42	
HMCS *Chedabucto* †	29 Sep 41	Sunk in collision, 21 Oct 43
HMCS *Chignecto*	12 Dec 40	
HMCS *Clayoquot* †	3 Oct 40	Torpedoed 24 Dec 44
HMCS *Courtenay*	21 Mar 42	
HMCS *Cowichan*	9 Aug 40	
HMCS *Drummondville*	30 Oct 41	
HMCS *Fort William*	25 Aug 42	
HMCS *Gananoque*	8 Nov 41	
HMCS *Georgian*	28 Jan 41	
HMCS *Goderich*	23 Nov 41	
HMCS *Grandmère*	11 Dec 41	
HMCS *Guysborough* †	22 Apr 42	Torpedoed 12 Mar 45
HMCS *Ingonish*	8 Aug 42	
HMCS *Kelowna*	5 Feb 42	
HMCS *Kenora*	6 Aug 42	
HMCS *Kentville*	10 Oct 42	
HMCS *Lockeport*	27 May 42	
HMCS *Mahone*	29 Sep 41	
HMCS *Malpeque*	4 Aug 41	
HMCS *Medicine Hat*	4 Dec 41	
HMCS *Milltown*	18 Sep 42	
HMCS *Minas*	2 Aug 41	
HMCS *Miramichi*	26 Nov 41	
HMCS *Mulgrave* †	4 Nov 42	Mined, 8 Oct 44, declared a constructive loss
HMCS *Nipigon*	26 Nov 41	
HMCS *Outarde*	4 Dec 41	
HMCS *Port Hope*	30 Feb 42	
HMCS *Quatsino*	3 Nov 41	
HMCS *Quinte*	30 Aug 41	
HMCS *Red Deer*	24 Nov 41	
HMCS *Sarnia*	13 Aug 42	
HMCS *Stratford*	29 Aug 42	
HMCS *Swift Current*	11 Nov 41	
HMCS *Thunder*	14 Oct 41	
HMCS *Ungava*	5 Sep 41	

[8.] Originally constructed and commissioned as HM Ships but Britian's inability to man them led to a request to the RCN to take them over.

HMCS *Vegreville*	11 Nov 41	
HMCS *Wasaga*	30 Jun 41	
HMCS *Westmount*	15 Sep 42	

Bangor Class (Diesel, 1940-1941 Program)

(D = 592 L = 162 S = 16 C = 83 A = 1 x 12-pdr, 2 x 20mm. AAS = DC)

HMCS *Brockville*	19 Sep 42	
HMCS *Digby*	26 Jul 42	
HMCS *Esquimalt* †	26 Oct 42	Torpedoed, 16 Apr 45
HMCS *Granby*	2 May 42	
HMCS *Lachine*	20 Jun 42	
HMCS *Melville*	4 Dec 41	
HMCS *Noranda*	15 May 41	
HMCS *Transcona*	25 Nov 42	
HMCS *Trois-Rivières*	12 Aug 42	
HMCS *Truro*	27 Aug 42	

Fundy Class

(D = 460 L = 163 S = 12 C = 38 A = 1 x 12 pdr)

HMCS *Comox*	23 Nov 38	
HMCS *Fundy*	1 Sep 38	
HMCS *Gaspé*	21 Oct 38	
HMCS *Nootka/Nanoose*	6 Dec 38	Renamed *Nanoose* on 1 Apr 43

Llewellyn Class

(D = 228 L = 119 S = 12 C = 23 A = 4 x .50 MG)

HMCS *Coquitlam*	25 Jul 45	
HMCS *Cranbrook*	12 May 44	
HMCS *Daerwood*	22 Apr 44	
HMCS *Kalamalka*	2 Oct 44	
HMCS *Lavallee*	21 Jun 44	
HMCS *Llewellyn*	24 Aug 42	
HMCS *Lloyd George*	24 Aug 42	
HMCS *Revelstoke*	4 Jul 44	
HMCS *Rossland*	15 Jul 44	
HMCS *St. Joseph*	24 May 44	

ANTI-SUBMARINE TRAWLERS

Western Isles Class

(D=530 L=164 S=12 C=40 A=1 x 12 pd., 3 x 20mm AA)

HMCS *Anticosti*	10 Aug 42	
HMCS *Baffin*	26 Aug 42	
HMCS *Cailiff*	17 Sep 42	
HMCS *Ironbound*	16 Oct 42	

HMCS *Liscomb*	8 Sep 42
HMCS *Magdalen*	28 Aug 42
HMCS *Manitoulin*	28 Sep 42
HMCS *Miscou*	17 Oct 42

MOTOR VESSELS

British Power Boat 72-Foot G Type Motor Torpedo Boat

(D = 44 L = 71 S = 39 C = 17 A = 1 x 6-pdr.; 2 x 20mm; 2 x 18-inch TT)

Eleven boats (Nos. *459* to *466, 485* and *486, 491*) commissioned in the 29th RCN MTB Flotilla in early 1944 and served in the English Channel in 1944-1945. Two boats (*Nos. 460 and 463*) destroyed by mines on 1 and 7 Jul 44. Five boats (*Nos. 459, 461, 462, 465 and 466*) destroyed in fire at Ostend on 14 Feb 45.

Fairmile D Type Motor Torpedo Boat

(D = 102 L = 115 S = 29 C = 32 A = 2 x 6-pdr; 2 x 20mm; 2 x 18-inch TT)

Ten boats (Nos. *726, 727, 735, 736, 743, 744, 745, 746, 748* and *797*) commissioned in the 65th RCN MTB Flotilla in early 1944 and served in the English Channel in 1944-1945.

Fairmile B Type Motor Launch

(D = 79 L = 112 S = 20/22 C = 17 A = 3 x 20mm)

Eighty examples of this type (Pennant Nos. *Q 050* to *Q 129*) were constructed in Canada between 1941 and 1944 to serve as patrol craft on the Gulf of St. Lawrence and Atlantic coast and, for a time in the Caribbean. Nos. *052, 062* and *063* were transferred to the Free French marine forces in February 1943.

Other Motor Craft

CMTB 1

(D = 32; L = 70 S = 40 C = 11 A = 4 x .50 mg; 4 x 18-inch TT)

British Power Boat 70-foot craft shipped to Canada in 1940 as a prototype for the construction of similar MTBs in Canada. This boat served briefly at Halifax in 1940-1941 and was turned over to the RN in that year.

S-09

(D = 45 L = 70 S = 22)

A British Power Boat 70-foot craft constructed for the USN in 1941. Turned over to the RCN by the RN, this vessel served as a patrol craft on the Alantic coast and Gulf of St. Lawrence before being designated a firing range control vessel on Lake Ontario.

Landing Craft, Infantry (Large)

(D = 380 L-158 S = 14 C = 22 A = 4 x 40 mm)

Thirty craft of this type were loaned to the RCN by the USN and RN in late 1943 and early 1944 for the express purpose of serving in three Canadian Landing Craft Flotillas for the Normandy invasion. All were present at D-Day and served until September 1944 when they were returned to the USN. Their numbers in Canadian service were: *115, 117, 118, 121, 125, 135, 166, 177, 249, 250, 252, 255, 262, 263, 266, 270, 271, 276, 285, 288, 295, 298, 299, 301, 302, 305, 310,* and *311.*

ARMED YACHTS

(Each of these vessels varied in size, armament and complement)

	Commissioned	Function/Comment
HMCS *Ambler*	6 May 40	Patrol, tender, training
HMCS *Beaver*	1 Apr 41	Training and patrol. Paid off, 17 Oct 44
HMCS *Caribou*	27 May 40	Guardship, patrol, training
HMCS *Cougar*	11 Sep 40	Patrol, examination vessel
HMCS *Elk*	10 Sep 40	Escort, training
HMCS *Grizzly*	17 Jul 41	Guard ship. Paid off, 17 June 44
HMCS *Husky*	23 Jul 40	Training and patrol
HMCS *Lynx*	26 Aug 40	Patrol. Paid off, 23 Apr 43
HMCS *Moose*	8 Sep 40	Patrol, training, examination
HMCS *Otter* †	2 Oct 40	Patrol. Destroyed in fire, 26 Mar 41
HMCS *Raccoon* †	31 Dec 40	Patrol. Torpedoed, 7 Sep 42
HMCS *Reindeer*	25 Jul 40	Patrol, training
HMCS *Renard*	27 May 40	Patrol, training. Paid off, 1 Aug 44
HMCS *Sans Peur*	5 Mar 40	Patrol, training
HMCS *Vison*	5 Oct 40	Patrol, training
HMCS *Wolf*	2 Oct 40	Patrol, training

AUXILIARY VESSELS

(These vessels varied in size, complement and armament)

	Type	Commissioned	Served As/Comment
Adversus †	RCMP Vessel	1939	Patrol craft. Wrecked 20 Dec 41
Alachasse	RCMP Vessel	1939	Patrol craft
Andrée Dupré	Trawler	1939	Examination vessel
Arleux/Gate Vessel 16	Trawler	13 Sep 39	Gate vessel
Armentières	Trawler	1927	Examination vessel
Arras/Gate Vessel 15	Trawler	11 Sep 39	Gate vessel
Bras D'Or †	Trawler	15 Sep 39	Minesweeper, patrol vessel. Sunk, 19 Oct 40
Dundalk	Tanker	13 Nov 43	Tanker
Dundurn	Tanker	25 Nov 43	Tanker
Eastore	Freighter	7 Dec 44	Supply vessel
Festubert/Gate Vessel 17	Trawler	1939	Gate vessel
Fleur de Lis	RCMP vessel	16 Nov 39	Patrol and examination
French	RCMP vessel	18 Sep 39	Patrol and examination
Givenchy	Trawler	15 Apr 39	Accommodation ship. Decommissioned 7 Dec 43
Jalobert		1939?	Examination vessel
Laurier	RCMP vessel	1939	Patrol, escort, examination
Loos/Gate Vessel 14	Trawler	12 Dec 40	Gate vessel
Macdonald	RCMP vessel	11 Oct 39	Patrol. Paid off, 28 Jan 45
Macsin	Trawler	1940	Examination vessel
Marvita	Rumrunner	1941	Examination vessel
Mastadon	Dredge	9 Dec 42	Auxiliary tanker
Mont Joli		5 Jul 40	Examination vessel
Moonbeam		Dec 40	Fuel oil carrier
Murray Stewart		1942	Examination vessel
Nitinat	Fishery patrol	Sep 39	Examination vessel
Norsal			Various
Preserver	Supply ship	11 Jul 42	Motor Launch base ship
Provider	Supply ship	1 Dec 42	Motor Launch base ship
Rayon D'Or	Trawler	11 Sep 39	Minesweeping and loop laying
Reo II	Rumrunner	23 Jan 41	Minesweeper, examination vessel
Ross Norman	Coaster	19 Jun 40	Minesweeper, towing craft
St. Eloi/Gate Vessel 12	Trawler	1940	Gate vessel
Sankaty	Ferry	24 Sep 40	Minelaying, looplaying
Shulamite	Rumrunner		Examination vessel
Skidegate	Training vessel	25 Jul 38	Training vessel. Paid off, 18 Feb 42
Standard Coaster	Coaster	11 Feb 42	Towing vessel
Star XVI	Whale catcher	Aug 41	Patrol vessel
Suderoy IV	Whale catcher	Jun 40	Patrol vessel
Suderoy V	Whale catcher	2 Jun 41	Patrol vessel
Suderoy VI	Whale catcher	19 Mar 41	Patrol vessel
Sunbeam	Barge	11 Nov 40	Fuel oil carrier
Vencedor			Miscellaneous auxiliary
Venosta		17 Nov 39	Gate vessel, minesweeper. Paid off, 22 Jan 42
Venture/ Harbour Craft 190	Schooner	25 Oct 37	Guardship/accommodation vessel
Venture II	Yacht	7 Dec 39	Depot ship
Vimy/Gate Vessel 1	Trawler		Gate vessel
Viernoe		11 Oct 39	Boom defence vessel
Whitethroat	Trawler	7 Dec 44	
Ypres/Gate Vessel 1	Trawler	1923	Gate vessel. Sunk in collision, 12 May 1940

Sources

Information from Directorate of History and Heritage, DND; Ken Macpherson and John Burgess, *The Ships of Canada's Naval Forces 1910-1985* (Toronto, 1981); Robert Darlington and Fraser McKee, *The Canadian Naval Chronicle* (St. Catharines, 1996); Gilbert Tucker, *The Naval Service of Canada.* Volume II. (Ottawa, 1952).

Abbreviations Used in the Notes

Adm   Admiralty

DHH   Directorate of History and Heritage, Department of National Defence, Ottawa

MG   Manuscript Group

NAC   National Archives of Canada, Ottawa

NHS   Naval Historical Section

NSHQ   Naval Service Headquarters, Ottawa

PRO   Public Record Office, UK

RG   Record Group

vol   volume

Chapter 1: Canada and the Sea: 1600-1918

Unless otherwise noted, this chapter is based on the following sources: Corelli Barnett, *Engage the Enemy More Closely: The Royal Navy in the Second World War* (London, 1991), 1-19; Clay Blair, *Hitler's U-Boat War. Vol. I: The Hunters, 1939-1942* (New York, 2000), 3-28; James A. Boutilier, ed., *The RCN in Retrospect, 1910-1968* (Vancouver, 1982), 1-61; W.A.B. Douglas, ed., *The RCN in Transition, 1910-1985* (Vancouver, 1988), 90-125; Tony German, *The Sea is at Our Gates: The History of the Canadian Navy* (Toronto, 1990), 13-34; Donald Goodspeed, *The Armed Forces of Canada, 1867-1967: A Century of Achievement* (Ottawa, 1967), 23-25; G.W.L. Nicholson, *Canadian Expeditionary Force 1914-1919* (Ottawa, 1964), 546-548; Thomas H. Raddall, *Halifax: Warden of the North* (New York, 1965), 247-256; Michael Hadley and Roger Sarty, *Tin Pots and Pirate Ships: Canadian Naval Forces and German Sea-Raiders 1880-1918* (Montreal, 1991), 3-29, 181-262; Roger Sarty, *Canada and the Battle of the Atlantic* (Montreal, 1998), 18-26; C.P. Stacey, *Quebec 1759: The Siege and the Battle. Edited*

and with new material by Donald E. Graves (Toronto, 2002), 215-231; Gilbert Tucker, *The Naval Service of Canada. Its Official History. Vol I: Origins and Early Years* (Ottawa, 1952), 1-301; J.M. Winter, *The Experience of World War I* (Oxford, 1988), 86-88.

Information on Canadian warships is from relevant entries in John Burgess and Ken Macpherson, *The Ships of Canada's Naval Forces 1910-1985. A Complete Pictorial History of Canadian Warships* (Toronto, 1981).

1 Information on the burial that took place on HMCS *Ottawa* on 13 September is from Commander L.B. Jenson, RCN (Retd.), who, as a member of the destroyer's crew, attended the service.

2 See C.P. Stacey, *Quebec 1759. The Siege and the Battle. Updated by Donald E. Graves,* (Toronto, 2002).

3 Resolution, House of Commons, 29 March 1909, Ottawa, quoted in Tony German, *The Sea is at Our Gates. The History of the Canadian Navy* (Toronto, 1990), 25.

4 Recruiting poster dated 1911 reproduced in Donald Goodspeed, *The Armed Forces of Canada, 1867-1967. A Century of Achievement* (Ottawa, 1967), 24.

5 Quoted in Goodspeed, *The Armed Forces of Canada, 1867-1967,* 69.

6 Michael Hadley and Roger Sarty, *Tin-Pots and Pirate Ships. Canadian Naval Forces & German Sea Raiders 1880-1918* (Montreal, 1991), 268-269.

7 DHH, NHS "Halifax 1905-20," quoted in Hadley and Sarty, *Tin-Pots,* 269.

8 Hose to Secretary of the Navy, 21 Sep 1918, quoted in *Hadley and Sarty,* Tin-Pots, 223.

Chronicle 1: The Early Days to 1918

1 DHH, NHS Files, HMCS *Stadacona* (Ship) File, A.H. Wickens to E.C. Russell, 16 November 1955.

2 Patrick W. Brock, "Commander E.A.E Nixon and the Royal Naval College of Canada," in Boutilier, ed., *The RCN in Retrospect, 1910-1968* (Vancouver, 1982), 37.

3 DHH, Biography Files, F.H. Houghton, "A Sailor's Life for Me."

4 Patrick W. Brock in *The RCN in Retrospect,* 38-39.

5 DHH, NHS Files, HMCS *Stadacona* (Ship) File, A.H. Wickens to E.C. Russell, 16 November 1955.

6 DHH, NHS Files, HMCS *Hochelaga,* McLaurin to Russell, 11 February 1963.

7 Statement of Captain Joseph Mesquita of the Schooner *Francis J. O'Hara,* regarding the loss of that vessel, 20 August 1918, in Roger Sarty and Michael Hadley, *Tin-Pots & Pirate Ships. Canadian Naval Forces & German Sea Raiders* (Montreal, 1983), 266.

8 NAC, Record Group 24, Box 2532, HQC, 1686, vol. 2, G. Meister to Militia Headquarters, 4 September 1918.

Chapter 2: Long, Slow Years: The Royal Canadian Navy between the Wars, 1919-1939

Unless otherwise noted, this chapter is based on the following sources: Corelli Barnett, *Engage the Enemy More Closely: The Royal Navy in the Second World War* (London, 1991), 19-56; Clay Blair, *Hitler's U-Boat War. Vol. II: The Hunters, 1939-1945* (New York, 2000), 29-56; J.A. Boutilier, ed, *The RCN in Retrospect, 1910-1968* (Vancouver, 1982), 62-104; *The Defeat of the Enemy Attack on Shipping 1939-1945. A Study of Policy and Operations. Vol 1A* (London, 1957), 3-16; Karl Dönitz, *Memoirs: Ten*

Years and Twenty Days (New York, 1997), 1-50; W.A.B. Douglas, ed., *The RCN in Transition, 1910-1985* (Vancouver, 1988), 3-14; W.A.B. Douglas and Brereton Greenhous, *Out of the Shadows. Canada in the Second World War. Revised Edition* (Toronto, 1995), 11-39; Tony German, *The Sea is at Our Gates: The History of the Canadian Navy* (Toronto, 1990), 55-70; Donald Goodspeed, *The Armed Forces of Canada, 1867-1967: A Century of Achievement* (Ottawa, 1967), 91-92, 96-101; Marc Milner, *The North Atlantic Run: The Royal Canadian Navy and the Battle for the Convoys* (Toronto, 1990), 12-38: Roger Sarty, *Canada and the Battle of the Atlantic* (Montreal, 1998), 26-36; C.P. Stacey, *Arms, Men and Governments. The War Policies of Canada, 1939-1945* (Toronto, 1970), 1-5, 67-80; 93-95; Gilbert Tucker, *The Naval Service of Canada. Its Official History. Vol I: Origins and Early Years* (Ottawa, 1952), 304-370.

Information on Canadian warships is from relevant entries in John Burgess and Ken Macpherson, *The Ships of Canada's Naval Forces 1910-1985. A Complete Pictorial History of Canadian Warships* (Toronto, 1981).

1 German, *Sea is at Our Gates*, 55.
2 Statement by Paymaster Commander J.E.A. Woodhouse, RN quoted in James Eayrs, *In Defence of Canada. Vol I: From the Great War to the Great Depression* (Toronto, 1964), 171.
3 Cited in J.W.H. Knox, "An Engineer's Outline of RCN History: Part I," in Boutilier, ed., *The RCN in Retrospect. 1910-1968* (Vancouver, 1982), 102.
4 Article 22 of the London Naval Treaty, 1930.
5 "Defence of Trade," Memorandum by Nelles, 12 Feb 1937, NAC, MG 27, III, B5, vol 37, file D-26, quoted in Marc Milner, *The North Atlantic Run: The Royal Canadian Navy and the Battle of the Atlantic* (Toronto, 1990), 9.
6 DHH, NHS 1650 (Operations General), pt 2, NSHQ Signal, 1 Sep 1939.
7 H.F. Pullen, "The RCN Between the Wars," in Boutilier, *The RCN in Retrospect*, 71.
8 Signal, NSHQ to all commands, 1 Sep 1939 quoted in H.F. Pullen, "The RCN Between the Wars," in Boutilier, *RCN in Retrospect*, 72.

Chronicle 2: The Interwar Period

1 DHH, Biography Files, F.H. Houghton, "A Sailor's Life for Me."
2 Hewitt and Mansfield in *Salty Dips*, Vol 1 (Ottawa, 1983), 55-56.
3 R. Houliston in *Salty Dips*, vol 1, 183.
4 F. Sherwood in *Salty Dips*, vol 1, 11-12.
5 C.H. Little in *Salty Dips*, vol 2 (Ottawa, 1985), 112.
6 DHH, Biography Files, F.H. Houghton, "A Sailor's Life for Me."
7 E. Brand in *Salty Dips*, vol 3 (Ottawa, 1988), 77-78.
8 W.B. Creery in *Salty Dips*, vol 3, 7.
9 J. Anderson in *Salty Dips*, vol 1, 7.

Chapter 3: Opening Rounds: The Royal Canadian Navy at War, September 1939–May 1941

Unless otherwise noted, this chapter is based on the following sources: Corelli Barnett, *Engage the Enemy More Closely: The Royal Navy in the Second World War* (London, 1991), 272-277; 429-457; Clay Blair, *Hitler's U-Boat War. Vol I: The Hunters, 1939-1942* (New York, 1996), 53-261; J.A. Boutilier, ed, *The RCN in Retrospect, 1910-1968* (Vancouver, 1982), 138-157, 175-188; *The Defeat of the Enemy Attack on Shipping 1939-1945. A Study of Policy and Operations. Vol 1A* (London, 1957), 40, 69-77; Karl Dönitz, *Memories: Ten Years and Twenty Days* (New York, 1997), 37-127; W.A.B. Douglas, *The Creation of a National Air Force: The Official History of the Royal Canadian Air Force* Volume II (Ottawa, 1986), 471-492; W.A.B. Douglas and Brereton Greenhous, *Out of the Shadows. Canada in the Second World War. Revised Edition* (Toronto, 1995), 72-82; Tony German, *The Sea is at Our Gates: The History of the Canadian Navy* (Toronto, 1990), 93-120; Marc Milner, *The North Atlantic Run: The Royal Canadian Navy and the Battle for the Convoys* (Toronto, 1990), 64-128: Roger Sarty, *Canada and the Battle of the Atlantic* (Montreal, 1998), 65-130; Joseph Schull, *The Far Distant Ships: An Official Account of Canadian Naval Operations in the Second World War* (Ottawa, 1952), 66-83; Gilbert Tucker, *The Naval Service of Canada. Its Official History. Vol II: Activities on Shore During the Second World War* (Ottawa, 1952), 33-65, 2333-254.

Information on Canadian warships is from relevant entries in John Burgess and Ken Macpherson, *The Ships of Canada's Naval Forces 1910-1985. A Complete Pictorial History of Canadian Warships* (Toronto, 1981).

1 Karl Dönitz, *Memoirs: Ten Years and Twenty Days*, (New York, 1997), 47.
2 Massey to the Canadian Government, 23 May 1940, quoted in Roger Sarty, *Canada and the Battle of the Atlantic*, (Montreal, 1998), 49.
3 Mackenzie King Diary, 24 May 1940, quoted in Sarty, *Battle of the Atlantic*, 49.
4 Report of *Kapitänleutnant* Otto Kretschmer, U-99, quoted in Clay Blair, *Hitler's U-Boat War. Vol. 1. The Hunters, 1939-1942* (New York, 1998), 198.
5 Quoted in Milner, *North Atlantic Run*, 27.
6 Churchill to Roosevelt, 31 Jan 1940, quoted in Corelli Barnett, *Engage the Enemy More Closely: The Royal Navy in the Second World War* (London, 1991), 201-202.
7 Barnett, *Engage the Enemy More Closely*, 271.
8 Dönitz, *Ten Years and Twenty Days*, 142.

Chronicle 3: The First Months of War, 1939-1940

1 J. Anderson in *Salty Dips*, vol 1, 2, 9-10.
2 F. Sherwood in *Salty Dips*, vol 1, 14.
3 O. Robertson in *Salty Dips*, vol 3, 38.
4 R. Houliston in *Salty Dips*, vol 1, 185.
5 Gregory W. Pritchard, ed., *Memories of Basic Training and Other Dips* (Lunenburg, 2000), 18-19.
6 Robertson in *Salty Dips*, vol 3, 42.
7 R. Hennessy in *Salty Dips*, vol 2, 9-10.
8 W.B. Creery in *Salty Dips*, vol 3, 6-7.
9 R. Timbrell in *Salty Dips*, vol 3, 22-24.
10 DHH, Biography Files, J. Lawrence Interview with R. Welland.
11 W.B. Creery in *Salty Dips*, vol 3, 7-8.
12 R. Timbrell in *Salty Dips*, vol 3, 27.
13 L. Audette in *Salty Dips*, vol 2, 60-61.
14 Edward O'Connor, ed., *The Corvette Years: The Lower Deck Story* (Vancouver, 1995), 67-68.

Chapter 4: Time of Trial: The Royal Canadian Navy and the Battle of the Atlantic, May 1941–May 1942

Unless otherwise noted, this chapter is based on the following sources: Corelli Barnett, *Engage the Enemy More Closely: The Royal Navy in the Second World War* (London, 1991), 272-277; 429-457; Clay Blair, *Hitler's U-Boat War. Vol. I. The Hunters* (New York, 1996), 218-339; J.A. Boutilier, ed, *The RCN in Retrospect, 1910-1968* (Vancouver, 1982), 138-157, 175-188; *The Defeat of the Enemy Attack on Shipping 1939-1945. A Study of Policy and Operations. Vol 1A* (London, 1957), 40, 69-77; Karl Dönitz, *Memoirs: Ten Years and Twenty Days* (New York, 1997), 127-194; W.A.B. Douglas, *The Creation of a National Air Force: The Official History of the Royal Canadian Air Force Volume II* (Ottawa, 1986), 471-492; W.A.B. Douglas and Brereton Greenhous, *Out of the Shadows. Canada in the Second World War. Revised Edition* (Toronto, 1995), 72-82; Tony German, *The Sea is at Our Gates: The History of the Canadian Navy* (Toronto, 1990), 93-120; Marc Milner, *The North Atlantic Run: The Royal Canadian Navy and the Battle for the Convoys* (Toronto, 1990), 64-128; Roger Sarty, *Canada and the Battle of the Atlantic* (Montreal, 1998), 65-130; Joseph Schull, *The Far Distant Ships: An Official Account of Canadian Naval Operations in the Second World War* (Ottawa, 1952), 66-83; Gilbert Tucker, *The Naval Service of Canada. Its Official History. Vol II: Activities on Shore During the Second World War* (Ottawa, 1952), 33-65, 233-254.

Information on Canadian warships is from relevant entries in John Burgess and Ken Macpherson, *The Ships of Canada's Naval Forces 1910-1985. A Complete Pictorial History of Canadian Warships* (Toronto, 1981).

1 Sarty, *Battle of the Atlantic*, 75.
2 Commander O.M. Read, USN, 22 Aug 1941, quoted in Sarty, *Battle of the Atlantic*, 75.
3 Captain (D), Newfoundland, Sep 41, quoted in Milner, *North Atlantic Run*, 39.
4 PRO, Adm 237/187, HMCS *Shediac*, Report of Proceedings, SC 48, quoted in Milner, *North Atlantic Run*, 82.
5 NAC, RG 24, vol 11929, file 00-220-3-6, Prentice to Captain (D), Newfoundland, 4 Nov 1941.

6 NAC, RG 24, vol 11929, file 00-220-3-6, Murray to Naval Secretary, 6 Nov 41.
7 NAC, RG 24, vol 11929, file 00-220-3-6, Captain E.B.K. Stevens to Murray, 16 Oct 41.
8 DCNS to CNS, Nov 41, quoted in Sarty, *Battle of the Atlantic*, 92.
9 DNP to CNS, 19 Nov 41, quoted in Sarty, *Battle of the Atlantic*, 92.
10 Quoted in Blair, *The Hunters*, 519.
11 Blair, *The Hunters*, 470.

Chronicle 4: 1941

1 Alan Easton, *50 North*: Canada's Atlantic Battleground (Toronto, 1963), 15-16.
2 Mac Johnston, *Corvettes Canada. Convoy Veterans of WWII Tell Their True Stories* (Whitby, 1994), 104.
3 Johnston, *Corvettes Canada*, 123-124.
4 Johnston, *Corvettes Canada*, 14.
5 O. Robertson in *Salty Dips*, vol 3, 43-44.
6 S.T. Richards, *Operation Sick Bay* (West Vancouver, 1994), 121-112.
7 Johnston, *Corvettes Canada*, 43-44.
8 NAC, RG 24, vol 11334, file 8280-SC42, Grubb to Captain (D), Newfoundland, 6 Nov 1941.
9 DHH, Biography Files. H. Lawrence interview with W.H. Willson.
10 James Lamb, *The Corvette Navy* (Toronto, 1977), 23-24.
11 Johnston, *Corvettes Canada*, 113-114.
12 Richards, *Operation Sick Bay*, 123.
13 S.T. Richards, *Operation Sick-Bay*, 126.
14 Easton, *50 North*, 60-61
15 Johnston, *Corvettes Canada*, 59-60.
16 Easton, *50 North*, 88.
17 NAC, RG 24, vol 11929, file 00-220-3-6, Stevens to Commanding Officer, Newfoundland, 16 Oct 1941.
18 R. Hennessy in *Salty Dips*, vol 2, 14.

Chapter 5: "If We Lose the War at Sea, We Lose the War:" The Ordeal, May–November 1942

Unless otherwise noted, this chapter is based on the following sources: Corelli Barnett, *Engage the Enemy More Closely: The Royal Navy in the Second World War* (London, 1991), 476-490; Clay Blair, *Hitler's U-Boat War* (New York, 1996): *Vol. I, The Hunters*, 431-691; *Vol. II. The Hunted* 9-152; J.A. Boutilier, ed, *The RCN in Retrospect, 1910-1968* (Vancouver, 1982), 138-157, 175-188; *The Defeat of the Enemy Attack on Shipping 1939-1945. A Study of Policy and Operations. Vol 1A* (London, 1957), 40-42, 78-83; Karl Dönitz, *Memoirs: Ten Years and Twenty Days* (New York, 1997), 195-299; W.A.B. Douglas and Brereton Greenhous, *Out of the Shadows. Canada in the Second World War. Revised Edition* (Toronto, 1995), 72-82; Tony German, *The Sea is at Our Gates: The History of the Canadian Navy* (Toronto, 1990), 93-120; Marc Milner, *The North Atlantic Run: The Royal Canadian Navy and the Battle for the Convoys* (Toronto, 1990), 96-107; Roger Sarty, *Canada and the Battle of the Atlantic* (Montreal, 1998), 89-125; Joseph Schull, *The Far Distant Ships: An Official Account of Canadian Naval Operations in the Second World War* (Ottawa, 1952), 122-142; Gilbert Tucker, *The Naval Service of Canada. Its Official History. Vol II: Activities on Shore During the Second World War* (Ottawa, 1952), 33-65, 233-254.

Information on Canadian warships is from relevant entries in John Burgess and Ken Macpherson, *The Ships of Canada's Naval Forces 1910-1985. A Complete Pictorial History of Canadian Warships* (Toronto, 1981).

1 Air Council to Chief of Air Staff, n.d. [c. Sep 41], quoted in John Terraine, *The Right of the Line: The Royal Air Force in the European War, 1939-1945* (London, 1985), 413.
2 Air Requirements for the Successful Prosecution of the War at Sea, 5 Mar 1942, quoted in Barnett, *Engage the Enemy More Closely*, 460.
3 Anglo-American Air Strategy, 30 Oct 42, quoted in Barnett, *Engage the Enemy More Closely*, 473.
4 Alan Easton, *50 North: Canada's Atlantic Battleground* (Toronto, 1963), 141.
5 Erich Topp, *Fackel über dem Atlantik* (Hereford, 1990), 85. Translation by the Canadian Naval Memorial Trust.
6 Easton, *50 North*, 164.
7 Lieutenant R.L. Hennessy, in *Salty Dips*, vol 2 (Ot-

tawa, 1985), 11.

8 Lieutenant R. Hennessy, in *Salty Dips*, vol 2, 11.

9 DHH, NHS 1650, "U-210," Lieutenant-Commander J.H. Stubbs, Report of Proceedings, HMCS *Assiniboine*, 10 Aug 42.

10 DHH, NHS 8000, "Assiniboine I," RCN Press Release, 19 Sep 42

11 Hennessy, *Salty Dips*, vol 2, 12.

12 T.C. Pullen and W.A.B. Douglas, "Convoy ON 127 and the loss of HMCS *Ottawa*, 13 September 1942," *Northern Mariner*, vol 2 (Apr 1992).

13 Latham B. Jenson, *Tin Hats, Oilskins and Seaboots. A Naval Journey, 1938-1945* (Toronto, 2000), 136.

14 German Radio broadcast quoted in German, *The Sea is at Our Gates*, 119.

15 Audette in *Salty Dips*, vol 2, 65-66.

16 First Lord to Churchill, 15 Dec 1942, quoted in Milner, *North Atlantic Run*, 196.

17 Churchill to Mackenzie King, 17 Dec 42, quoted in Milner, *North Atlantic Run*, 197.

Chronicle 5: 1942

1 Johnston, *Corvettes Canada*, 76.

2 O'Connor, *Corvette Years*, 37.

3 Latham B. Jenson, *Tin Hats, Oilskins and Seaboots*, (Toronto, 2000), 125-126.

4 Frank Curry, *War at Sea: A Canadian Seaman on the North Atlantic* (Toronto, 1990), 53-54.

5 Lamb, *Corvette Navy*, 90-91.

6 Joseph Schull, *The Far Distant Ships* (Ottawa, 1952), 131-133.

7 DHH, NHS 1650 Files, U-210, J.C. Stubbs, Report of Proceedings, HMCS *Assiniboine*, 10 Aug 1942.

8 Jenson, *Tin Hats*, 135-136.

9 Thomas Lynch, *Fading Memories: Canadian Sailors and the Battle of the Atlantic* (Yarmouth, 1993), 118.

10 Jenson, *Tin Hats*, 139-140.

11 Lynch, *Fading Memories*, 118.

12 Jenson, *Tin Hats*, 141.

13 Curry, *War at Sea*, 70-71.

14 Jenson, *Tin Hats*, 124.

15 Audette in *Salty Dips*, vol 2, 65-66.

16 Johnston, *Corvettes Canada*, 173-174.

17 Easton, *50 North*, 165.

18 Frank Curry, *War at Sea: A Canadian Seaman on the North Atlantic* (Toronto, 1990), 66-67.

Chapter 6: "The Battle of The Atlantic is Getting Harder:" Victory in Mid-Ocean, December 1942–May 1943

Unless otherwise noted, this chapter is based on the following sources: Corelli Barnett, *Engage the Enemy More Closely: The Royal Navy in the Second World War* (London, 1991), 458-490, 573-613; Clay Blair, *Hitler's U-Boat War. Vol II. The Hunted* (New York, 1998), 158-295; J.A. Boutilier, ed, *The RCN in Retrospect, 1910-1968* (Vancouver, 1982), 138-234; 175-186; *The Defeat of the Enemy Attack on Shipping 1939-1945. A Study of Policy and Operations. Vol 1A* (London, 1957), 42, 83-97; Karl Dönitz, *Memoirs: Ten Years and Twenty Days* (New York, 1997), 315-342; W.A.B. Douglas, *The Creation of a National Air Force: The Official History of the Royal Canadian Air Force Volume II* (Ottawa, 1986), 537-567; W.A.B. Douglas, ed, *The RCN in Transition, 1910-1985* (Vancouver, 1988), 126-158; W.A.B. Douglas and Brereton Greenhous, *Out of the Shadows. Canada in the Second World War. Revised Edition* (Toronto, 1995), 73-90; Michael Gannon, *Black May: The Epic Story of the Allies' Defeat of the German U-Boats in May 1943* (New York, 1989), 49-59, 61-64, 66-76, 83-86, 165-168; Tony German, *The Sea is at Our Gates: The History of the Canadian Navy* (Toronto, 1990), 128-143; Marc Milner, *The North Atlantic Run: The Royal Canadian Navy and the Battle for the Convoys* (Toronto, 1990), 157-241; Roger Sarty, *Canada and the Battle of the Atlantic* (Montreal, 1998), 117-130; Joseph Schull, *The Far Distant Ships: An Official Account of Canadian Naval Operations in the Second World War* (Ottawa, 1952), 161-174; C.P. Stacey, *Arms, Men and Governments. The War Policies of Canada, 1939-1945* (Toronto, 1970), 307-310; Gilbert Tucker, *The Naval Service of Canada. Its Official History. Vol II: Activities on Shore During the Second World War* (Ottawa, 1952), 436-445.

Information on Canadian warships is from relevant entries in John Burgess and Ken Macpherson, *The Ships of Canada's Naval Forces 1910-1985. A Complete Pictorial History of Canadian Warships* (Toronto, 1981).

1 Captain Eric Brand, RN, quoted in Sarty, *Battle of the Atlantic*, 128.

2 NAC, RG 24, vol 11968, file 222-1, Minutes of Conference, Washington, 30 Dec 42.

3 Henderson quoted in Milner, *North Atlantic Run*, 209.

4 Milner, *North Atlantic Run*, 209.

5 Milner, *North Atlantic Run*, 213.

6 DHH, NS 8440-60, Nelles to Pound, 7 Jan 43.

7 DHH, NS 8440, Churchill to Mackenzie King, 18 Jan 43.

8 Quoted in Milner, *North Atlantic Run*, 213.

9 Quoted in Dönitz, *Memoirs*, 327.

10 War Diary, Commander of U-Boats, 24 May 43, quoted in Barnett, *Engage the Enemy More Closely*, 611.

11 Quoted in Barnett, *Engage the Enemy More Closely*, 603.

12 Signal, U-Boat Command, 22 May 43, quoted in Barnett, *Engage the Enemy More Closely*, 610.

13 U-Boat Command War Diary, 24 May 43, quoted in Barnett, *Engage the Enemy More Closely*, 612.

14 U-Boat Command War Diary, 24 May 43, quoted in Barnett, *Engage the Enemy More Closely*, 612.

15 Barnett, *Engage the Enemy More Closely*, 613.

Chronicle 6: 1943

1 Jenson, *Tin Hats, Oilskins and Seaboots* (Toronto, 2000), 189-190.

2 Johnston, *Corvettes Canada*, 208-209.

3 Jenson, *Tin Hats*, 174-175.

4 O'Connor, *Corvette Years*, 107-108.

5 O'Connor, *Corvette Years*, 102-103.

6 Lamb, *Corvette Navy*, 127-128.

7 CPO Bonner in Lynch, *Fading Memories*, 75.

8 NAC, MG 32m C 71, vol 2, file 2-6, Diary, June to December 1943.

9 Mike Parker, *Running the Gauntlet* (Halifax, 1994), 62.

10 Parker, *Running the Gauntlet*, 64.

11 Parker, *Running the Gauntlet*, 245.

12 Parker, *Running the Gauntlet*, 82-83.

13 Parker, *Running the Gauntlet*, 170.

14 Parker, *Running the Gauntlet*, 267.

15 Parker, *Running the Gauntlet*, 83.

Chapter 7: The Royal Canadian Navy Comes of Age: June 1943–April 1944

Unless otherwise noted, this chapter is based on the following sources: Clay Blair, *Hitler's U-Boat War. Vol II. The Hunted* (New York, 1998), 478-509; J.A. Boutilier, ed, *The RCN in Retrospect, 1910-1968* (Vancouver, 1982), 138-174; 175-186; *The Defeat of the Enemy Attack on Shipping 1939-1945. A Study of Policy and Operations. Vol 1A* (London, 1957), 98-116; Karl Dönitz, *Memoirs: Ten Years and Twenty Days* (New York, 1997), 406-425; W.A.B. Douglas, ed, *The RCN in Transition, 1910-1985* (Vancouver, 1988), 159-186; Tony German, *The Sea is at Our Gates: The History of the Canadian Navy* (Toronto, 1990), 144-145; Marc Milner, *The North Atlantic Run: The Royal Canadian Navy and the Battle for the Convoys* (Toronto, 1990), 242-268; Marc Milner, *The U-Boat Hunters. The Royal Canadian Navy and the Offensive against Germany's Submarines* (Toronto, 1994), 21-133; Roger Sarty, *Canada and the Battle of the Atlantic* (Montreal, 1998), 131-155; Joseph Schull, *The Far Distant Ships: An Official Account of Canadian Naval Operations in the Second World War* (Ottawa, 1952), 175-181; C.P. Stacey, *Arms, Men and Governments. The War Policies of Canada, 1939-1945* (Toronto, 1970), 315-319, 590-591; Gilbert Tucker, *The Naval Service of Canada. Its Official History. Vol II: Activities on Shore During the Second World War* (Ottawa, 1952), 242-335, 402-417.

Information on Canadian warships is from relevant entries in John Burgess and Ken Macpherson, *The Ships of Canada's Naval Forces 1910-1985. A Complete Pictorial History of Canadian Warships* (Toronto, 1981).

1 NAC, RG 24, vol 3997, file NSS 1057-3-24, pt 1, Comments on the Operation and Performance of HMC Ships, 1 Jun 43.

2 DHH 79/446, KTB, Bdv, 31 Jul 43.

3 Appreciation of the U-Boat Situation, 1 Aug 43, quoted in W.A.B. Douglas and Jurgen Rohwer, "Canada and the Wolf Packs, September 1943," in W.A.B. Douglas, ed, *The RCN in Transition, 1910-1985* (Vancouver, 1988), 163.

4 Dönitz, Signal, 20 Sep 43, quoted in Douglas and Rohwer, "Canada and the Wolf Packs," 168.

5 Signal, 19 Sep 43, quoted in Douglas and Rohwer, "Canada and the Wolf Packs," 168.

6 Signal, 19 Sep 43, in Douglas and Rohwer, "Canada and the Wolf Packs," 168.

7 Quoted in Marc Milner, *The U-Boat Hunters. The Royal Canadian Navy and the Offensive Against Germany's Submarines* (Montreal, 1998), 66.

8 Quoted in Milner, *U-Boat Hunters*, 67.

9 Rohwer and Douglas, "Canada and the Wolfpacks," 176.

10 Alec Douglas, *The Creation of a National Air Force. The Official History of the Royal Canadian Air Force. Vol. II* (Ottawa, 19860, 564.

11 Quoted in Douglas and Rohwer, 179

12 Quoted in Douglas and Rohwer, "Canada and the Wolfpacks," 179.

13 NAC, MG 32, C71, vol 3, file 3-14, Memo for the Minister in Connolly's handwriting, 30 Nov 43.

14 Schull

Chronicle 7: 1944

1 Easton, *50 North*, 223-225.

2 Diary of Commander A. Layard, RN, Royal Naval Museum, Portsmouth, UK. All Layard quotations are from this source.

3 Easton, *50 North*, 265-268.

4 Allen W. Stevens, *Glory of Youth*, (Author, 1995), 81.

5 Stevens, *Glory of Youth*, 87.

6 Stevens, *Glory of Youth*, 165-168.

7 Lynch, *Fading Memories*, 90-91.

8 Richards, *Operation Sick Bay*, 133.

9 Barbard Dundas, *A History of Women in the Canadian Military* (Montreal, 2000), 63.

10 Rosamond Greer, *The Girls of the King's Navy*, (*), 53-54.

11 Lynch, *Fading Memories*, 178.

12 Greer, *The Girls*, 118, 119.

13 Lynch, *Fading Memories*, 177.

14 Lynch, *Fading Memories*, 178.

15 Greer, *The Girls*, 101.

Chapter 8: Victory: May 1944–May 1945

Unless otherwise noted, this chapter is based on the following sources: Clay Blair, *Hitler's U-Boat War. Vol II. The Hunted, 1942-1945* (New York, 2000)), 570-689; *The Defeat of the Enemy Attack on Shipping 1939-1945. A Study of Policy and Operations. Vol 1A* (London, 1957), 124-130; Karl Dönitz, *Memories: Ten Years and Twenty Days* (New York, 1997), 406-429; W.A.B. Douglas, *The Creation of a National Air Force: The Official History of the Royal Canadian Air Force Volume II* (Ottawa, 1986), 569-597; W.A.B. Douglas, ed, *The RCN in Transition, 1910-1985* (Vancouver, 1988), 143-158, 159-186; Tony German, *The Sea is at Our Gates: The History of the Canadian Navy* (Toronto, 1990), 155-195; Marc Milner, *The U-Boat Hunters. The Royal Canadian Navy and the Offensive against Germany's Submarines* (Toronto, 1994), 134-255; Roger Sarty, *Canada and the Battle of the Atlantic* (Montreal, 1998), 143-154; Joseph Schull, *The Far Distant Ships: An Official Account of Canadian Naval Operations in the Second World War* (Ottawa, 1952), 215-227, 239-285.

Information on Canadian warships is from relevant entries in John Burgess and Ken Macpherson, *The Ships of Canada's Naval Forces 1910-1985. A Complete Pictorial History of Canadian Warships* (Toronto, 1981).

1 U-Boat Command, Jun 1944, quoted in Clay Blair, *Hitler's U-Boat War. Vol. II. The Hunted, 1942-1945* (New York, 1998), 589.

2 Quoted in Milner, *U-Boat Hunters*, 221.

3 DHH 79/446, KTB, Bdv, 1 Jan 45.

4 DHH 79/446, KTB, Bdv, 1 Jan 45.

5 U-Boat Command War Diary, 28 Aug 43, quoted in *Defeat of the Enemy Attack on Shipping 1939-1945. A Study of Policy and Operations, Vol. 1 A* (London, 1957), 125.

6 Quoted in Milner, *U-Boat Hunters*, 240.

7 Samuel E. Morison, *History of the United States Naval*

Operations in World War II. Vol 10. The Atlantic Battle Won, May 1943-May 1945 (Boston, 1956), 328.

8 Unpublished memoir of Werner Hirschmann.

9 Unpublished memoir of Werner Hirschmann.

10 Edward O'Connor, *The Corvette Years*: The Lower Deck Story (Vancouver, 1995), 169.

11 Diary of Commander A.F.C. Layard, RN, Royal Naval Museum, Portsmouth, 16 May 45.

Chronicle 8: 1945

1 Lynch, *Fading Memories*, 43.

2 Account of the sinking of *Esquimalt* by Terence Manuel from the website "HMCS Esquimalt."

3 Audette in *Salty Dips*, vol 2, 74.

Epilogue: Triumph and Tragedy: The Legacy of the Battle of the Atlantic

Unless otherwise noted, the epilogue is based on Tony German, *The Sea is At Our Gates. The History of the Canadian Navy* (Toronto, 1990), 195-199; Marc Milner, *HMCS Sackville 1941-1985* (Halifax, 1998); Thomas Raddall, *Halifax: Warden of the North* (New York, 1965), 297-311.

1 German, *The Sea is At Our Gates*, 199.

2 Lieutenant P. Evans, commanding officer of HMCS *Trillium*, Feb 1943, quoted in Milner, *North Atlantic Run*, 214.

Chronicle 9: The Aftermath

1 Lieutenant Commander A. Griffin, "A Naval Officer's War." Episode 7, *Starshell* (No. 12). Autumn 2000.

2 Greer, *The Girls*, 120-121.

3 O. Robertson in *Salty Dips*, vol 3, 56.

4 O. Robertson in *Salty Dips*, vol 3, 55.

5 O'Connor, *Corvette Years*, 43-44.

6 Easton, *50 North*, 286, 287.

7 Greer, *The Girls*, 141-142.

8 Curry, *War at Sea*, 146-147.

9 Stevens, *Glory of Youth*, 218-219.

10 Johnston, *Corvettes Canada*, 286.

11 Lamb, *Corvette Navy*, 175, 176.

Unpublished Sources

Directorate of History and Heritage, DND, Ottawa
Biography Files
DHH 79/446, Translation of *Kriegestagebuch, Befehls-haber der Unterseeboote*, War Diary, Commander of Submarines
Memorandum, "Relative Naval Strength, 1945," c. 1994
NHS (Naval Historical Section) Files

Hirschmann, Werner. Unpublished memoirs.

Manuel, Terence, "HCS *Esquimalt*" Web Site

National Archives of Canada, Ottawa
Manuscript Group 32, C 71, Papers of John Connolly
Record Group 24, Records of the Department of Militia and Defence, RCN Records

Royal Naval Museum, Portsmouth, United Kingdom
Diary of Commander A.F.C. Layard, RN, 1944-1945

Published Sources

Admiralty, Historical Section. *The Defeat of the Enemy Attack on Shipping 1939-1945: A Study of Policy and Operations. Volumes 1A and 1B*. London: Admiralty, 1957.

Barnett, Corelli. *Engage the Enemy More Closely: The Royal Navy in the Second World War*. New York: Norton, 1991

Blair, Clay. *Hitler's U-Boat War. Vol I. The Hunters, 1939-1942. Vol. II. The Hunted, 1942-1945*. New York: Modern LIbrary, 1998

Boutilier, James A. ed. *The RCN in Retrospect, 1910-1968*. Vancouver: UBC Press, 1982

Burgess, Donald and Ken Macpherson. *The Ships of Canada's Naval Forces, 1910-1985*. Toronto: Collins, 1985

Curry, Frank. *War at Sea: A Canadian Seaman on the North Atlantic*. Toronto: Lugus Press, 1990.

Darlington, Robert and Fraser Mckee. *The Canadian Naval Chronicle 1939-1945*. St. Catharines, Vanwell, 1996.

Dönitz, Karl. *Memoirs: Ten Years and Twenty Days*. New York: Da Capo, 1997

Douglas, W.A.B. *The Creation of a National Air Force: The Official History of the Royal Canadian Air Force. Volume II*. Toronto: University of Toronto Press, 1986

———, ed. *The RCN in Transition, 1910-1985*. Vancouver: UBC Press, 1988.

——— and Brereton Greenhous. *Out of the Shadows: Canada in the Second World War*. Toronto: Dundurn, 1995.

Dundas, Barbara. *A History of Women in the Canadian Military*. Montreal: Art Global, 2000.

Easton, Alan. *50 North: Canada's Atlantic Battleground*. Toronto: Ryerson, 1963.

Eayrs, James. *In Defence of Canada: From the Great War to the Great Depression*. Toronto: University of Toronto Press, 1964.

Gannon, Michael. *Black May: The Epic Story of the Allies' Defeat of the German U-Boats in May 1943*. New York: Harper Collins, 1989

German, Tony. *The Sea is at Our Gates: The History of the Canadian Navy*. Toronto: McClelland and Stewart, 1990.

Goodspeed, Donald J. *Century of Achievement: The Armed Forces of Canada, 1867 to 1967*. Ottawa: Department of National Defence, 1968.

Greer, Rosamond. *The Girls of the King's Navy*. Victoria: Sono Nis Press, 1983.

Griffin, Anthony. "A Naval Officer's War. Episode 7," *Starshell*, 7 (No 12), Autumn 2000.

Hadley, Michael and Roger Sarty. *Tin-Pots and Pirate Ships: Canadian Naval Forces and German Sea Raiders, 1880-1918*. Montreal: McGill-Queen's, 1991.

Hughes, Terry and John Costello. *The Battle of the Atlantic*. New York: Dial, 1977.

Jenson, Latham B. *Tin Hats, Oilskins & Seaboots: A Naval Journey, 1938-1945*. Toronto: Robin Brass Studio, 2000.

Johnston, Mac. *Corvettes Canada: Convoy Veterans of World War II Tell Their Stories*. Toronto: McGraw-Hill Ryerson, 1994.

Lamb, James B. *The Corvette Navy: Canadian Sailors and the Battle of the Atlantic*. Toronto: Macmillan, 1977.

Lynch, Thomas G., ed. *Fading Memories: Canadian Sailors and the Battle of the Atlantic*. Halifax: Atlantic Chiefs and Petty Officers' Association, 1993.

Milner, Marc. *North Atlantic Run: The Royal Canadian Navy and the Battle for the Convoys*. Toronto: Penguin, 1990.

——— . *The U-Boat Hunters: The Royal Canadian Navy and the Offensive Against Germany's Submarines*. Toronto: University of Toronto, 1994.

——— . *HMCS Sackville, 1941-1985*. Halifax: Canadian Naval Memorial Trust, 1998.

Morison, Samuel E. *History of the United States Naval Operations in World War II. Vol. 10: The Atlantic Battle Won*, May 1943-May 1945. Boston: Little, Brown, 1956.

Nicholson, G.W.L. *Canadian Expeditionary Force 1914-1919: Official History of the Canadian Army in the*

First World War. Ottawa: Department of National Defence, 1964.

O'Connor, Edward. *The Corvette Years: The Lower Deck Story*. Vancouver: Cordillera, 1995.

Parker, Mike. *Running the Gauntlet*. Halifax: Nimbus Press, 1994.

Pritchard, Gregory, ed. *Memories of Basic Training and Other Dips*. Lunenburg: South Shore Naval Association, 2000

Pullen, T.C. and W.A.B. Douglas, "Convoy ON 127 and the loss of HMCS *Ottawa*, 13 September 1942," *Northern Mariner*, vol 2 (April 1992), 15

Raddall, Thomas. *Halifax: Warden of the North*. New York: Doubleday, 1965.

Richards, S.T. *Operation Sick Bay*. West Vancouver: Cordillera Publishing, 1994.

Salty Dips. Volumes I, II and III. Ottawa: Naval Officers' Association of Canada, Ottawa Branch, 1983-1985.

Sarty, Roger. *Canada and the Battle of the Atlantic*. Montreal: Art Global, 1998.

Schull, Joseph. *The Far Distant Ships*. Ottawa: Queen's Printer, 1952.

Stacey, C.P. *Arms, Men and Governments: The War Policies of Canada, 1939-1945*. Ottawa: Department of National Defence, 1970

Stevens, Allen W. *Glory of Youth*. Author, 1995.

Terraine, John. *The Right of the Line: The Royal Air Force in the European War, 1939-1945*. London: Hodder & Stoughton, 1985

Topp, Erich. *Fackel uber dem Atlantic*. Hereford, UK: 1990.

Tucker, Gilbert. *The Naval Service of Canada: Its Official History. Volume II: Activities on Shore During the Second World War*. Ottawa: Department of National Defence, 1952.

About the author

DONALD E. GRAVES is the director of Ensign Heritage, a company specializing in heritage consulting and travel, and lives with his author wife, Dianne, near Ottawa.

He is also an internationally recognized military historian whose many books on land warfare have garnered praise from readers and reviewers alike. Graves's *Field of Glory* was described by one reviewer as "history at its best: exciting, entertaining, and readable," while his study of the bloody 1814 battle of Lundy's Lane, *Where Right and Glory Lead,* was termed an "excellent example of the 'sharp end' of military history" and his *South Albertas: A Canadian Regiment at War* was praised "as one of the finest unit histories ever published" which "in fact transcends the genre to rate as a truly great history of Canada at war."

In Peril on the Sea is Graves's first book of naval history, although he has published a number of articles on naval topics which arose out of his experience as an historian on the team researching and writing the history of the Royal Canadian Navy in the Second World War.

His current project is to edit a second volume in the *Fighting for Canada* series. For more information on Donald E. Graves and his writing, see "Sword and Pen," the author's website at <*http://www.ensigngroup.ca*>.

PHOTO BY DIANNE GRAVES

Books by Donald E. Graves

ORIGINAL WORKS

Guns Across the River: The Battle of the Windmill, 1838
(Friends of Windmill Point / Robin Brass Studio, 2001)

South Albertas: A Canadian Regiment at War
(Robin Brass Studio, 1998)

Redcoats and Grey Jackets: The Battle of Chippawa, 1814
(Dundurn Press, 1994)

(with Michael Whitby) *Normandy 1944: The Canadian Summer*
(Art Global, 1994)

FORGOTTEN SOLDIERS:
THE WAR OF 1812 IN THE NORTH TRILOGY

I: *Field of Glory: The Battle of Crysler's Farm, 1813*
(Robin Brass Studio, 1999)

II: *Where Right and Glory Lead! The Battle of Lundy's Lane, 1814*
(Robin Brass Studio, 1997)

III: A third volume is in preparation.

EDITED WORKS

Quebec, 1759: The Siege and the Battle by C.P. Stacey
(Updated by Donald E. Graves; Robin Brass Studio, 2002)

The Incredible War of 1812: A Military History by J.M. Hitsman
(Updated by Donald E. Graves; Robin Brass Studio, 1999)

Soldiers of 1814: American Enlisted Men's Memoirs of the Niagara Campaign
(Old Fort Niagara Press, 1996)

Merry Hearts Make Light Days: The War of 1812 Memoirs of Lieutenant John Le Couteur, 104th Foot
(Carleton University Press, 1993; distributed by Robin Brass Studio)

1885. Experiences of the Halifax Battalion in the North-West
(Museum Restoration Service, 1985)

Tin Hats, Oilskins & Seaboots
A Naval Journey, 1938-1945

Latham B. Jenson

Tin Hats, Oilskins & Seaboots tells the story of the wartime naval career of popular author/artist L.B. Jenson. Born in Calgary in 1921, "Yogi" Jenson joined the Royal Canadian Navy in 1938 as an officer cadet. Wartime service took him to the South Atlantic searching for the *Graf Spee* and Norway engaging the *Scharnhorst* and *Gneisenau*. In 1941, he was appointed to HMCS *Ottawa*, which was sunk a year later with great loss of life in a battle with German submarines. Surviving this, he continued on convoy duties in the North Atlantic before going in early 1944 to the destroyer *Algonquin* as executive officer, attacking German ships, including the *Tirpitz*, and being one of the first ships to open fire on the shore defences in the invasion of Normandy.

The book, illustrated with Jenson's luminous line drawings, is a valuable record not only of how ships fought the battles of the Atlantic, but of life on board, where men had to live under difficult conditions for weeks on end, all seen through the eyes of an engaging young officer.

The author

After retiring from the RCN, Latham B. Jenson settled in Nova Scotia and illustrated a number of much-loved books, including *Vanishing Halifax*, *Nova Scotia Sketchbook*, *Fishermen of Nova Scotia* and *Saga of the Great Fishing Schooners*. As vice-president of the Heritage Trust of Nova Scotia, he took part in a successful campaign to stop the demolition of historic waterfront buildings in Halifax. He was a member of the board of governors of the first Schooner Bluenose Foundation and was chairman of the advisory council of the Maritime Museum of the Atlantic. In this capacity he instigated the acquisition of HMCS *Sackville*, the last corvette remaining from the Second World War, and its restoration to its wartime configuration as a memorial to those who fought and won the Battle of the Atlantic. L.B. Jenson lives near Halifax.

312 pages

8 x 9 inches, landscape

More than 170 illustrations

Index

ISBN 1-896941-14-1

Paperback: $24.95

"This isn't just a moving autobiography; it's also a wonderful visual record.…
This really is a feast of a book." *Halifax Chronicle Herald*